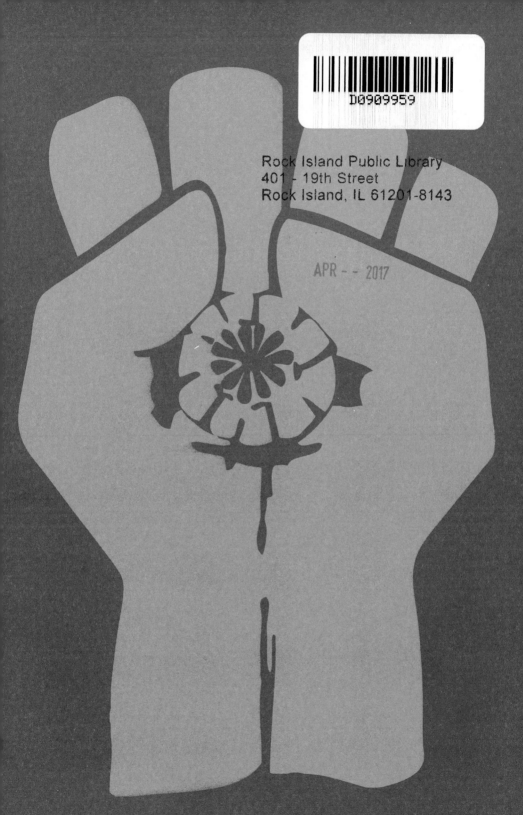

TO NATHAN

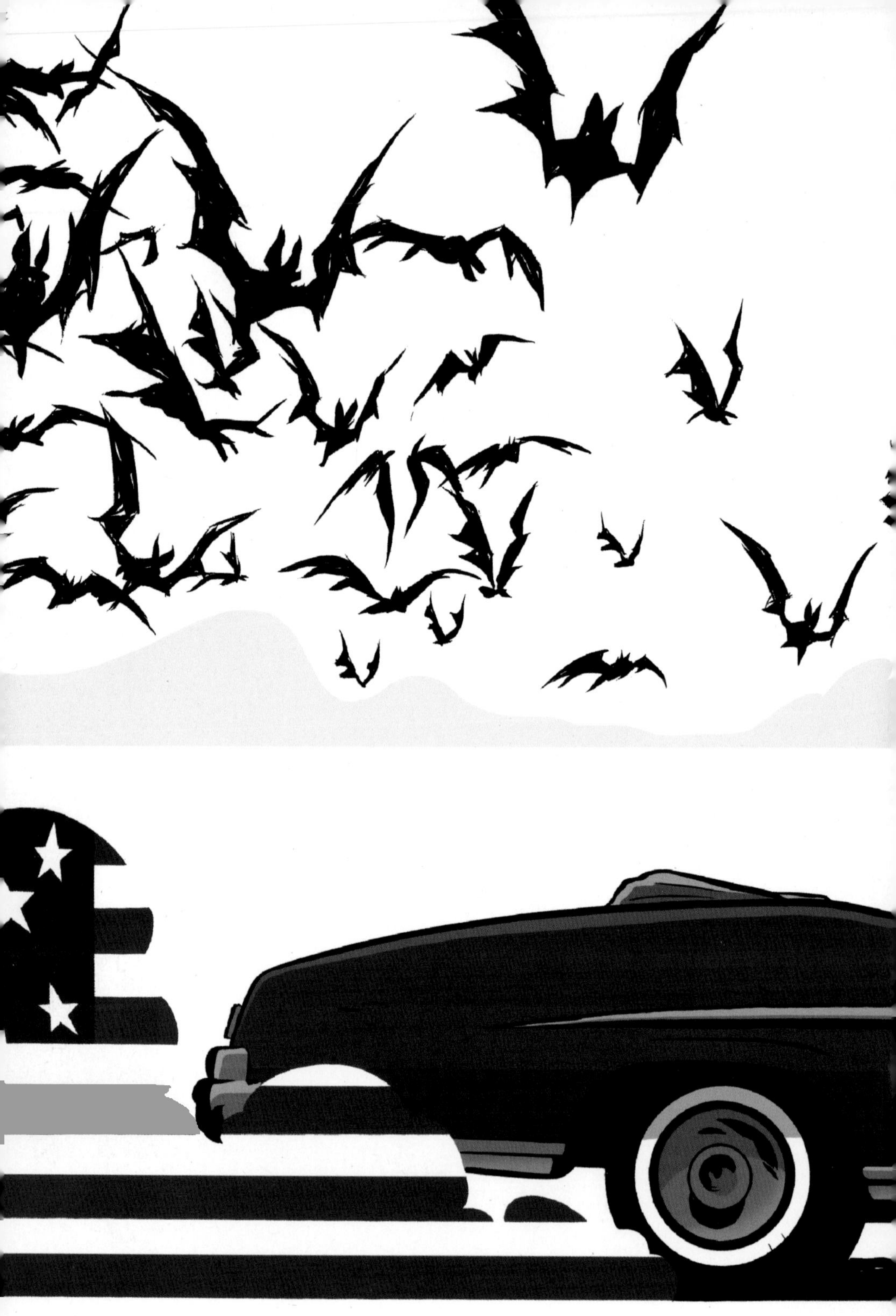

Hunter S. Thompson's

Fear and Loathing in Las Vegas

ADAPTED BY
TROY LITTLE

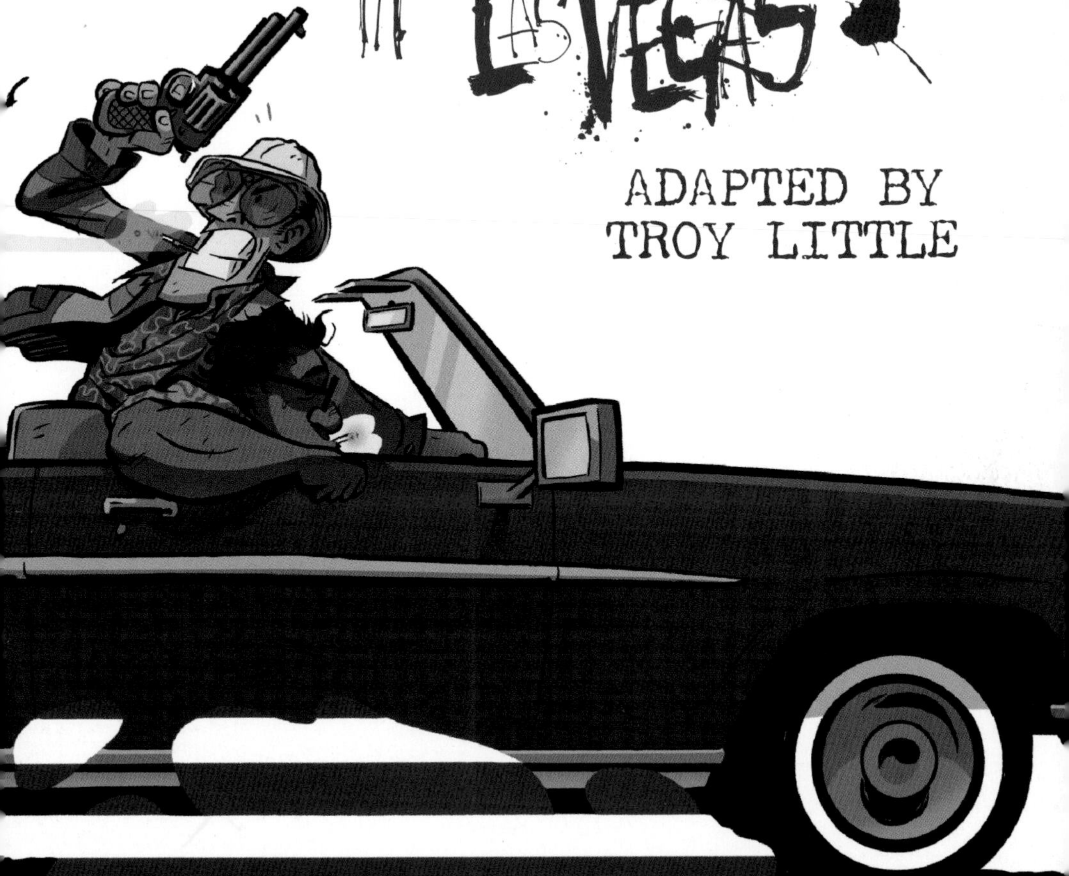

A Savage Journey to the Heart of the American Dream

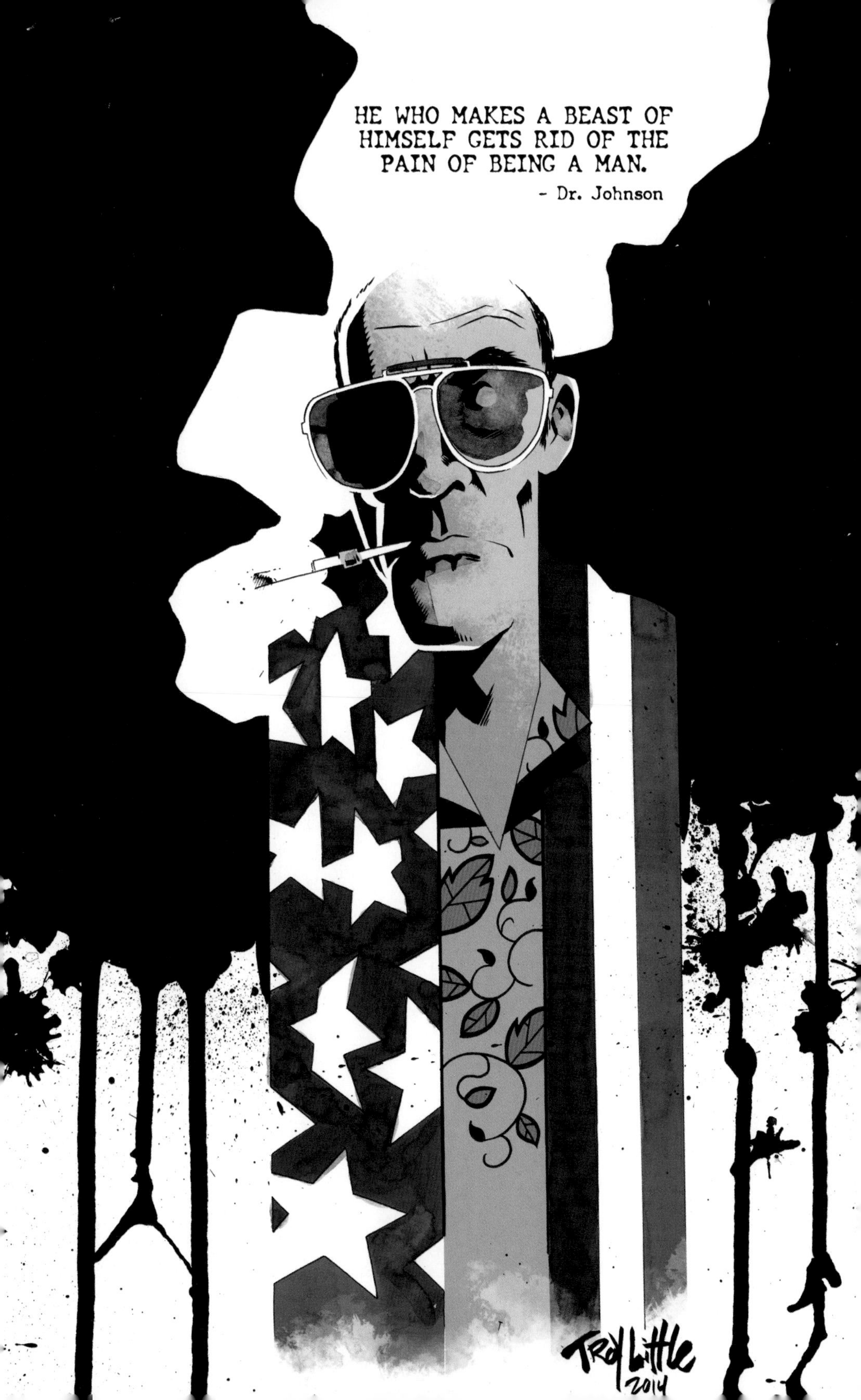
HE WHO MAKES A BEAST OF HIMSELF GETS RID OF THE PAIN OF BEING A MAN.
- Dr. Johnson
TROY LITTLE
2014

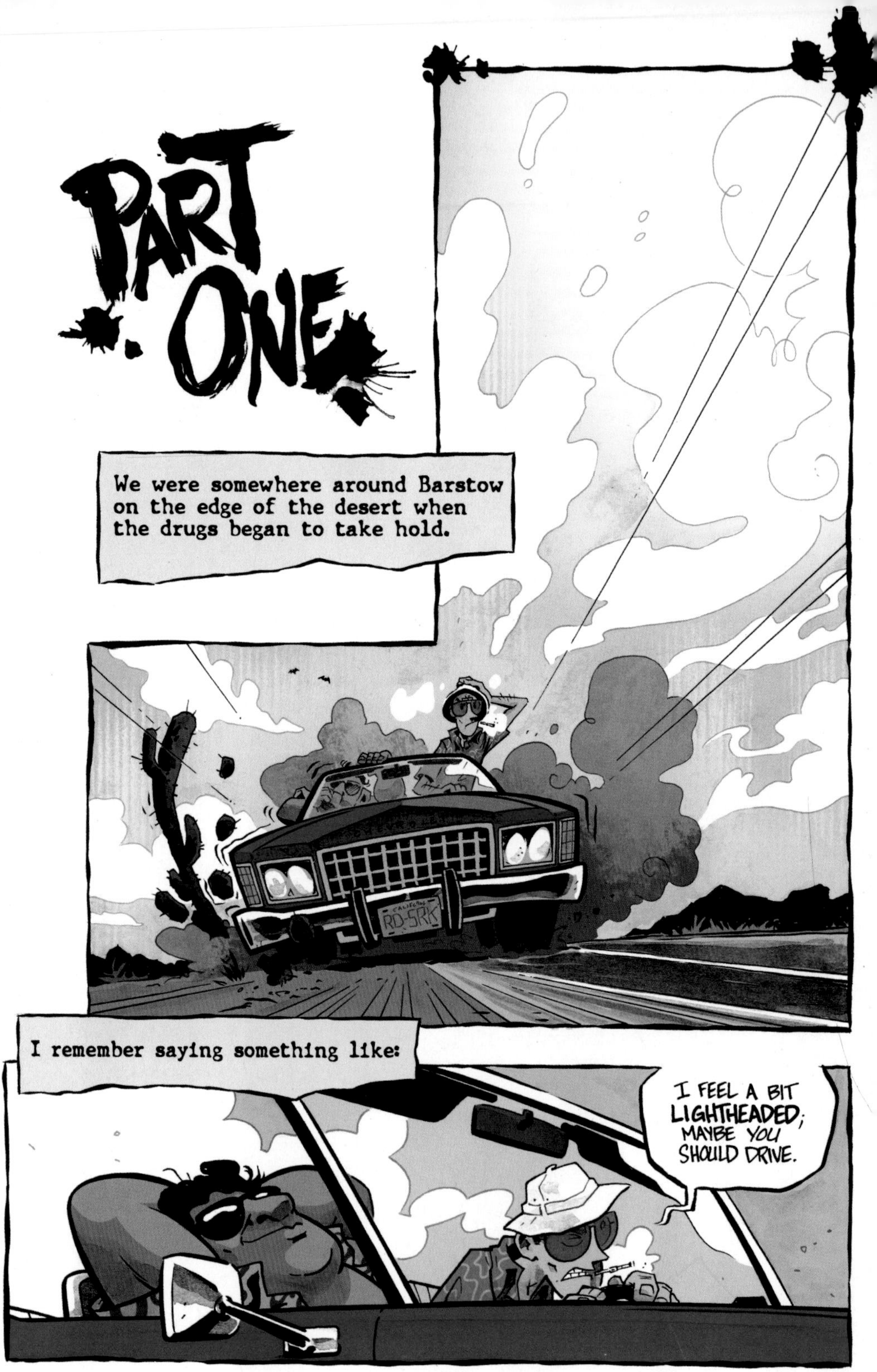
PART ONE
We were somewhere around Barstow on the edge of the desert when the drugs began to take hold.
RD-5RK
I remember saying something like:
I FEEL A BIT LIGHTHEADED; MAYBE YOU SHOULD DRIVE.

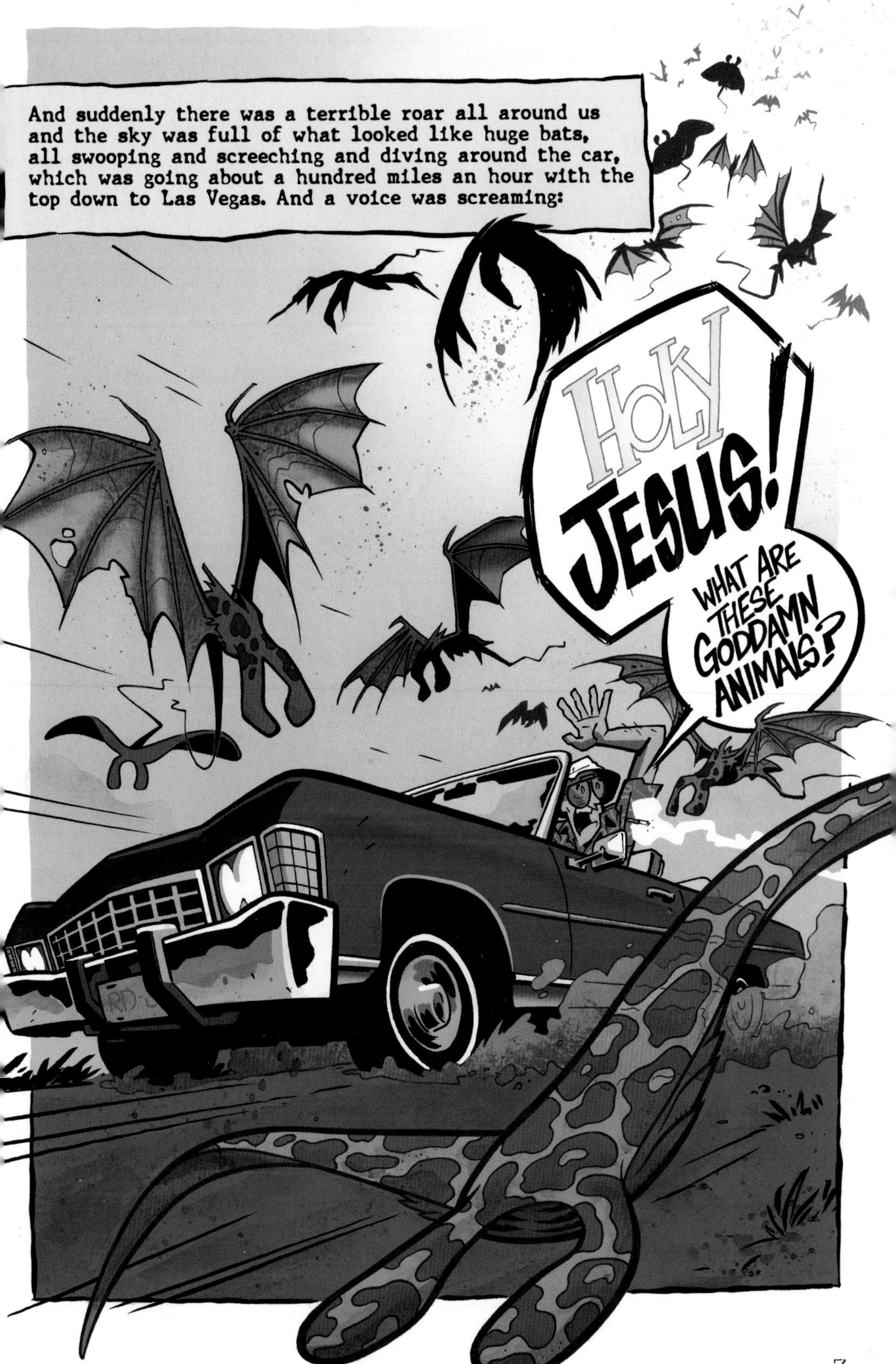
And suddenly there was a terrible roar all around us and the sky was full of what looked like huge bats, all swooping and screeching and diving around the car, which was going about a hundred miles an hour with the top down to Las Vegas. And a voice was screaming:
HOLY JESUS!
WHAT ARE THESE GODDAMN ANIMALS?

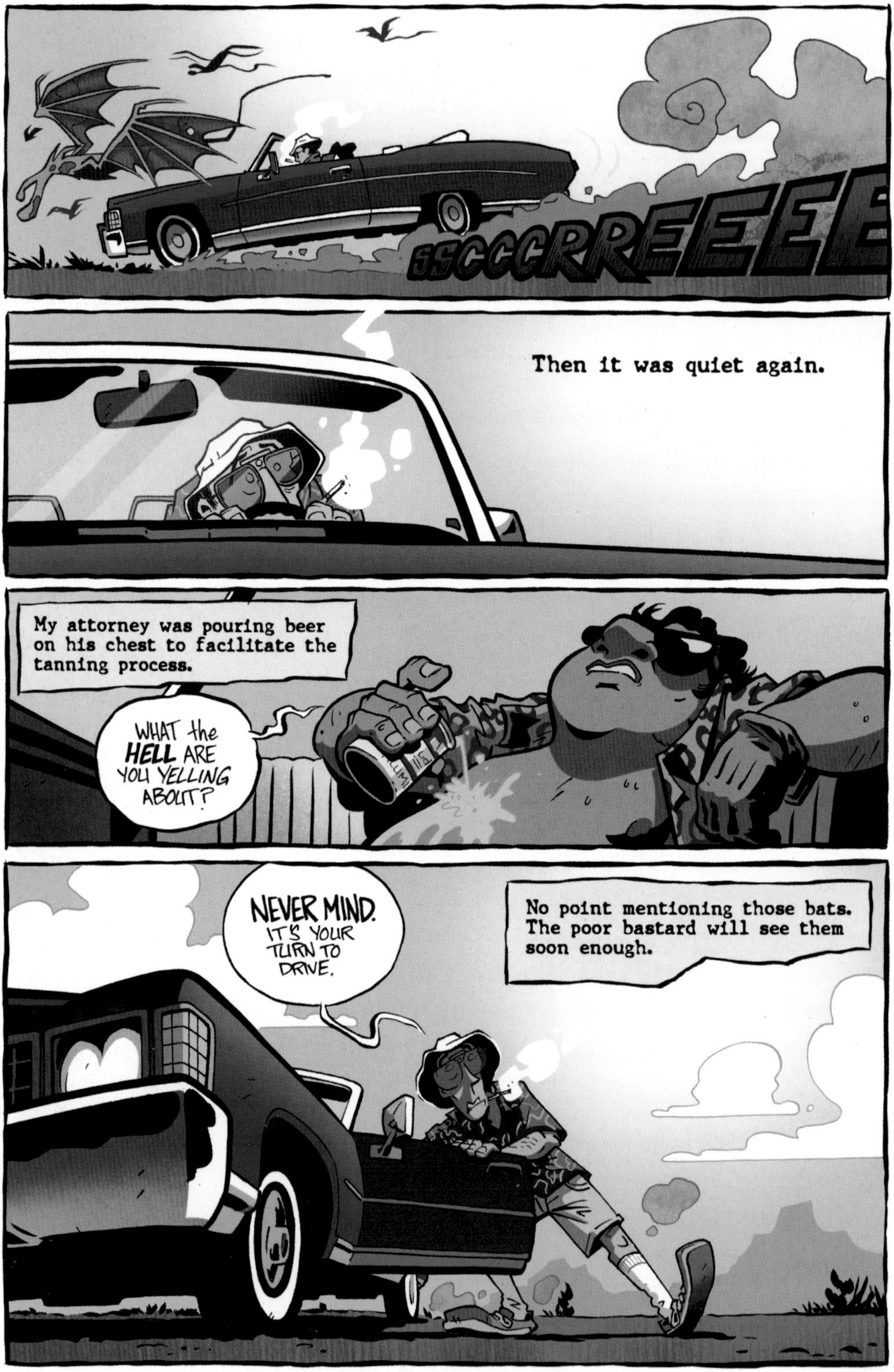
SSCCCRRREEEEE
Then it was quiet again.
My attorney was pouring beer on his chest to facilitate the tanning process.
WHAT the HELL ARE YOU YELLING ABOUT?
NEVER MIND. IT'S YOUR TURN TO DRIVE.
No point mentioning those bats. The poor bastard will see them soon enough.

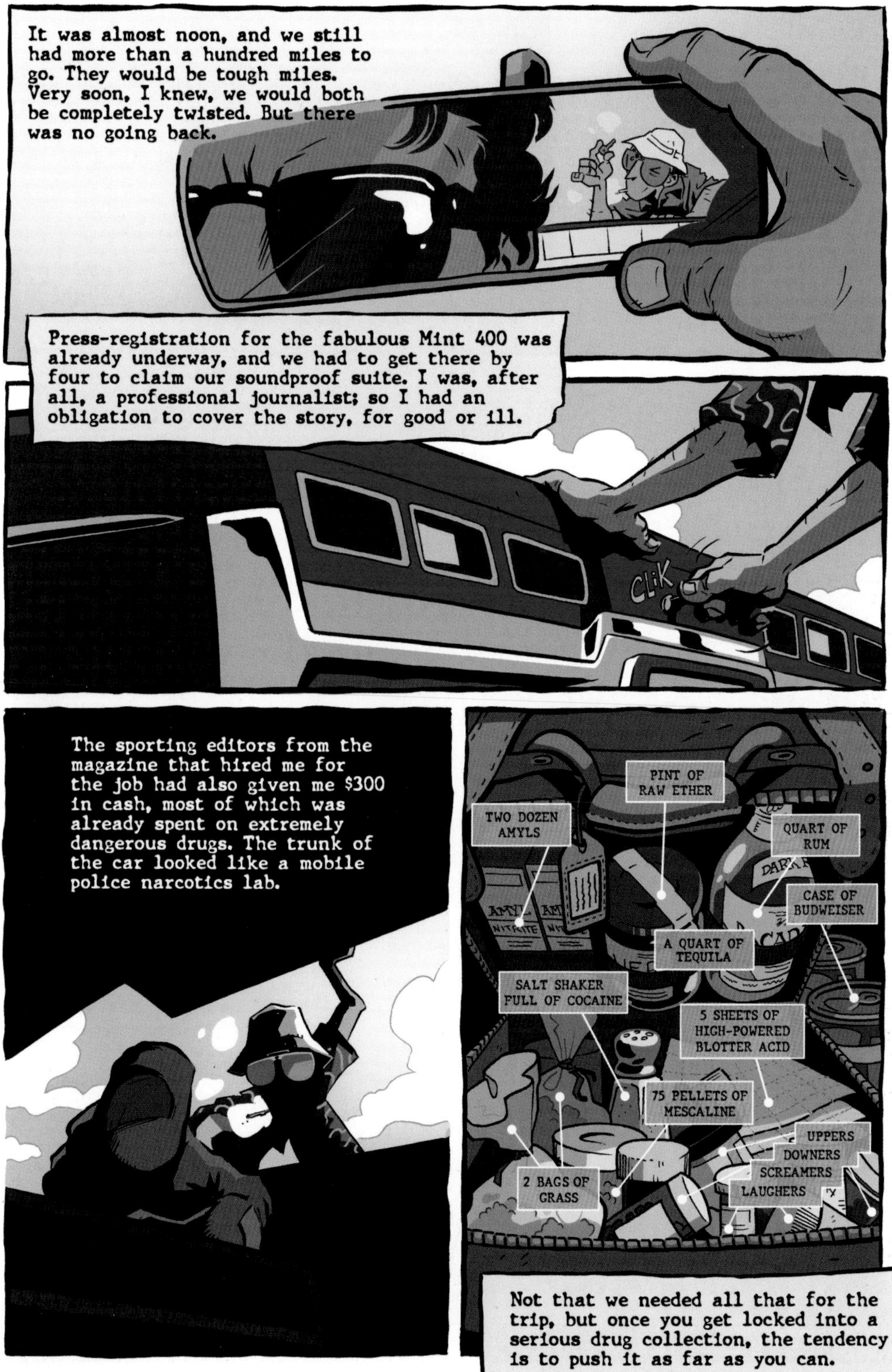
It was almost noon, and we still had more than a hundred miles to go. They would be tough miles. Very soon, I knew, we would both be completely twisted. But there was no going back.
Press-registration for the fabulous Mint 400 was already underway, and we had to get there by four to claim our soundproof suite. I was, after all, a professional journalist; so I had an obligation to cover the story, for good or ill.
CLIK
The sporting editors from the magazine that hired me for the job had also given me $300 in cash, most of which was already spent on extremely dangerous drugs. The trunk of the car looked like a mobile police narcotics lab.
PINT OF RAW ETHER
TWO DOZEN AMYLS
QUART OF RUM
CASE OF BUDWEISER
A QUART OF TEQUILA
SALT SHAKER FULL OF COCAINE
5 SHEETS OF HIGH-POWERED BLOTTER ACID
75 PELLETS OF MESCALINE
2 BAGS OF GRASS
UPPERS
DOWNERS
SCREAMERS
LAUGHERS
Not that we needed all that for the trip, but once you get locked into a serious drug collection, the tendency is to push it as far as you can.

The only thing that really worried me was the ether.

There is nothing in the world more helpless and irresponsible and depraved than a man in the depths of an ether binge.

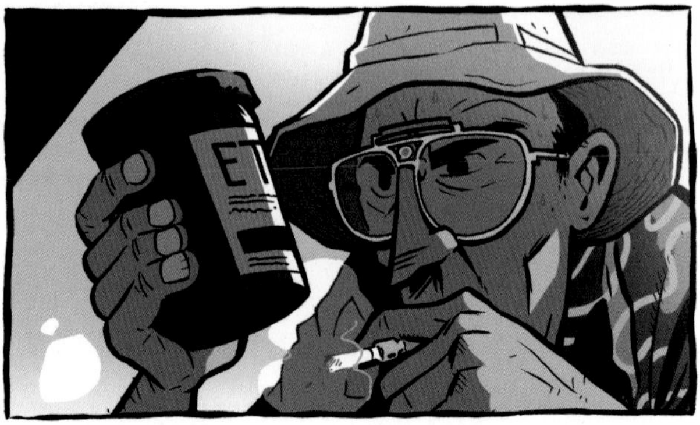

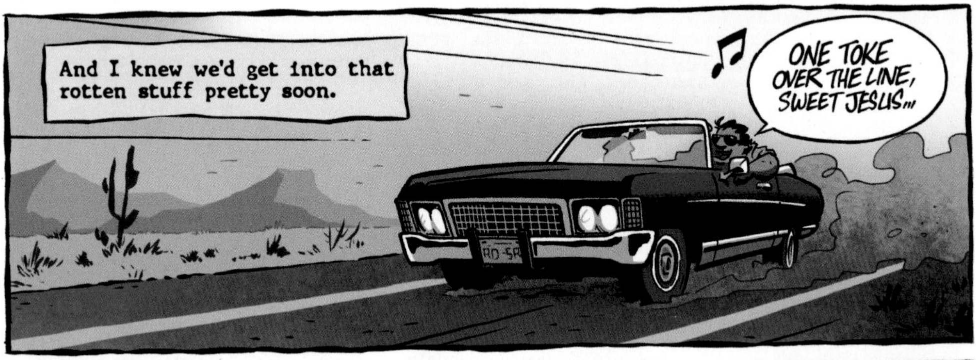

And I knew we'd get into that rotten stuff pretty soon.
ONE TOKE OVER THE LINE, SWEET JESUS...

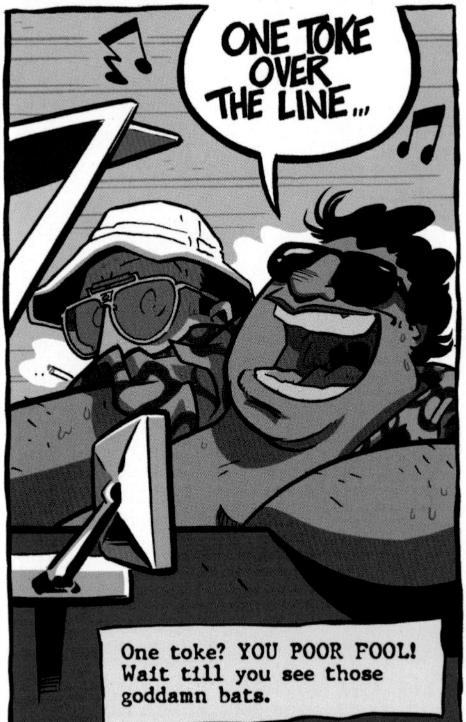

ONE TOKE OVER THE LINE...
One toke? YOU POOR FOOL! Wait till you see those goddamn bats.

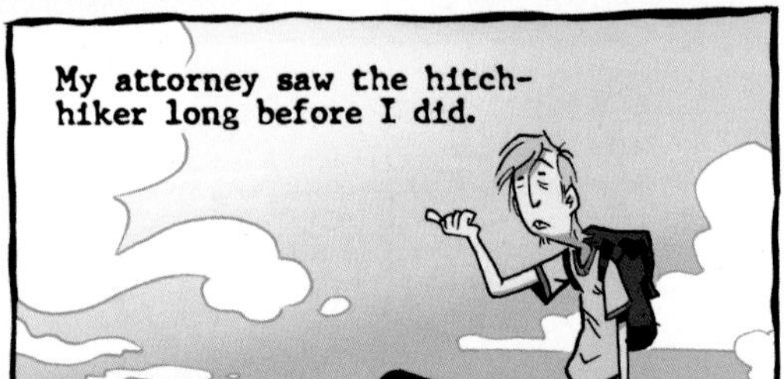

My attorney saw the hitch-hiker long before I did.

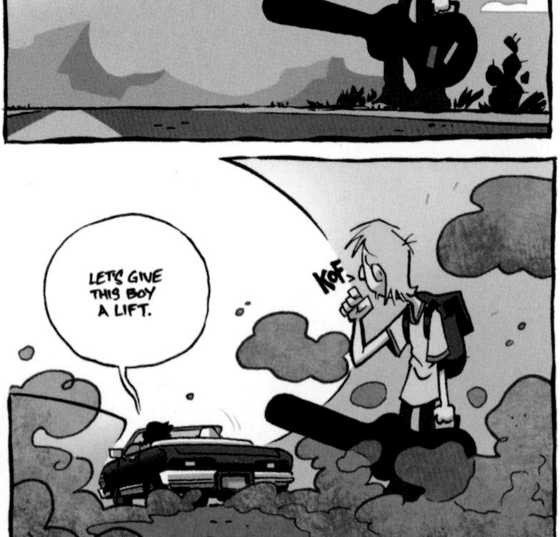

LET'S GIVE THIS BOY A LIFT.
KOF

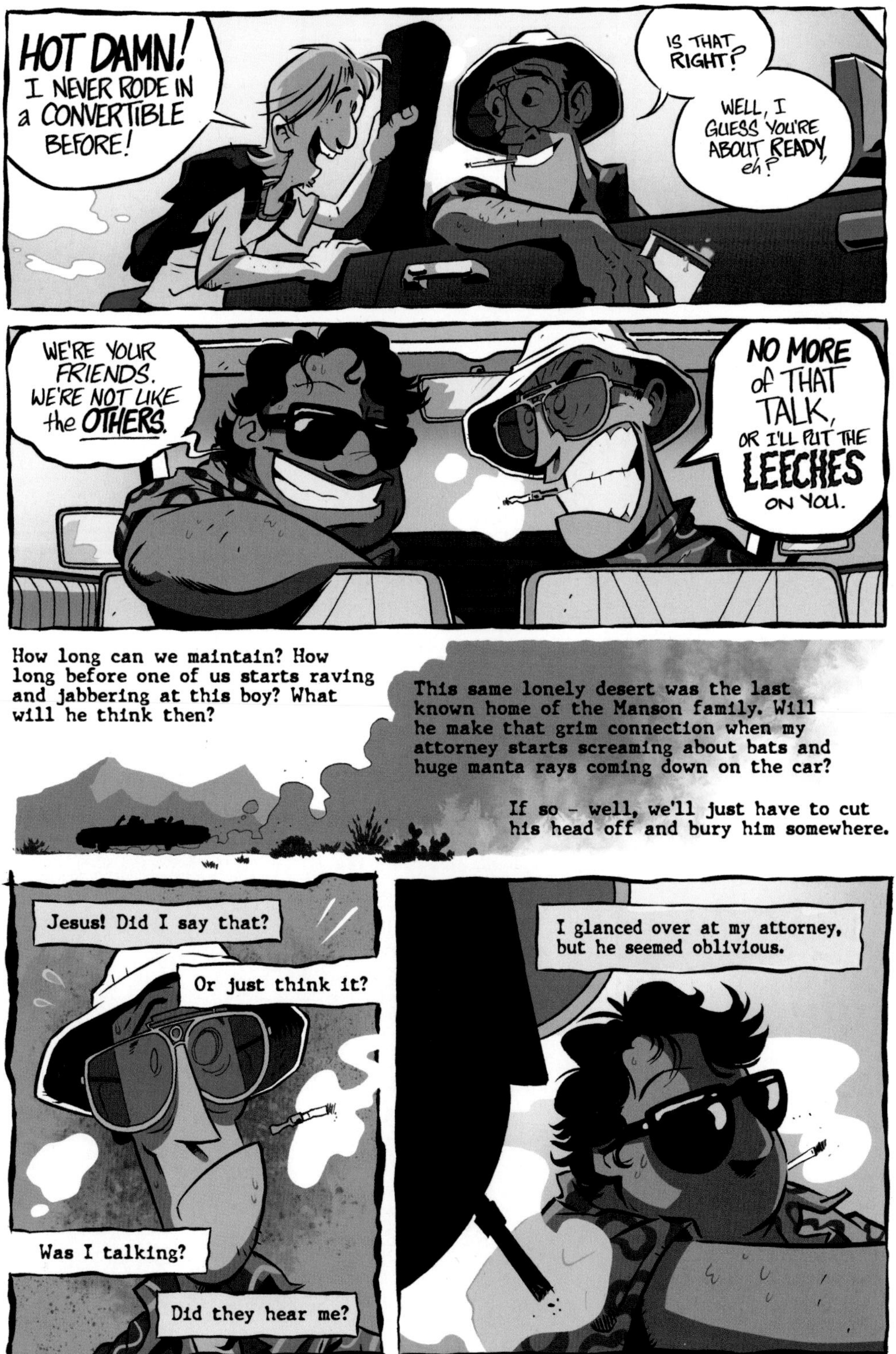
HOT DAMN! I NEVER RODE IN a CONVERTIBLE BEFORE!
IS THAT RIGHT?
WELL, I GUESS YOU'RE ABOUT READY, eh?
WE'RE YOUR FRIENDS. WE'RE NOT LIKE the OTHERS.
NO MORE of THAT TALK, OR I'LL PUT THE LEECHES ON YOU.
How long can we maintain? How long before one of us starts raving and jabbering at this boy? What will he think then?
This same lonely desert was the last known home of the Manson family. Will he make that grim connection when my attorney starts screaming about bats and huge manta rays coming down on the car?
If so - well, we'll just have to cut his head off and bury him somewhere.
Jesus! Did I say that?
Or just think it?
Was I talking?
Did they hear me?
I glanced over at my attorney, but he seemed oblivious.

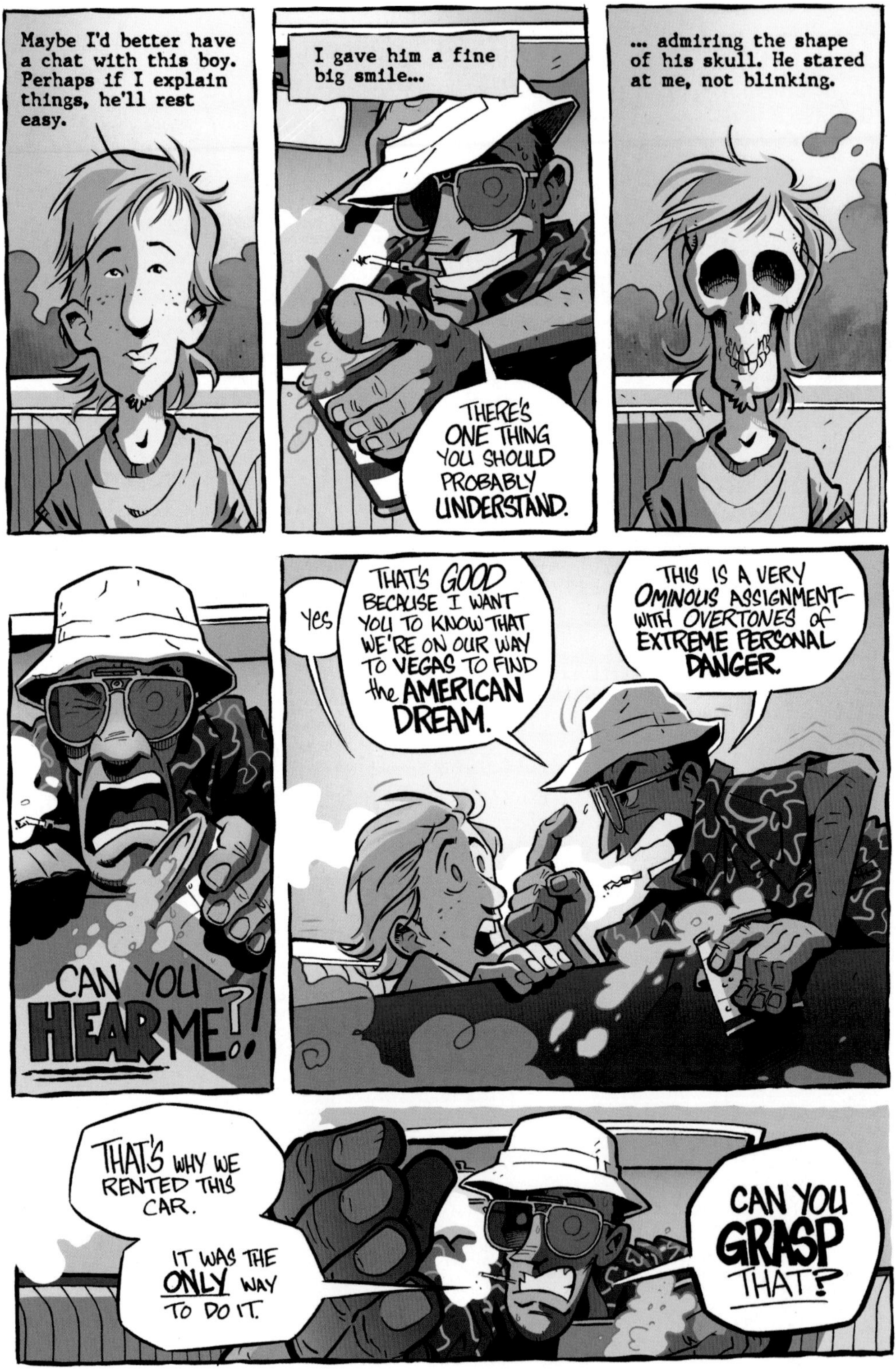

Maybe I'd better have a chat with this boy. Perhaps if I explain things, he'll rest easy.
I gave him a fine big smile...
THERE'S ONE THING YOU SHOULD PROBABLY UNDERSTAND.
... admiring the shape of his skull. He stared at me, not blinking.
CAN YOU HEAR ME?!
Yes
THAT'S GOOD BECAUSE I WANT YOU TO KNOW THAT WE'RE ON OUR WAY TO VEGAS TO FIND the AMERICAN DREAM.
THIS IS A VERY OMINOUS ASSIGNMENT- WITH OVERTONES of EXTREME PERSONAL DANGER.
THAT'S WHY WE RENTED THIS CAR.
IT WAS THE ONLY WAY TO DO IT.
CAN YOU GRASP THAT?

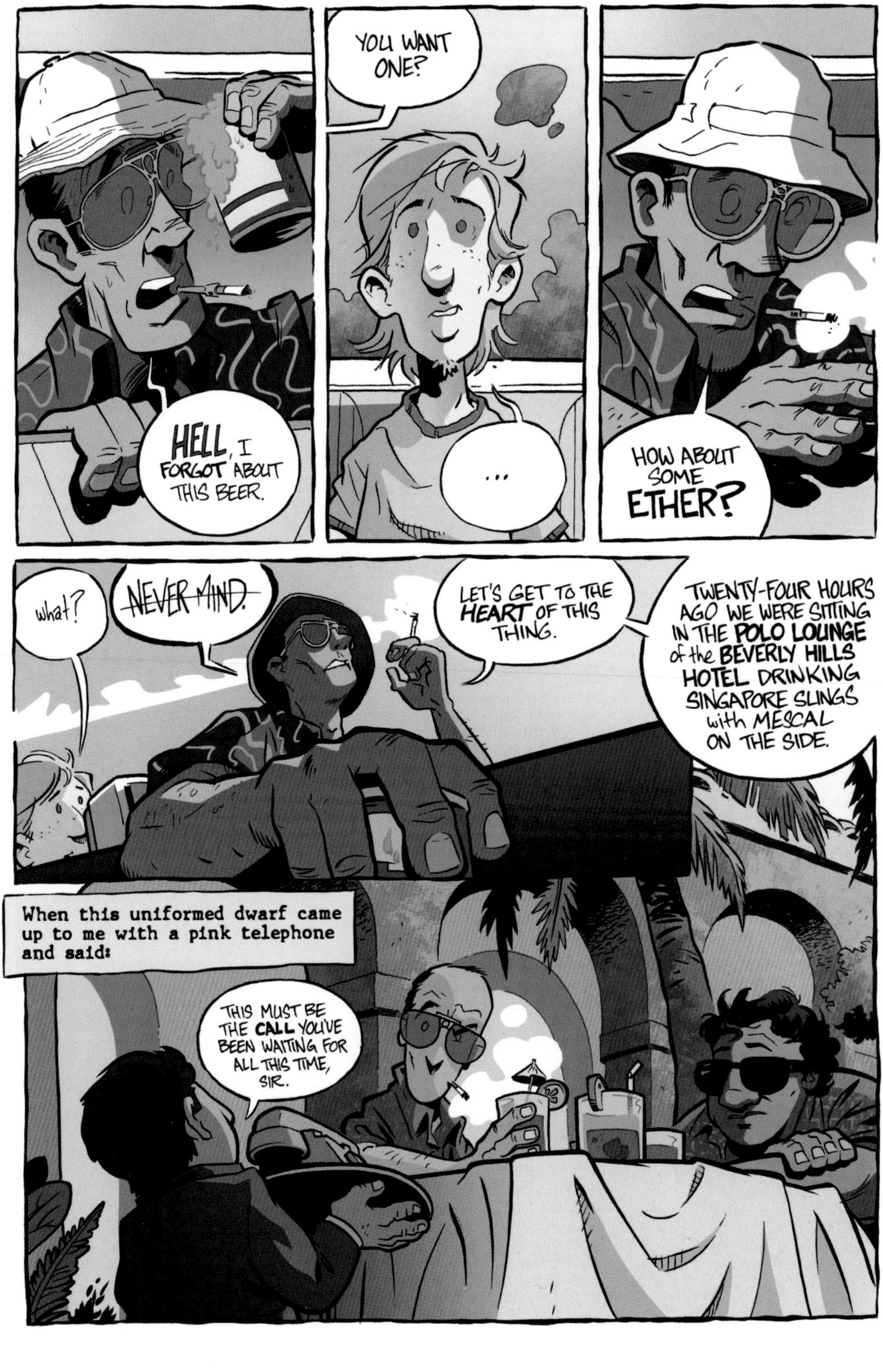
HELL, I FORGOT ABOUT THIS BEER.
YOU WANT ONE?
...
HOW ABOUT SOME ETHER?
what?
NEVER MIND.
LET'S GET TO THE HEART OF THIS THING.
TWENTY-FOUR HOURS AGO WE WERE SITTING IN THE POLO LOUNGE of the BEVERLY HILLS HOTEL DRINKING SINGAPORE SLINGS with MESCAL ON THE SIDE.
When this uniformed dwarf came up to me with a pink telephone and said:
THIS MUST BE THE CALL YOU'VE BEEN WAITING FOR ALL THIS TIME, SIR.

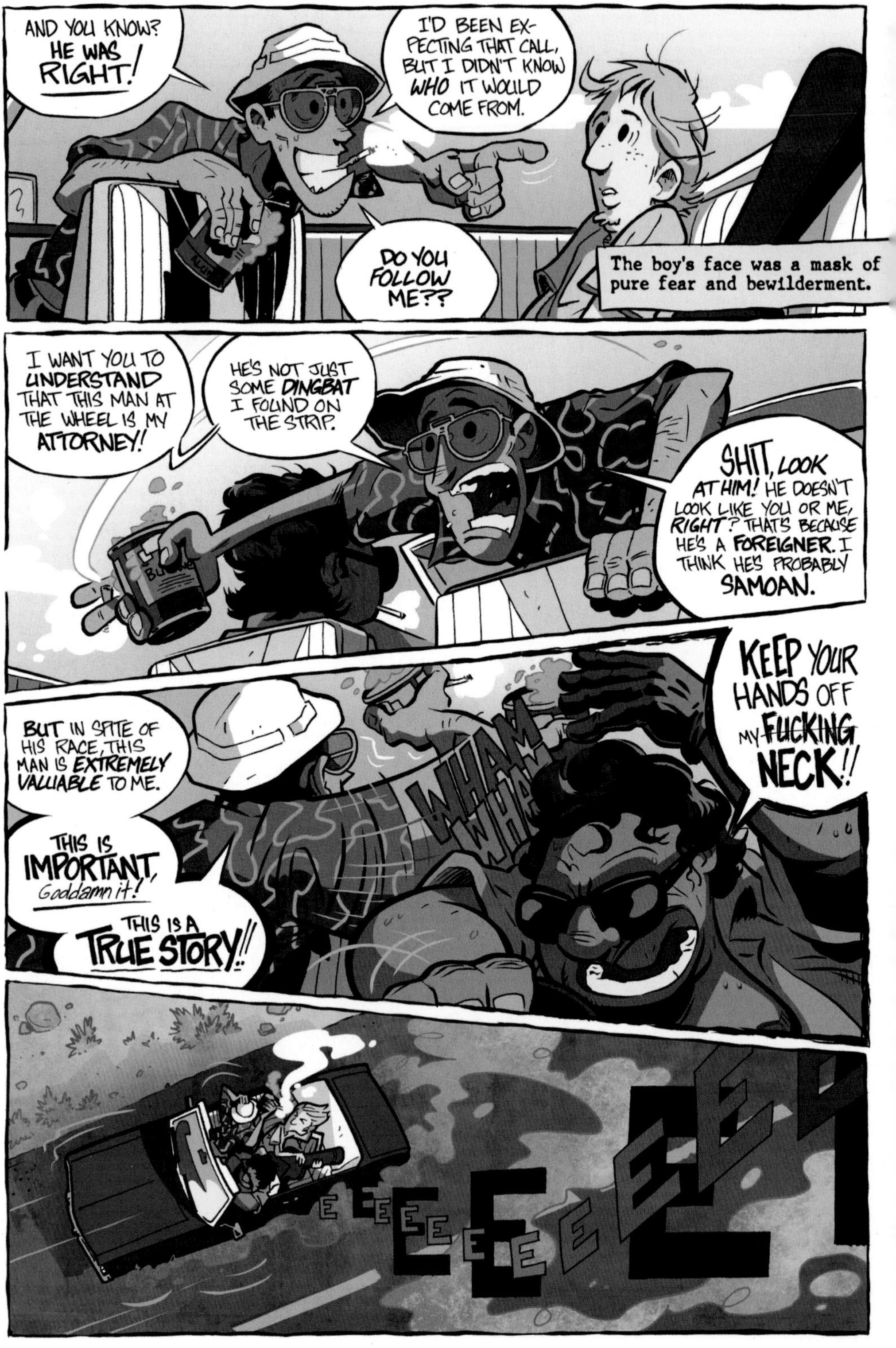

AND YOU KNOW? HE WAS RIGHT!
I'D BEEN EXPECTING THAT CALL, BUT I DIDN'T KNOW WHO IT WOULD COME FROM.
DO YOU FOLLOW ME??
The boy's face was a mask of pure fear and bewilderment.
I WANT YOU TO UNDERSTAND THAT THIS MAN AT THE WHEEL IS MY ATTORNEY!
HE'S NOT JUST SOME DINGBAT I FOUND ON THE STRIP.
SHIT, LOOK AT HIM! HE DOESN'T LOOK LIKE YOU OR ME, RIGHT? THAT'S BECAUSE HE'S A FOREIGNER. I THINK HE'S PROBABLY SAMOAN.
BUT IN SPITE OF HIS RACE, THIS MAN IS EXTREMELY VALUABLE TO ME.
WHAM WHAM
KEEP YOUR HANDS OFF MY FUCKING NECK!!
THIS IS IMPORTANT, Goddamn it!
THIS IS A TRUE STORY!!
EEEEEEEEEEEEEEEE

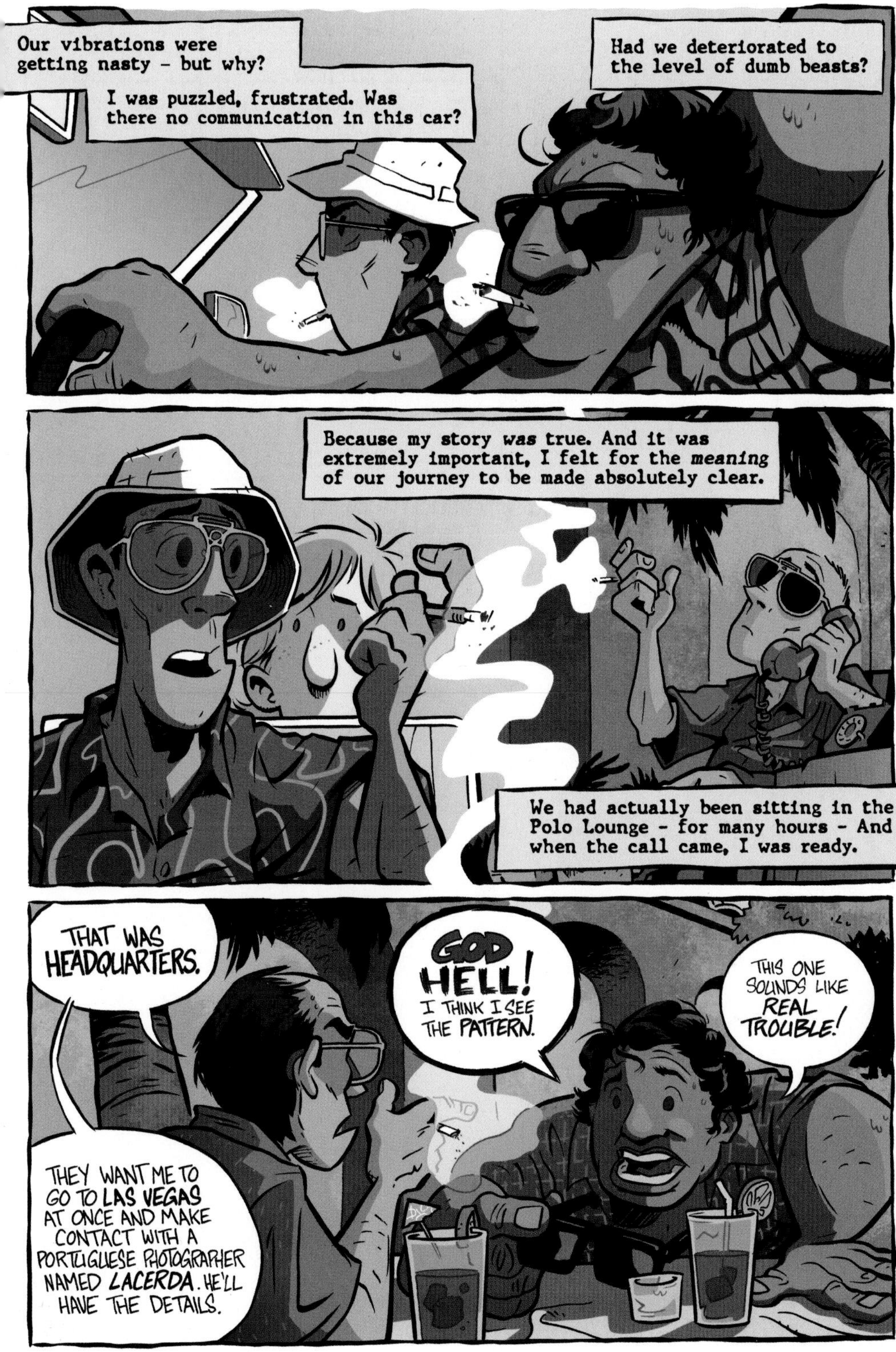

Our vibrations were getting nasty - but why?
I was puzzled, frustrated. Was there no communication in this car?
Had we deteriorated to the level of dumb beasts?
Because my story *was* true. And it was extremely important, I felt for the *meaning* of our journey to be made absolutely clear.
We had actually been sitting in the Polo Lounge - for many hours - And when the call came, I was ready.
THAT WAS HEADQUARTERS.
THEY WANT ME TO GO TO LAS VEGAS AT ONCE AND MAKE CONTACT WITH A PORTUGUESE PHOTOGRAPHER NAMED LACERDA. HE'LL HAVE THE DETAILS.
GOD HELL! I THINK I SEE THE PATTERN.
THIS ONE SOUNDS LIKE REAL TROUBLE!

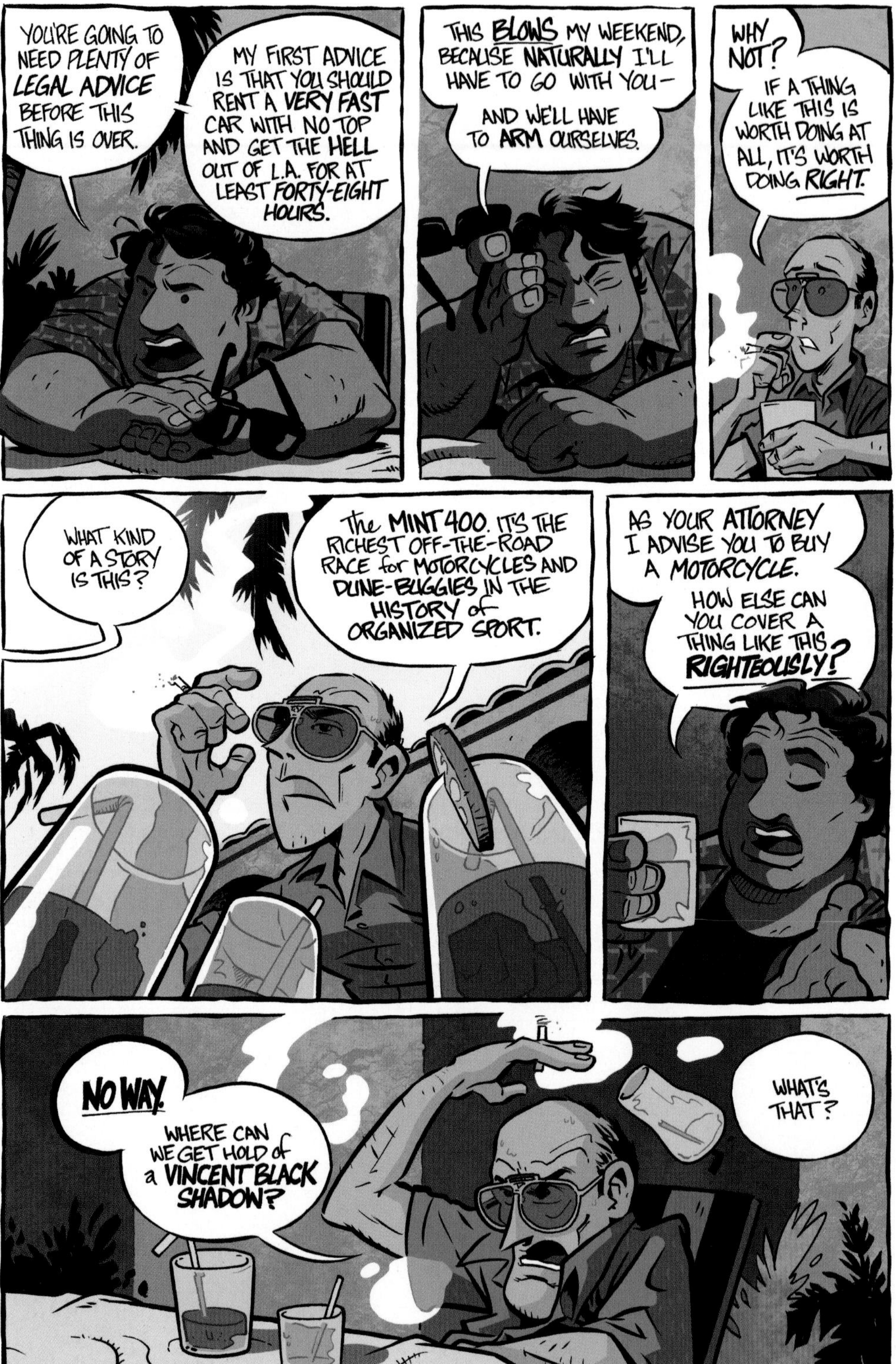
YOU'RE GOING TO NEED PLENTY OF LEGAL ADVICE BEFORE THIS THING IS OVER.
MY FIRST ADVICE IS THAT YOU SHOULD RENT A VERY FAST CAR WITH NO TOP AND GET THE HELL OUT OF L.A. FOR AT LEAST FORTY-EIGHT HOURS.
THIS BLOWS MY WEEKEND, BECAUSE NATURALLY I'LL HAVE TO GO WITH YOU—
AND WE'LL HAVE TO ARM OURSELVES.
WHY NOT?
IF A THING LIKE THIS IS WORTH DOING AT ALL, IT'S WORTH DOING RIGHT.
WHAT KIND OF A STORY IS THIS?
The MINT 400. IT'S THE RICHEST OFF-THE-ROAD RACE for MOTORCYCLES AND DUNE-BUGGIES IN THE HISTORY of ORGANIZED SPORT.
AS YOUR ATTORNEY I ADVISE YOU TO BUY A MOTORCYCLE.
HOW ELSE CAN YOU COVER A THING LIKE THIS RIGHTEOUSLY?
NO WAY.
WHERE CAN WE GET HOLD of a VINCENT BLACK SHADOW?
WHAT'S THAT?

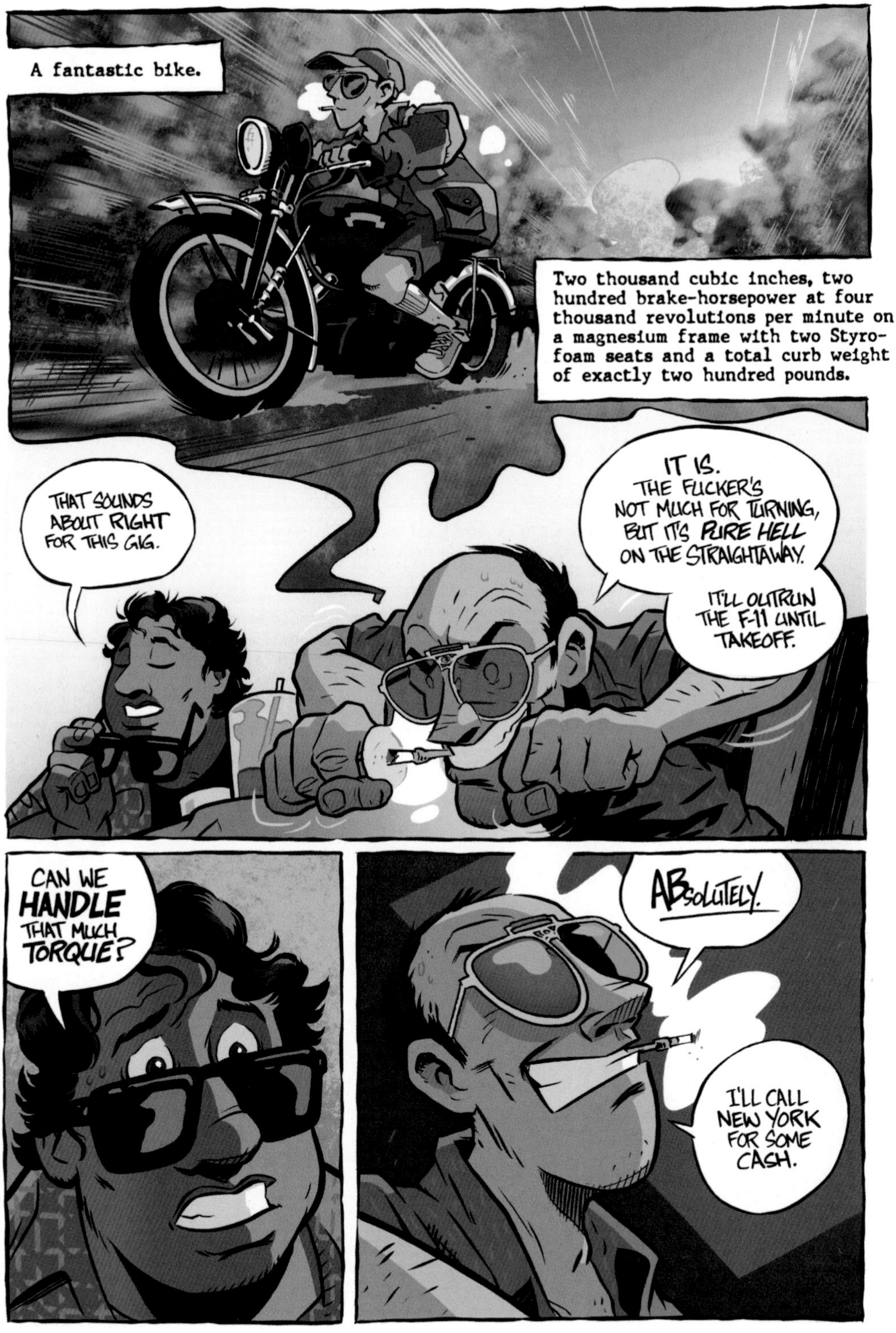
A fantastic bike.
Two thousand cubic inches, two hundred brake-horsepower at four thousand revolutions per minute on a magnesium frame with two Styrofoam seats and a total curb weight of exactly two hundred pounds.
THAT SOUNDS ABOUT RIGHT FOR THIS GIG.
IT IS. THE FUCKER'S NOT MUCH FOR TURNING, BUT IT'S PURE HELL ON THE STRAIGHTAWAY.
IT'LL OUTRUN THE F-11 UNTIL TAKEOFF.
CAN WE HANDLE THAT MUCH TORQUE?
ABSOLUTELY.
I'LL CALL NEW YORK FOR SOME CASH.

2. The Seizure of $300 from a Pig Woman in Beverly Hills

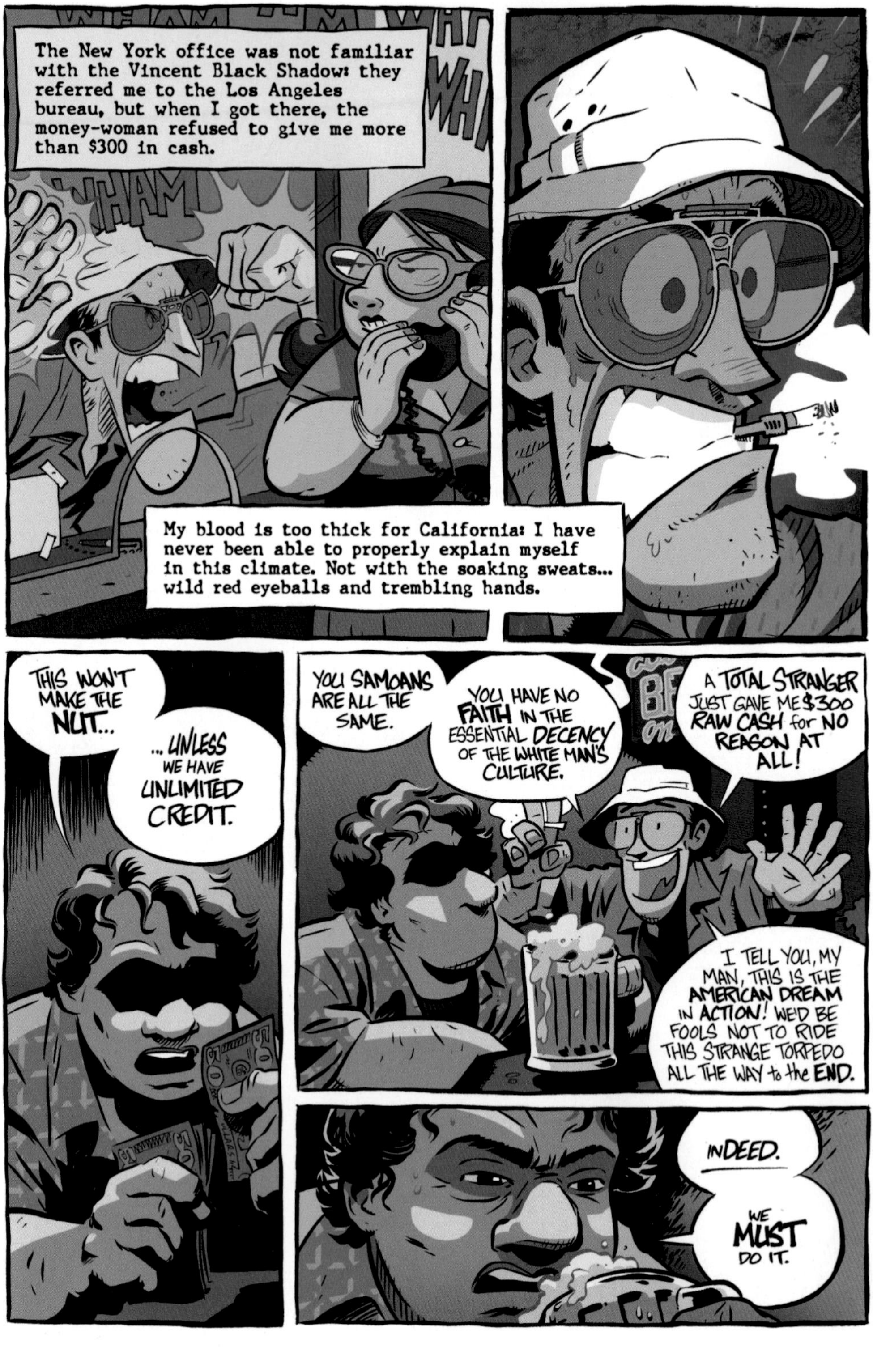
The New York office was not familiar with the Vincent Black Shadow: they referred me to the Los Angeles bureau, but when I got there, the money-woman refused to give me more than $300 in cash.
WHAM
My blood is too thick for California: I have never been able to properly explain myself in this climate. Not with the soaking sweats... wild red eyeballs and trembling hands.
THIS WON'T MAKE THE NUT...
...UNLESS WE HAVE UNLIMITED CREDIT.
YOU SAMOANS ARE ALL THE SAME.
YOU HAVE NO FAITH IN THE ESSENTIAL DECENCY OF THE WHITE MAN'S CULTURE.
A TOTAL STRANGER JUST GAVE ME $300 RAW CASH for NO REASON AT ALL!
I TELL YOU, MY MAN, THIS IS THE AMERICAN DREAM IN ACTION! WE'D BE FOOLS NOT TO RIDE THIS STRANGE TORPEDO ALL THE WAY to the END.
INDEED.
WE MUST DO IT.

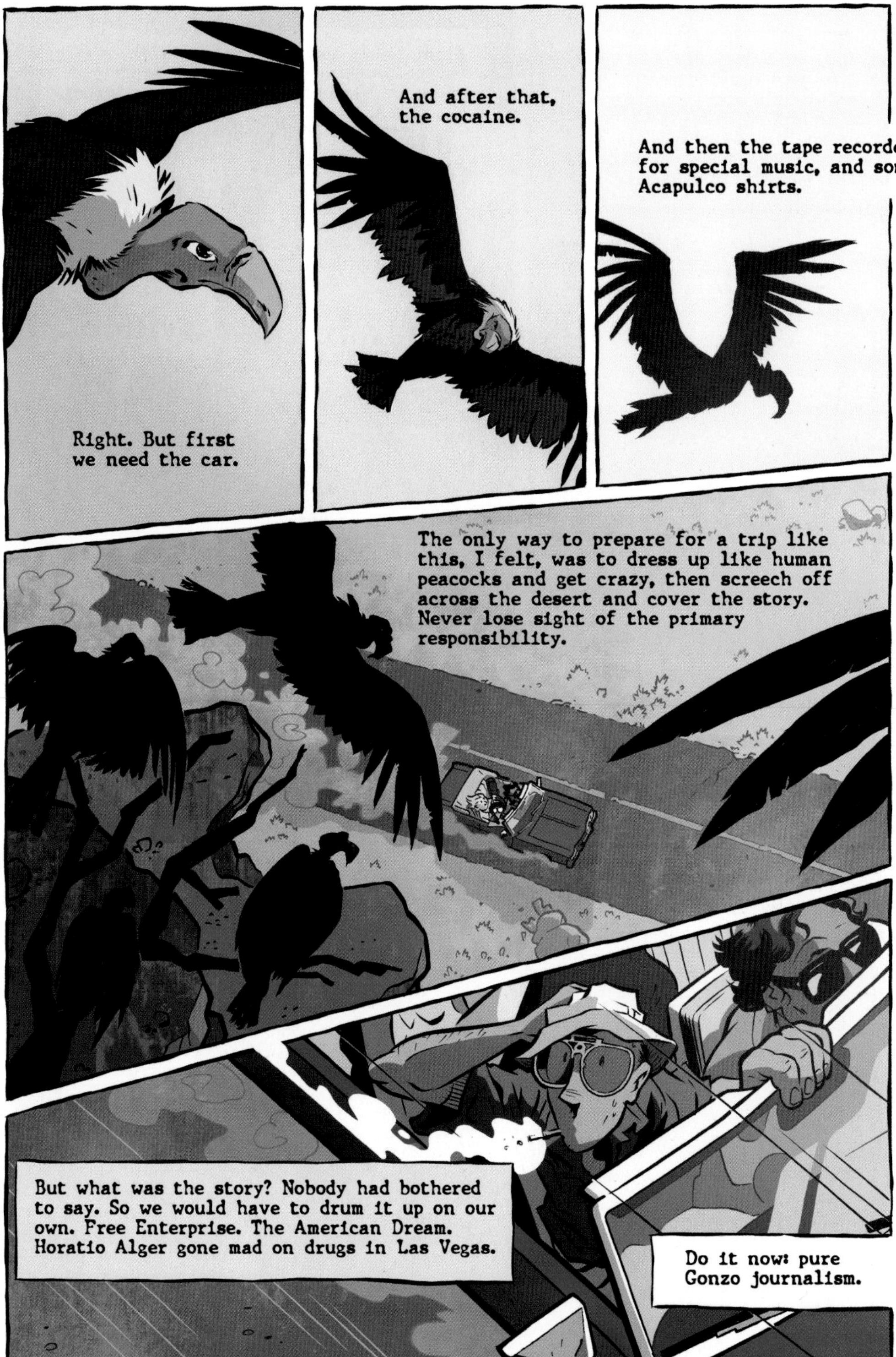
Right. But first
we need the car.
And after that,
the cocaine.
And then the tape recorder,
for special music, and some
Acapulco shirts.
The only way to prepare for a trip like
this, I felt, was to dress up like human
peacocks and get crazy, then screech off
across the desert and cover the story.
Never lose sight of the primary
responsibility.
But what was the story? Nobody had bothered
to say. So we would have to drum it up on our
own. Free Enterprise. The American Dream.
Horatio Alger gone mad on drugs in Las Vegas.
Do it now: pure
Gonzo journalism.

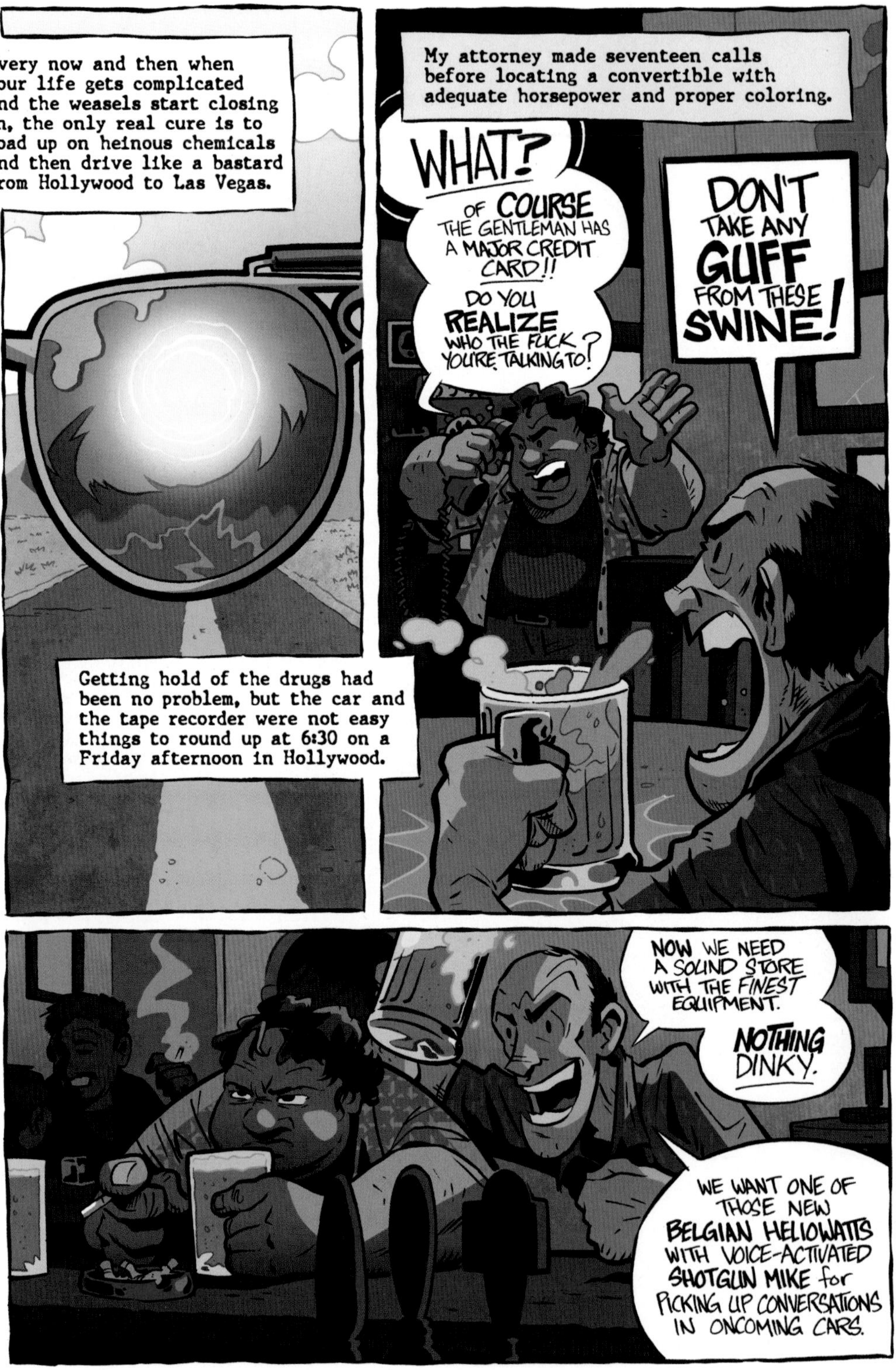
Every now and then when your life gets complicated and the weasels start closing in, the only real cure is to load up on heinous chemicals and then drive like a bastard from Hollywood to Las Vegas.
Getting hold of the drugs had been no problem, but the car and the tape recorder were not easy things to round up at 6:30 on a Friday afternoon in Hollywood.
My attorney made seventeen calls before locating a convertible with adequate horsepower and proper coloring.
WHAT?
OF COURSE THE GENTLEMAN HAS A MAJOR CREDIT CARD!!
DO YOU REALIZE WHO THE FUCK YOU'RE TALKING TO?
DON'T TAKE ANY GUFF FROM THESE SWINE!
NOW WE NEED A SOUND STORE WITH THE FINEST EQUIPMENT.
NOTHING DINKY.
WE WANT ONE OF THOSE NEW BELGIAN HELIOWATTS WITH VOICE-ACTIVATED SHOTGUN MIKE for PICKING UP CONVERSATIONS IN ONCOMING CARS.

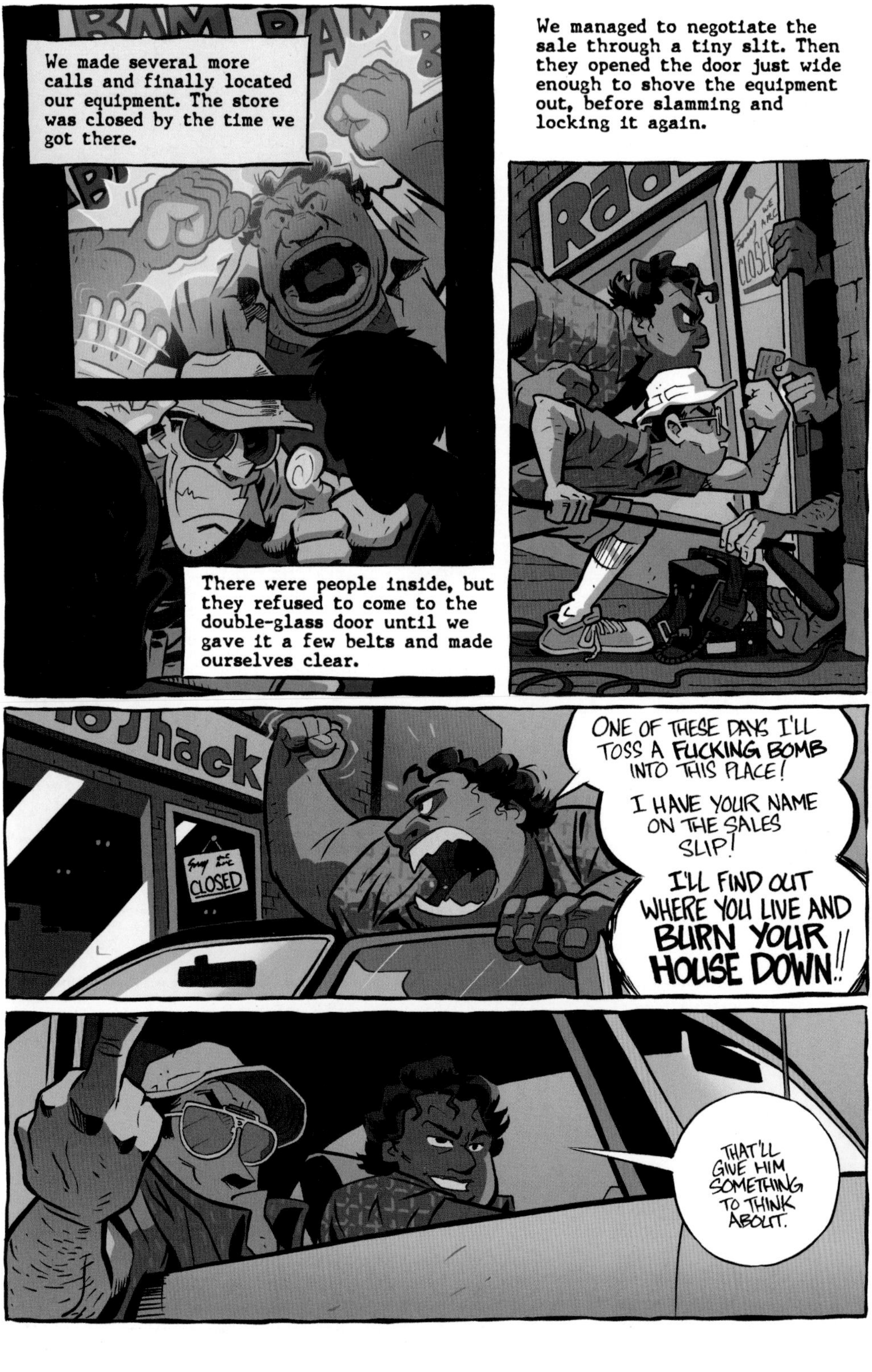
We made several more calls and finally located our equipment. The store was closed by the time we got there.
There were people inside, but they refused to come to the double-glass door until we gave it a few belts and made ourselves clear.
We managed to negotiate the sale through a tiny slit. Then they opened the door just wide enough to shove the equipment out, before slamming and locking it again.
CLOSED
ONE OF THESE DAYS I'LL TOSS A FUCKING BOMB INTO THIS PLACE!
I HAVE YOUR NAME ON THE SALES SLIP!
I'LL FIND OUT WHERE YOU LIVE AND BURN YOUR HOUSE DOWN!!
THAT'LL GIVE HIM SOMETHING TO THINK ABOUT.

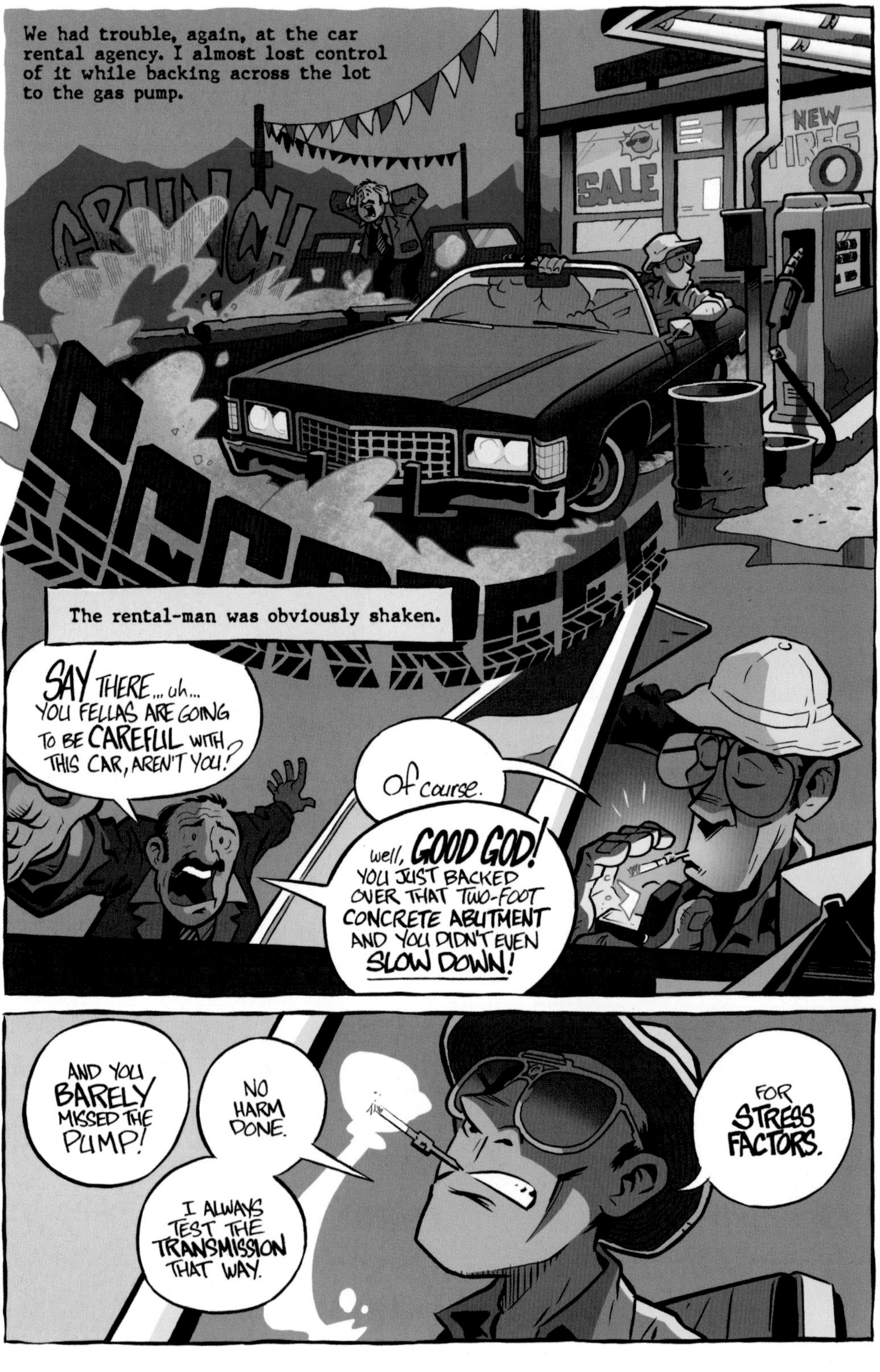
We had trouble, again, at the car rental agency. I almost lost control of it while backing across the lot to the gas pump.
NEW
SALE
The rental-man was obviously shaken.
SAY THERE... uh... YOU FELLAS ARE GOING TO BE CAREFUL WITH THIS CAR, AREN'T YOU?
Of course.
well, GOOD GOD! YOU JUST BACKED OVER THAT TWO-FOOT CONCRETE ABUTMENT AND YOU DIDN'T EVEN SLOW DOWN!
AND YOU BARELY MISSED THE PUMP!
NO HARM DONE.
I ALWAYS TEST THE TRANSMISSION THAT WAY.
FOR STRESS FACTORS.

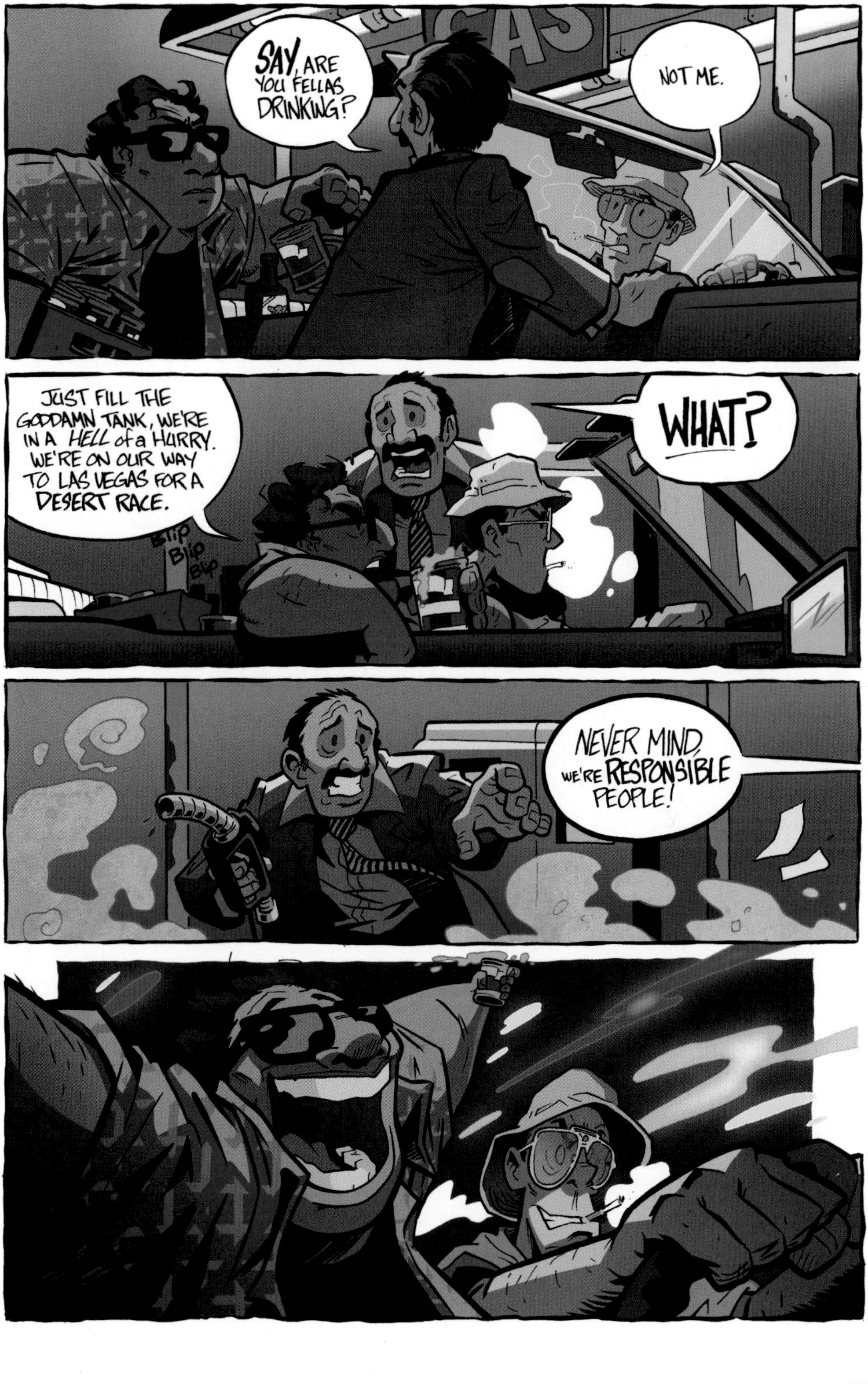
SAY, ARE YOU FELLAS DRINKING?
NOT ME.
JUST FILL THE GODDAMN TANK, WE'RE IN A HELL of a HURRY. WE'RE ON OUR WAY TO LAS VEGAS FOR A DESERT RACE.
Blip Blip Blip
WHAT?
NEVER MIND, WE'RE RESPONSIBLE PEOPLE!

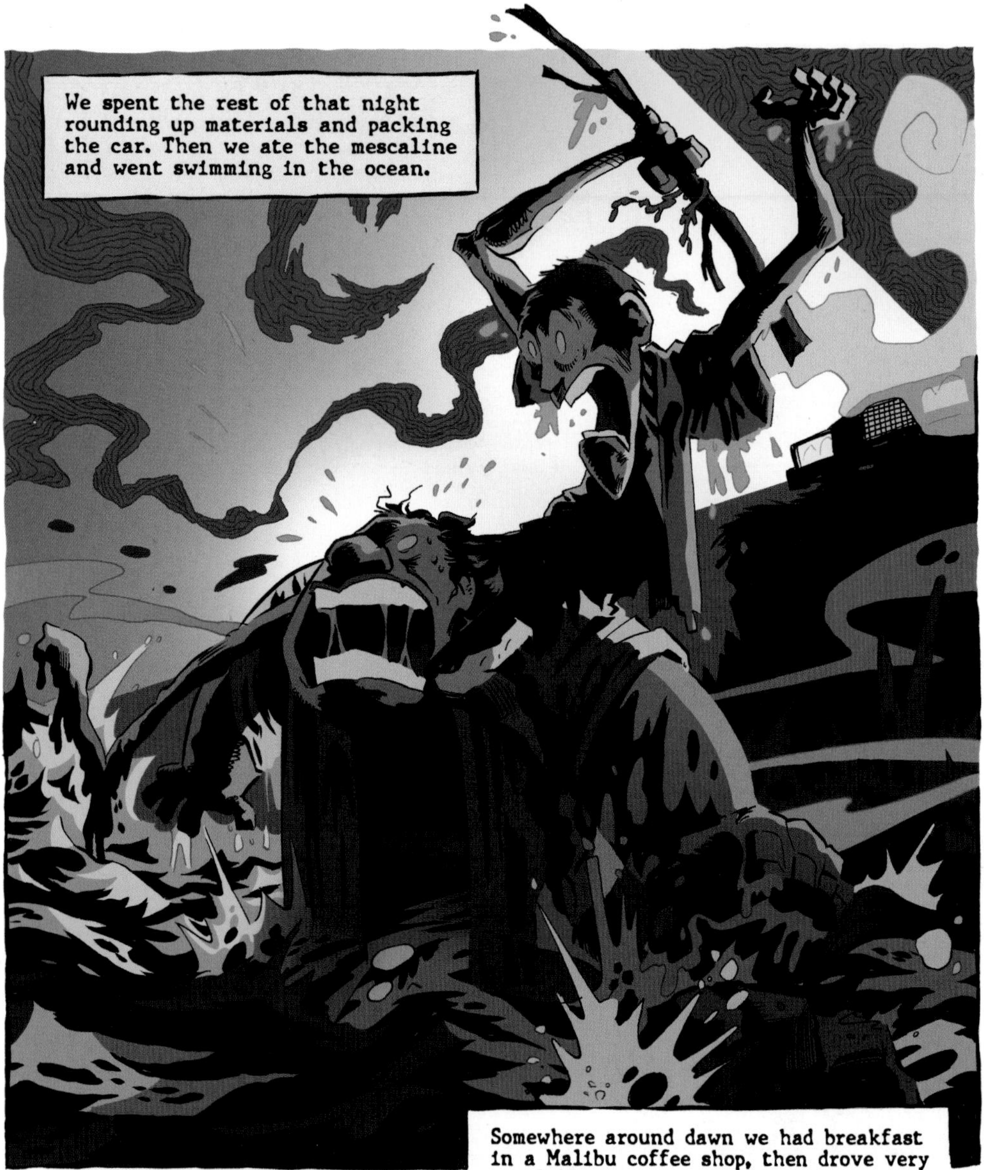
We spent the rest of that night rounding up materials and packing the car. Then we ate the mescaline and went swimming in the ocean.

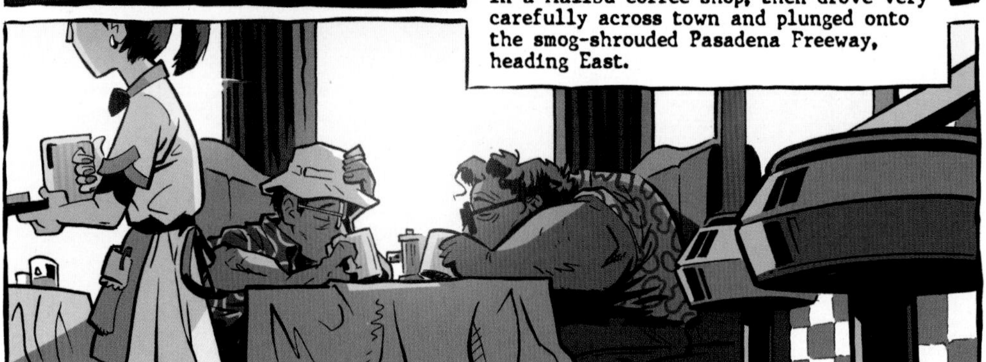
Somewhere around dawn we had breakfast in a Malibu coffee shop, then drove very carefully across town and plunged onto the smog-shrouded Pasadena Freeway, heading East.

3. Strange Medicine on the Desert... a Crisis of Confidence

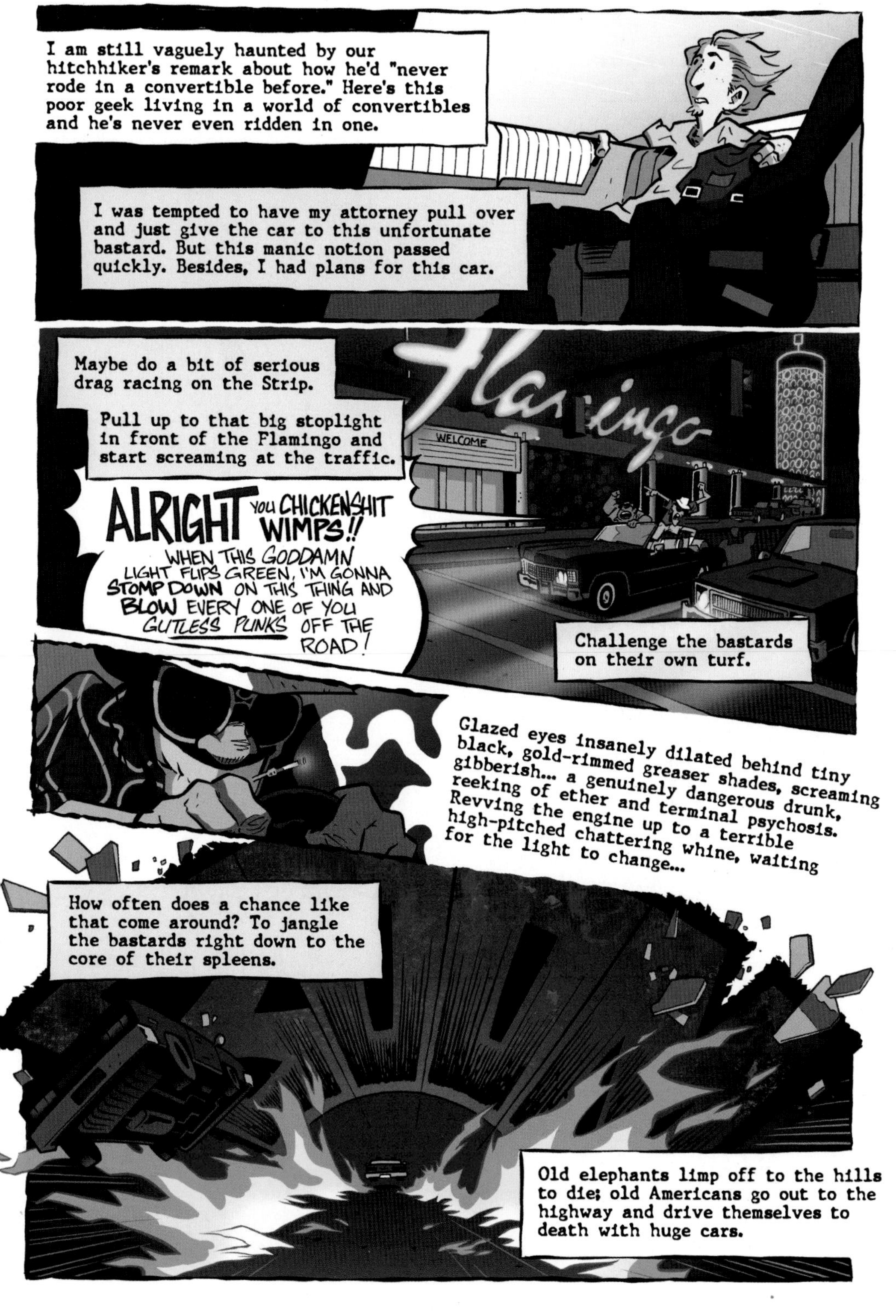
I am still vaguely haunted by our hitchhiker's remark about how he'd "never rode in a convertible before." Here's this poor geek living in a world of convertibles and he's never even ridden in one.
I was tempted to have my attorney pull over and just give the car to this unfortunate bastard. But this manic notion passed quickly. Besides, I had plans for this car.
Flamingo
Maybe do a bit of serious drag racing on the Strip.
Pull up to that big stoplight in front of the Flamingo and start screaming at the traffic.
WELCOME
ALRIGHT YOU CHICKENSHIT WIMPS!! WHEN THIS GODDAMN LIGHT FLIPS GREEN, I'M GONNA STOMP DOWN ON THIS THING AND BLOW EVERY ONE OF YOU GUTLESS PUNKS OFF THE ROAD!
Challenge the bastards on their own turf.
Glazed eyes insanely dilated behind tiny black, gold-rimmed greaser shades, screaming gibberish... a genuinely dangerous drunk, reeking of ether and terminal psychosis. Revving the engine up to a terrible high-pitched chattering whine, waiting for the light to change...
How often does a chance like that come around? To jangle the bastards right down to the core of their spleens.
Old elephants limp off to the hills to die; old Americans go out to the highway and drive themselves to death with huge cars.

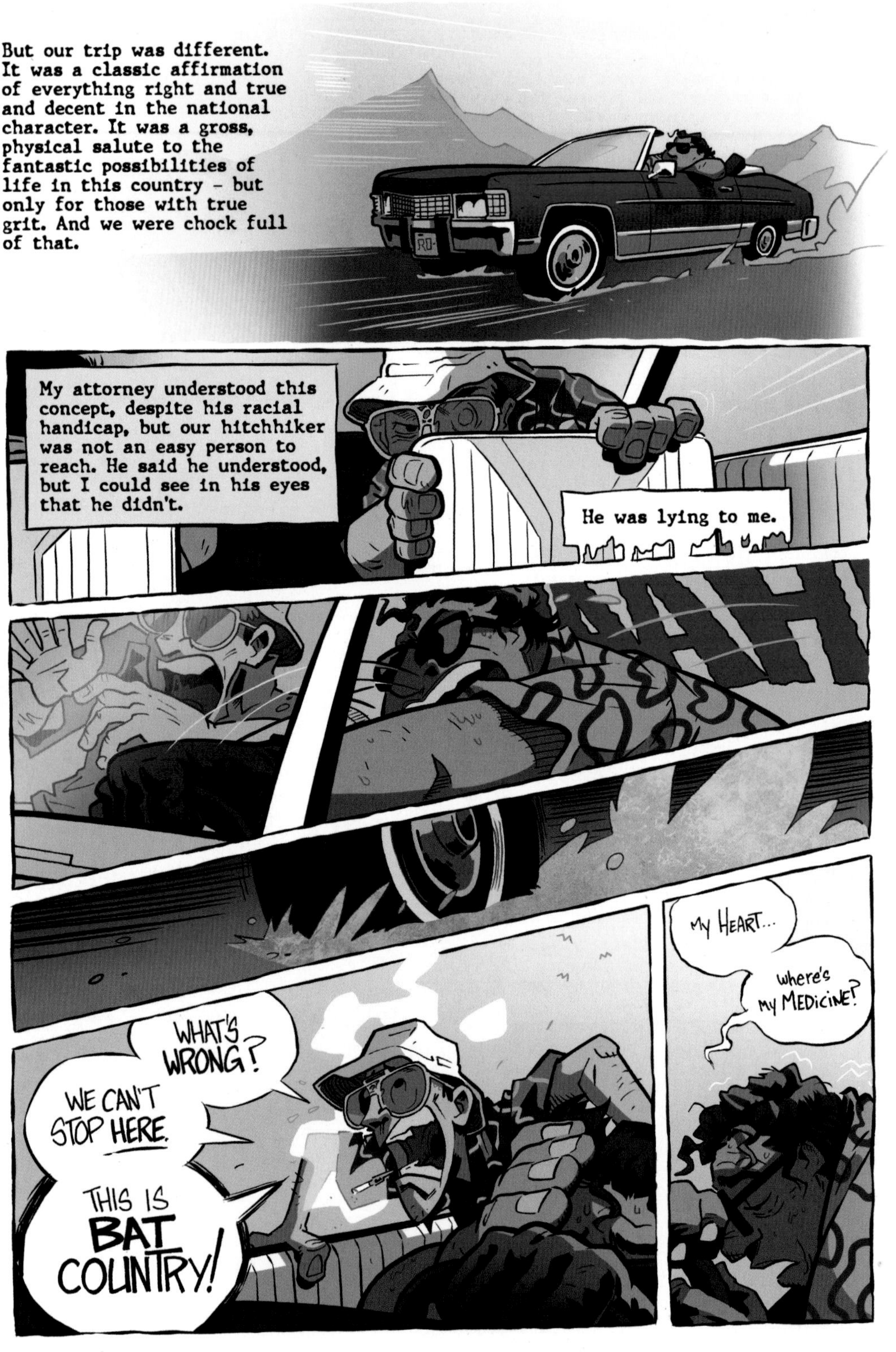
But our trip was different. It was a classic affirmation of everything right and true and decent in the national character. It was a gross, physical salute to the fantastic possibilities of life in this country - but only for those with true grit. And we were chock full of that.
My attorney understood this concept, despite his racial handicap, but our hitchhiker was not an easy person to reach. He said he understood, but I could see in his eyes that he didn't.
He was lying to me.
MY HEART...
where's my MEDICINE?
WHAT'S WRONG?
WE CAN'T STOP HERE.
THIS IS BAT COUNTRY!

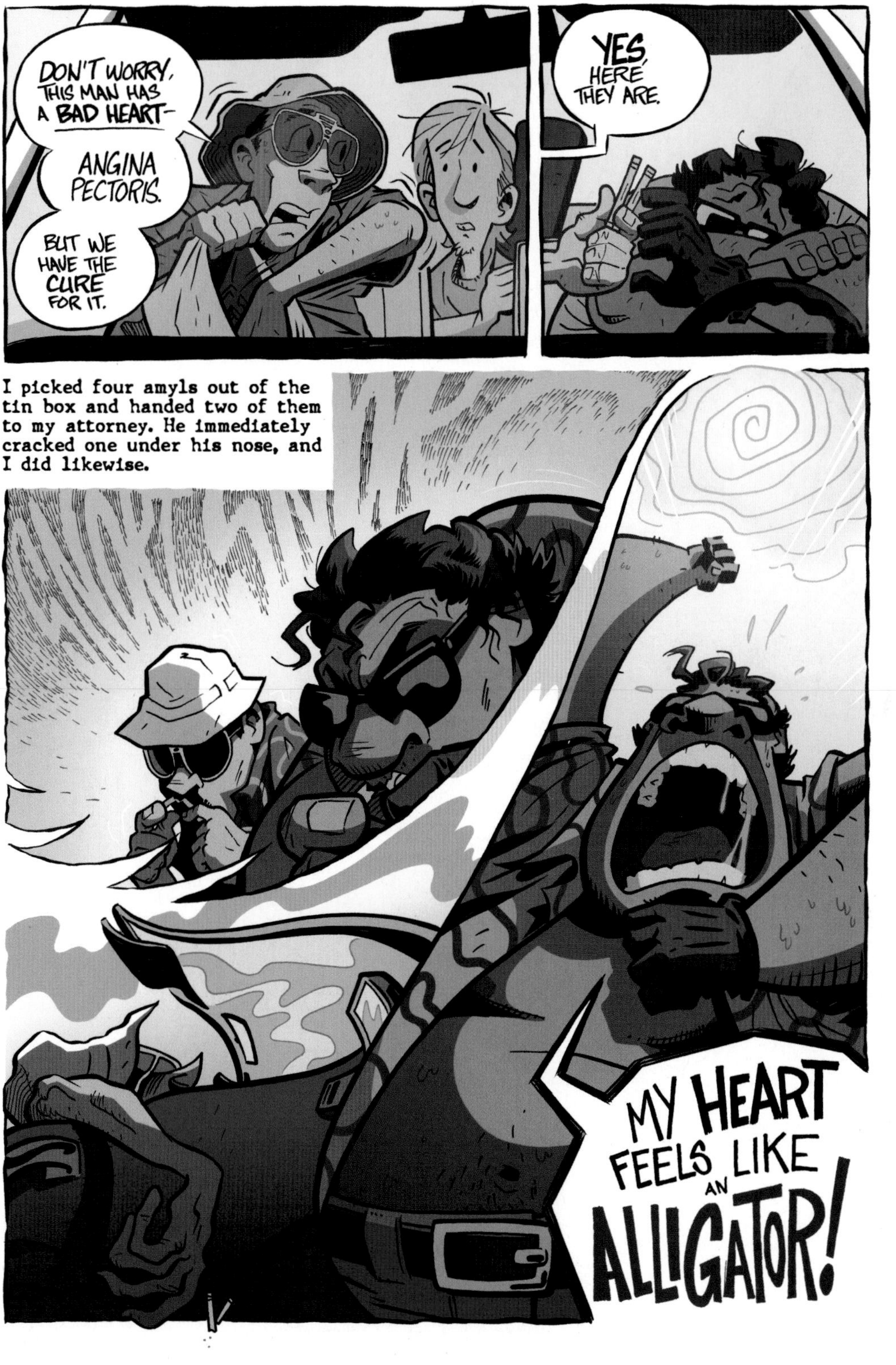
DON'T WORRY, THIS MAN HAS A BAD HEART-
ANGINA PECTORIS.
BUT WE HAVE THE CURE FOR IT.
YES, HERE THEY ARE.
I picked four amyls out of the tin box and handed two of them to my attorney. He immediately cracked one under his nose, and I did likewise.
MY HEART FEELS LIKE AN ALLIGATOR!

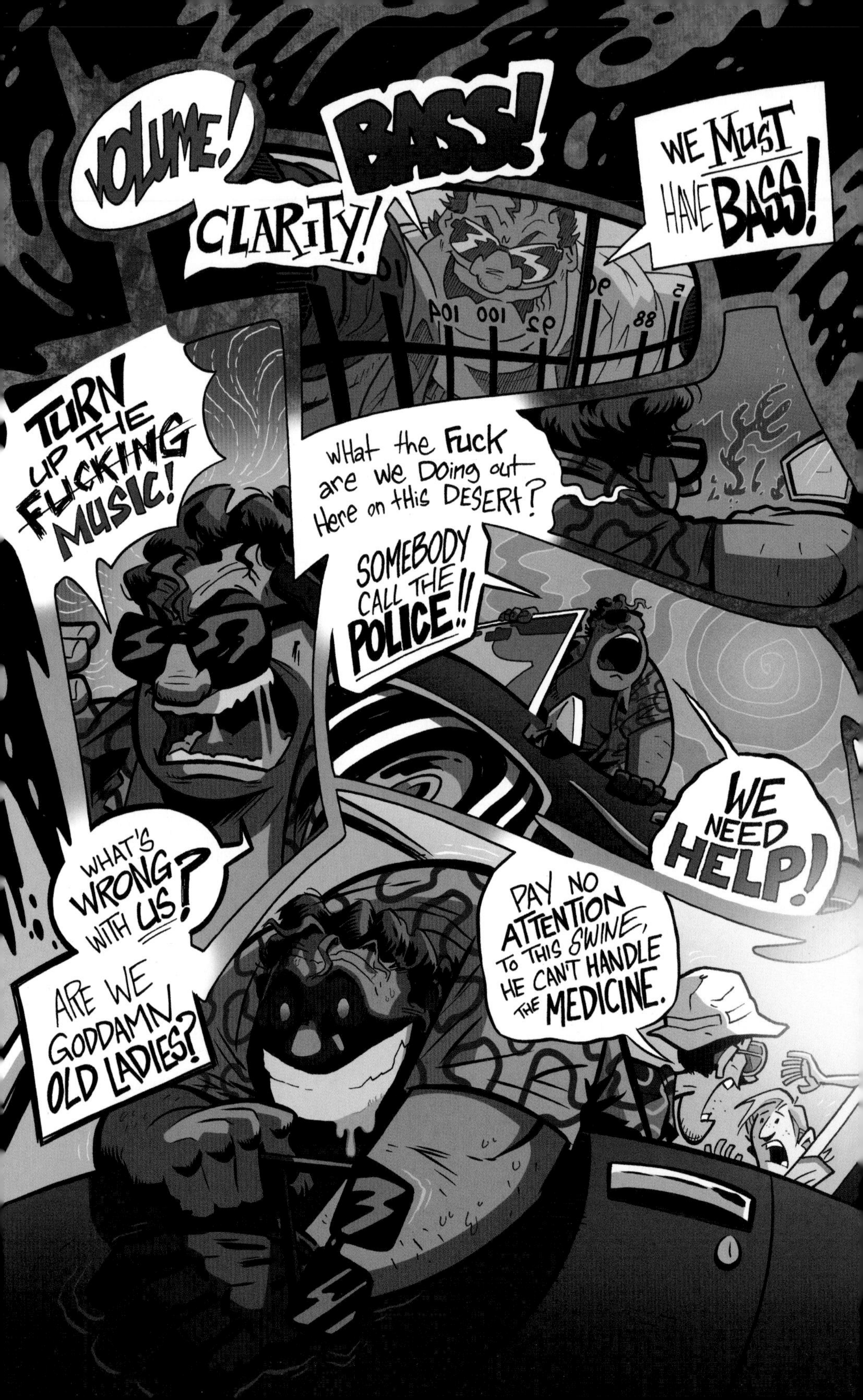
VOLUME!
CLARITY!
BASS!
WE MUST HAVE BASS!
TURN UP THE FUCKING MUSIC!
WHAT the FUCK are we DOING out Here on tHIS DESERT?
SOMEBODY CALL THE POLICE!!
WE NEED HELP!
WHAT'S WRONG WITH US?
ARE WE GODDAMN OLD LADIES?
PAY NO ATTENTION TO THIS SWINE, HE CAN'T HANDLE THE MEDICINE.

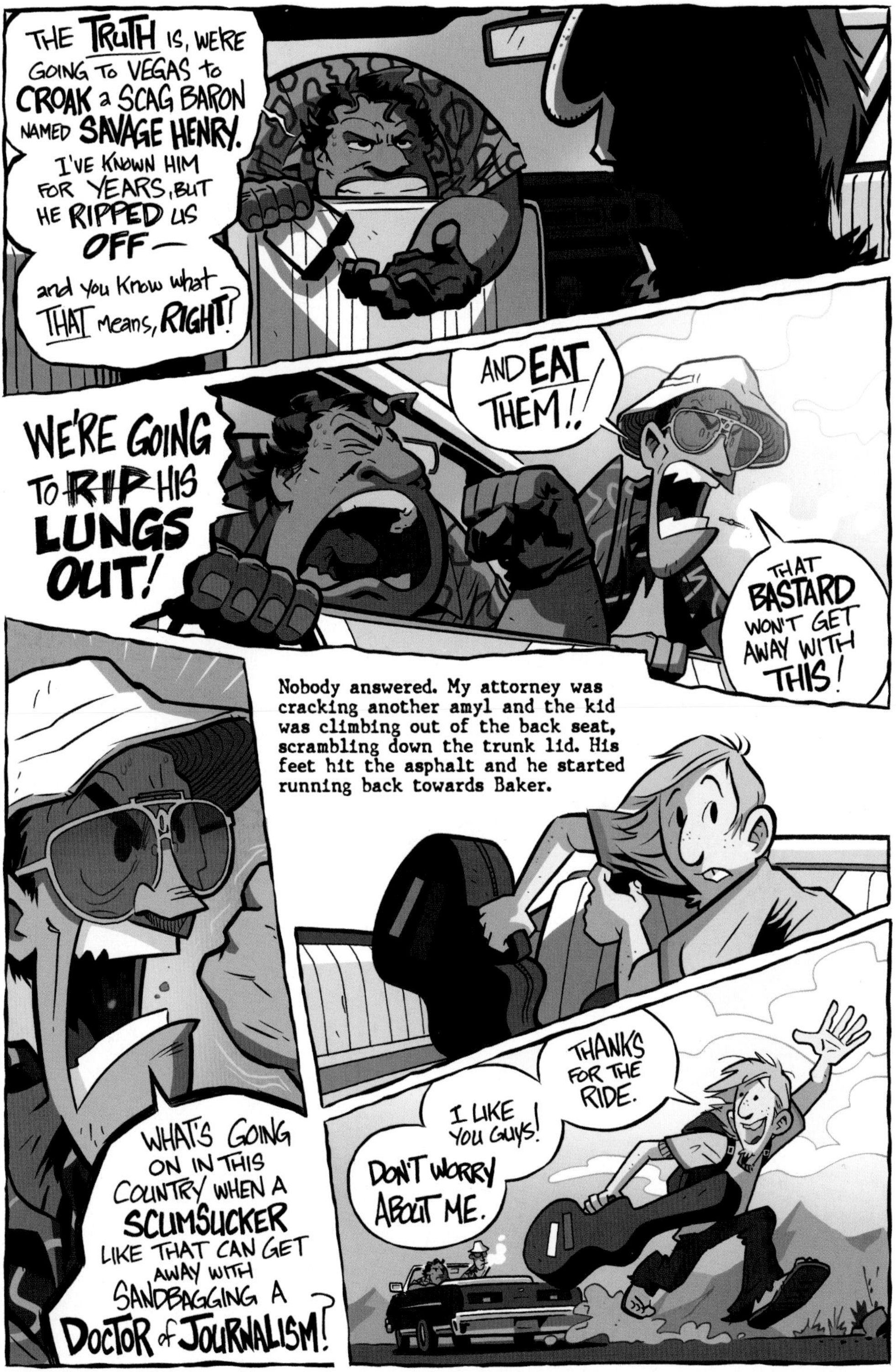
THE TRUTH IS, WE'RE GOING TO VEGAS to CROAK a SCAG BARON NAMED SAVAGE HENRY. I'VE KNOWN HIM FOR YEARS, BUT HE RIPPED US OFF—
and you Know what THAT means, RIGHT?
AND EAT THEM!!
WE'RE GOING TO RIP HIS LUNGS OUT!
THAT BASTARD WON'T GET AWAY WITH THIS!
Nobody answered. My attorney was cracking another amyl and the kid was climbing out of the back seat, scrambling down the trunk lid. His feet hit the asphalt and he started running back towards Baker.
WHAT'S GOING ON IN THIS COUNTRY WHEN A SCUMSUCKER LIKE THAT CAN GET AWAY WITH SANDBAGGING A DOCTOR of JOURNALISM?
THANKS FOR THE RIDE.
I LIKE YOU GUYS!
DON'T WORRY ABOUT ME.

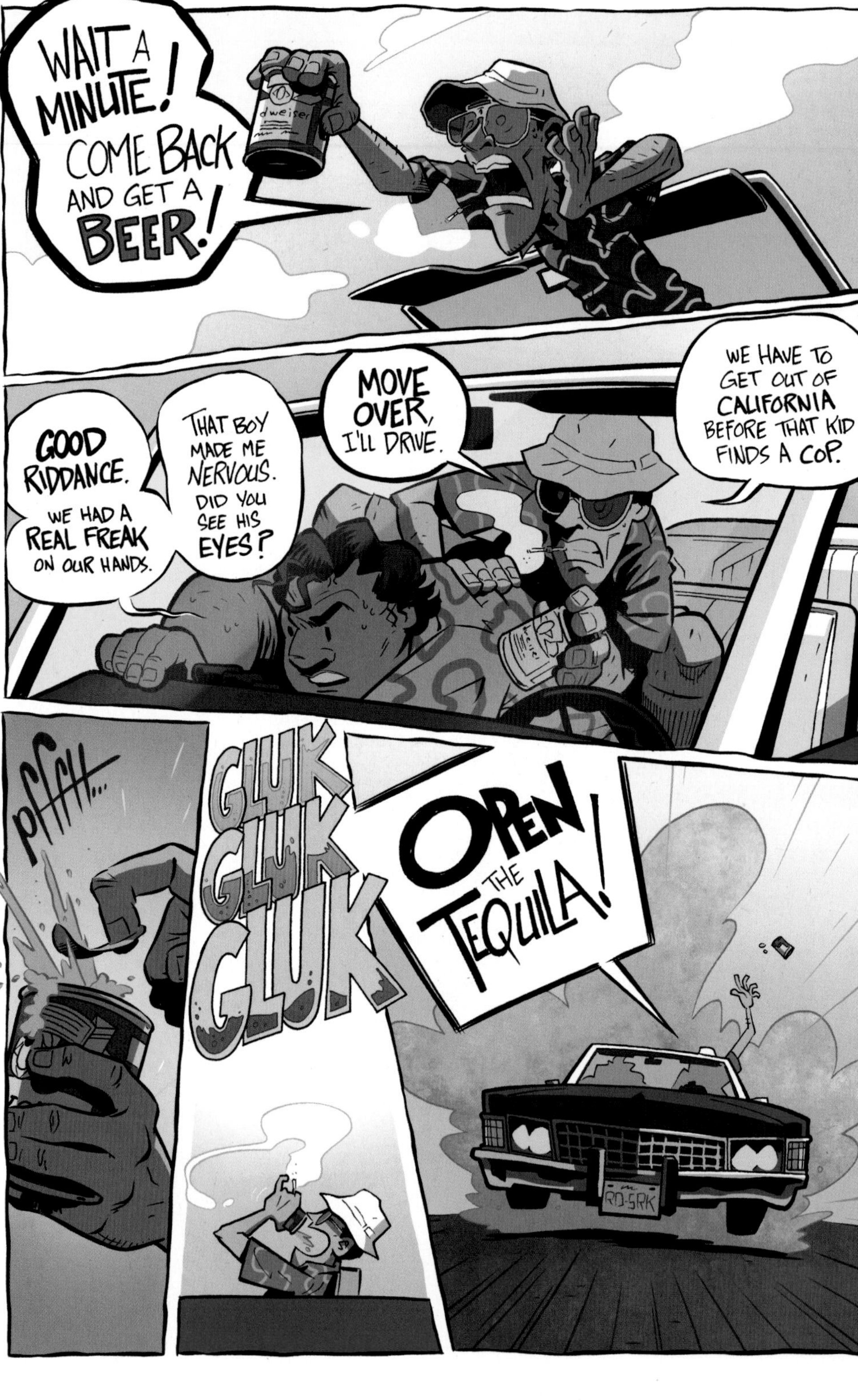
WAIT A MINUTE! COME BACK AND GET A BEER!
GOOD RIDDANCE. WE HAD A REAL FREAK ON OUR HANDS.
THAT BOY MADE ME NERVOUS. DID YOU SEE HIS EYES?
MOVE OVER, I'LL DRIVE.
WE HAVE TO GET OUT OF CALIFORNIA BEFORE THAT KID FINDS A COP.
pffftt...
GLUK GLUK GLUK
OPEN THE TEQUILA!
RD-SRK

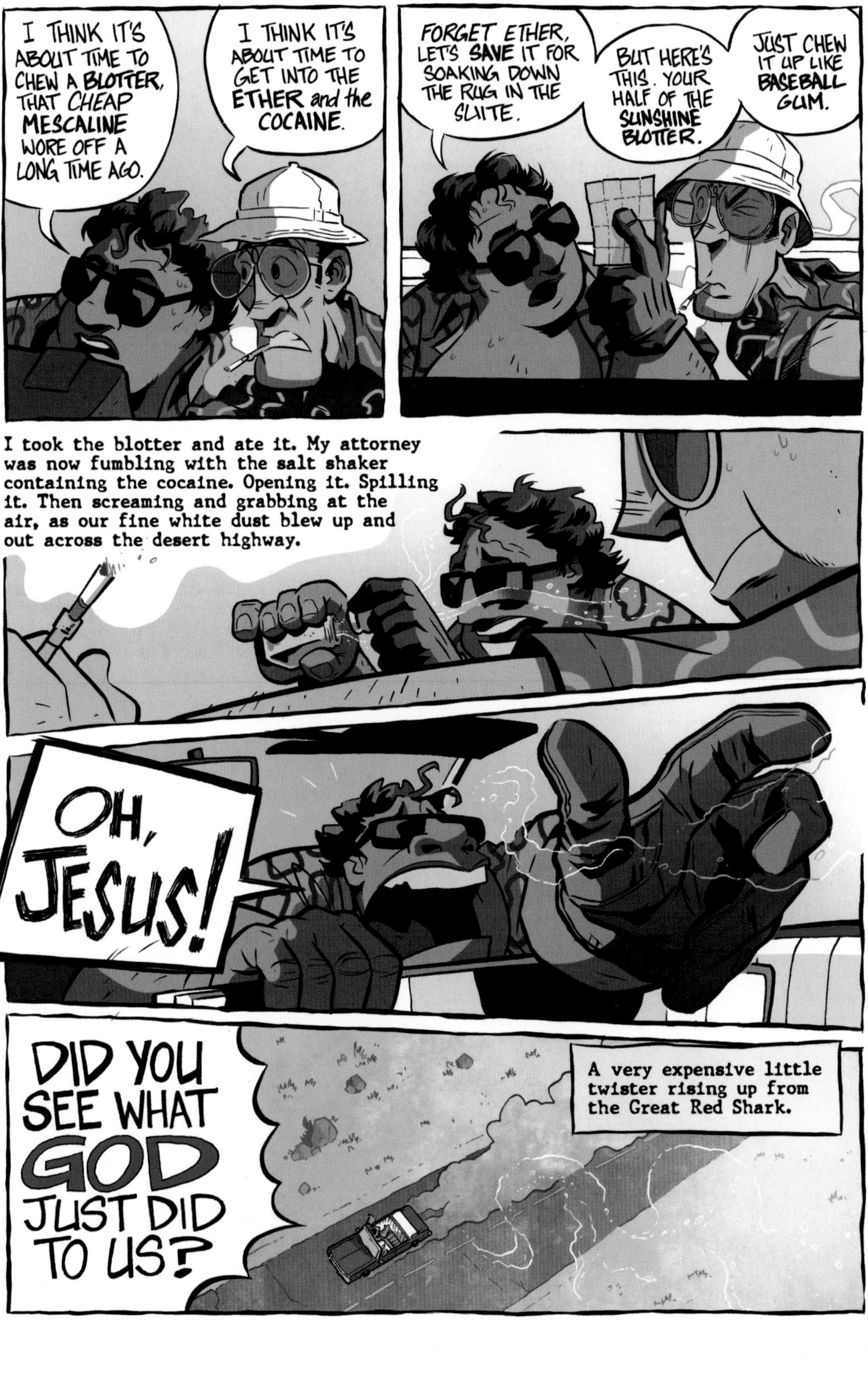
I THINK IT'S ABOUT TIME TO CHEW A BLOTTER, THAT CHEAP MESCALINE WORE OFF A LONG TIME AGO.
I THINK IT'S ABOUT TIME TO GET INTO THE ETHER and the COCAINE.
FORGET ETHER, LET'S SAVE IT FOR SOAKING DOWN THE RUG IN THE SUITE.
BUT HERE'S THIS. YOUR HALF OF THE SUNSHINE BLOTTER.
JUST CHEW IT UP LIKE BASEBALL GUM.
I took the blotter and ate it. My attorney was now fumbling with the salt shaker containing the cocaine. Opening it. Spilling it. Then screaming and grabbing at the air, as our fine white dust blew up and out across the desert highway.
OH, JESUS!
DID YOU SEE WHAT GOD JUST DID TO US?
A very expensive little twister rising up from the Great Red Shark.

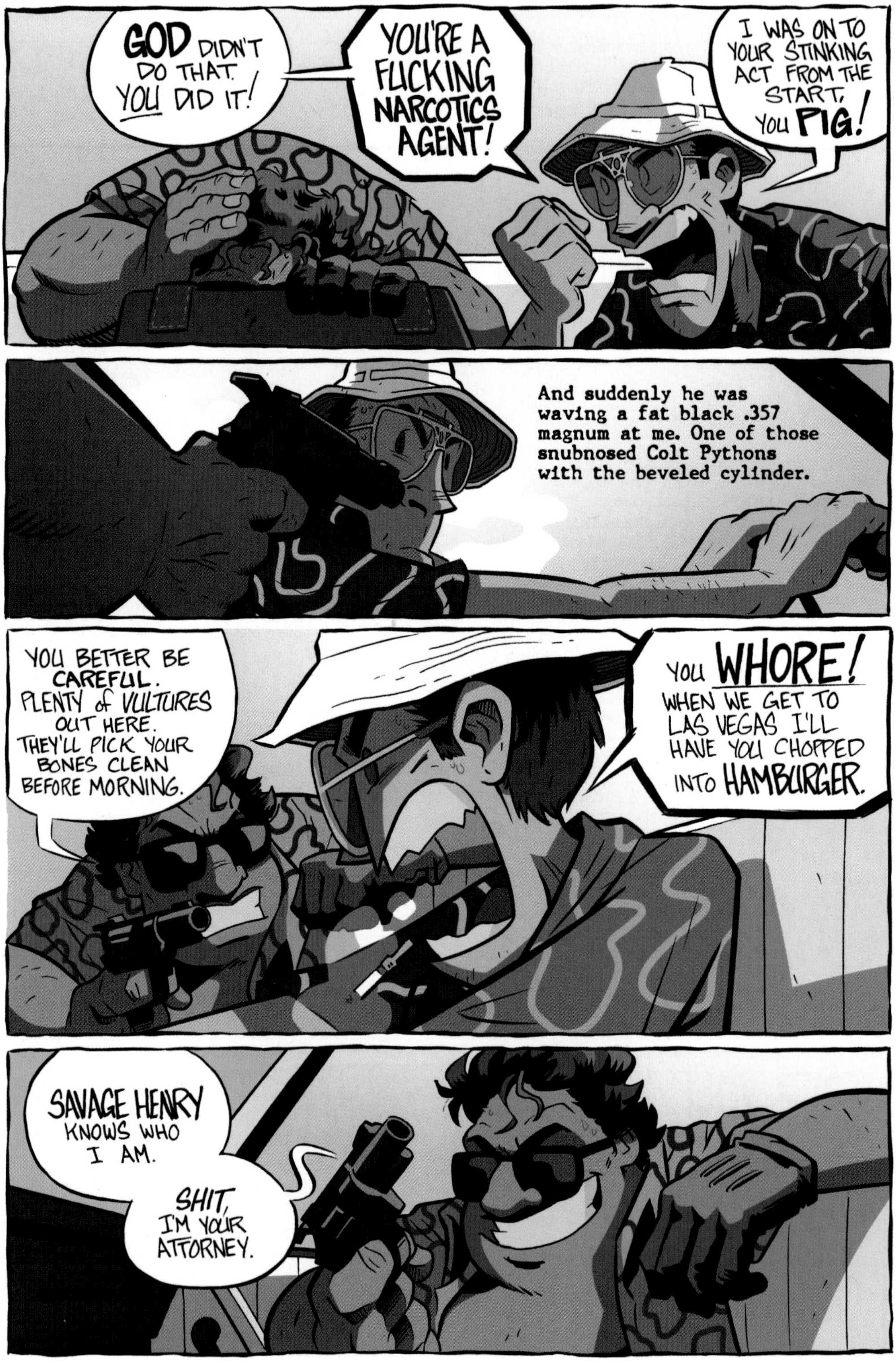
GOD DIDN'T DO THAT. YOU DID IT!
YOU'RE A FUCKING NARCOTICS AGENT!
I WAS ON TO YOUR STINKING ACT FROM THE START, YOU PIG!
And suddenly he was waving a fat black .357 magnum at me. One of those snubnosed Colt Pythons with the beveled cylinder.
YOU BETTER BE CAREFUL. PLENTY of VULTURES OUT HERE. THEY'LL PICK YOUR BONES CLEAN BEFORE MORNING.
YOU WHORE! WHEN WE GET TO LAS VEGAS I'LL HAVE YOU CHOPPED INTO HAMBURGER.
SAVAGE HENRY KNOWS WHO I AM.
SHIT, I'M YOUR ATTORNEY.

YOU'RE FULL OF ACID, YOU FOOL. IT'LL BE A GODDAMN MIRACLE IF WE CAN GET TO THE HOTEL BEFORE YOU TURN INTO A WILD ANIMAL.

ARE YOU READY FOR THAT!

HOW LONG DO WE HAVE?

MAYBE THIRTY MORE MINUTES.

AS YOUR ATTORNEY I ADVISE YOU TO DRIVE AT TOP SPEED.

Thirty minutes. It was going to be very close. The objective was the big tower of the Mint Hotel, downtown — and if we didn't get there before we lost all control, there was also the Nevada State prison upstate in Carson City.

CALIFORNIA

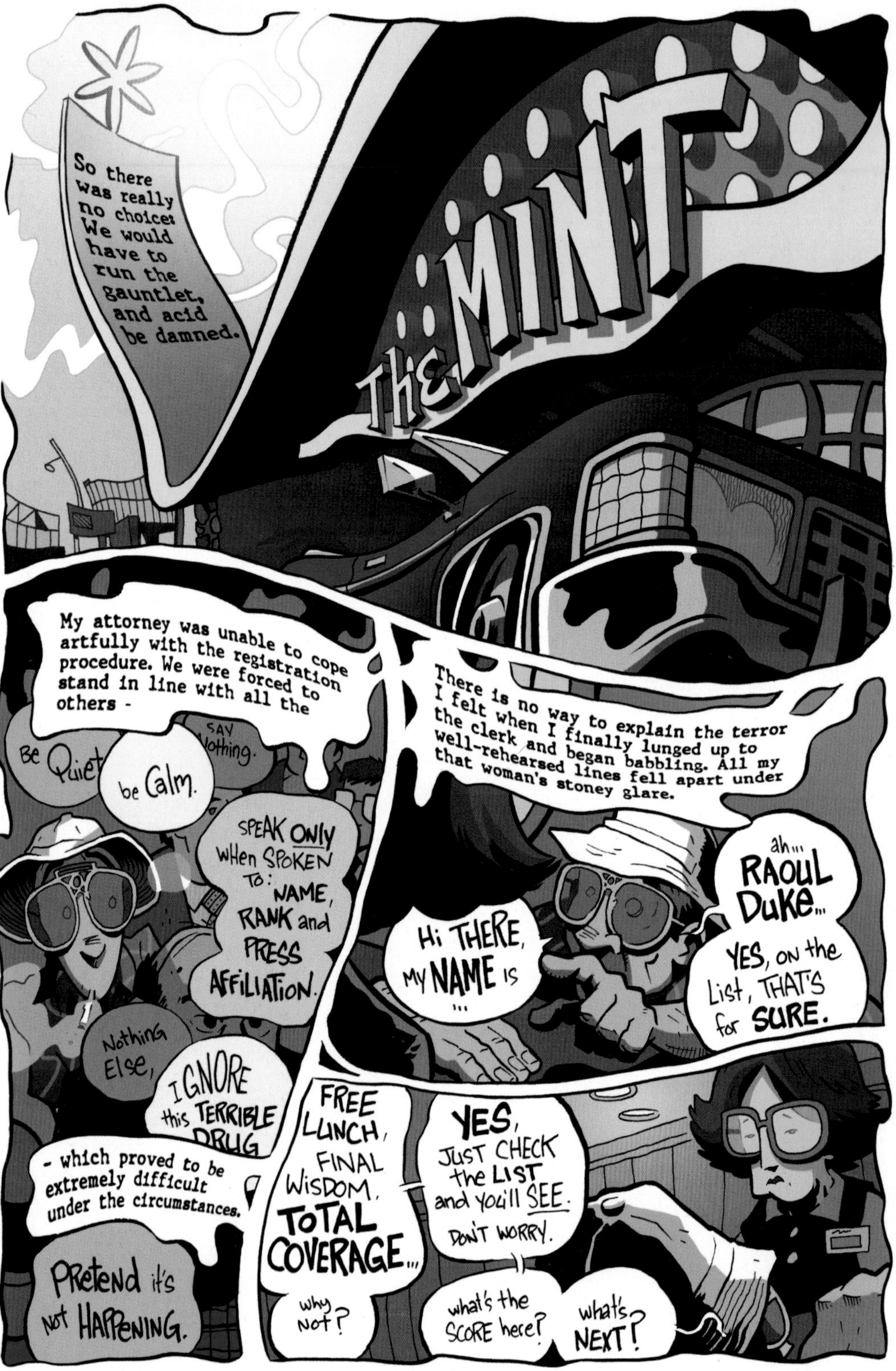
So there was really no choice: We would have to run the gauntlet, and acid be damned.
The MINT
My attorney was unable to cope artfully with the registration procedure. We were forced to stand in line with all the others -
Be Quiet
SAY Nothing.
be Calm.
SPEAK ONLY WHEN SPOKEN TO: NAME, RANK and PRESS AFFILIATION.
Nothing Else,
IGNORE this TERRIBLE DRUG
- which proved to be extremely difficult under the circumstances.
PRETEND it's NOT HAPPENING.
There is no way to explain the terror I felt when I finally lunged up to the clerk and began babbling. All my well-rehearsed lines fell apart under that woman's stoney glare.
Hi THERE, MY NAME IS ...
ah... RAOUL DUKE...
YES, ON the List, THAT'S for SURE.
FREE LUNCH, FINAL WISDOM, TOTAL COVERAGE...
why not?
YES, JUST CHECK the LIST and you'll SEE. DON'T WORRY.
what's the SCORE here?
what's NEXT?

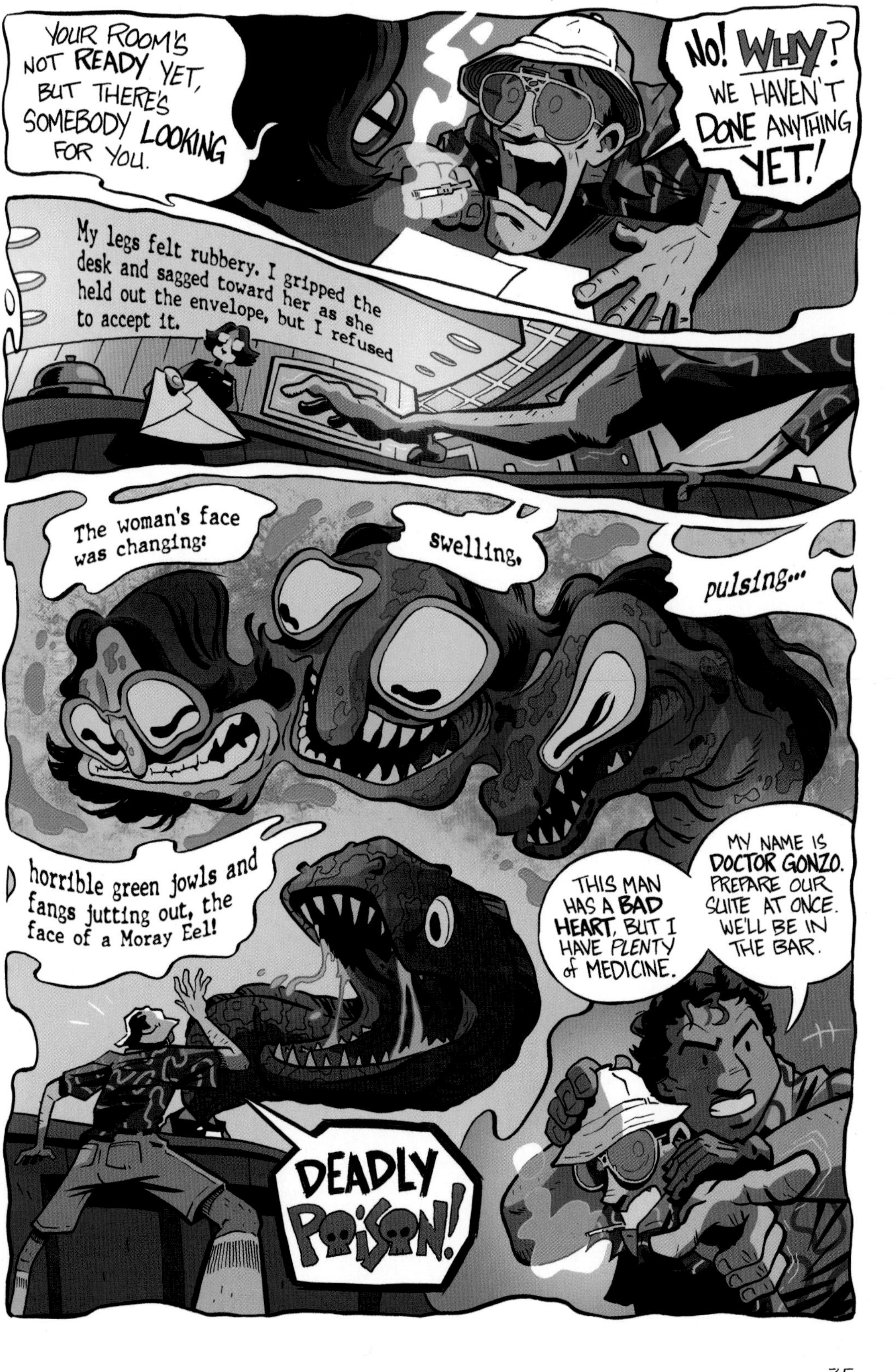
YOUR ROOM'S NOT READY YET, BUT THERE'S SOMEBODY LOOKING FOR YOU.
NO! WHY? WE HAVEN'T DONE ANYTHING YET!
My legs felt rubbery. I gripped the desk and sagged toward her as she held out the envelope, but I refused to accept it.
The woman's face was changing:
swelling,
pulsing...
horrible green jowls and fangs jutting out, the face of a Moray Eel!
DEADLY POISON!
THIS MAN HAS A BAD HEART, BUT I HAVE PLENTY of MEDICINE.
MY NAME IS DOCTOR GONZO. PREPARE OUR SUITE AT ONCE. WE'LL BE IN THE BAR.

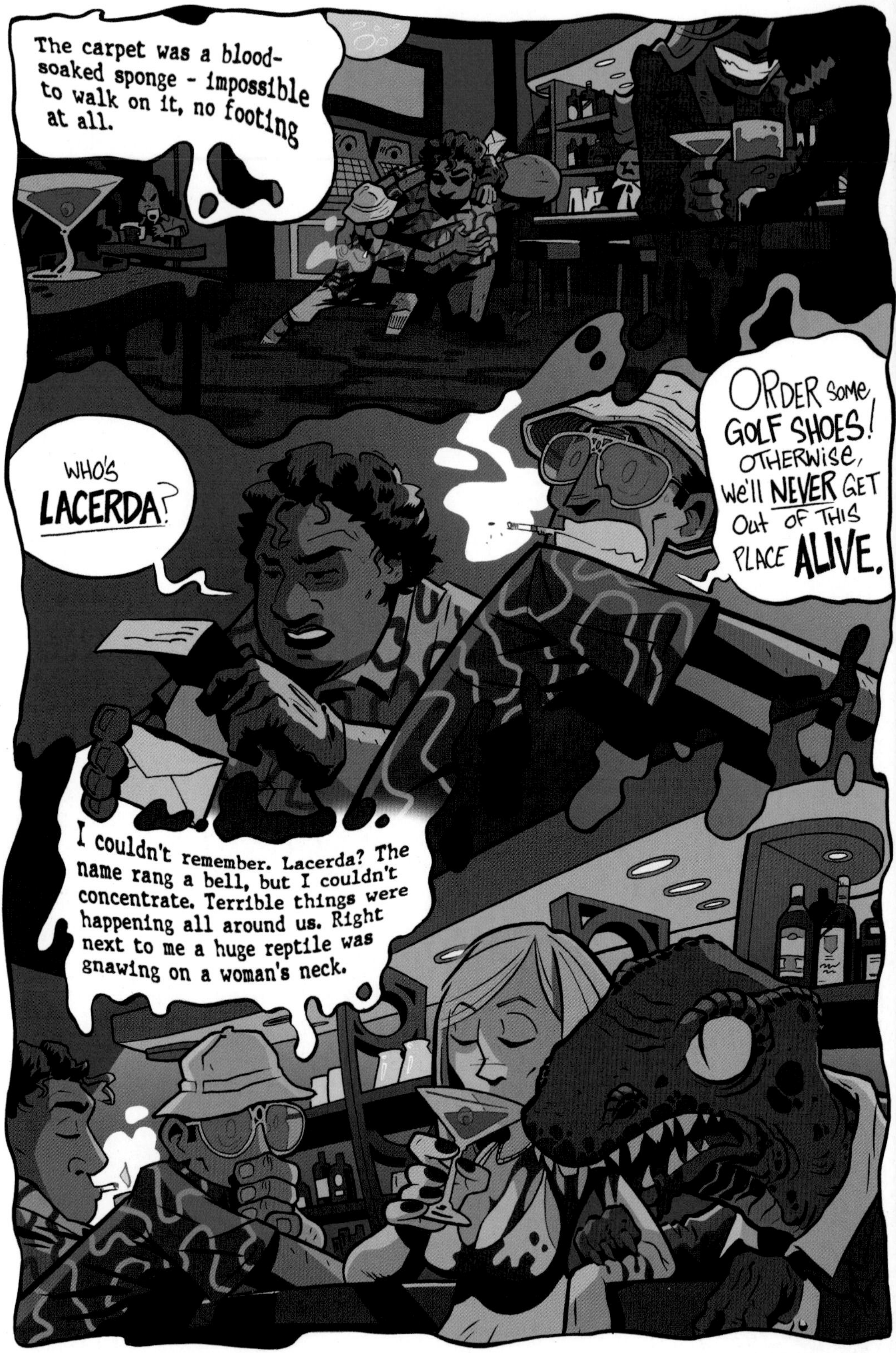
The carpet was a blood-soaked sponge - impossible to walk on it, no footing at all.
WHO'S LACERDA?
ORDER some GOLF SHOES! OTHERWISE, We'll NEVER GET Out OF THIS PLACE ALIVE.
I couldn't remember. Lacerda? The name rang a bell, but I couldn't concentrate. Terrible things were happening all around us. Right next to me a huge reptile was gnawing on a woman's neck.

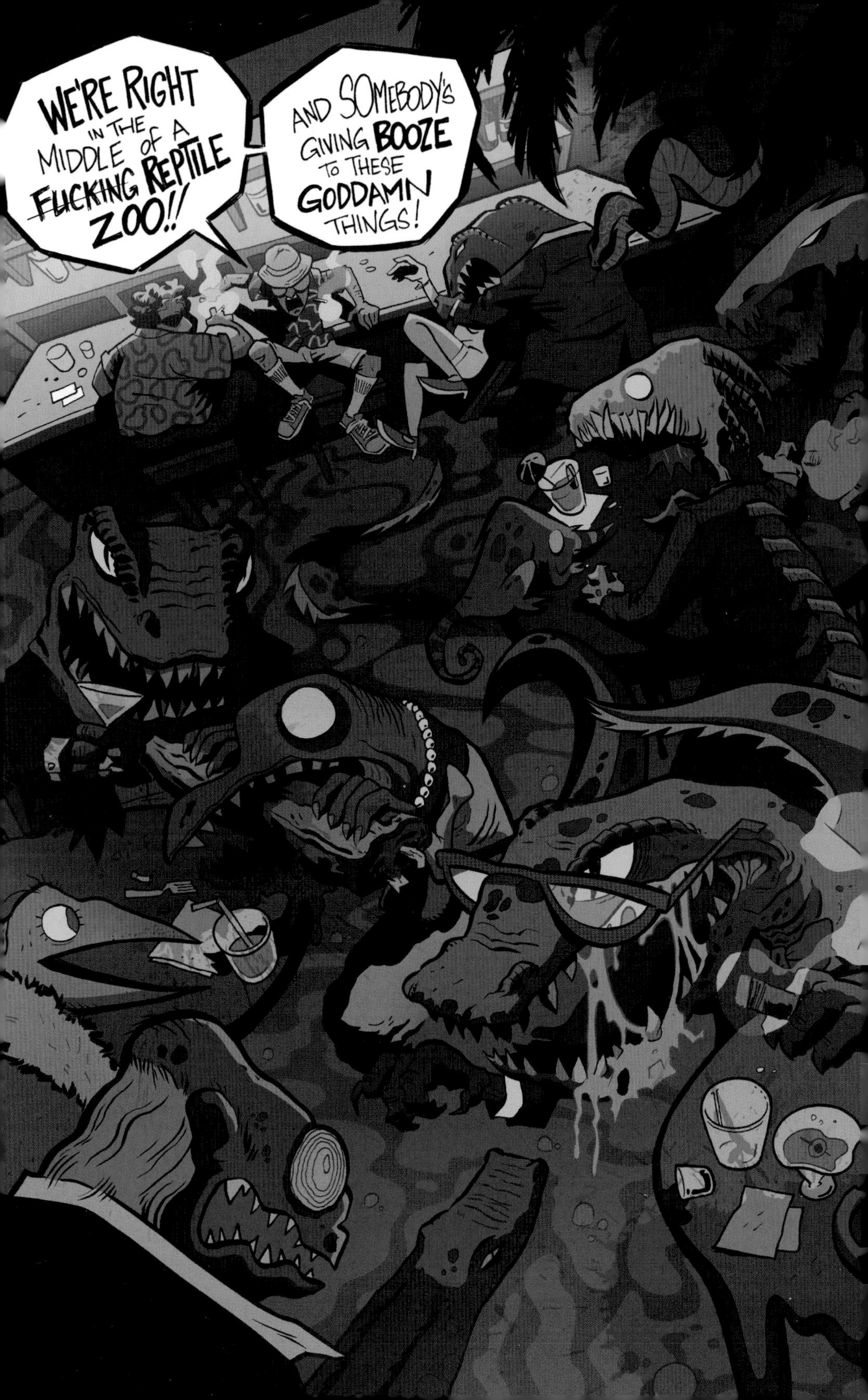
WE'RE RIGHT IN THE MIDDLE OF A FUCKING REPTILE ZOO!!
AND SOMEBODY'S GIVING BOOZE TO THESE GODDAMN THINGS!

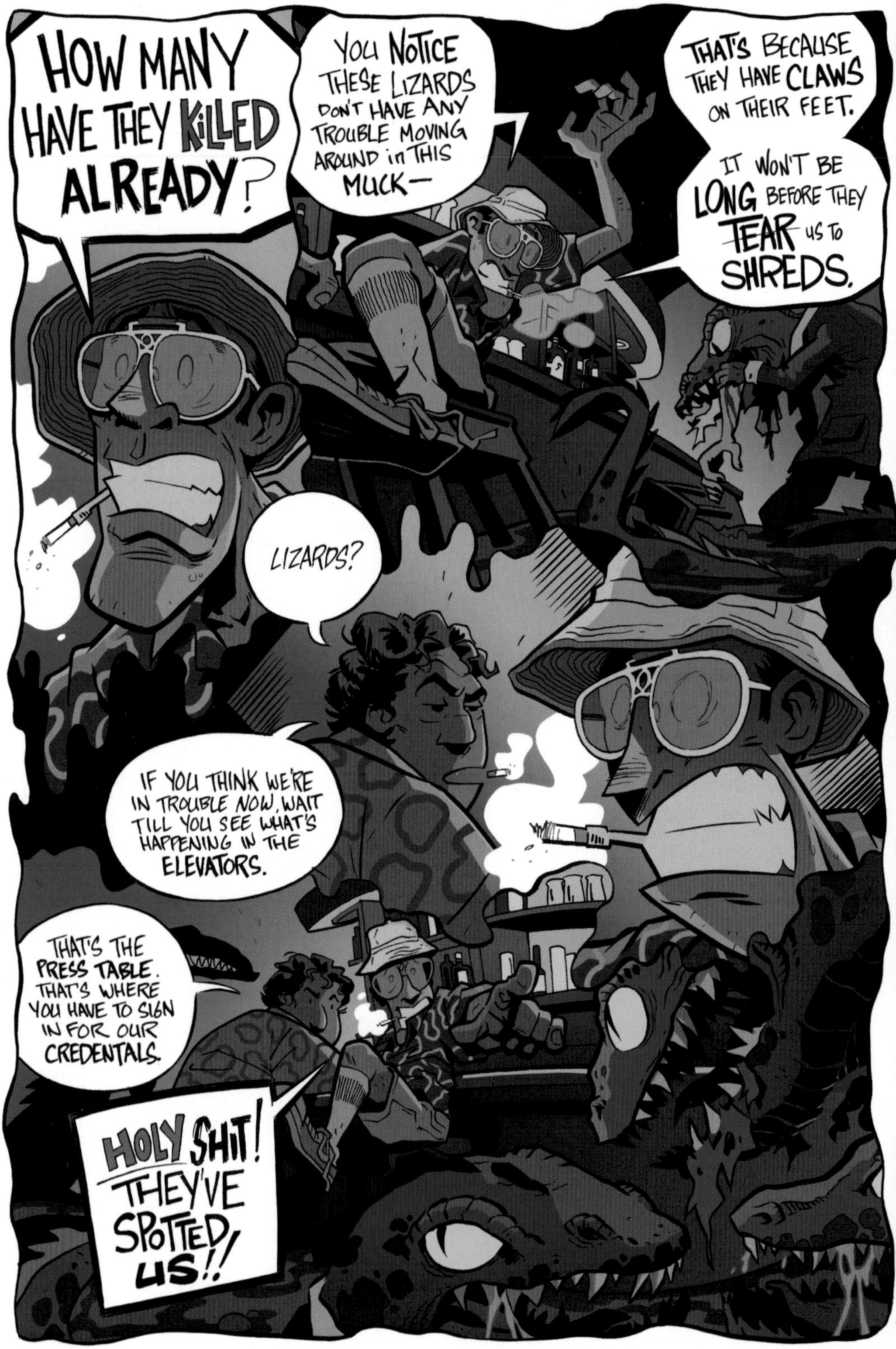
HOW MANY HAVE THEY KILLED ALREADY?
YOU NOTICE THESE LIZARDS DON'T HAVE ANY TROUBLE MOVING AROUND IN THIS MUCK—
THAT'S BECAUSE THEY HAVE CLAWS ON THEIR FEET.
IT WON'T BE LONG BEFORE THEY TEAR US TO SHREDS.
LIZARDS?
IF YOU THINK WE'RE IN TROUBLE NOW, WAIT TILL YOU SEE WHAT'S HAPPENING IN THE ELEVATORS.
THAT'S THE PRESS TABLE. THAT'S WHERE YOU HAVE TO SIGN IN FOR OUR CREDENTALS.
HOLY SHIT! THEY'VE SPOTTED US!!

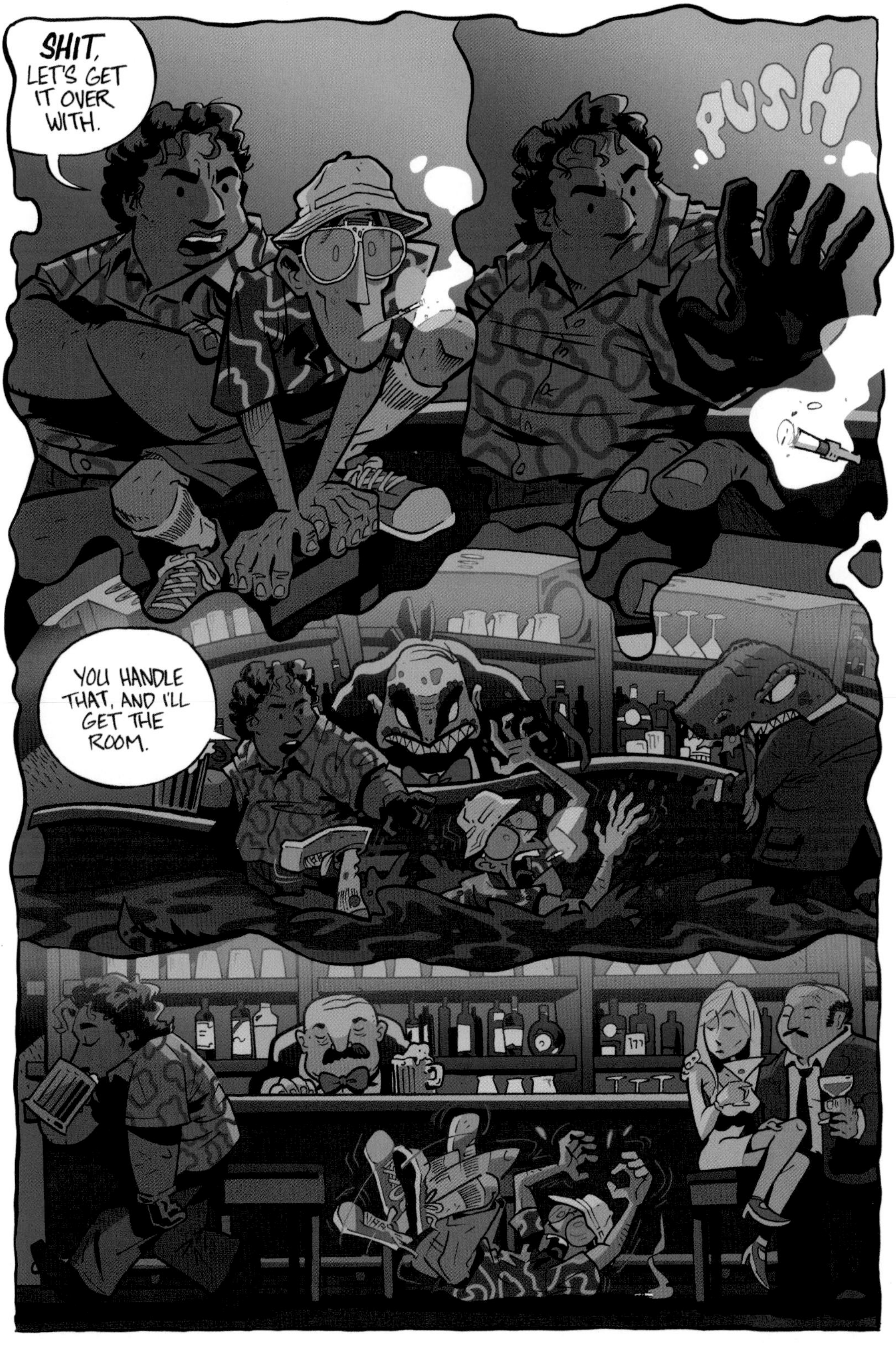
SHIT, LET'S GET IT OVER WITH.
PUSH
YOU HANDLE THAT, AND I'LL GET THE ROOM.

4. Hideous Music and the Sound of Many Shotguns... Rude Vibes on a Saturday Evening in Vegas

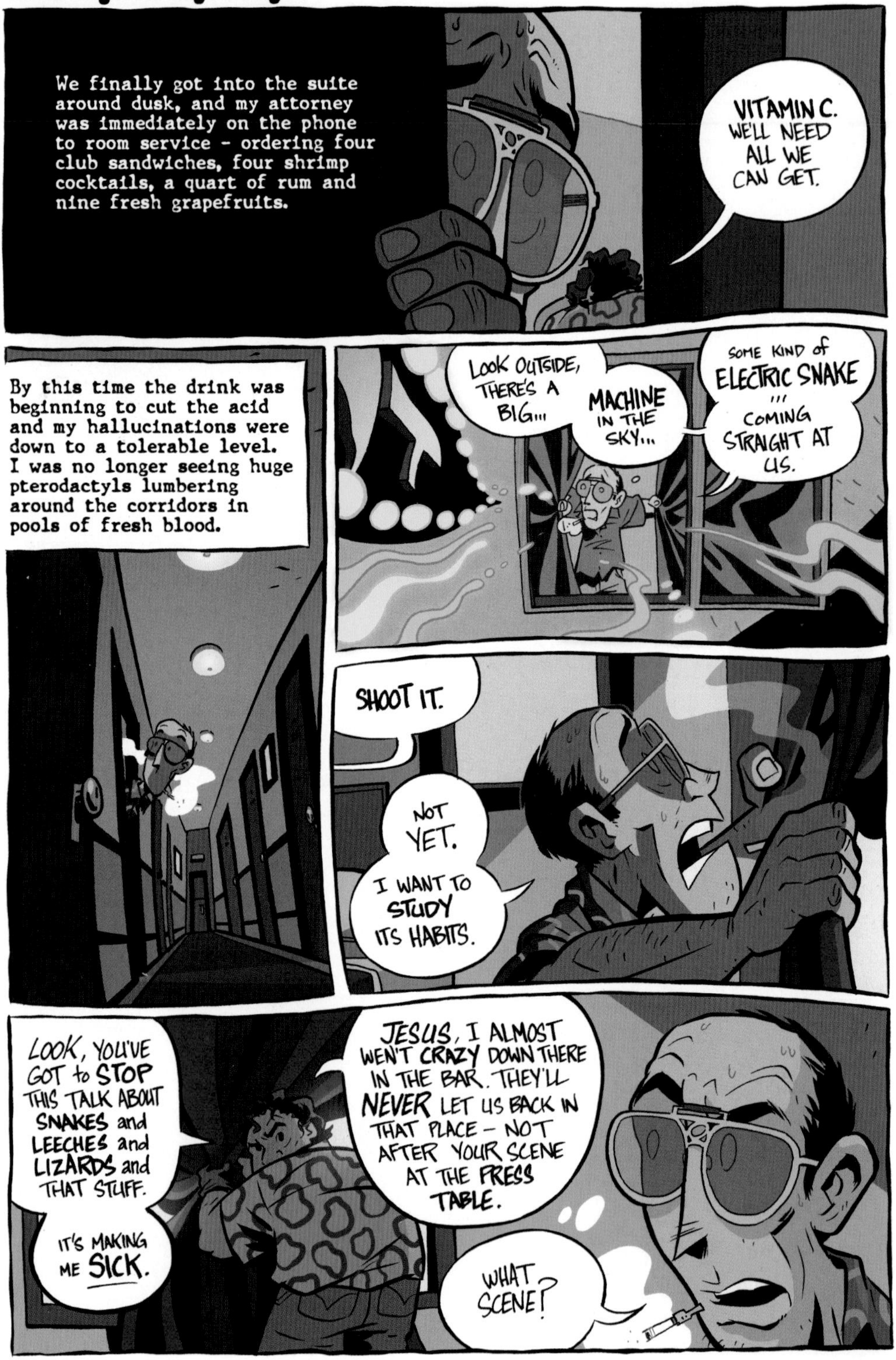

We finally got into the suite around dusk, and my attorney was immediately on the phone to room service - ordering four club sandwiches, four shrimp cocktails, a quart of rum and nine fresh grapefruits.
VITAMIN C. WE'LL NEED ALL WE CAN GET.
By this time the drink was beginning to cut the acid and my hallucinations were down to a tolerable level. I was no longer seeing huge pterodactyls lumbering around the corridors in pools of fresh blood.
LOOK OUTSIDE, THERE'S A BIG...
MACHINE IN THE SKY...
SOME KIND OF ELECTRIC SNAKE ... COMING STRAIGHT AT US.
SHOOT IT.
NOT YET.
I WANT TO STUDY ITS HABITS.
LOOK, YOU'VE GOT TO STOP THIS TALK ABOUT SNAKES AND LEECHES AND LIZARDS AND THAT STUFF.
IT'S MAKING ME SICK.
JESUS, I ALMOST WENT CRAZY DOWN THERE IN THE BAR. THEY'LL NEVER LET US BACK IN THAT PLACE - NOT AFTER YOUR SCENE AT THE PRESS TABLE.
WHAT SCENE?

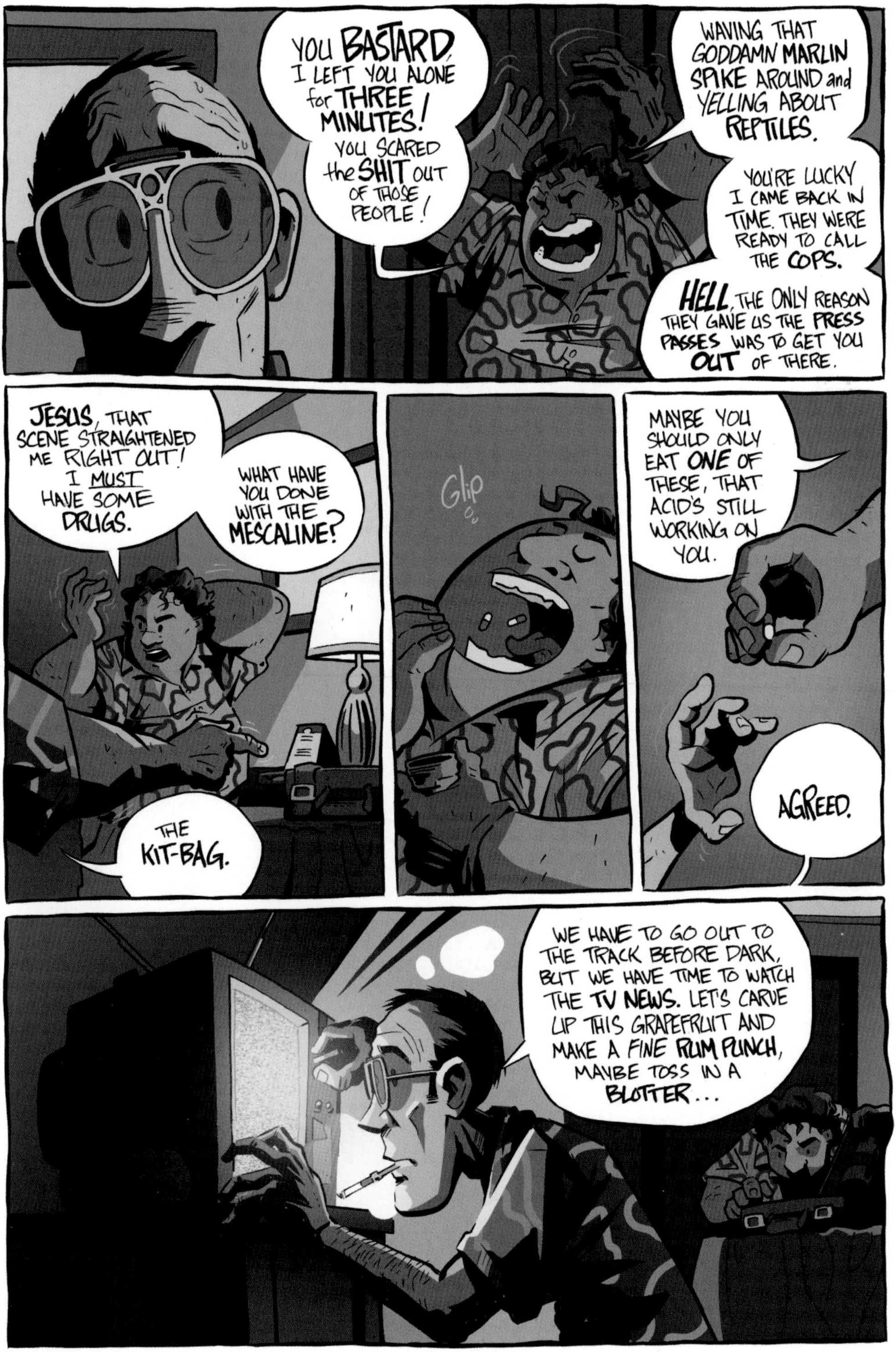
YOU BASTARD, I LEFT YOU ALONE for THREE MINUTES!
YOU SCARED the SHIT OUT OF THOSE PEOPLE!
WAVING THAT GODDAMN MARLIN SPIKE AROUND and YELLING ABOUT REPTILES.
YOU'RE LUCKY I CAME BACK IN TIME. THEY WERE READY TO CALL THE COPS.
HELL, THE ONLY REASON THEY GAVE US THE PRESS PASSES WAS TO GET YOU OUT OF THERE.
JESUS, THAT SCENE STRAIGHTENED ME RIGHT OUT! I MUST HAVE SOME DRUGS.
WHAT HAVE YOU DONE WITH THE MESCALINE?
THE KIT-BAG.
Glip
MAYBE YOU SHOULD ONLY EAT ONE OF THESE, THAT ACID'S STILL WORKING ON YOU.
AGREED.
WE HAVE TO GO OUT TO THE TRACK BEFORE DARK, BUT WE HAVE TIME TO WATCH THE TV NEWS. LET'S CARVE UP THIS GRAPEFRUIT AND MAKE A FINE RUM PUNCH, MAYBE TOSS IN A BLOTTER...

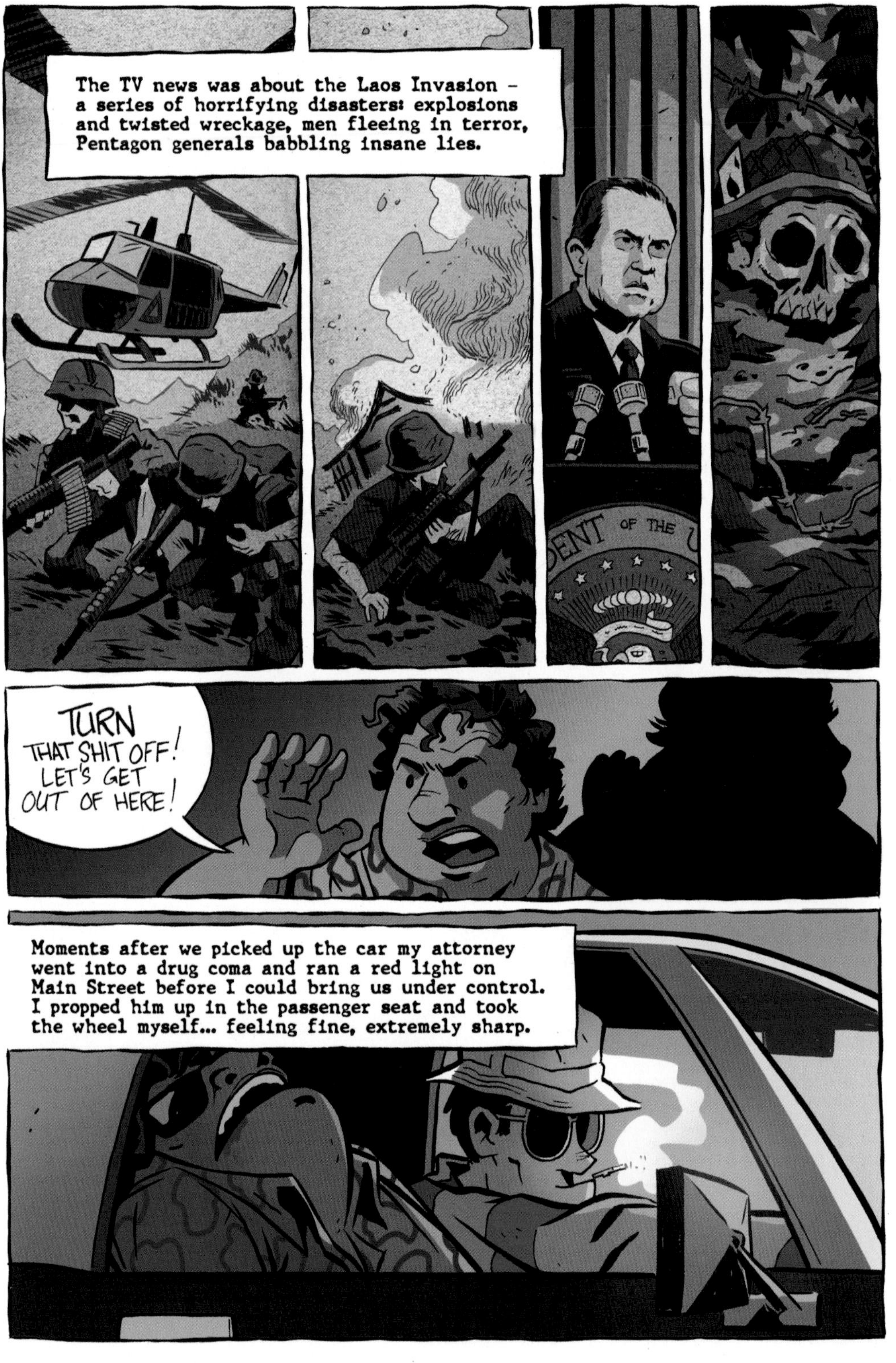
The TV news was about the Laos Invasion – a series of horrifying disasters: explosions and twisted wreckage, men fleeing in terror, Pentagon generals babbling insane lies.
DENT OF THE U
TURN THAT SHIT OFF! LET'S GET OUT OF HERE!
Moments after we picked up the car my attorney went into a drug coma and ran a red light on Main Street before I could bring us under control. I propped him up in the passenger seat and took the wheel myself... feeling fine, extremely sharp.

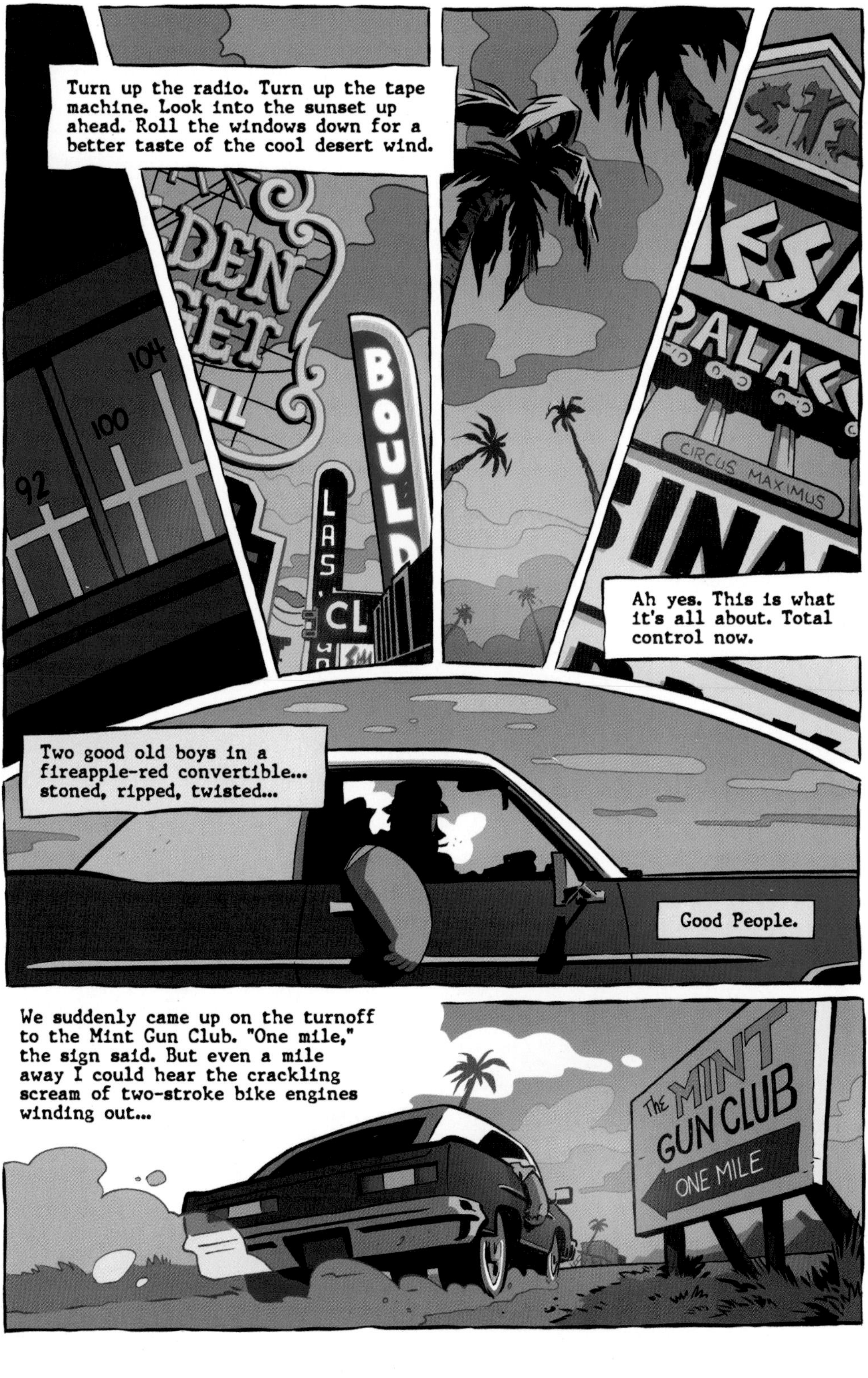
Turn up the radio. Turn up the tape machine. Look into the sunset up ahead. Roll the windows down for a better taste of the cool desert wind.
CIRCUS MAXIMUS
Ah yes. This is what it's all about. Total control now.
Two good old boys in a fireapple-red convertible... stoned, ripped, twisted...
Good People.
We suddenly came up on the turnoff to the Mint Gun Club. "One mile," the sign said. But even a mile away I could hear the crackling scream of two-stroke bike engines winding out...
The MINT GUN CLUB
ONE MILE

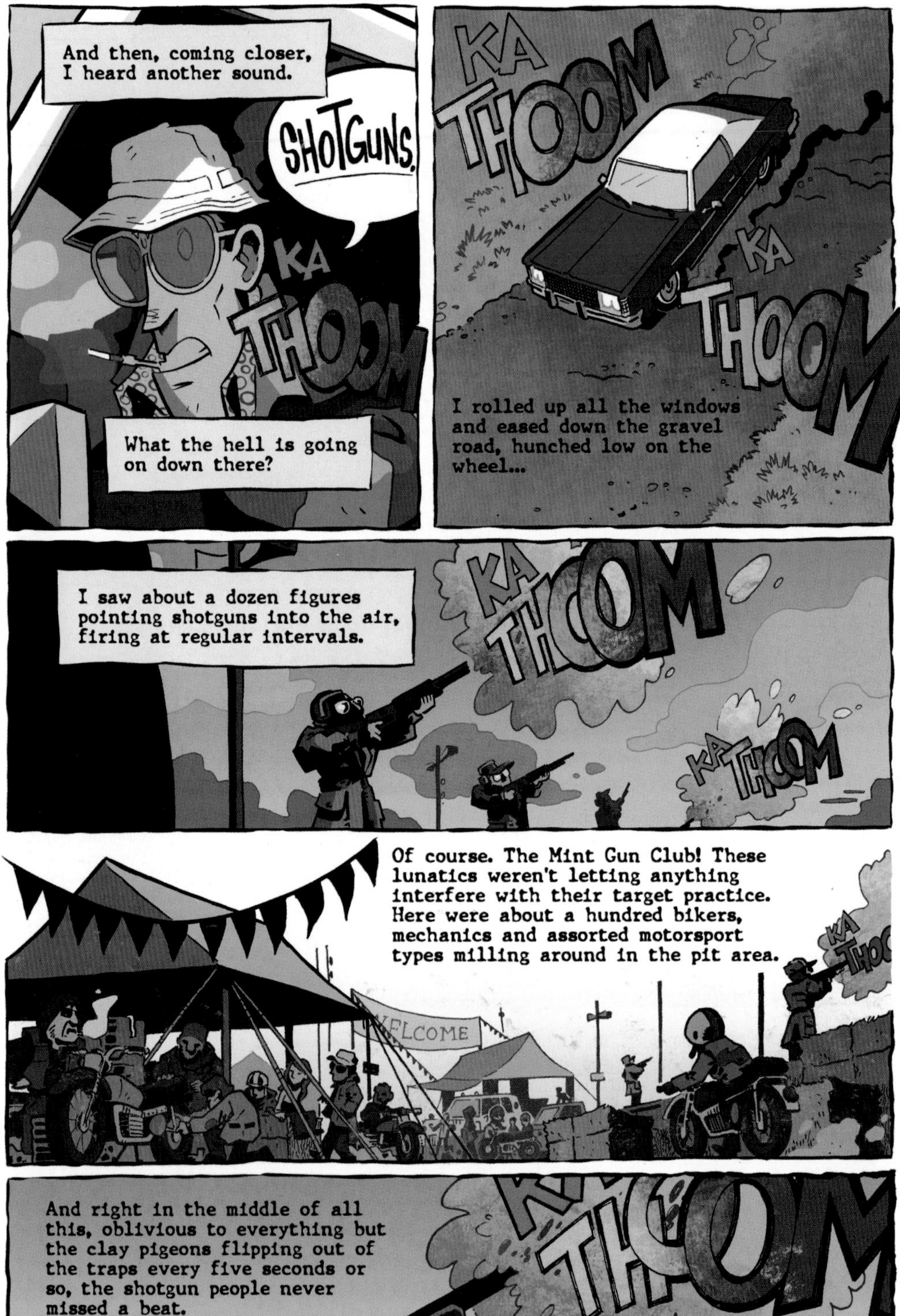
And then, coming closer, I heard another sound.
SHOTGUNS.
KA THOOM
What the hell is going on down there?
KA THOOM
KA THOOM
I rolled up all the windows and eased down the gravel road, hunched low on the wheel...
I saw about a dozen figures pointing shotguns into the air, firing at regular intervals.
KA THOOM
KA THOOM
Of course. The Mint Gun Club! These lunatics weren't letting anything interfere with their target practice. Here were about a hundred bikers, mechanics and assorted motorsport types milling around in the pit area.
WELCOME
And right in the middle of all this, oblivious to everything but the clay pigeons flipping out of the traps every five seconds or so, the shotgun people never missed a beat.
THOOM

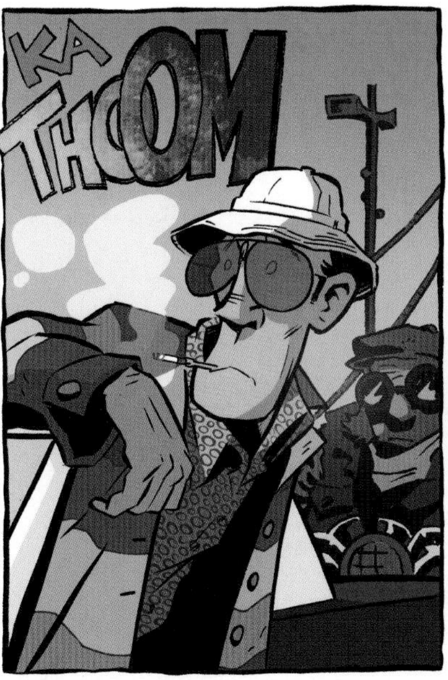
KA
THOOM

Well, why not?

The shooting provided a certain rhythm - sort of a steady bass-line - to the high-pitched chaos of the bike scene.

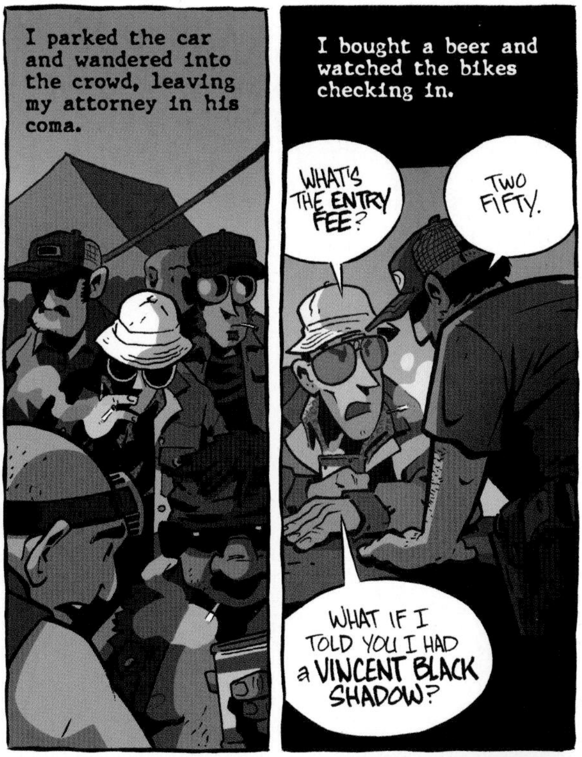
I parked the car and wandered into the crowd, leaving my attorney in his coma.
I bought a beer and watched the bikes checking in.
WHAT'S THE ENTRY FEE?
TWO FIFTY.
WHAT IF I TOLD YOU I HAD a VINCENT BLACK SHADOW?

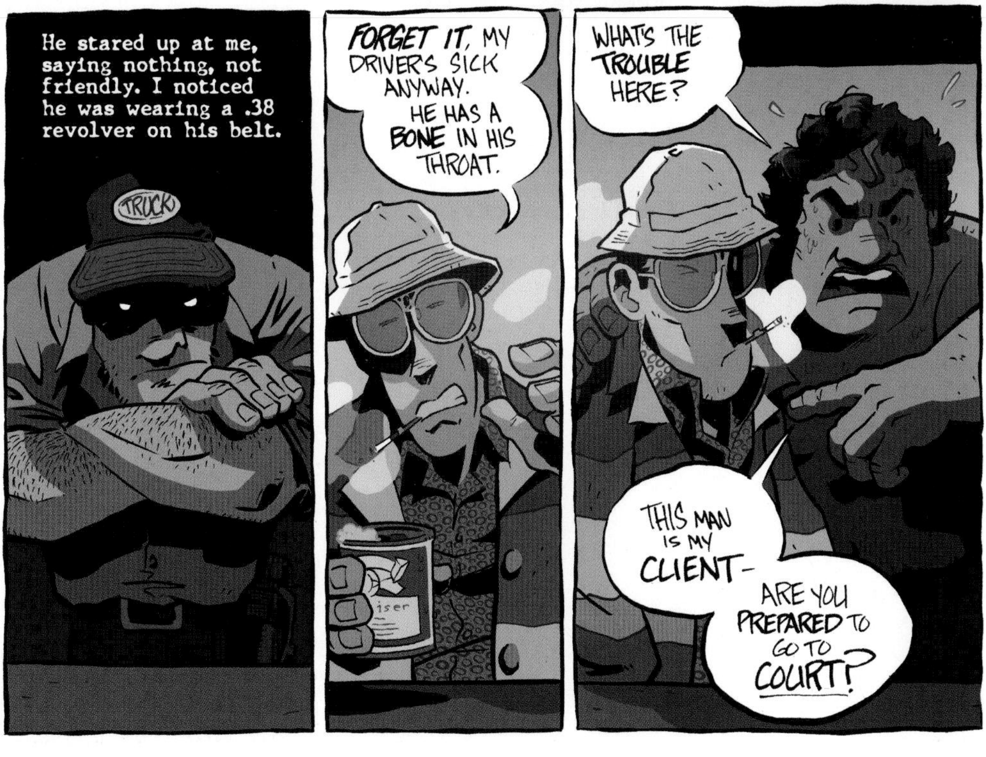
He stared up at me, saying nothing, not friendly. I noticed he was wearing a .38 revolver on his belt.
TRUCK
FORGET IT, MY DRIVER'S SICK ANYWAY. HE HAS A BONE IN HIS THROAT.
iser
WHAT'S THE TROUBLE HERE?
THIS MAN IS MY CLIENT-
ARE YOU PREPARED TO GO TO COURT?

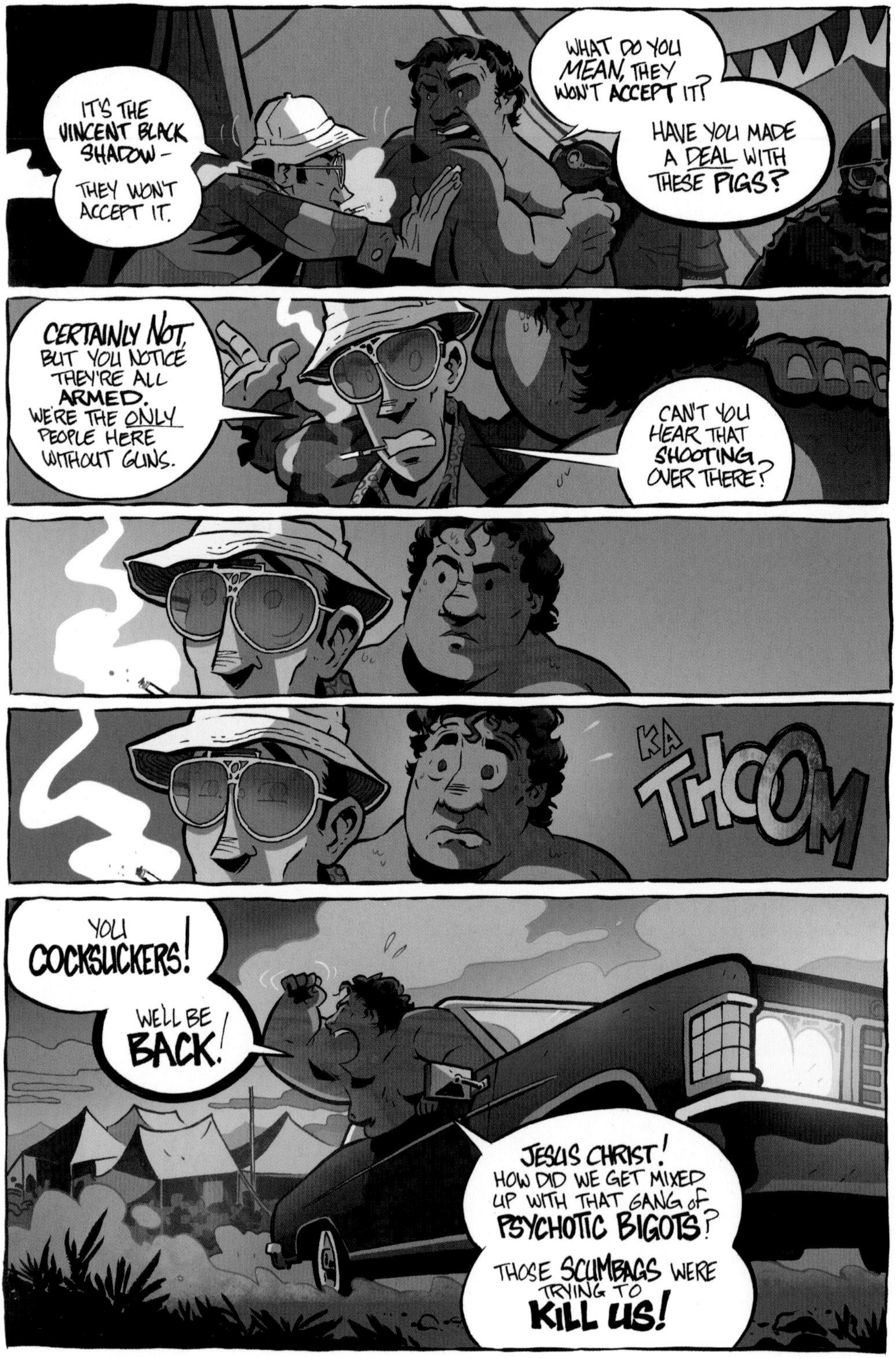
IT'S THE VINCENT BLACK SHADOW -
THEY WON'T ACCEPT IT.
WHAT DO YOU MEAN, THEY WON'T ACCEPT IT?
HAVE YOU MADE A DEAL WITH THESE PIGS?
CERTAINLY NOT, BUT YOU NOTICE THEY'RE ALL ARMED. WE'RE THE ONLY PEOPLE HERE WITHOUT GUNS.
CAN'T YOU HEAR THAT SHOOTING OVER THERE?
KA THOOM
YOU COCKSUCKERS!
WE'LL BE BACK!
JESUS CHRIST! HOW DID WE GET MIXED UP WITH THAT GANG of PSYCHOTIC BIGOTS?
THOSE SCUMBAGS WERE TRYING TO KILL US!

5. Covering the Story... A Glimpse of the Press in Action... Ugliness & Failure

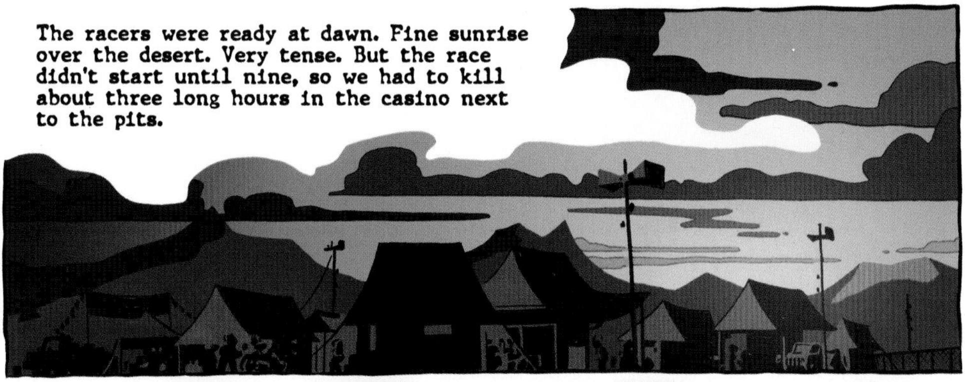

The racers were ready at dawn. Fine sunrise over the desert. Very tense. But the race didn't start until nine, so we had to kill about three long hours in the casino next to the pits.

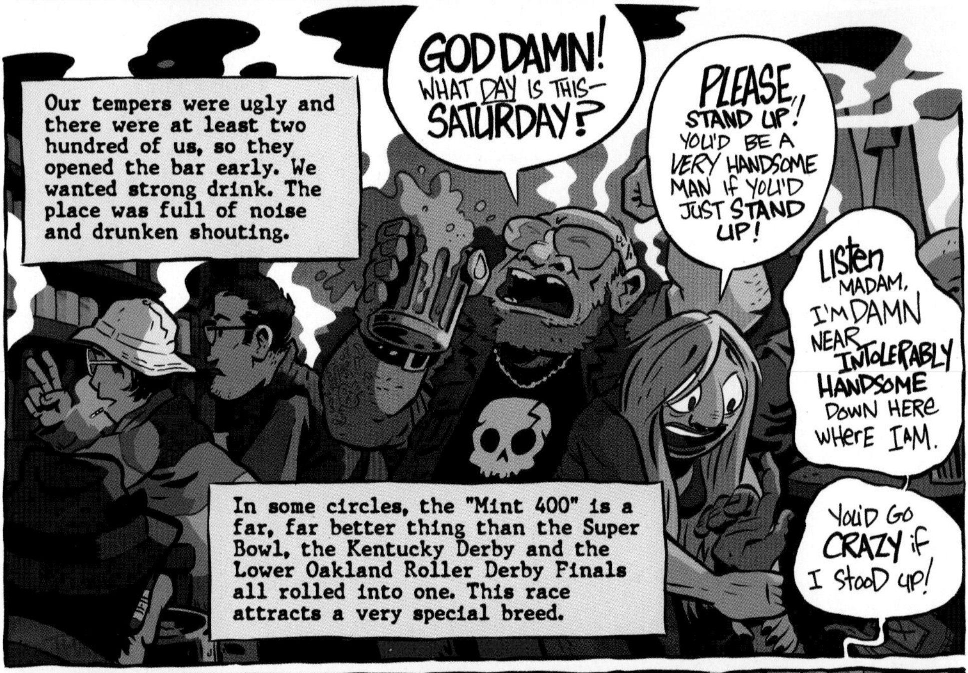

Our tempers were ugly and there were at least two hundred of us, so they opened the bar early. We wanted strong drink. The place was full of noise and drunken shouting.
GOD DAMN! WHAT DAY IS THIS— SATURDAY?
PLEASE, STAND UP! YOU'D BE A VERY HANDSOME MAN IF YOU'D JUST STAND UP!
LISTEN MADAM, I'M DAMN NEAR INTOLERABLY HANDSOME DOWN HERE WHERE I AM.
YOU'D GO CRAZY IF I STOOD UP!
In some circles, the "Mint 400" is a far, far better thing than the Super Bowl, the Kentucky Derby and the Lower Oakland Roller Derby Finals all rolled into one. This race attracts a very special breed.

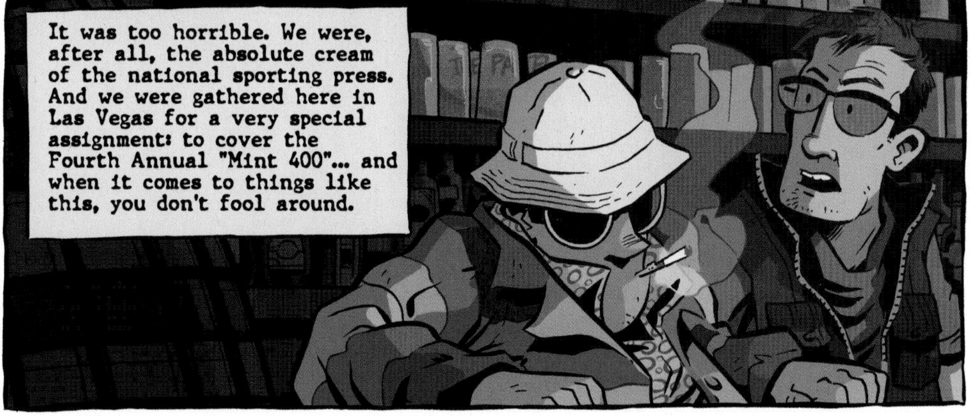

It was too horrible. We were, after all, the absolute cream of the national sporting press. And we were gathered here in Las Vegas for a very special assignment: to cover the Fourth Annual "Mint 400"... and when it comes to things like this, you don't fool around.

But now - even before the spectacle got under way - there were signs that we might be losing control of the situation... and with the race about to start, we were dangerously disorganized.

The first ten bikes blasted off on the stroke of nine. It was extremely exciting and we all went outside to watch.

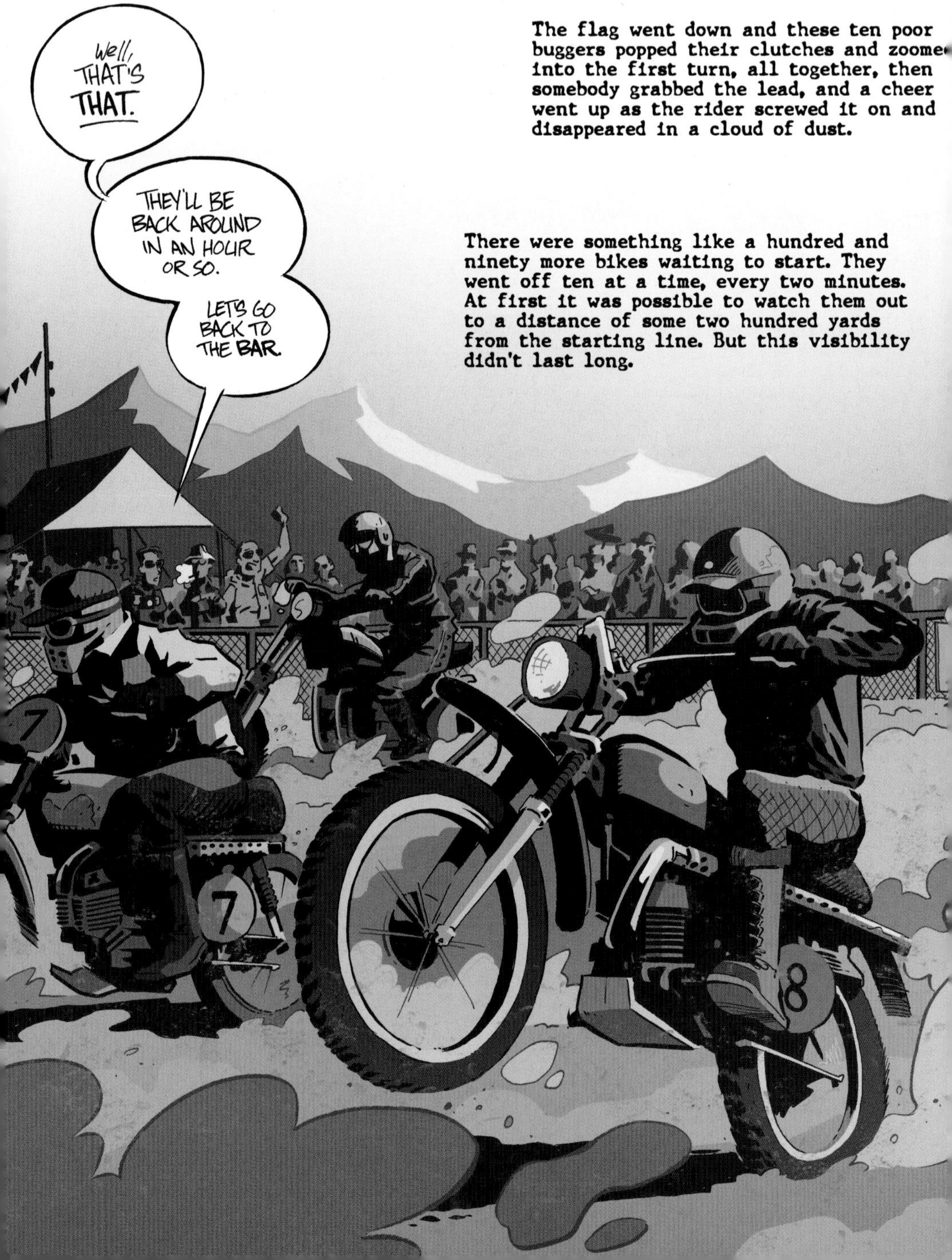
The flag went down and these ten poor buggers popped their clutches and zoome into the first turn, all together, then somebody grabbed the lead, and a cheer went up as the rider screwed it on and disappeared in a cloud of dust.
Well, THAT'S THAT.
THEY'LL BE BACK AROUND IN AN HOUR OR SO.
LET'S GO BACK TO THE BAR.
There were something like a hundred and ninety more bikes waiting to start. They went off ten at a time, every two minutes. At first it was possible to watch them out to a distance of some two hundred yards from the starting line. But this visibility didn't last long.
7
7
8

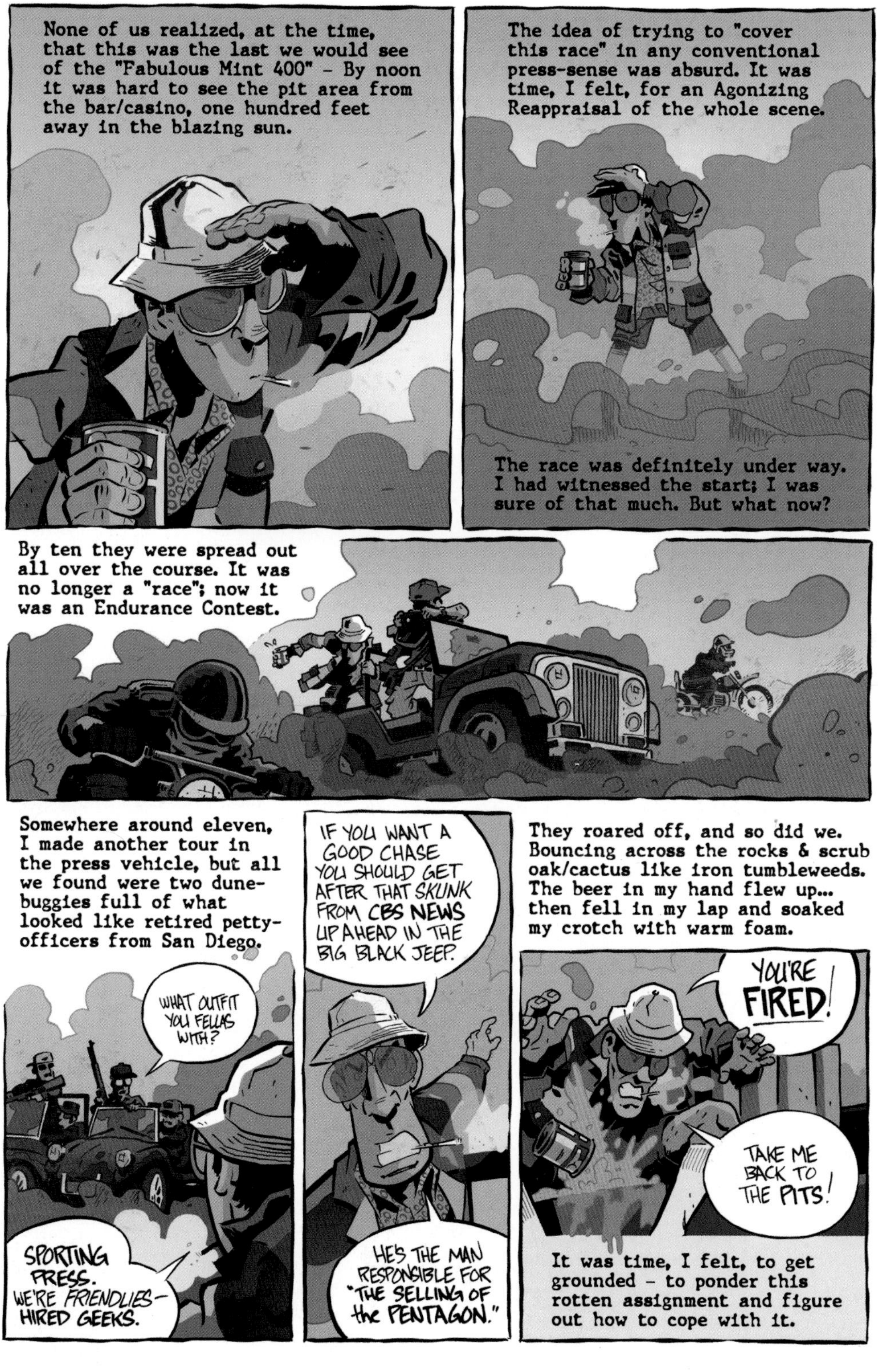
None of us realized, at the time, that this was the last we would see of the "Fabulous Mint 400" - By noon it was hard to see the pit area from the bar/casino, one hundred feet away in the blazing sun.
The idea of trying to "cover this race" in any conventional press-sense was absurd. It was time, I felt, for an Agonizing Reappraisal of the whole scene.
The race was definitely under way. I had witnessed the start; I was sure of that much. But what now?
By ten they were spread out all over the course. It was no longer a "race"; now it was an Endurance Contest.
Somewhere around eleven, I made another tour in the press vehicle, but all we found were two dune-buggies full of what looked like retired petty-officers from San Diego.
WHAT OUTFIT YOU FELLAS WITH?
SPORTING PRESS. WE'RE FRIENDLIES— HIRED GEEKS.
IF YOU WANT A GOOD CHASE YOU SHOULD GET AFTER THAT SKUNK FROM CBS NEWS UP AHEAD IN THE BIG BLACK JEEP.
HE'S THE MAN RESPONSIBLE FOR "THE SELLING OF the PENTAGON."
They roared off, and so did we. Bouncing across the rocks & scrub oak/cactus like iron tumbleweeds. The beer in my hand flew up... then fell in my lap and soaked my crotch with warm foam.
YOU'RE FIRED!
TAKE ME BACK TO THE PITS!
It was time, I felt, to get grounded - to ponder this rotten assignment and figure out how to cope with it.

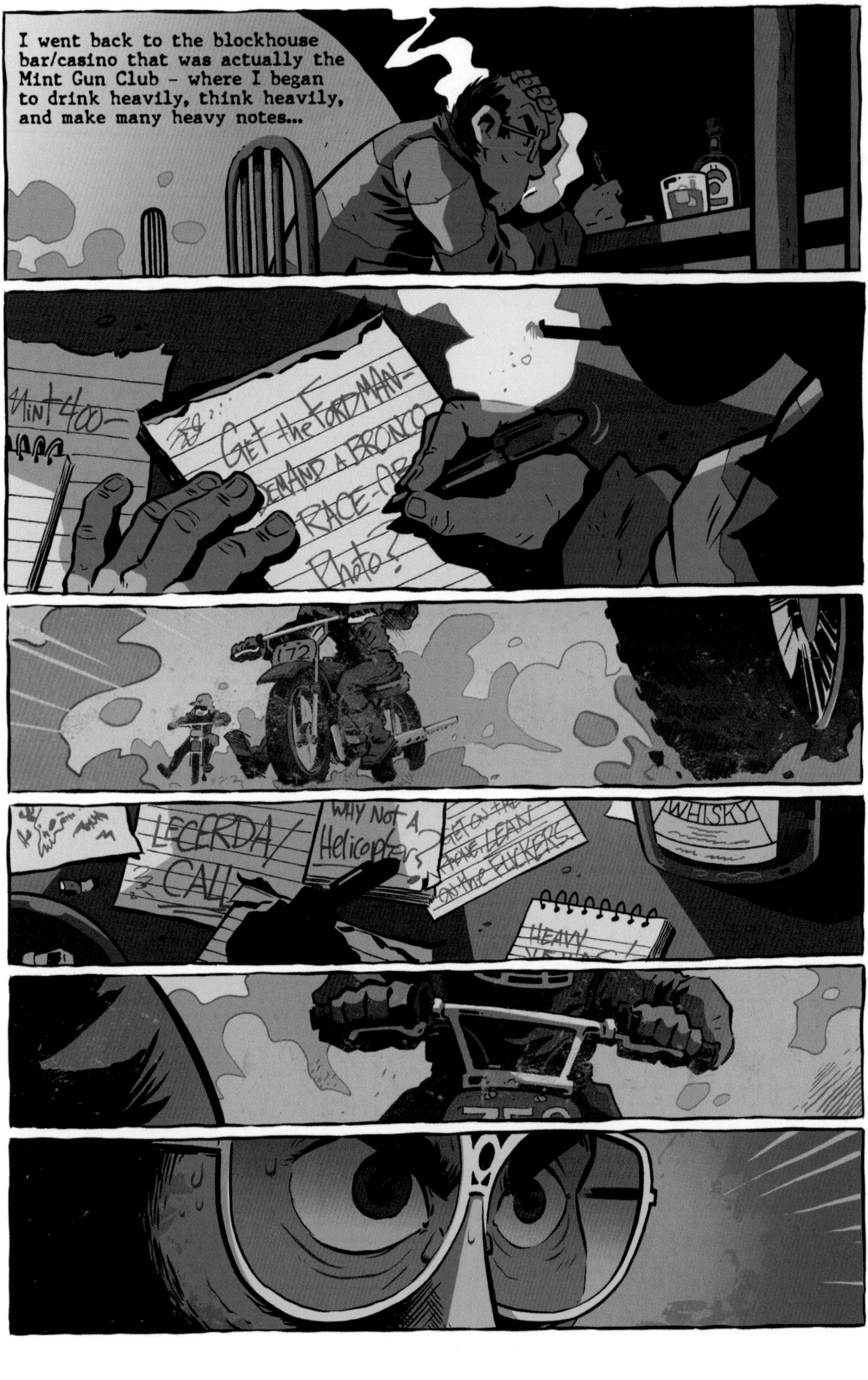
I went back to the blockhouse bar/casino that was actually the Mint Gun Club - where I began to drink heavily, think heavily, and make many heavy notes...
Mint 400-
Get the FORDMAN-
DEMAND A BRONCO
RACE-OR
Photo?
172
LECERDA/
CALL
WHY Not A Helicopters
GET ON THE PHONE. LEAN ON the FUCKERS.
HEAVY
WHISKY

8. A Night on the Town... Confrontation at the Desert Inn... Drug Frenzy at the Circus-Circus

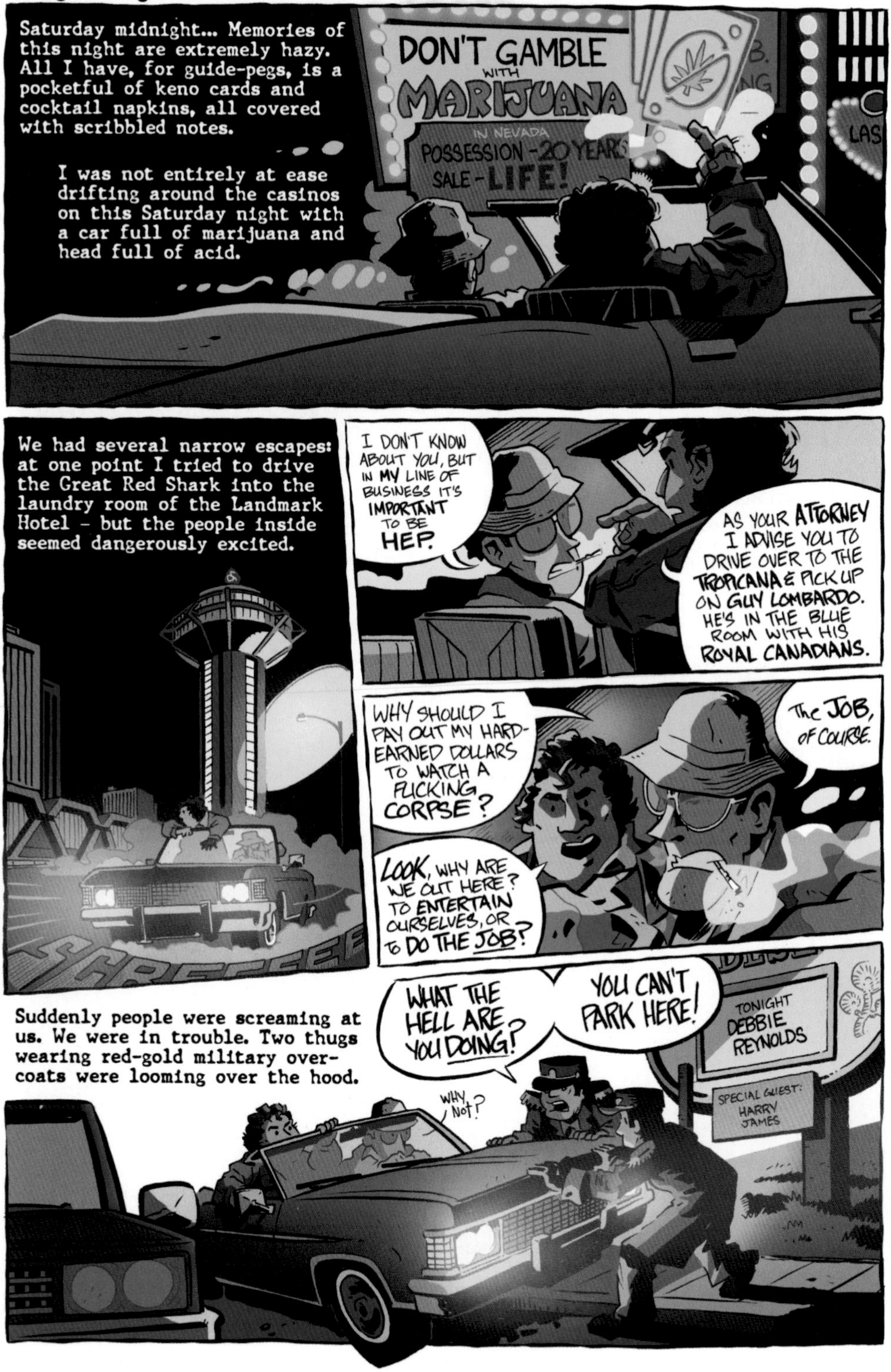
Saturday midnight... Memories of this night are extremely hazy. All I have, for guide-pegs, is a pocketful of keno cards and cocktail napkins, all covered with scribbled notes.
I was not entirely at ease drifting around the casinos on this Saturday night with a car full of marijuana and head full of acid.
DON'T GAMBLE WITH MARIJUANA
IN NEVADA
POSSESSION - 20 YEARS
SALE - LIFE!
We had several narrow escapes: at one point I tried to drive the Great Red Shark into the laundry room of the Landmark Hotel - but the people inside seemed dangerously excited.
SCREEEE
I DON'T KNOW ABOUT YOU, BUT IN MY LINE OF BUSINESS IT'S IMPORTANT TO BE HEP.
AS YOUR ATTORNEY I ADVISE YOU TO DRIVE OVER TO THE TROPICANA & PICK UP ON GUY LOMBARDO. HE'S IN THE BLUE ROOM WITH HIS ROYAL CANADIANS.
WHY SHOULD I PAY OUT MY HARD-EARNED DOLLARS TO WATCH A FUCKING CORPSE?
The JOB, OF COURSE.
LOOK, WHY ARE WE OUT HERE? TO ENTERTAIN OURSELVES, OR TO DO THE JOB?
Suddenly people were screaming at us. We were in trouble. Two thugs wearing red-gold military overcoats were looming over the hood.
WHAT THE HELL ARE YOU DOING?
YOU CAN'T PARK HERE!
WHY NOT?
TONIGHT DEBBIE REYNOLDS
SPECIAL GUEST: HARRY JAMES

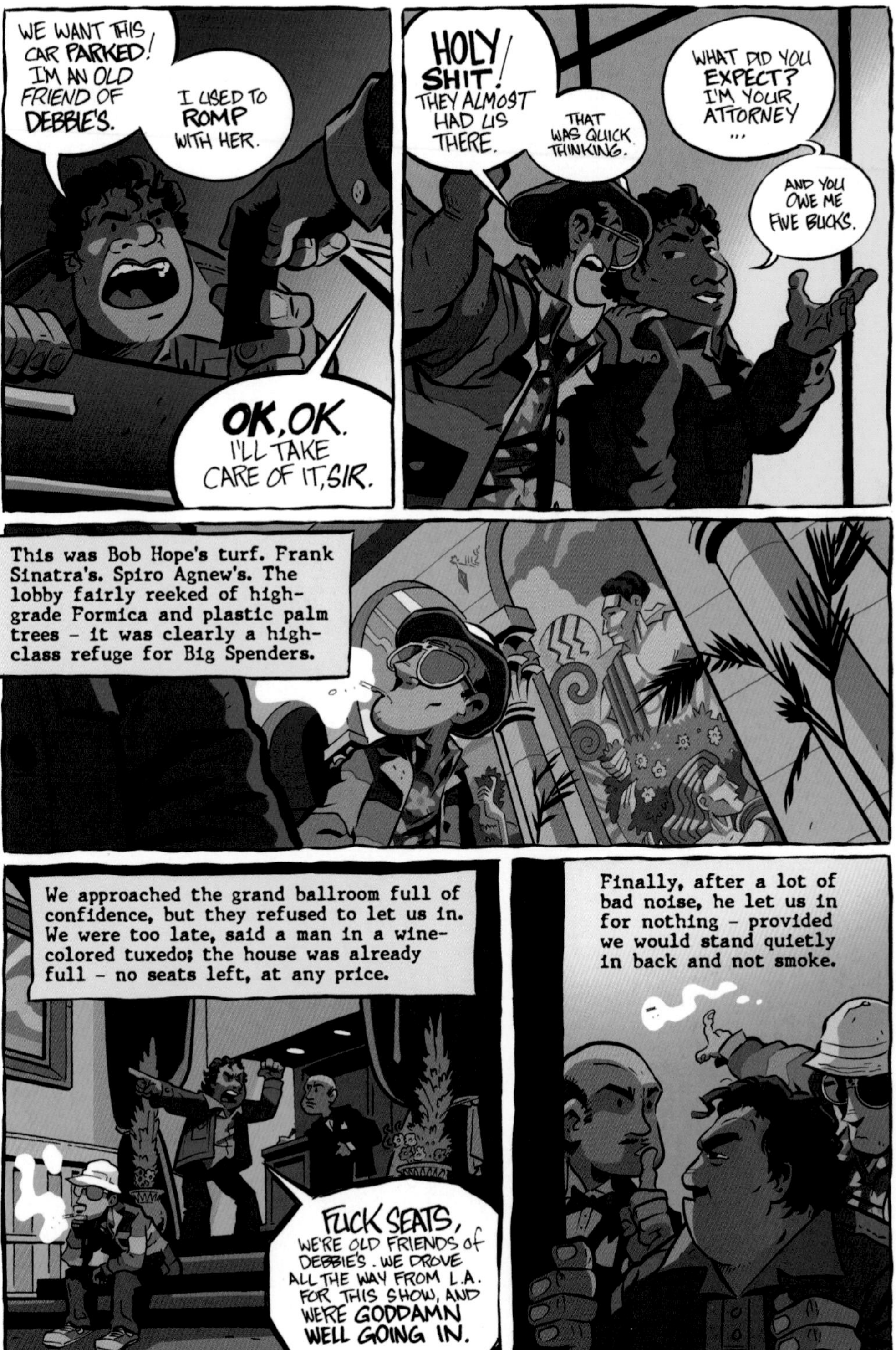
WE WANT THIS CAR PARKED! I'M AN OLD FRIEND OF DEBBIE'S.
I USED TO ROMP WITH HER.
OK, OK. I'LL TAKE CARE OF IT, SIR.
HOLY SHIT! THEY ALMOST HAD US THERE.
THAT WAS QUICK THINKING.
WHAT DID YOU EXPECT? I'M YOUR ATTORNEY ...
AND YOU OWE ME FIVE BUCKS.
This was Bob Hope's turf. Frank Sinatra's. Spiro Agnew's. The lobby fairly reeked of high-grade Formica and plastic palm trees - it was clearly a high-class refuge for Big Spenders.
We approached the grand ballroom full of confidence, but they refused to let us in. We were too late, said a man in a wine-colored tuxedo; the house was already full - no seats left, at any price.
FUCK SEATS, WE'RE OLD FRIENDS of DEBBIE'S. WE DROVE ALL THE WAY FROM L.A. FOR THIS SHOW, AND WE'RE GODDAMN WELL GOING IN.
Finally, after a lot of bad noise, he let us in for nothing - provided we would stand quietly in back and not smoke.

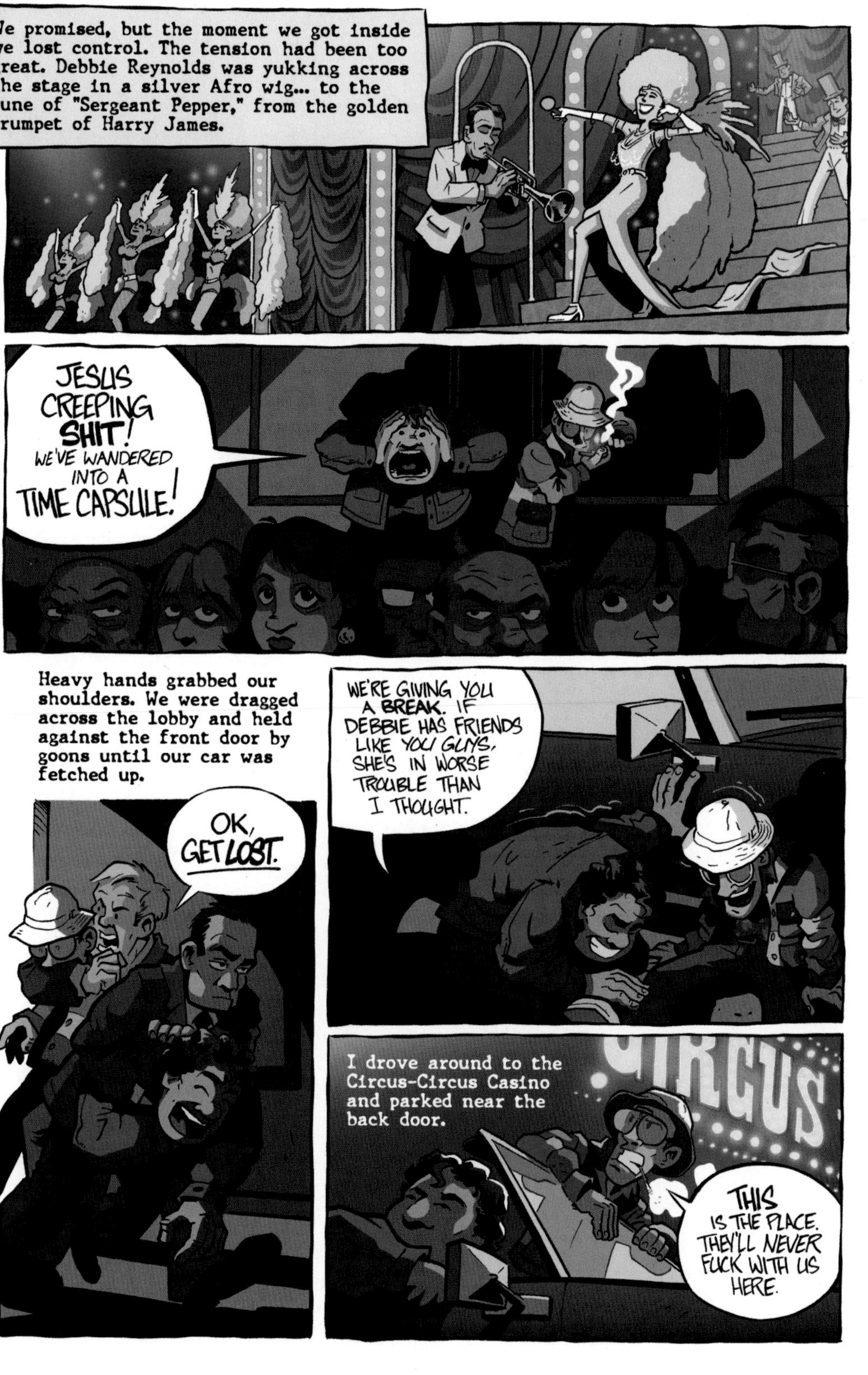
We promised, but the moment we got inside we lost control. The tension had been too great. Debbie Reynolds was yukking across the stage in a silver Afro wig... to the tune of "Sergeant Pepper," from the golden trumpet of Harry James.
JESUS CREEPING SHIT! WE'VE WANDERED INTO A TIME CAPSULE!
Heavy hands grabbed our shoulders. We were dragged across the lobby and held against the front door by goons until our car was fetched up.
OK, GET LOST.
WE'RE GIVING YOU A BREAK. IF DEBBIE HAS FRIENDS LIKE YOU GUYS, SHE'S IN WORSE TROUBLE THAN I THOUGHT.
I drove around to the Circus-Circus Casino and parked near the back door.
CIRCUS
THIS IS THE PLACE. THEY'LL NEVER FUCK WITH US HERE.

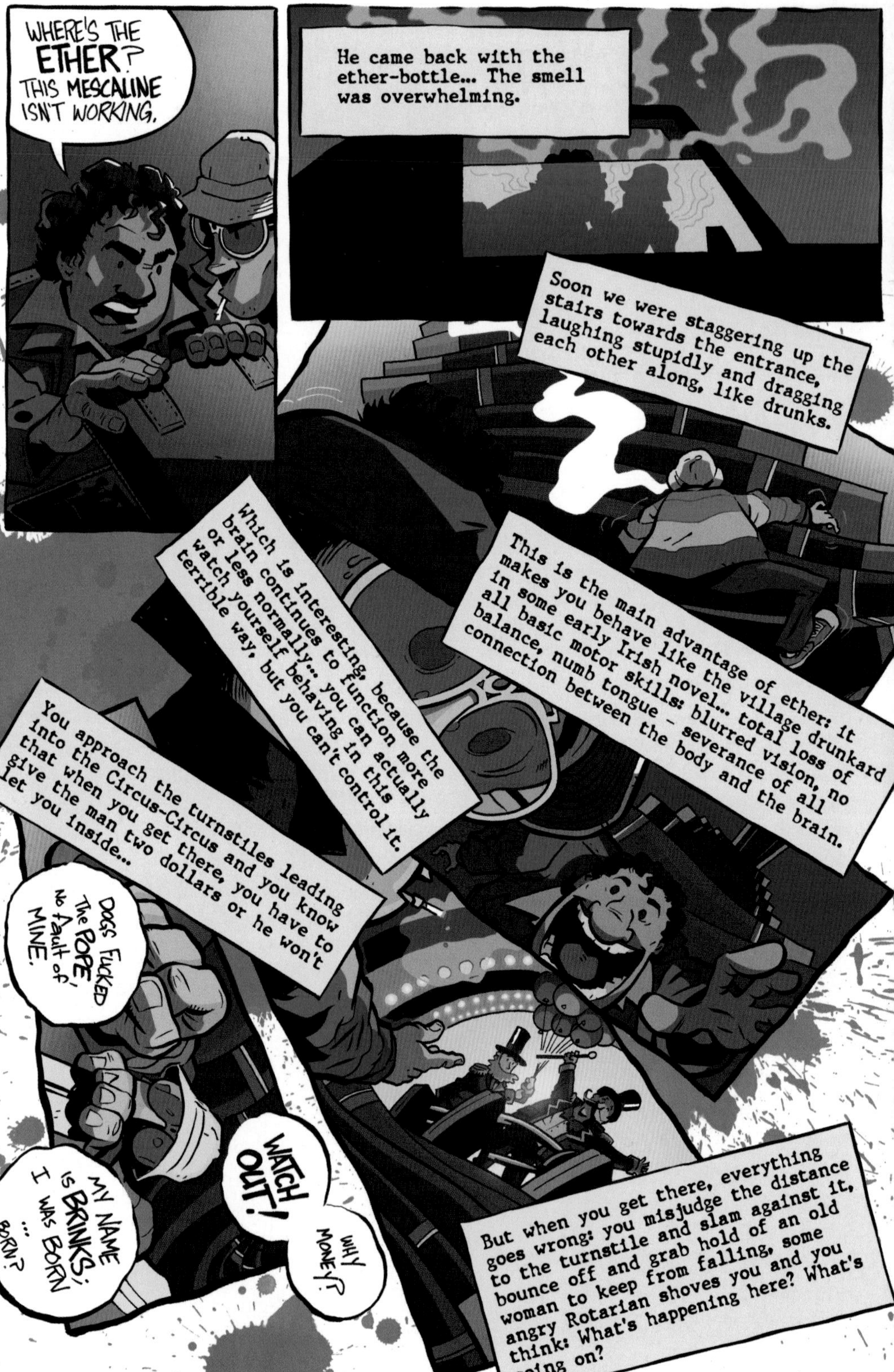
WHERE'S THE ETHER? THIS MESCALINE ISN'T WORKING.
He came back with the ether-bottle... The smell was overwhelming.
Soon we were staggering up the stairs towards the entrance, laughing stupidly and dragging each other along, like drunks.
This is the main advantage of ether: it makes you behave like the village drunkard in some early Irish novel... total loss of all basic motor skills: blurred vision, no balance, numb tongue - severance of all connection between the body and the brain.
Which is interesting, because the brain continues to function more or less normally... you can actually watch yourself behaving in this terrible way, but you can't control it.
You approach the turnstiles leading into the Circus-Circus and you know that when you get there, you have to give the man two dollars or he won't let you inside...
DOGS FUCKED The POPE, No fault of MINE.
WATCH OUT!
WHY MONEY?
MY NAME is BRINKS; I WAS BORN ... BORN?
But when you get there, everything goes wrong: you misjudge the distance to the turnstile and slam against it, bounce off and grab hold of an old woman to keep from falling, some angry Rotarian shoves you and you think: What's happening here? What's going on?

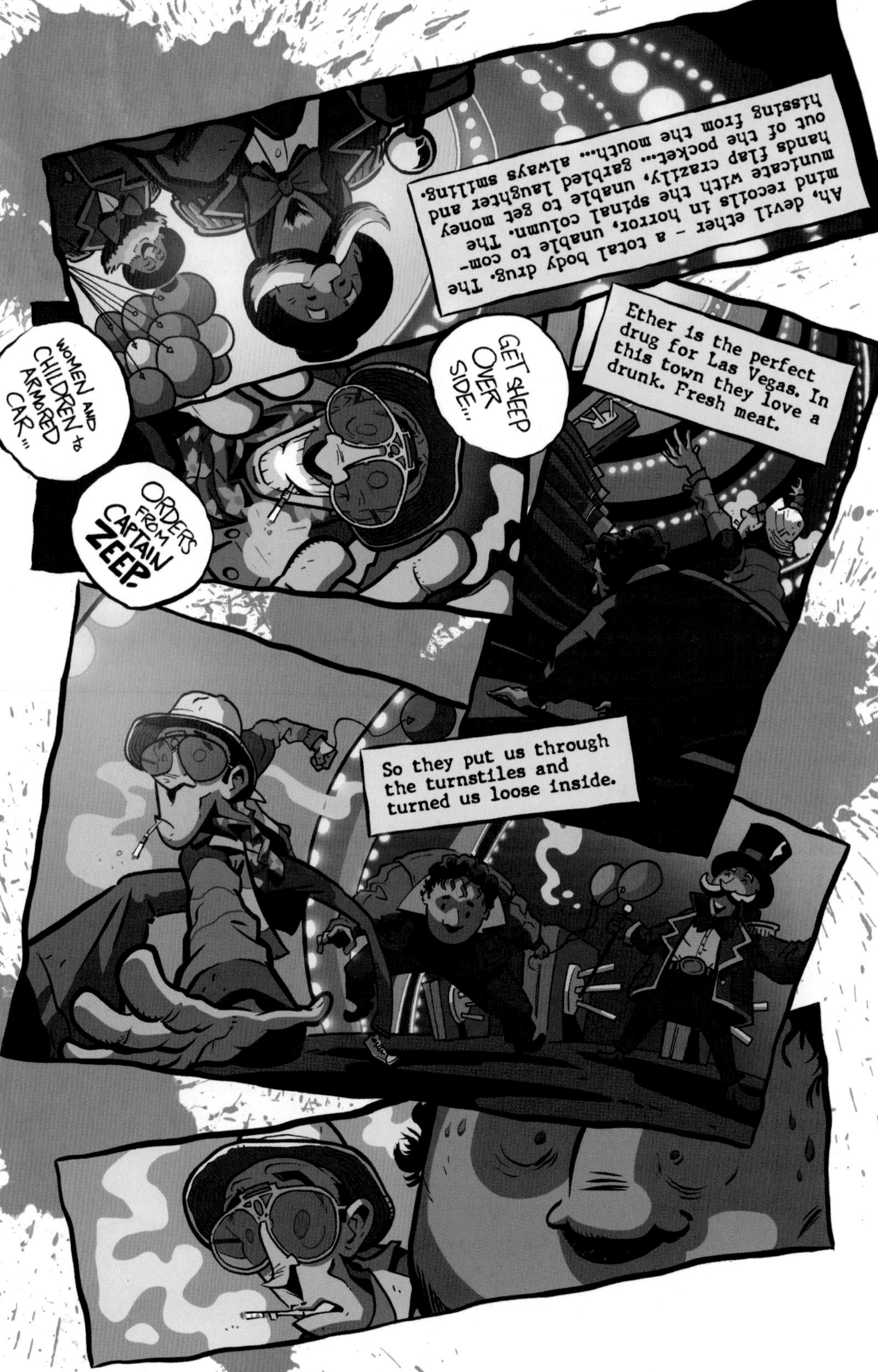
Ah, devil ether - a total body drug. The mind recoils in horror, unable to communicate with the spinal column. The hands flap crazily, unable to get money out of the pocket... garbled laughter and hissing from the mouth... always smiling.
Ether is the perfect drug for Las Vegas. In this town they love a drunk. Fresh meat.
GET SHEEP OVER SIDE...
WOMEN AND CHILDREN to ARMORED CAR...
ORDERS FROM CAPTAIN ZEEP.
So they put us through the turnstiles and turned us loose inside.

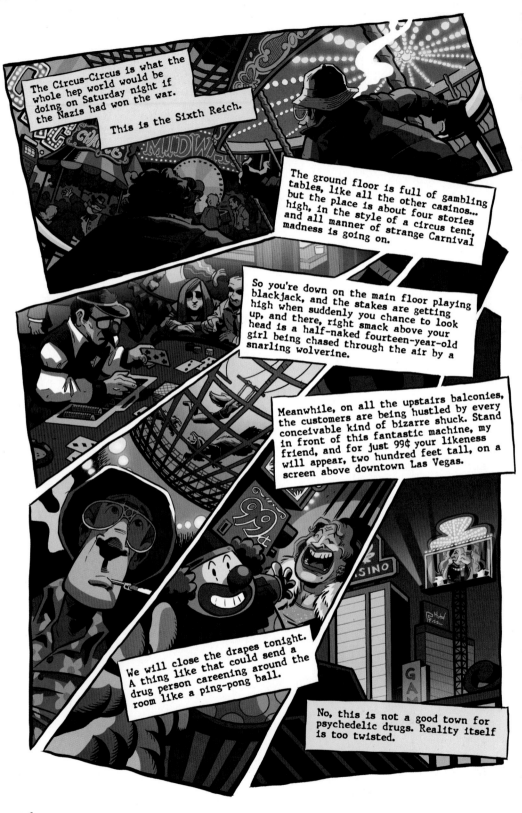

The Circus-Circus is what the whole hep world would be doing on Saturday night if the Nazis had won the war.

This is the Sixth Reich.

The ground floor is full of gambling tables, like all the other casinos... but the place is about four stories high, in the style of a circus tent, and all manner of strange Carnival madness is going on.

So you're down on the main floor playing blackjack, and the stakes are getting high when suddenly you chance to look up, and there, right smack above your head is a half-naked fourteen-year-old girl being chased through the air by a snarling wolverine.

Meanwhile, on all the upstairs balconies, the customers are being hustled by every conceivable kind of bizarre shuck. Stand in front of this fantastic machine, my friend, and for just 99¢ your likeness will appear, two hundred feet tall, on a screen above downtown Las Vegas.

We will close the drapes tonight. A thing like that could send a drug person careening around the room like a ping-pong ball.

No, this is not a good town for psychedelic drugs. Reality itself is too twisted.

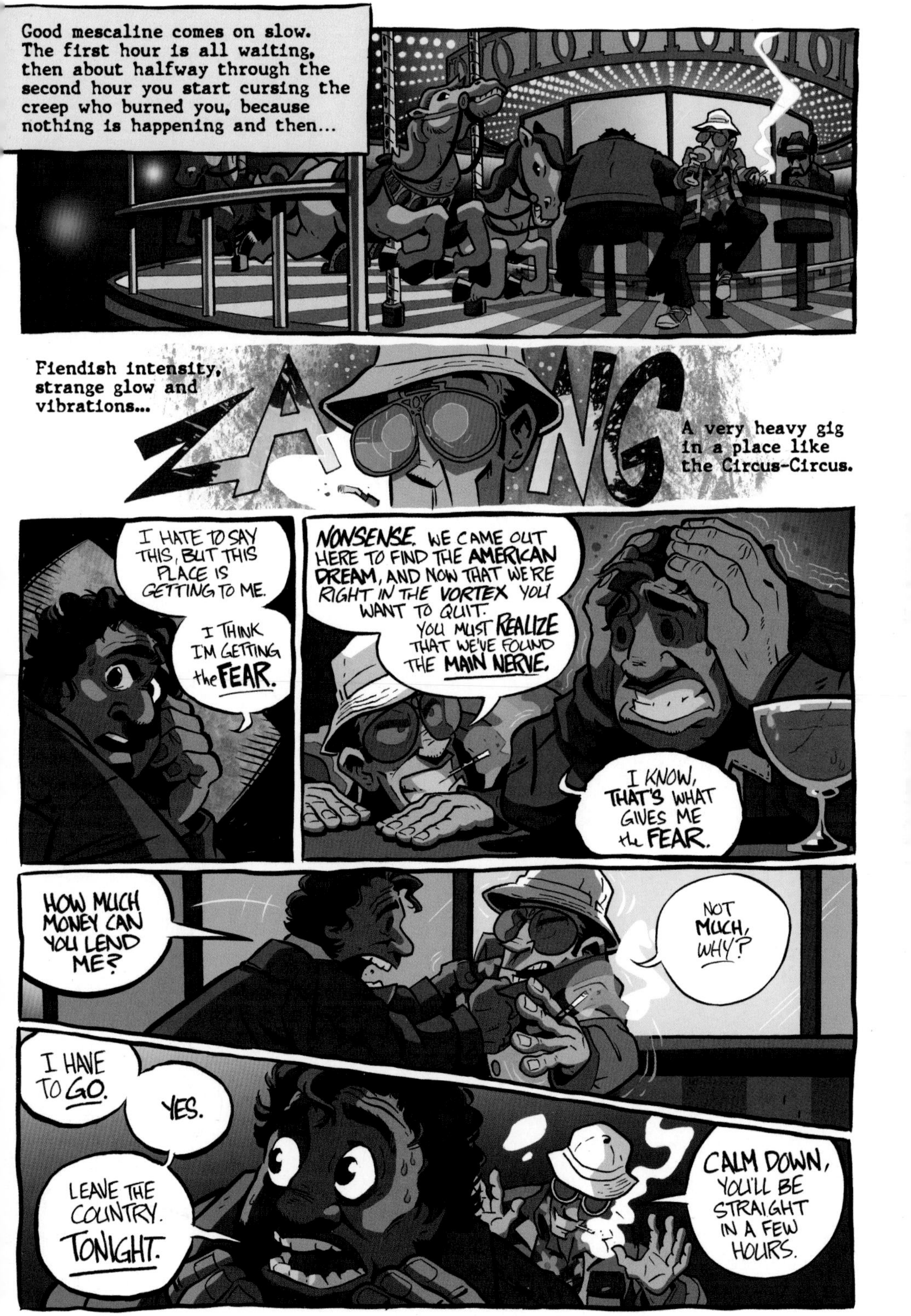
Good mescaline comes on slow. The first hour is all waiting, then about halfway through the second hour you start cursing the creep who burned you, because nothing is happening and then...
Fiendish intensity, strange glow and vibrations...
ZA-NG
A very heavy gig in a place like the Circus-Circus.
I HATE TO SAY THIS, BUT THIS PLACE IS GETTING TO ME.
I THINK I'M GETTING the FEAR.
NONSENSE. WE CAME OUT HERE TO FIND THE AMERICAN DREAM, AND NOW THAT WE'RE RIGHT IN THE VORTEX YOU WANT TO QUIT.
YOU MUST REALIZE THAT WE'VE FOUND THE MAIN NERVE.
I KNOW, THAT'S WHAT GIVES ME the FEAR.
HOW MUCH MONEY CAN YOU LEND ME?
NOT MUCH, WHY?
I HAVE TO GO.
YES.
LEAVE THE COUNTRY. TONIGHT.
CALM DOWN, YOU'LL BE STRAIGHT IN A FEW HOURS.

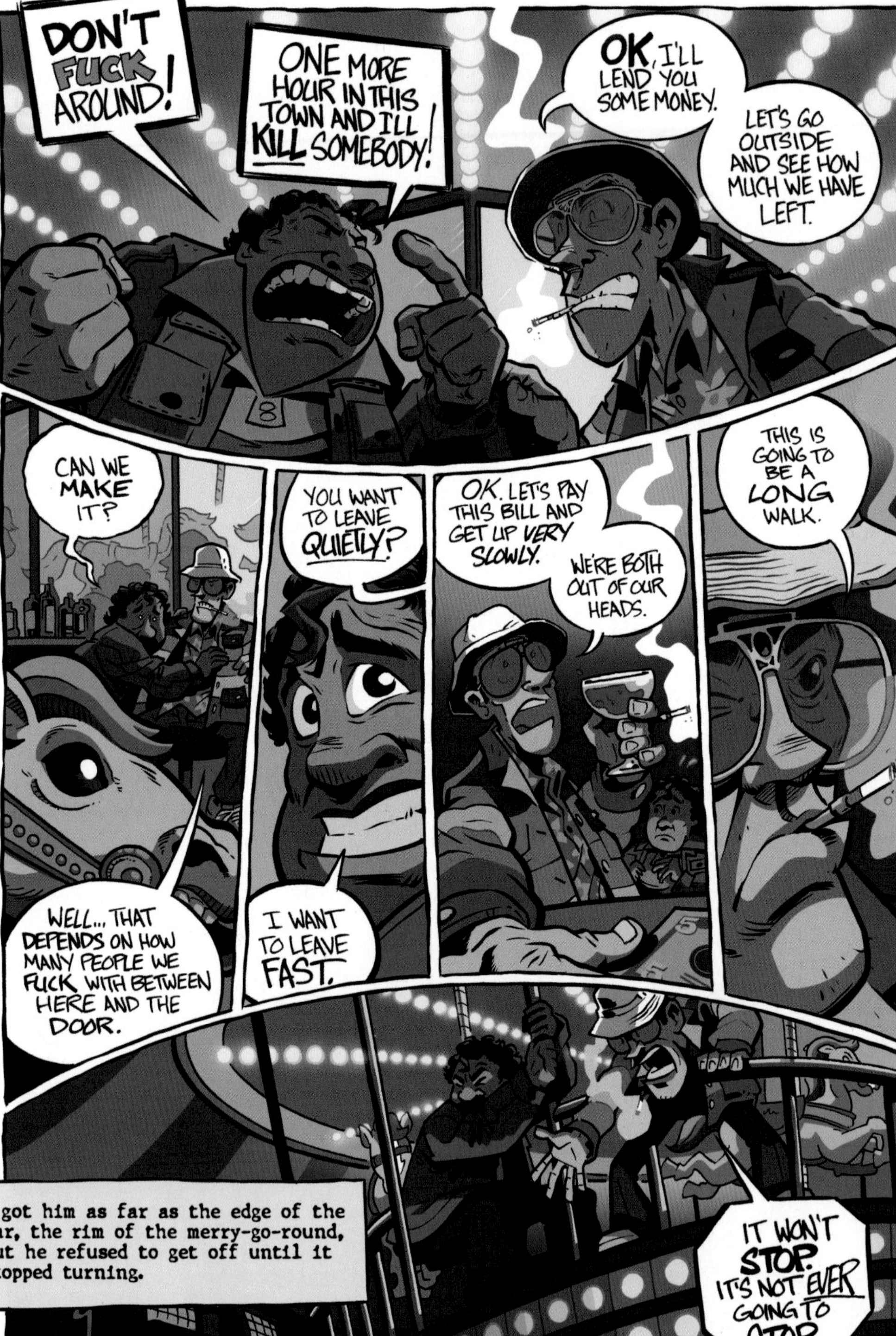
DON'T FUCK AROUND!
ONE MORE HOUR IN THIS TOWN AND I'LL KILL SOMEBODY!
OK, I'LL LEND YOU SOME MONEY.
LET'S GO OUTSIDE AND SEE HOW MUCH WE HAVE LEFT.
CAN WE MAKE IT?
WELL... THAT DEPENDS ON HOW MANY PEOPLE WE FUCK WITH BETWEEN HERE AND THE DOOR.
YOU WANT TO LEAVE QUIETLY?
I WANT TO LEAVE FAST.
OK. LET'S PAY THIS BILL AND GET UP VERY SLOWLY.
WE'RE BOTH OUT OF OUR HEADS.
THIS IS GOING TO BE A LONG WALK.
I got him as far as the edge of the bar, the rim of the merry-go-round, but he refused to get off until it stopped turning.
IT WON'T STOP. IT'S NOT EVER GOING TO STOP.

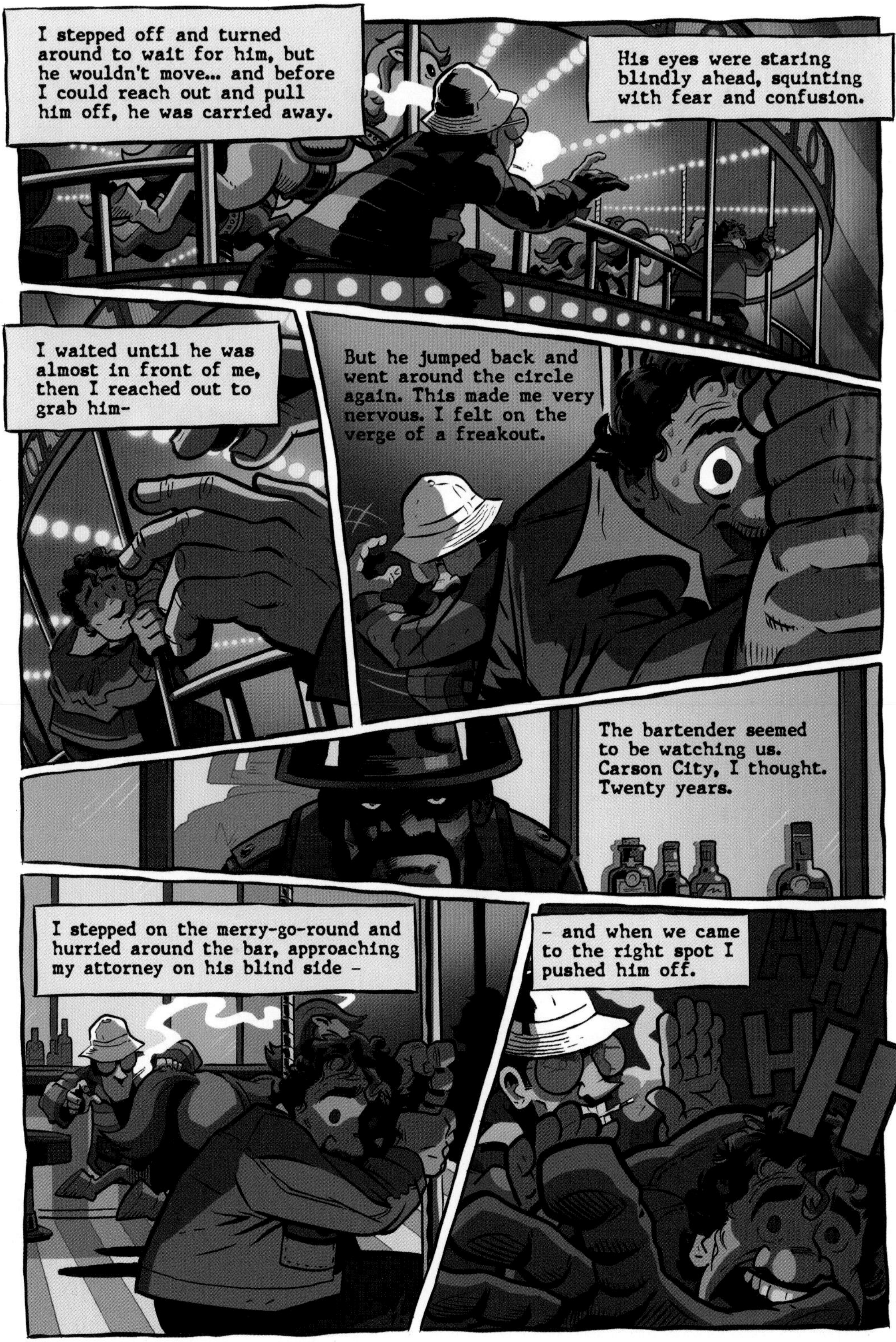
I stepped off and turned around to wait for him, but he wouldn't move... and before I could reach out and pull him off, he was carried away.
His eyes were staring blindly ahead, squinting with fear and confusion.
I waited until he was almost in front of me, then I reached out to grab him-
But he jumped back and went around the circle again. This made me very nervous. I felt on the verge of a freakout.
The bartender seemed to be watching us. Carson City, I thought. Twenty years.
I stepped on the merry-go-round and hurried around the bar, approaching my attorney on his blind side -
- and when we came to the right spot I pushed him off.

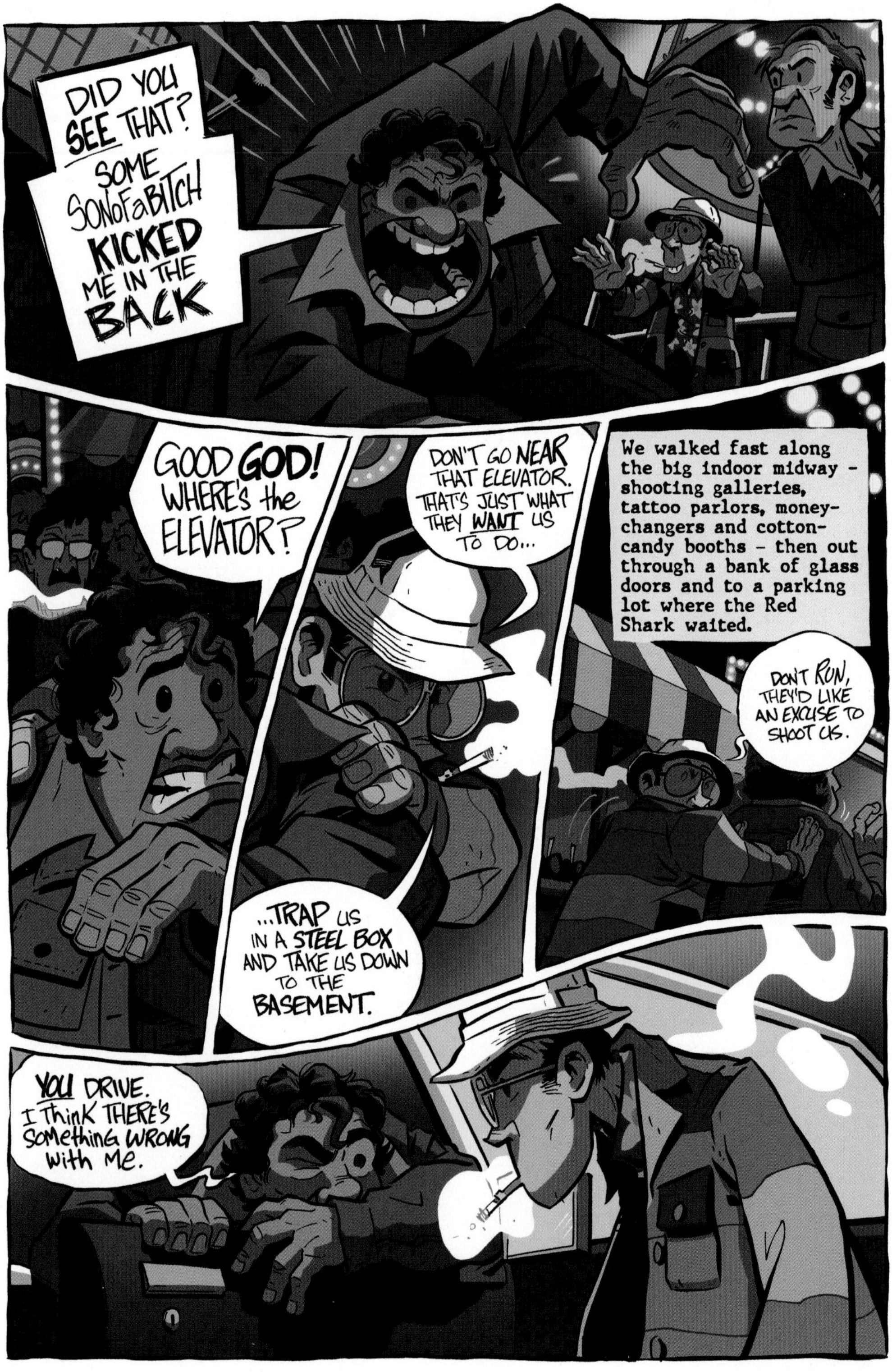
DID YOU SEE THAT? SOME SONofaBITCH KICKED ME IN THE BACK
GOOD GOD! WHERE'S the ELEVATOR?
DON'T GO NEAR THAT ELEVATOR. THAT'S JUST WHAT THEY WANT US TO DO...
...TRAP US IN A STEEL BOX AND TAKE US DOWN TO THE BASEMENT.
We walked fast along the big indoor midway - shooting galleries, tattoo parlors, money-changers and cotton-candy booths - then out through a bank of glass doors and to a parking lot where the Red Shark waited.
DON'T RUN, THEY'D LIKE AN EXCUSE TO SHOOT US.
YOU DRIVE. I Think THERE'S Something WRONG with Me.

7. Paranoid Terror... and the Awful Specter of Sodomy... A Flashing of Knives and Green Water

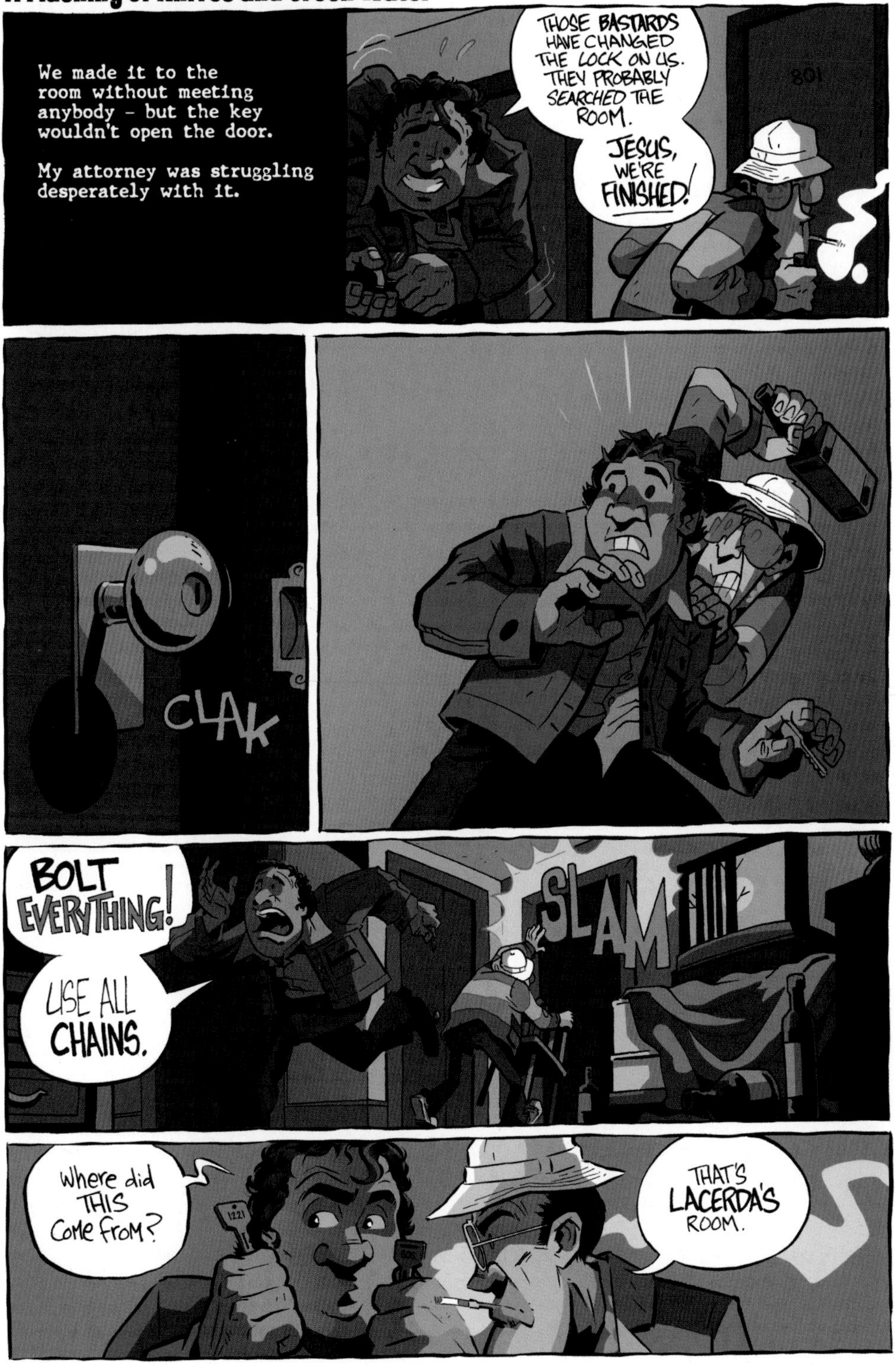
We made it to the room without meeting anybody - but the key wouldn't open the door.
My attorney was struggling desperately with it.
THOSE BASTARDS HAVE CHANGED THE LOCK ON US. THEY PROBABLY SEARCHED THE ROOM.
JESUS, WE'RE FINISHED!
801
CLAK
BOLT EVERYTHING!
USE ALL CHAINS.
SLAM
Where did THIS Come from?
THAT'S LACERDA'S ROOM.

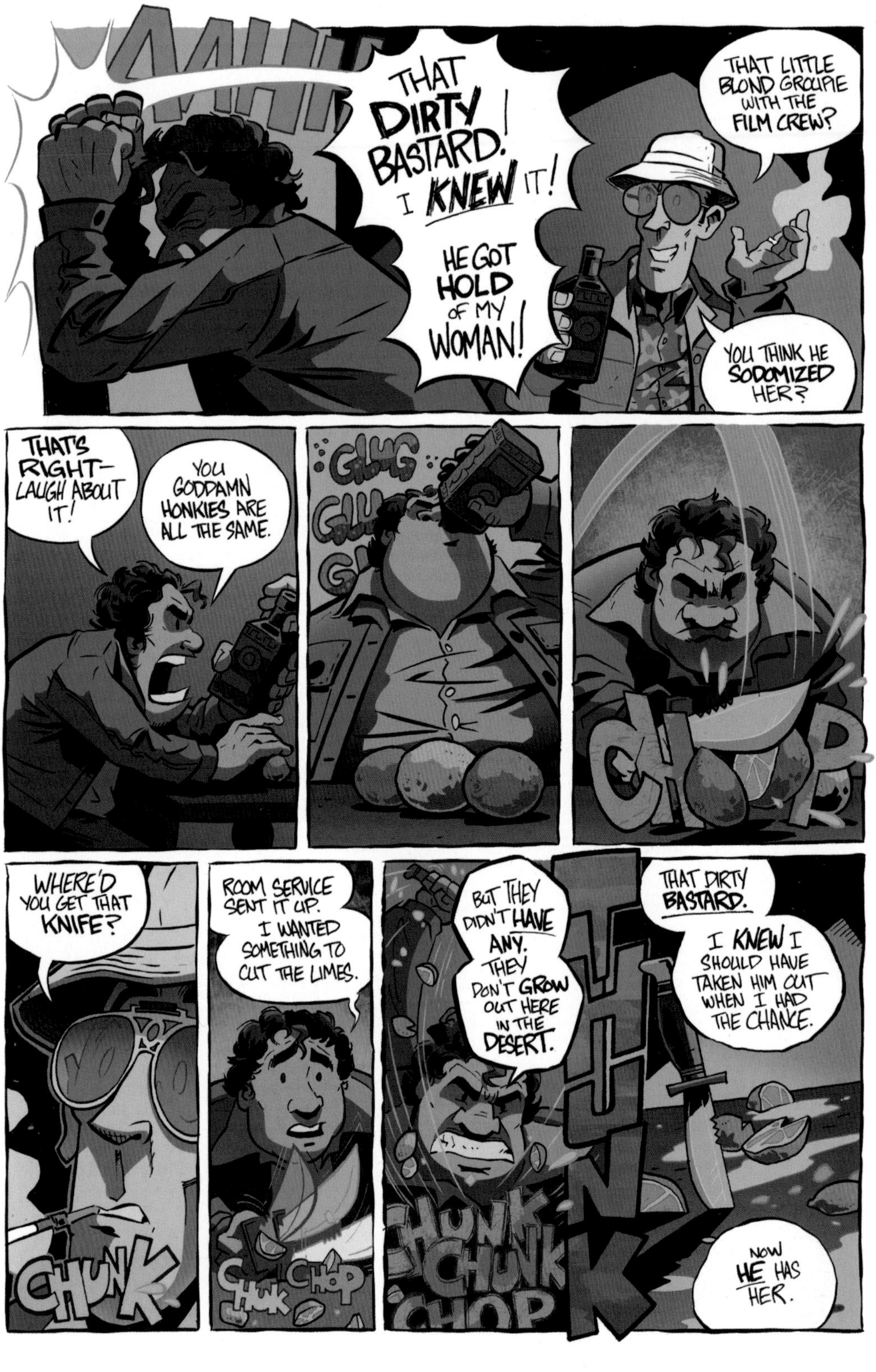
AAHH
THAT DIRTY BASTARD! I KNEW IT!
HE GOT HOLD OF MY WOMAN!
THAT LITTLE BLOND GROUPIE WITH THE FILM CREW?
YOU THINK HE SODOMIZED HER?
THAT'S RIGHT-LAUGH ABOUT IT!
YOU GODDAMN HONKIES ARE ALL THE SAME.
GLUG
GLUG
CHOP
WHERE'D YOU GET THAT KNIFE?
CHUNK
ROOM SERVICE SENT IT UP.
I WANTED SOMETHING TO CUT THE LIMES.
CHOP
BUT THEY DIDN'T HAVE ANY. THEY DON'T GROW OUT HERE IN THE DESERT.
CHUNK
CHUNK
CHOP
THUNK
THAT DIRTY BASTARD.
I KNEW I SHOULD HAVE TAKEN HIM OUT WHEN I HAD THE CHANCE.
NOW HE HAS HER.

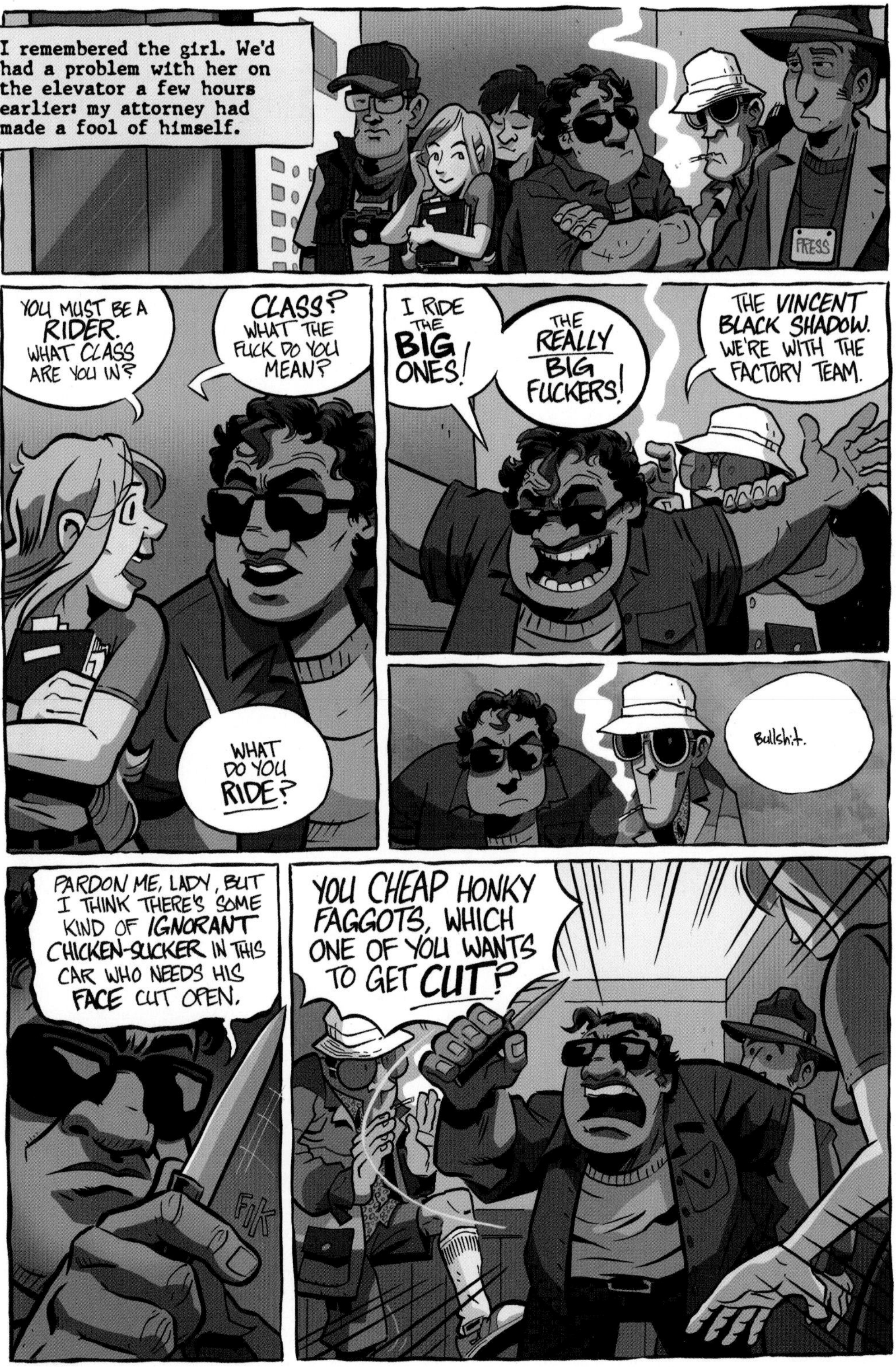
I remembered the girl. We'd had a problem with her on the elevator a few hours earlier: my attorney had made a fool of himself.
PRESS
YOU MUST BE A RIDER. WHAT CLASS ARE YOU IN?
CLASS? WHAT THE FUCK DO YOU MEAN?
WHAT DO YOU RIDE?
I RIDE THE BIG ONES!
THE REALLY BIG FUCKERS!
THE VINCENT BLACK SHADOW. WE'RE WITH THE FACTORY TEAM.
Bullshit.
PARDON ME, LADY, BUT I THINK THERE'S SOME KIND OF IGNORANT CHICKEN-SUCKER IN THIS CAR WHO NEEDS HIS FACE CUT OPEN.
FIK
YOU CHEAP HONKY FAGGOTS, WHICH ONE OF YOU WANTS TO GET CUT?

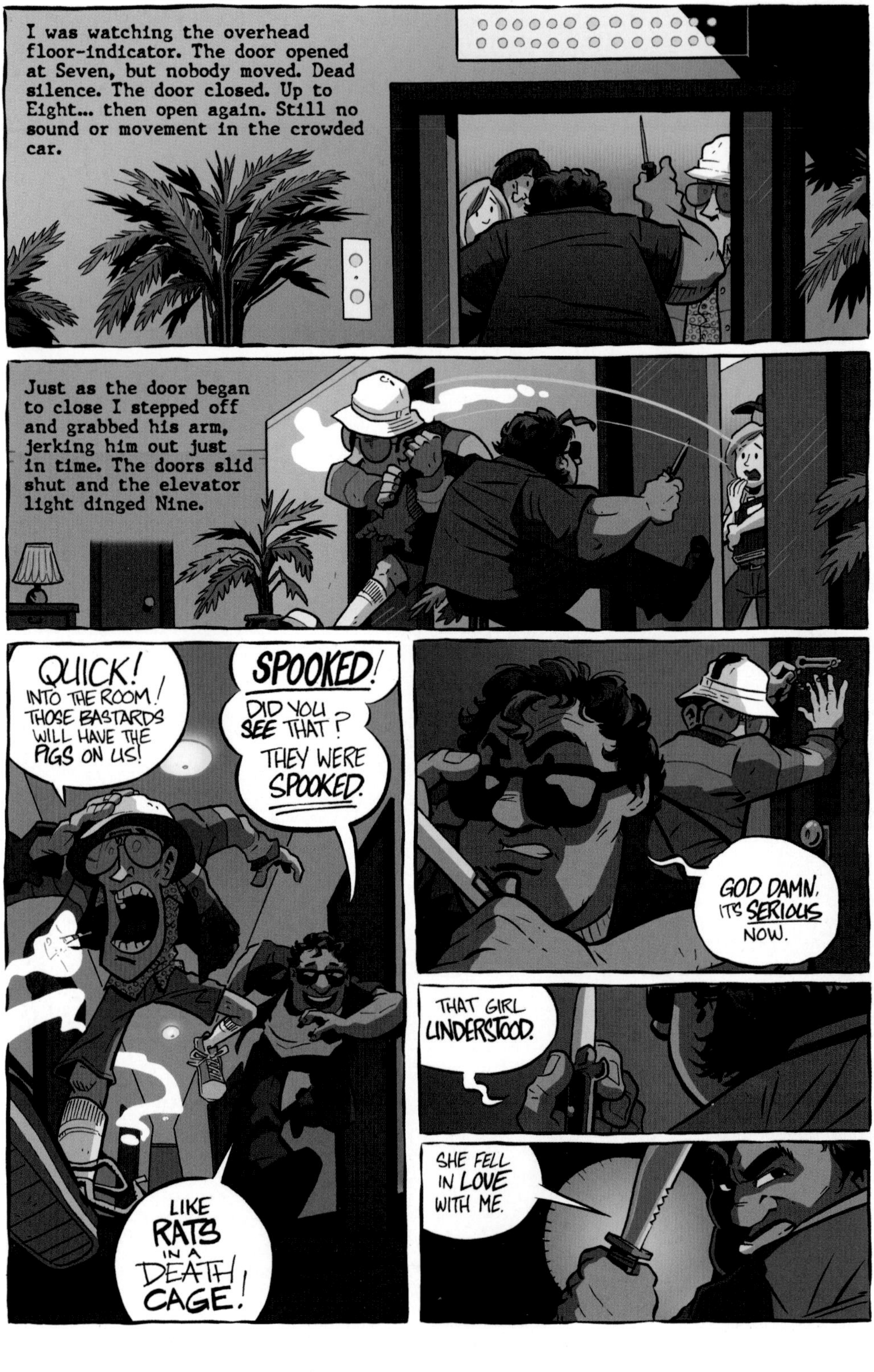
I was watching the overhead floor-indicator. The door opened at Seven, but nobody moved. Dead silence. The door closed. Up to Eight... then open again. Still no sound or movement in the crowded car.
Just as the door began to close I stepped off and grabbed his arm, jerking him out just in time. The doors slid shut and the elevator light dinged Nine.
QUICK! INTO THE ROOM! THOSE BASTARDS WILL HAVE THE PIGS ON US!
SPOOKED! DID YOU SEE THAT? THEY WERE SPOOKED.
LIKE RATS IN A DEATH CAGE!
GOD DAMN, IT'S SERIOUS NOW.
THAT GIRL UNDERSTOOD.
SHE FELL IN LOVE WITH ME.

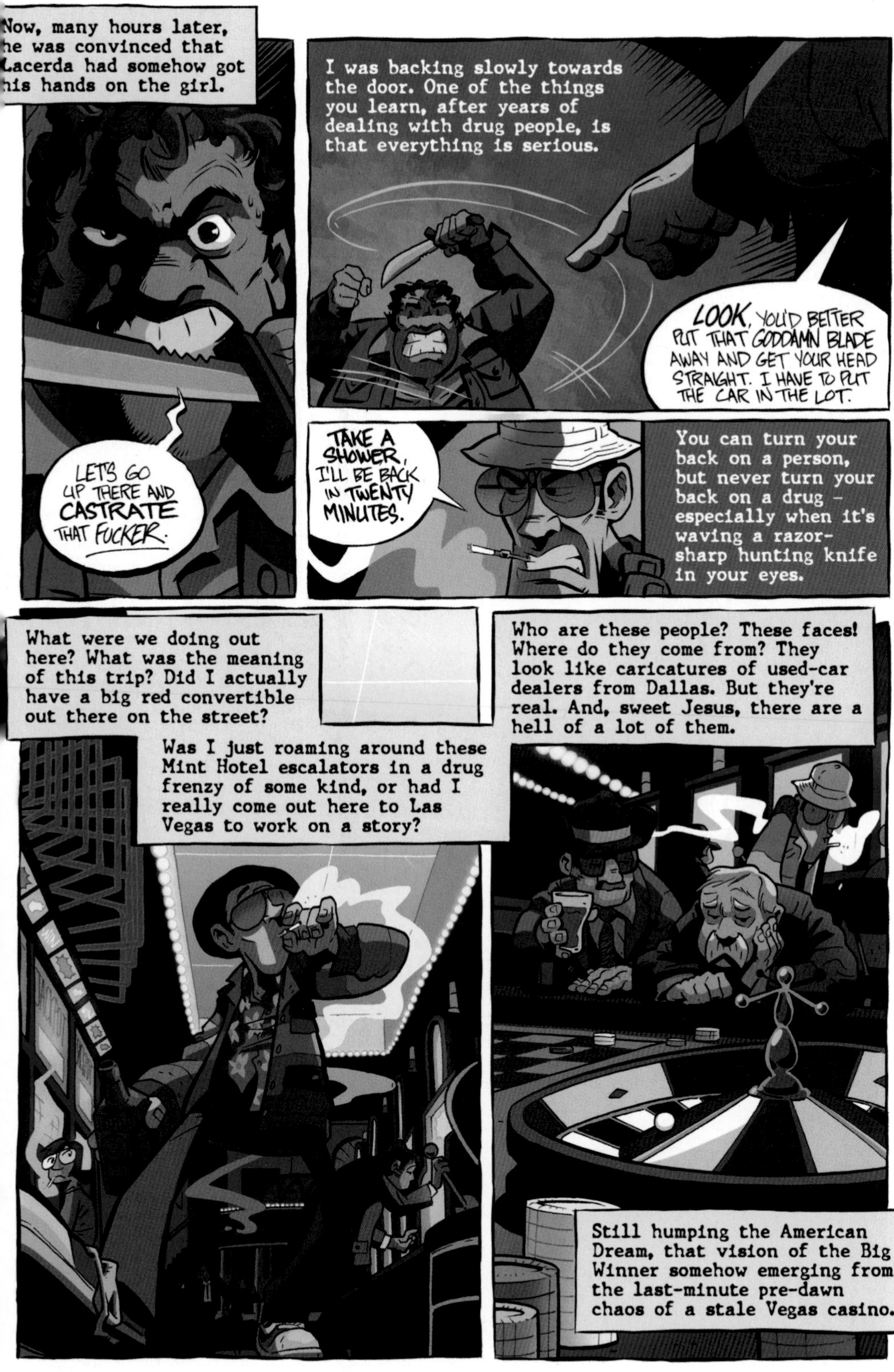

Now, many hours later, he was convinced that Lacerda had somehow got his hands on the girl.
LET'S GO UP THERE AND CASTRATE THAT FUCKER.
I was backing slowly towards the door. One of the things you learn, after years of dealing with drug people, is that everything is serious.
LOOK, YOU'D BETTER PUT THAT GODDAMN BLADE AWAY AND GET YOUR HEAD STRAIGHT. I HAVE TO PUT THE CAR IN THE LOT.
TAKE A SHOWER, I'LL BE BACK IN TWENTY MINUTES.
You can turn your back on a person, but never turn your back on a drug - especially when it's waving a razor-sharp hunting knife in your eyes.
What were we doing out here? What was the meaning of this trip? Did I actually have a big red convertible out there on the street?
Was I just roaming around these Mint Hotel escalators in a drug frenzy of some kind, or had I really come out here to Las Vegas to work on a story?
Who are these people? These faces! Where do they come from? They look like caricatures of used-car dealers from Dallas. But they're real. And, sweet Jesus, there are a hell of a lot of them.
Still humping the American Dream, that vision of the Big Winner somehow emerging from the last-minute pre-dawn chaos of a stale Vegas casino.

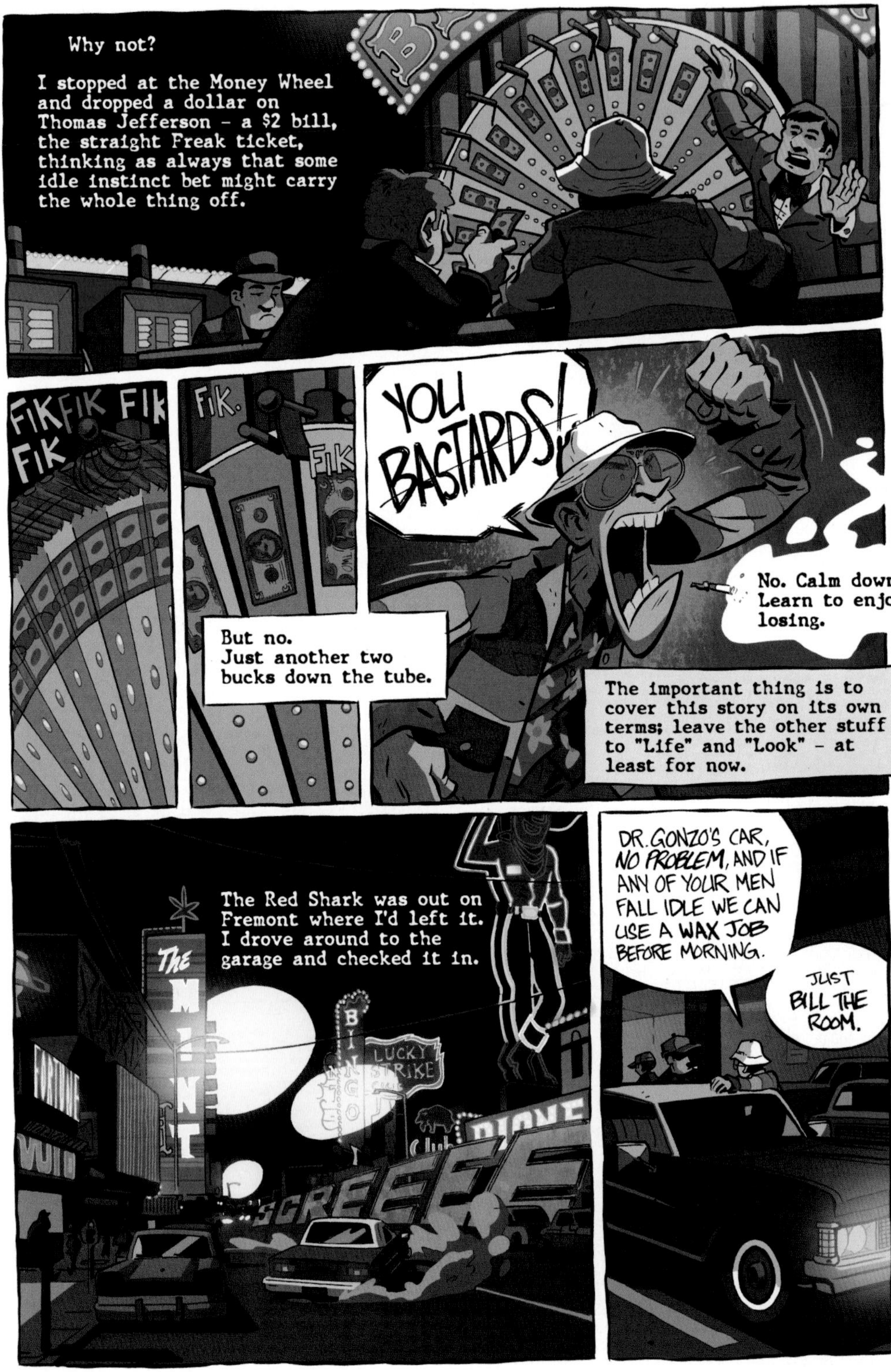
Why not?
I stopped at the Money Wheel and dropped a dollar on Thomas Jefferson - a $2 bill, the straight Freak ticket, thinking as always that some idle instinct bet might carry the whole thing off.
FIK FIK FIK FIK
FIK.
FIK
But no. Just another two bucks down the tube.
YOU BASTARDS!
No. Calm down. Learn to enjoy losing.
The important thing is to cover this story on its own terms; leave the other stuff to "Life" and "Look" - at least for now.
The Red Shark was out on Fremont where I'd left it. I drove around to the garage and checked it in.
THE MINT
FORTUNE
BINGO
LUCKY STRIKE
SCREEEE
DR. GONZO'S CAR, NO PROBLEM, AND IF ANY OF YOUR MEN FALL IDLE WE CAN USE A WAX JOB BEFORE MORNING.
JUST BILL THE ROOM.

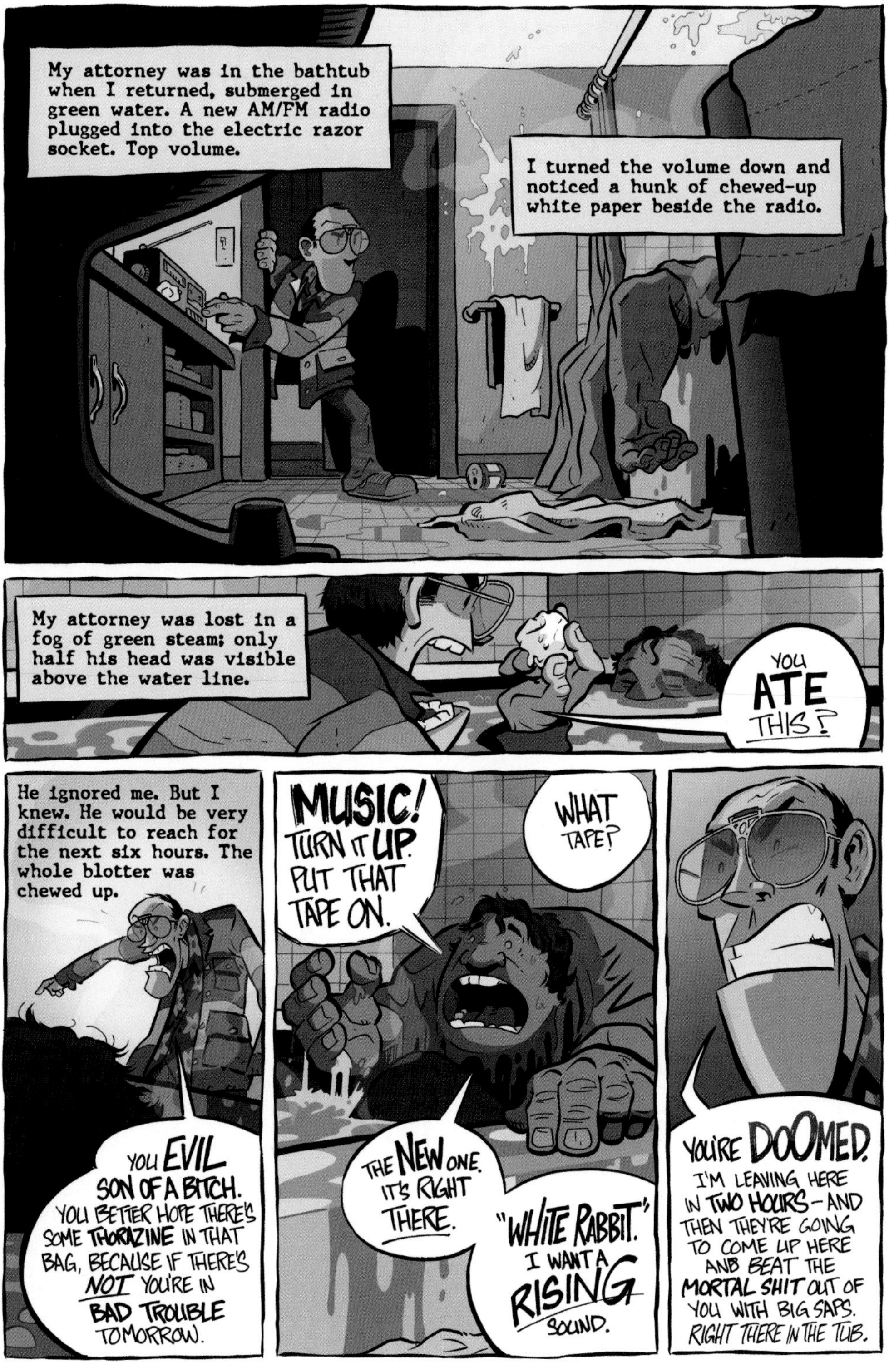
My attorney was in the bathtub when I returned, submerged in green water. A new AM/FM radio plugged into the electric razor socket. Top volume.
I turned the volume down and noticed a hunk of chewed-up white paper beside the radio.
My attorney was lost in a fog of green steam; only half his head was visible above the water line.
YOU ATE THIS?
He ignored me. But I knew. He would be very difficult to reach for the next six hours. The whole blotter was chewed up.
YOU EVIL SON OF A BITCH. YOU BETTER HOPE THERE'S SOME THORAZINE IN THAT BAG, BECAUSE IF THERE'S NOT YOU'RE IN BAD TROUBLE TOMORROW.
MUSIC! TURN IT UP. PUT THAT TAPE ON.
WHAT TAPE?
THE NEW ONE. IT'S RIGHT THERE.
"WHITE RABBIT." I WANT A RISING SOUND.
YOU'RE DOOMED. I'M LEAVING HERE IN TWO HOURS—AND THEN THEY'RE GOING TO COME UP HERE AND BEAT THE MORTAL SHIT OUT OF YOU WITH BIG SAPS. RIGHT THERE IN THE TUB.

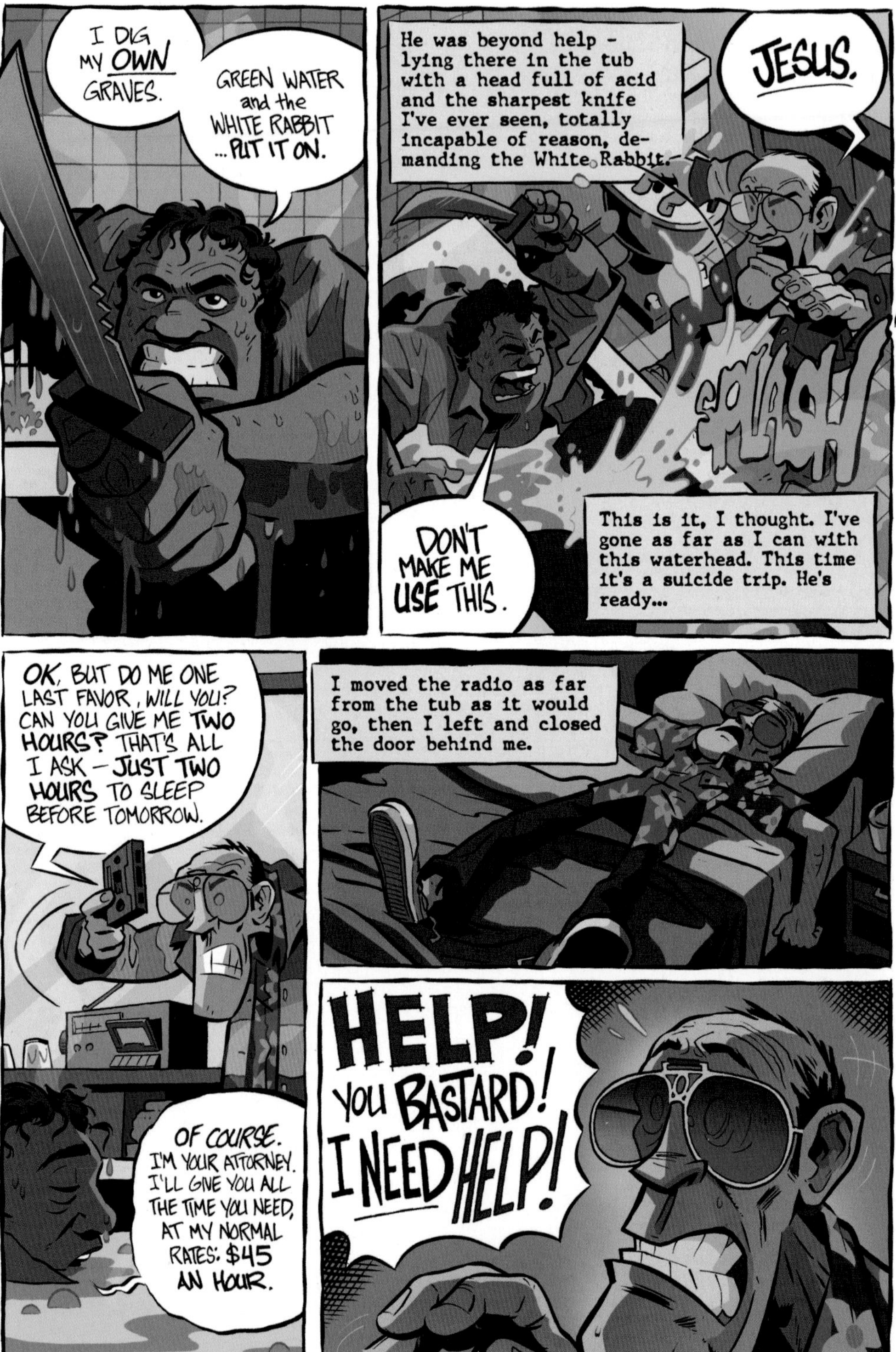
I DIG MY OWN GRAVES.
GREEN WATER and the WHITE RABBIT ...PUT IT ON.
He was beyond help - lying there in the tub with a head full of acid and the sharpest knife I've ever seen, totally incapable of reason, demanding the White Rabbit.
JESUS.
SPLASH
DON'T MAKE ME USE THIS.
This is it, I thought. I've gone as far as I can with this waterhead. This time it's a suicide trip. He's ready...
OK, BUT DO ME ONE LAST FAVOR, WILL YOU? CAN YOU GIVE ME TWO HOURS? THAT'S ALL I ASK - JUST TWO HOURS TO SLEEP BEFORE TOMORROW.
OF COURSE. I'M YOUR ATTORNEY. I'LL GIVE YOU ALL THE TIME YOU NEED, AT MY NORMAL RATES: $45 AN HOUR.
I moved the radio as far from the tub as it would go, then I left and closed the door behind me.
HELP! YOU BASTARD! I NEED HELP!

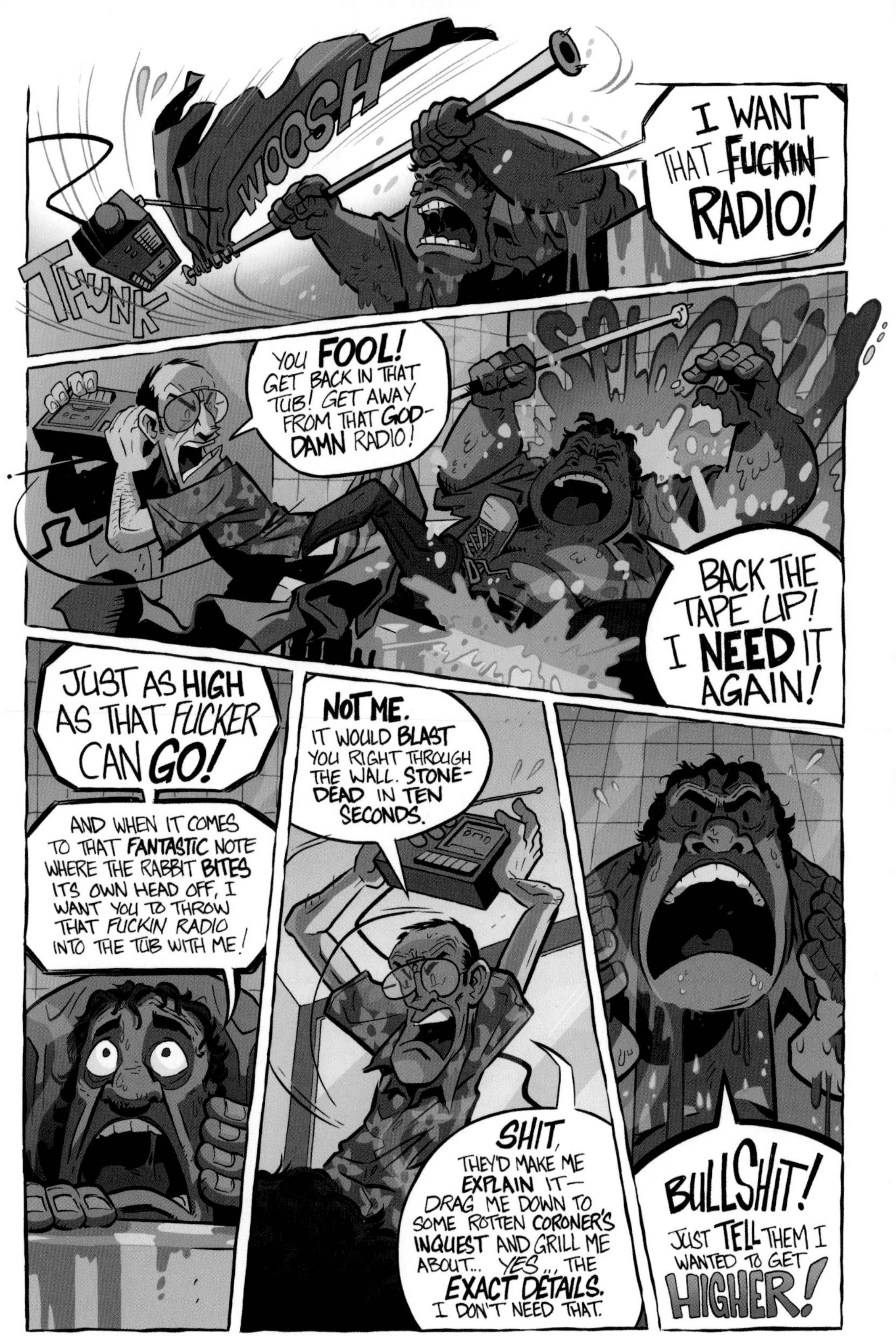

WOOSH
THUNK
I WANT THAT FUCKIN RADIO!
YOU FOOL! GET BACK IN THAT TUB! GET AWAY FROM THAT GOD-DAMN RADIO!
BACK THE TAPE UP! I NEED IT AGAIN!
JUST AS HIGH AS THAT FUCKER CAN GO!
AND WHEN IT COMES TO THAT FANTASTIC NOTE WHERE THE RABBIT BITES ITS OWN HEAD OFF, I WANT YOU TO THROW THAT FUCKIN RADIO INTO THE TUB WITH ME!
NOT ME. IT WOULD BLAST YOU RIGHT THROUGH THE WALL. STONE-DEAD IN TEN SECONDS.
SHIT, THEY'D MAKE ME EXPLAIN IT— DRAG ME DOWN TO SOME ROTTEN CORONER'S INQUEST AND GRILL ME ABOUT... YES... THE EXACT DETAILS. I DON'T NEED THAT.
BULLSHIT! JUST TELL THEM I WANTED TO GET HIGHER!

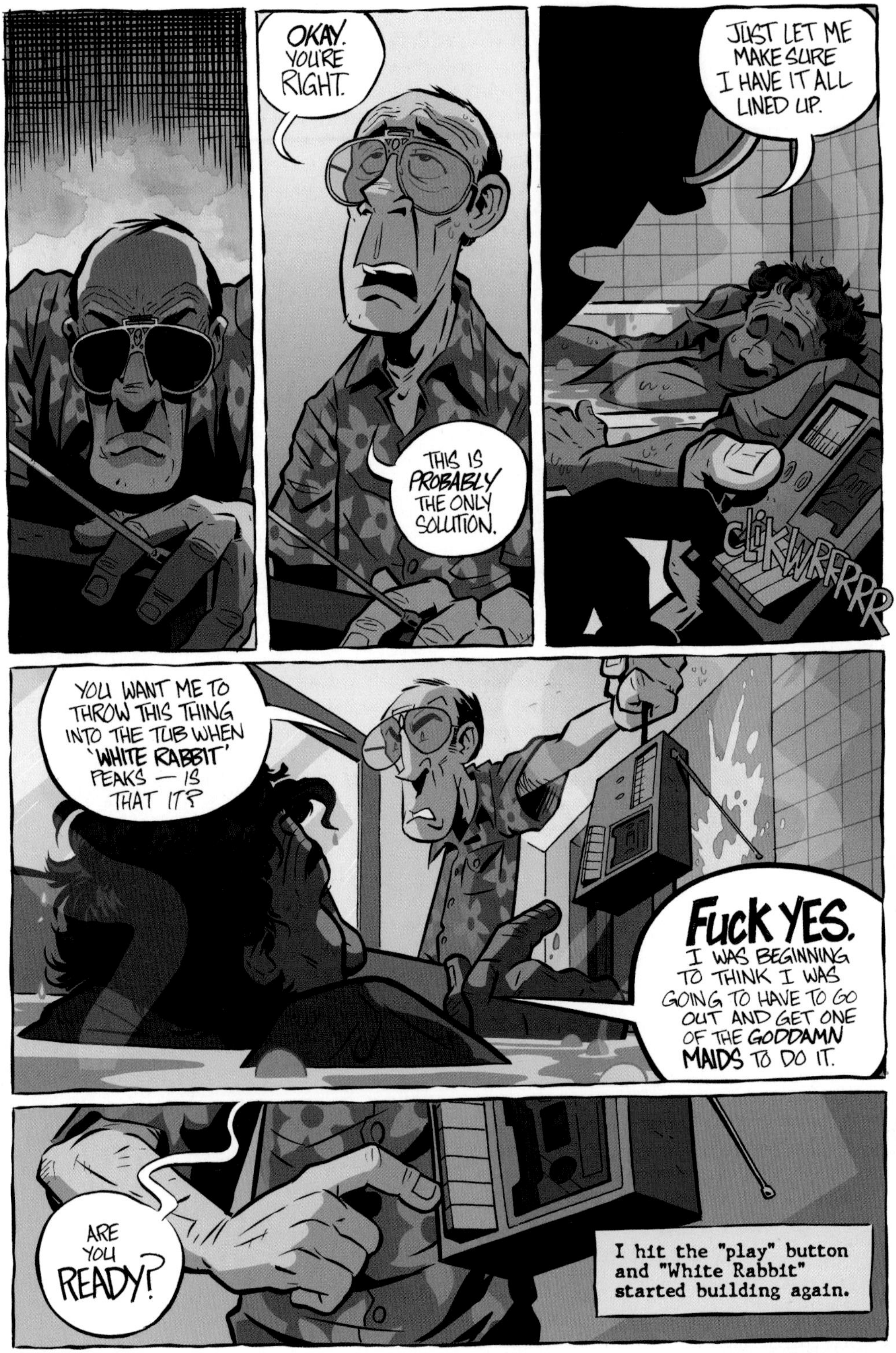
OKAY. YOU'RE RIGHT.
THIS IS PROBABLY THE ONLY SOLUTION.
JUST LET ME MAKE SURE I HAVE IT ALL LINED UP.
CLICK WRRRRR
YOU WANT ME TO THROW THIS THING INTO THE TUB WHEN 'WHITE RABBIT' PEAKS — IS THAT IT?
FUCK YES. I WAS BEGINNING TO THINK I WAS GOING TO HAVE TO GO OUT AND GET ONE OF THE GODDAMN MAIDS TO DO IT.
ARE YOU READY?
I hit the "play" button and "White Rabbit" started building again.

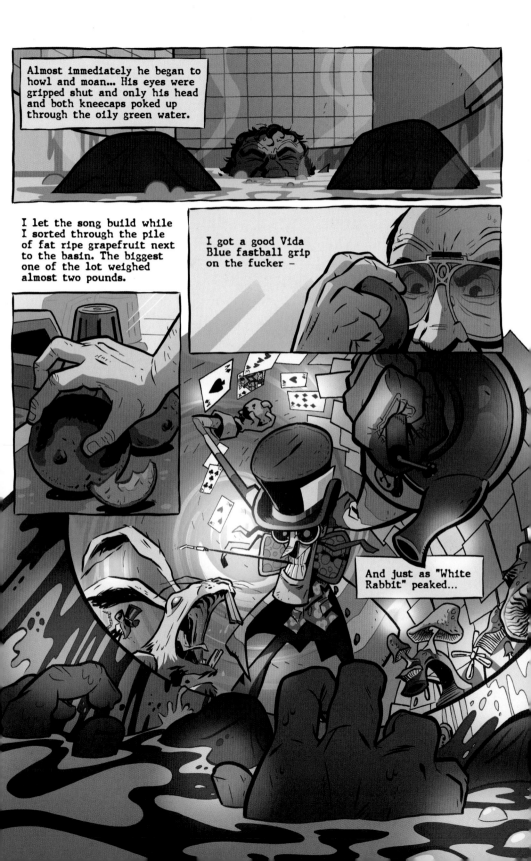

Almost immediately he began to howl and moan... His eyes were gripped shut and only his head and both kneecaps poked up through the oily green water.

I let the song build while I sorted through the pile of fat ripe grapefruit next to the basin. The biggest one of the lot weighed almost two pounds.

I got a good Vida Blue fastball grip on the fucker —

And just as "White Rabbit" peaked...

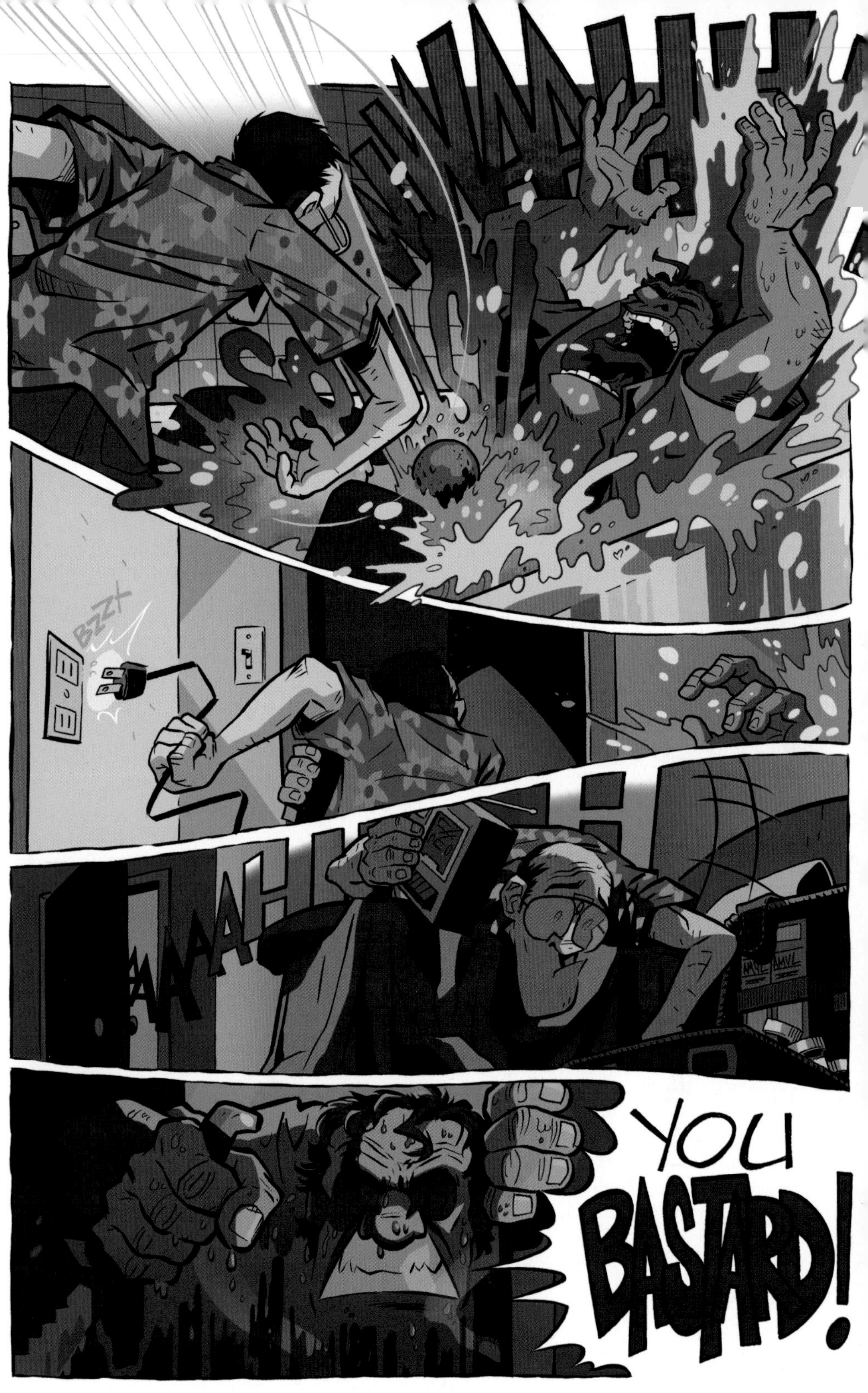
BZZT
YOU
BASTARD!

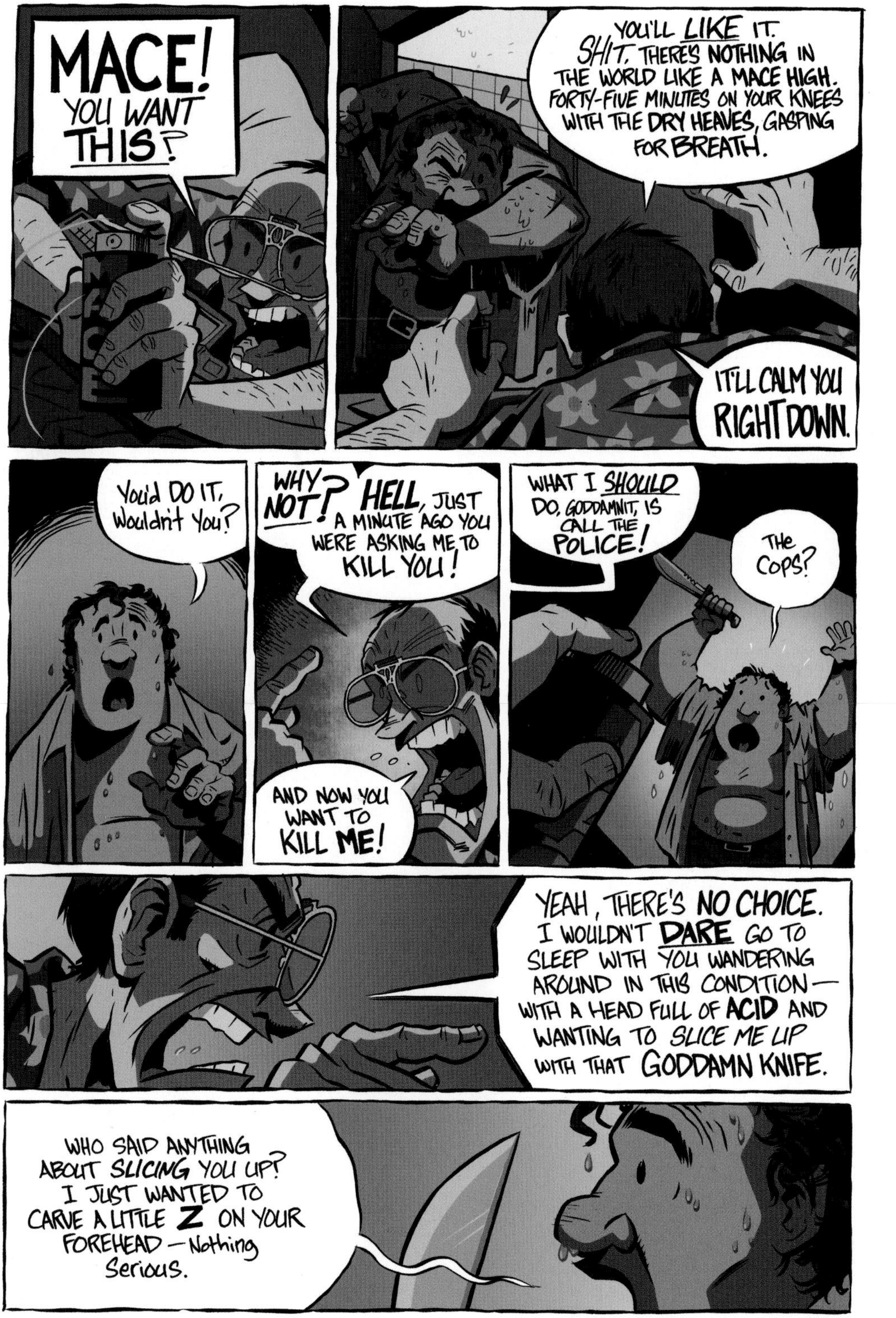
MACE! YOU WANT THIS?
YOU'LL LIKE IT. SHIT, THERE'S NOTHING IN THE WORLD LIKE A MACE HIGH. FORTY-FIVE MINUTES ON YOUR KNEES WITH THE DRY HEAVES, GASPING FOR BREATH.
IT'LL CALM YOU RIGHT DOWN.
You'd DO IT, Wouldn't You?
WHY NOT?! HELL, JUST A MINUTE AGO YOU WERE ASKING ME TO KILL YOU!
AND NOW YOU WANT TO KILL ME!
WHAT I SHOULD DO, GODDAMNIT, IS CALL THE POLICE!
The Cops?
YEAH, THERE'S NO CHOICE. I WOULDN'T DARE GO TO SLEEP WITH YOU WANDERING AROUND IN THIS CONDITION— WITH A HEAD FULL OF ACID AND WANTING TO SLICE ME UP WITH THAT GODDAMN KNIFE.
WHO SAID ANYTHING ABOUT SLICING YOU UP? I JUST WANTED TO CARVE A LITTLE Z ON YOUR FOREHEAD— Nothing Serious.

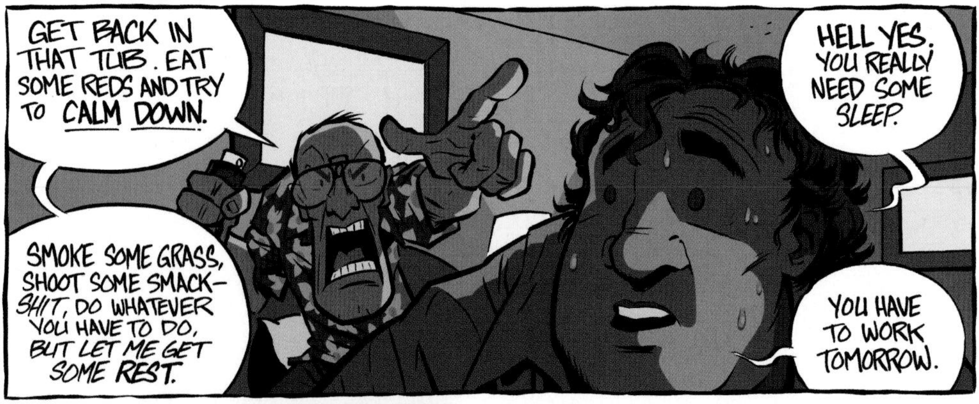
GET BACK IN THAT TUB. EAT SOME REDS AND TRY TO CALM DOWN.
SMOKE SOME GRASS, SHOOT SOME SMACK- SHIT, DO WHATEVER YOU HAVE TO DO, BUT LET ME GET SOME REST.
HELL YES. YOU REALLY NEED SOME SLEEP.
YOU HAVE TO WORK TOMORROW.

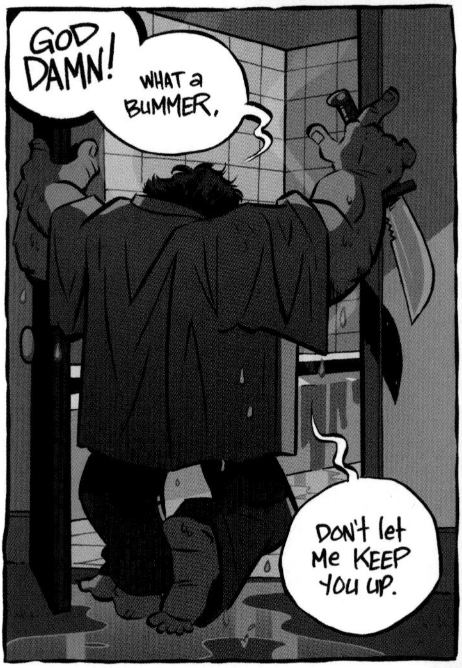
GOD DAMN!
WHAT a BUMMER.
DON'T let Me KEEP YOU UP.

I watched him shuffle back into the bathroom - still holding the blade, but now he seemed unaware of it. The acid had shifted gears on him; the next phase would probably be one of those hellishly intense introspection nightmares. Four hours or so of catatonic despair; but nothing physical, nothing dangerous.

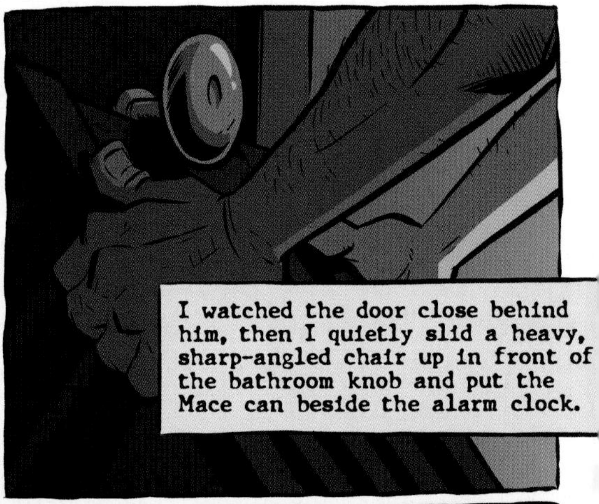
I watched the door close behind him, then I quietly slid a heavy, sharp-angled chair up in front of the bathroom knob and put the Mace can beside the alarm clock.

The room was very quiet. I walked over to the TV set and turned it on to a dead channel - white noise at maximum decibels, a fine sound for sleeping, a powerful continuous hiss to drown out everything strange.

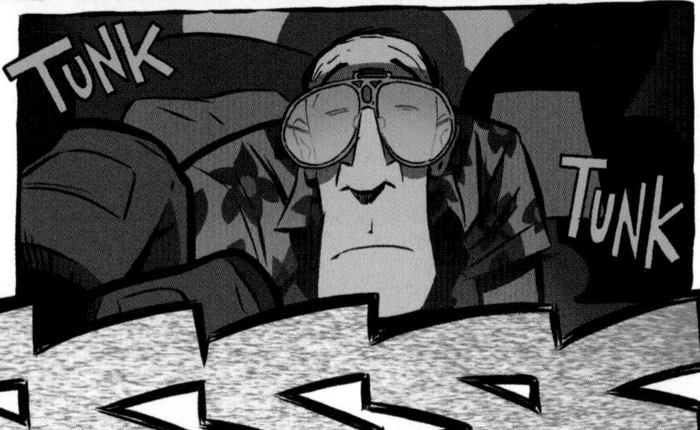
TUNK
TUNK

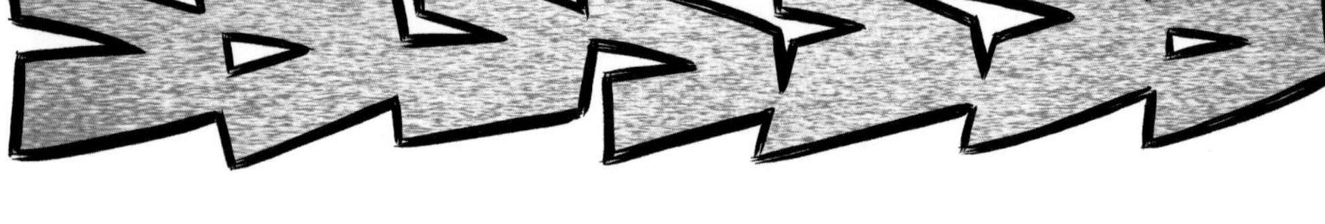
SSSSSS

8. "Genius 'Round the World Stands Hand in Hand, and One Shock of Recognition Runs the Whole Circle 'Round" - Art Linkletter

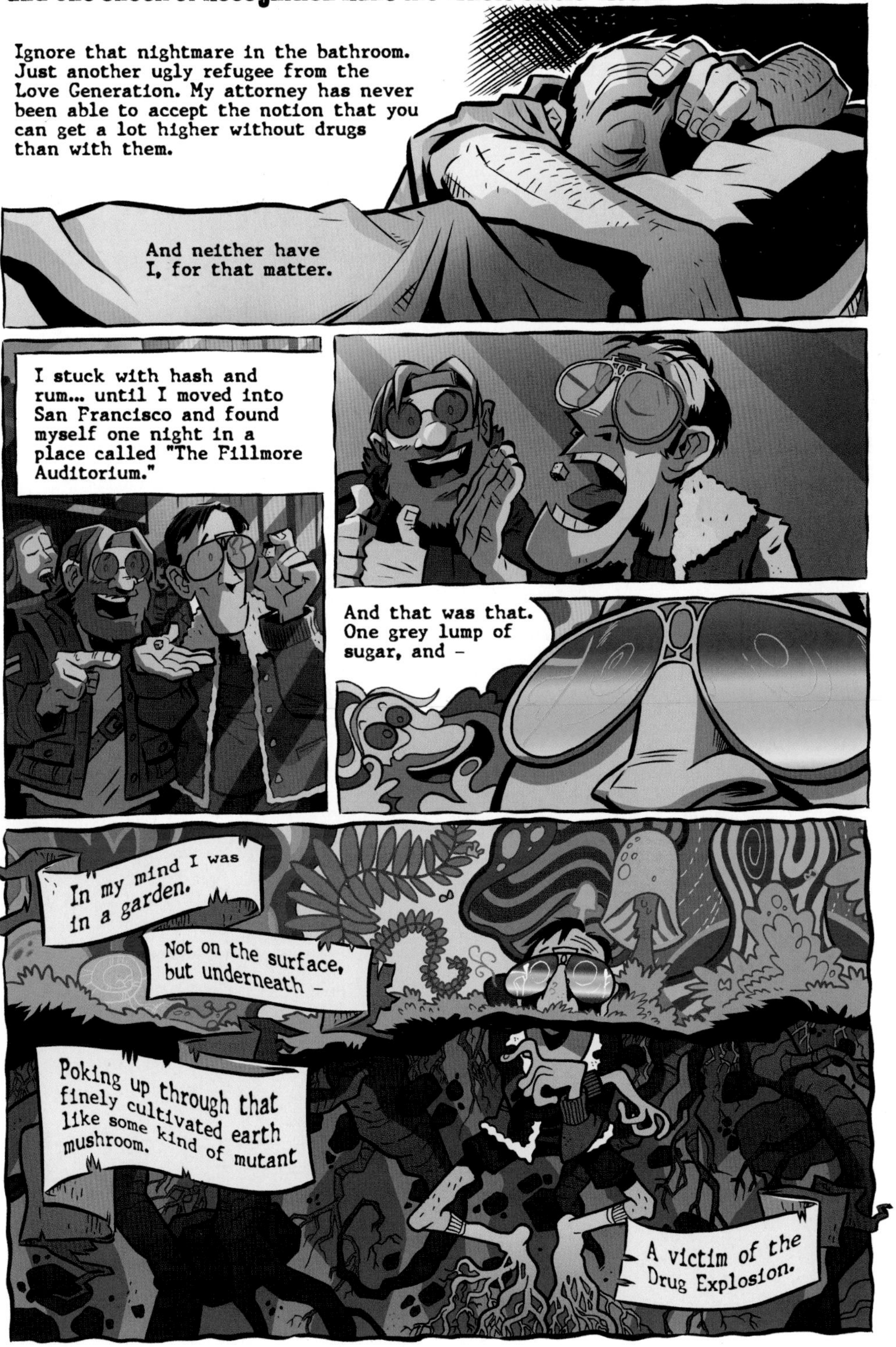
Ignore that nightmare in the bathroom. Just another ugly refugee from the Love Generation. My attorney has never been able to accept the notion that you can get a lot higher without drugs than with them.
And neither have I, for that matter.
I stuck with hash and rum... until I moved into San Francisco and found myself one night in a place called "The Fillmore Auditorium."
And that was that. One grey lump of sugar, and -
In my mind I was in a garden.
Not on the surface, but underneath -
Poking up through that finely cultivated earth like some kind of mutant mushroom.
A victim of the Drug Explosion.

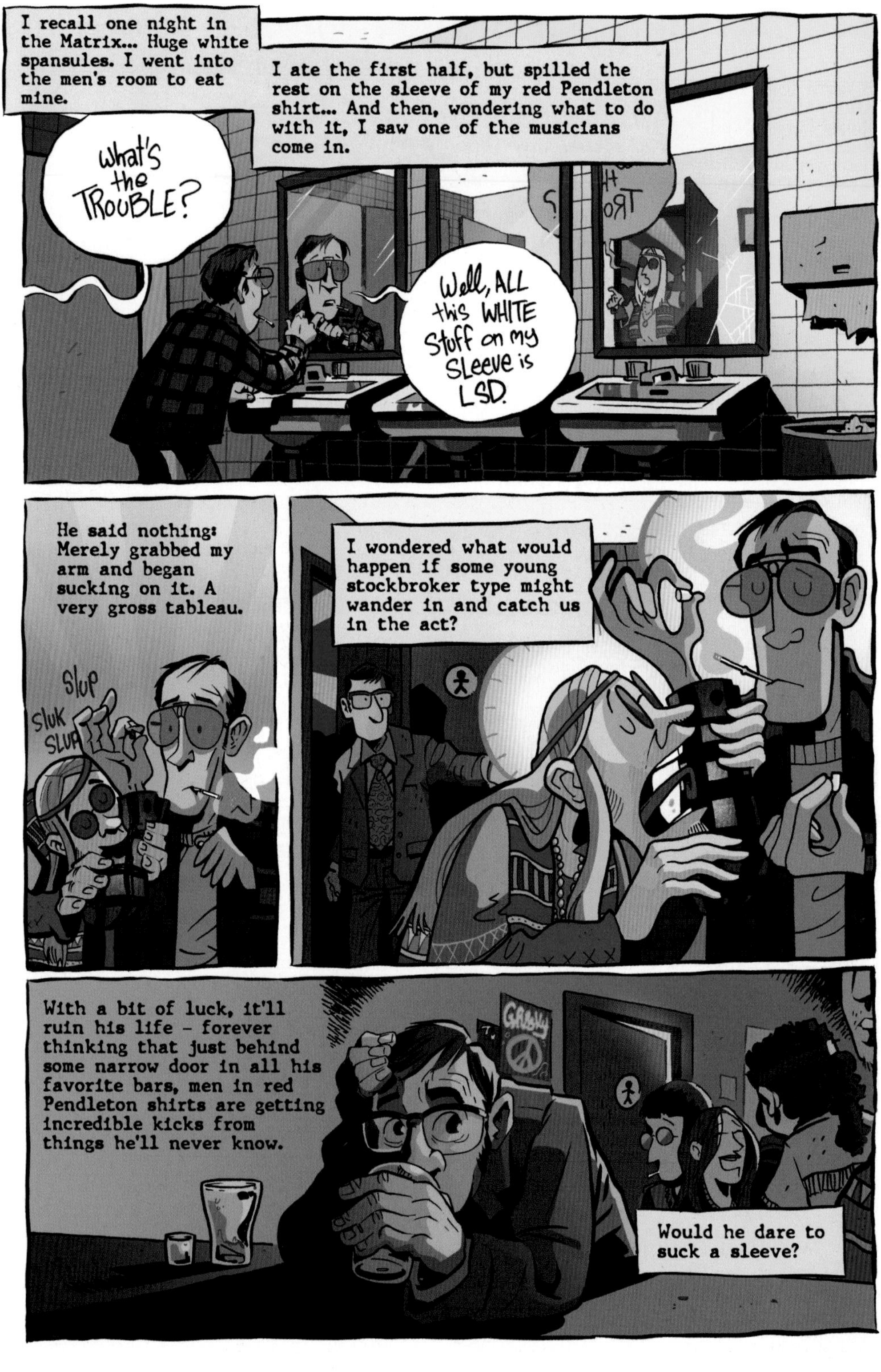
I recall one night in the Matrix... Huge white spansules. I went into the men's room to eat mine.
I ate the first half, but spilled the rest on the sleeve of my red Pendleton shirt... And then, wondering what to do with it, I saw one of the musicians come in.
What's the TROUBLE?
Well, ALL this WHITE Stuff on my SLeeve is LSD.
He said nothing: Merely grabbed my arm and began sucking on it. A very gross tableau.
SLUP
SLUK
SLUP
I wondered what would happen if some young stockbroker type might wander in and catch us in the act?
With a bit of luck, it'll ruin his life - forever thinking that just behind some narrow door in all his favorite bars, men in red Pendleton shirts are getting incredible kicks from things he'll never know.
Would he dare to suck a sleeve?

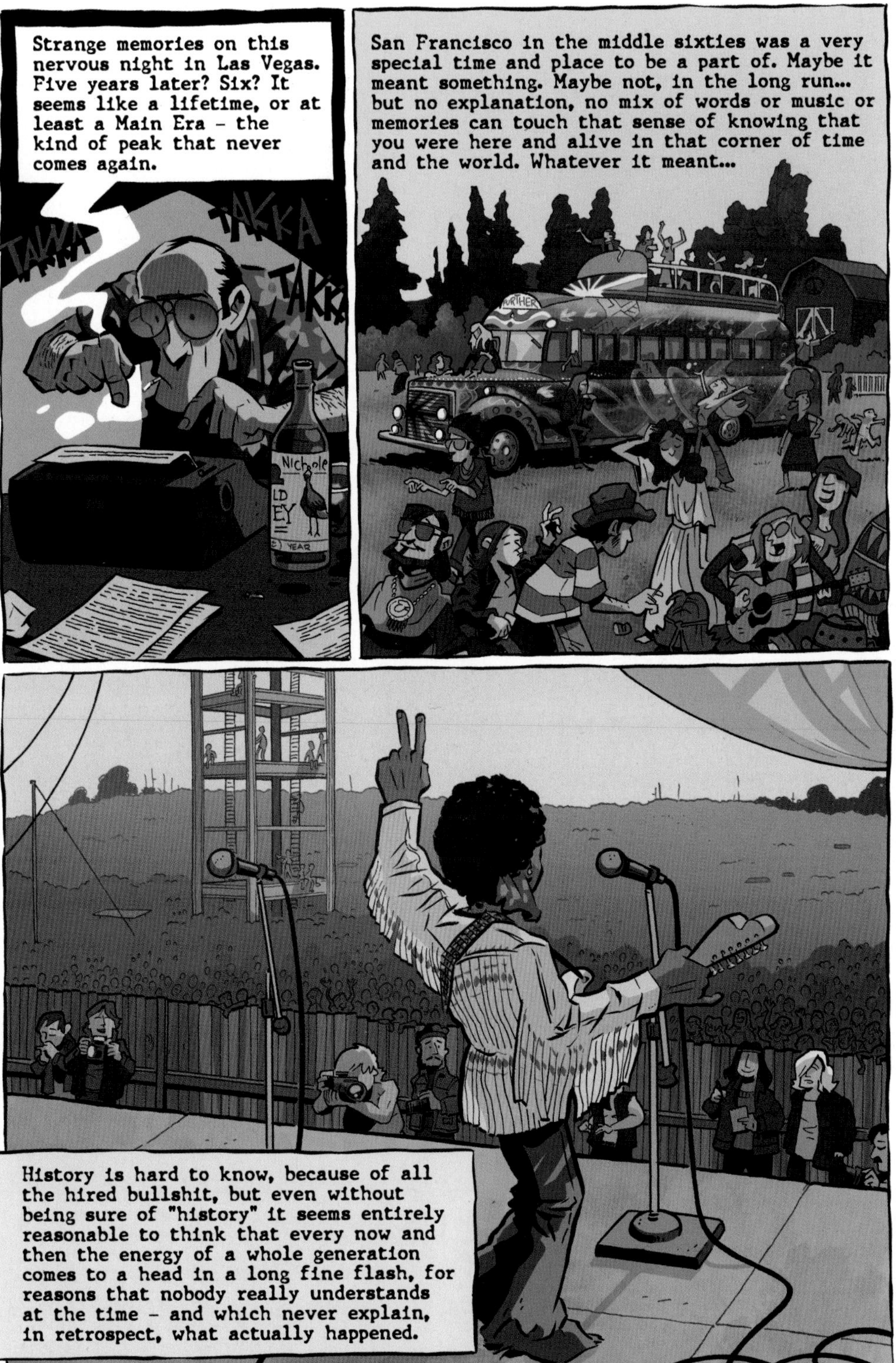
Strange memories on this nervous night in Las Vegas. Five years later? Six? It seems like a lifetime, or at least a Main Era - the kind of peak that never comes again.
TAKKA
TAKKA
TAKKA
San Francisco in the middle sixties was a very special time and place to be a part of. Maybe it meant something. Maybe not, in the long run... but no explanation, no mix of words or music or memories can touch that sense of knowing that you were here and alive in that corner of time and the world. Whatever it meant...
FURTHER
History is hard to know, because of all the hired bullshit, but even without being sure of "history" it seems entirely reasonable to think that every now and then the energy of a whole generation comes to a head in a long fine flash, for reasons that nobody really understands at the time - and which never explain, in retrospect, what actually happened.

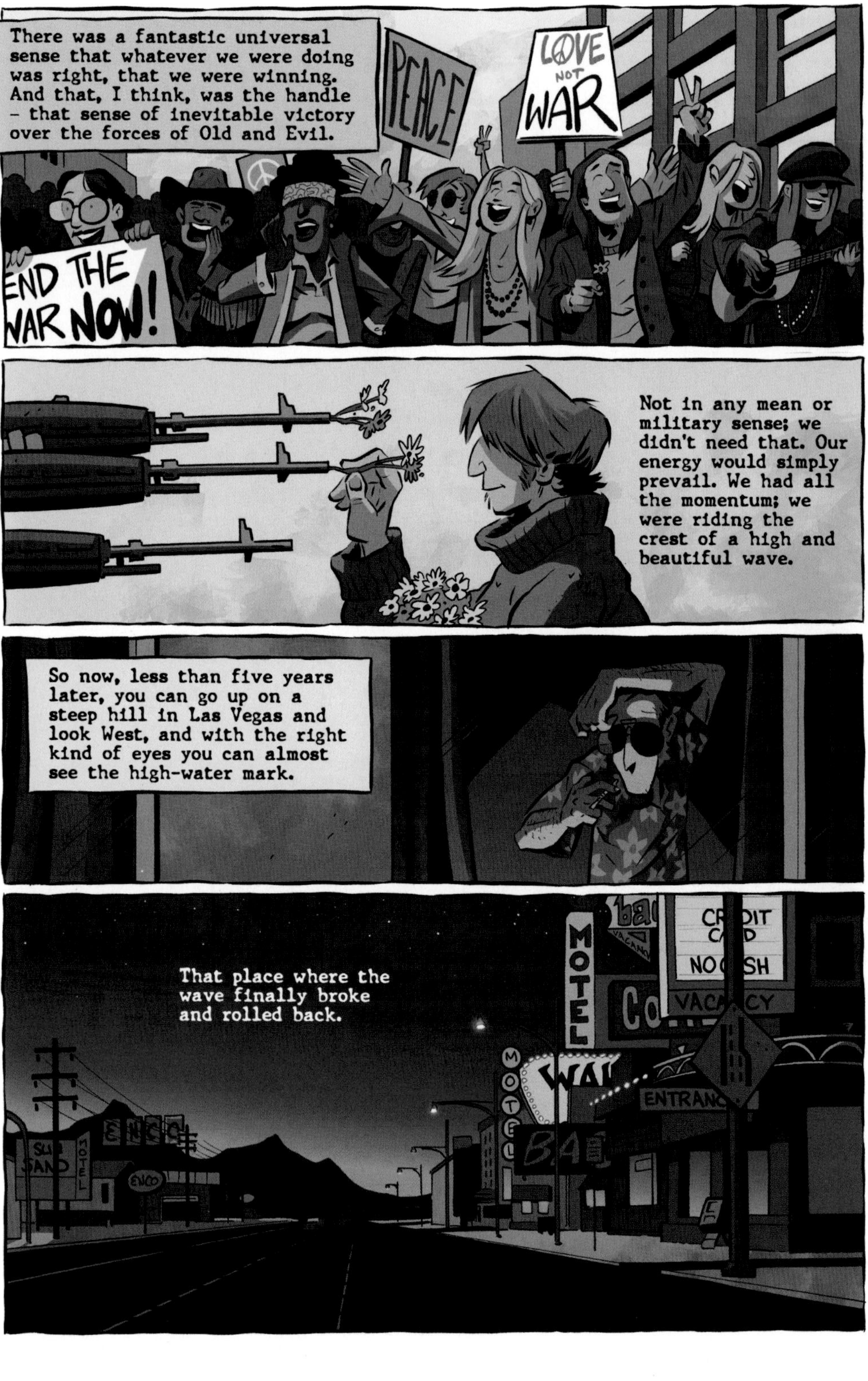
There was a fantastic universal sense that whatever we were doing was right, that we were winning. And that, I think, was the handle - that sense of inevitable victory over the forces of Old and Evil.
PEACE
LOVE NOT WAR
END THE WAR NOW!
Not in any mean or military sense; we didn't need that. Our energy would simply prevail. We had all the momentum; we were riding the crest of a high and beautiful wave.
So now, less than five years later, you can go up on a steep hill in Las Vegas and look West, and with the right kind of eyes you can almost see the high-water mark.
That place where the wave finally broke and rolled back.
MOTEL
MOTEL
MOTEL

9. No Sympathy for the Devil... Newsmen Tortured?... Flight into Madness

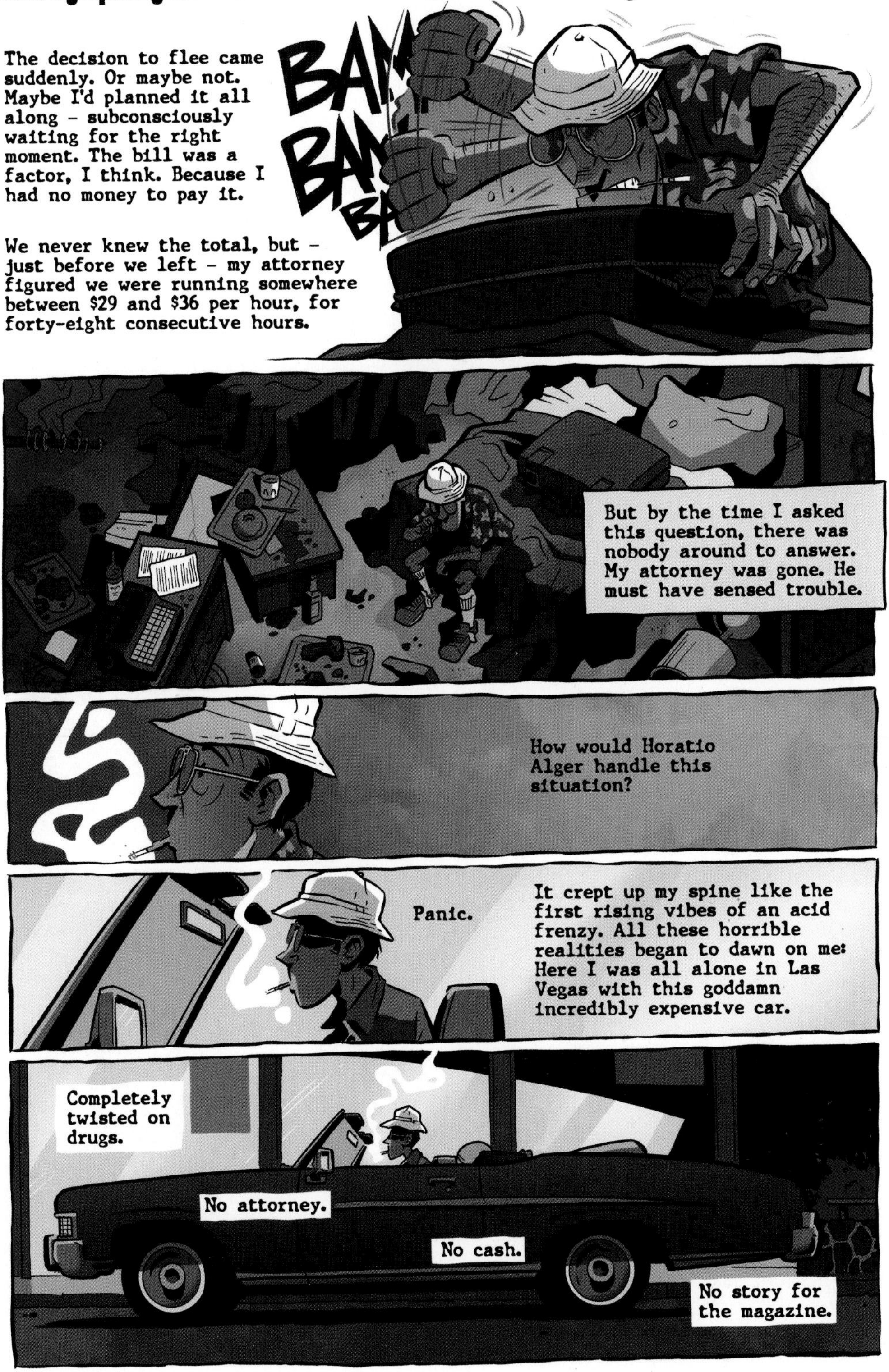
The decision to flee came suddenly. Or maybe not. Maybe I'd planned it all along – subconsciously waiting for the right moment. The bill was a factor, I think. Because I had no money to pay it.
BAM
BAM
BA
We never knew the total, but – just before we left – my attorney figured we were running somewhere between $29 and $36 per hour, for forty-eight consecutive hours.
But by the time I asked this question, there was nobody around to answer. My attorney was gone. He must have sensed trouble.
How would Horatio Alger handle this situation?
Panic.
It crept up my spine like the first rising vibes of an acid frenzy. All these horrible realities began to dawn on me: Here I was all alone in Las Vegas with this goddamn incredibly expensive car.
Completely twisted on drugs.
No attorney.
No cash.
No story for the magazine.

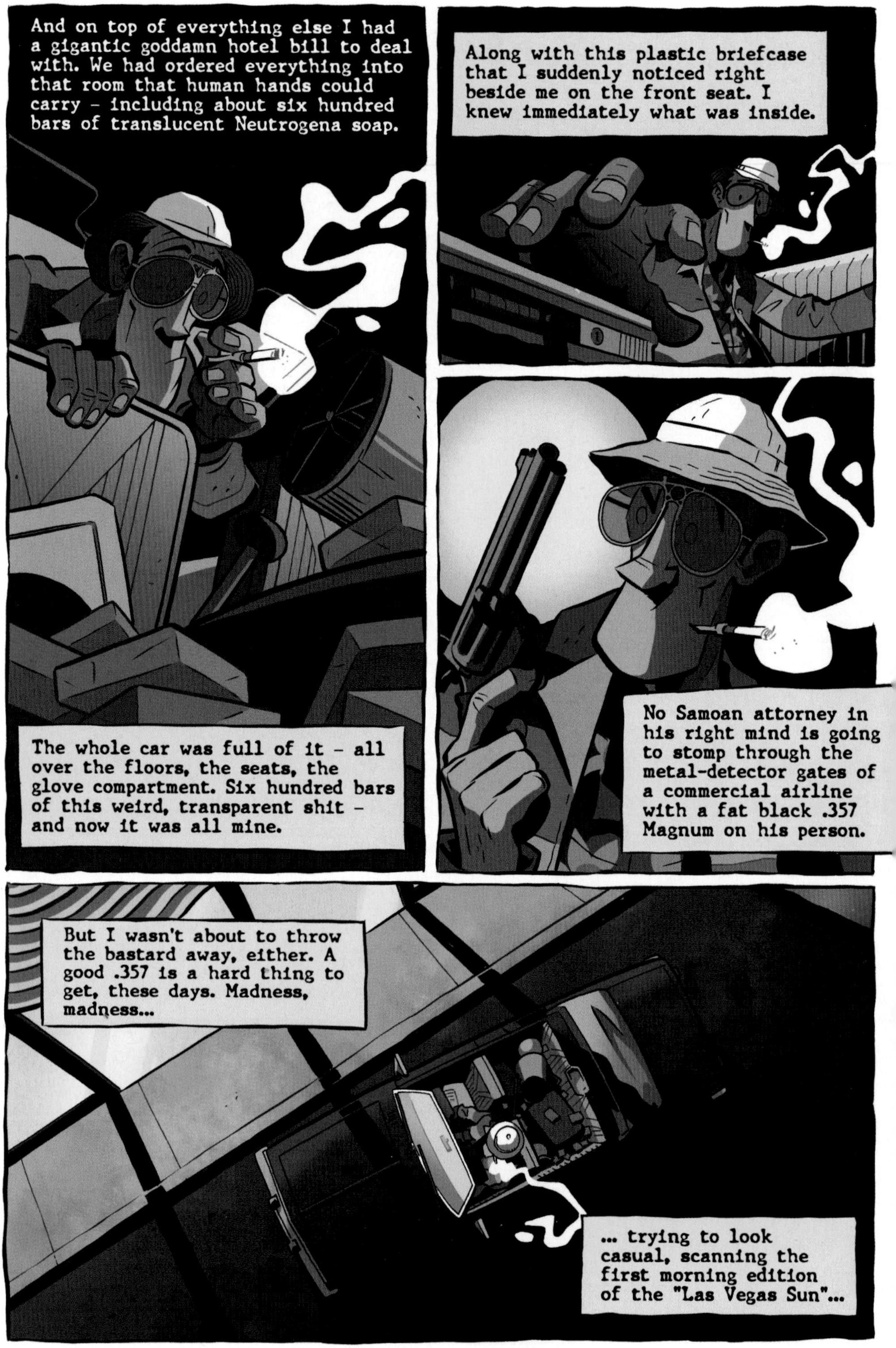
And on top of everything else I had a gigantic goddamn hotel bill to deal with. We had ordered everything into that room that human hands could carry - including about six hundred bars of translucent Neutrogena soap.
The whole car was full of it - all over the floors, the seats, the glove compartment. Six hundred bars of this weird, transparent shit - and now it was all mine.
Along with this plastic briefcase that I suddenly noticed right beside me on the front seat. I knew immediately what was inside.
No Samoan attorney in his right mind is going to stomp through the metal-detector gates of a commercial airline with a fat black .357 Magnum on his person.
But I wasn't about to throw the bastard away, either. A good .357 is a hard thing to get, these days. Madness, madness...
... trying to look casual, scanning the first morning edition of the "Las Vegas Sun"...

Weather
Sunny
High 78
Details A2

LAS VEGAS SUN

Wednesday
March 24, 1971
10 CENTS

Established 1950

Trio Re-Arrested in Beauty's Death

An overdose of heroin was listed as the official cause of death for pretty Diane Hamby, 19, whose body was found stuffed in a refrigerator last week, according to the Clark County Coroner's office. Investigators of the sheriff's homicide team who went to arrest the suspects said that one, a 24-year-old woman, attempted to fling herself through the glass doors of her trailer before being stopped by deputies. Officers said she was apparently hysterical and shouted, "You'll never take me alive." But officers handcuffed the woman and she apparently was not injured... CONTINUED ON PAGE 6

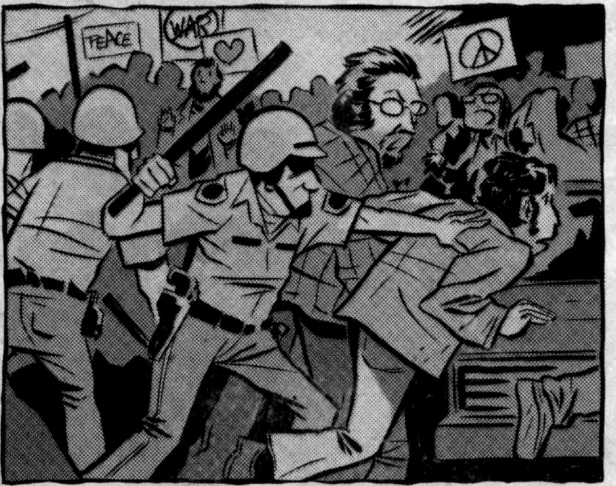
PEACE
WAR

Torture Tales Told in War Hearings

WASHINGTON – Volunteer witnesses told an informal congressional panel yesterday that while serving as military interrogators they routinely used electrical telephone hookups and helicopter drops to torture and kill Vietnamese prisoners. One Army intelligence specialist said the pistol slaying of his Chinese interpreter was defended by a superior who said, "She was just a slope, anyway," meaning she was an Asiatic....

GI Drug Deaths Claimed

WASHINGTON (AP) – A House Subcommittee report says illegal drugs killed 160 American GI's last year – 40 of them in Vietnam... Drugs were suspected, it said, in another 56 military deaths in Asia and the Pacific Command ... It said the heroin problem in Vietnam is increasing in seriousness, primarily because of processing laboratories in Laos, Thailand and Hong Kong. "Drug suppression in Vietnam is almost completely ineffective," the report said, "partially because of an ineffective local police force and partially because some presently unknown corrupt officials in public office are involved in the drug traffic."

Five wounded near NYC Tenement

An unidentified gunman fired from the roof of a building, for no apparent reason.

Pharmacy Owner Arrested in Probe

A result of a preliminary investigation (of a Las Vegas pharmacy) showing a shortage of over 100,000 ... dered danger-

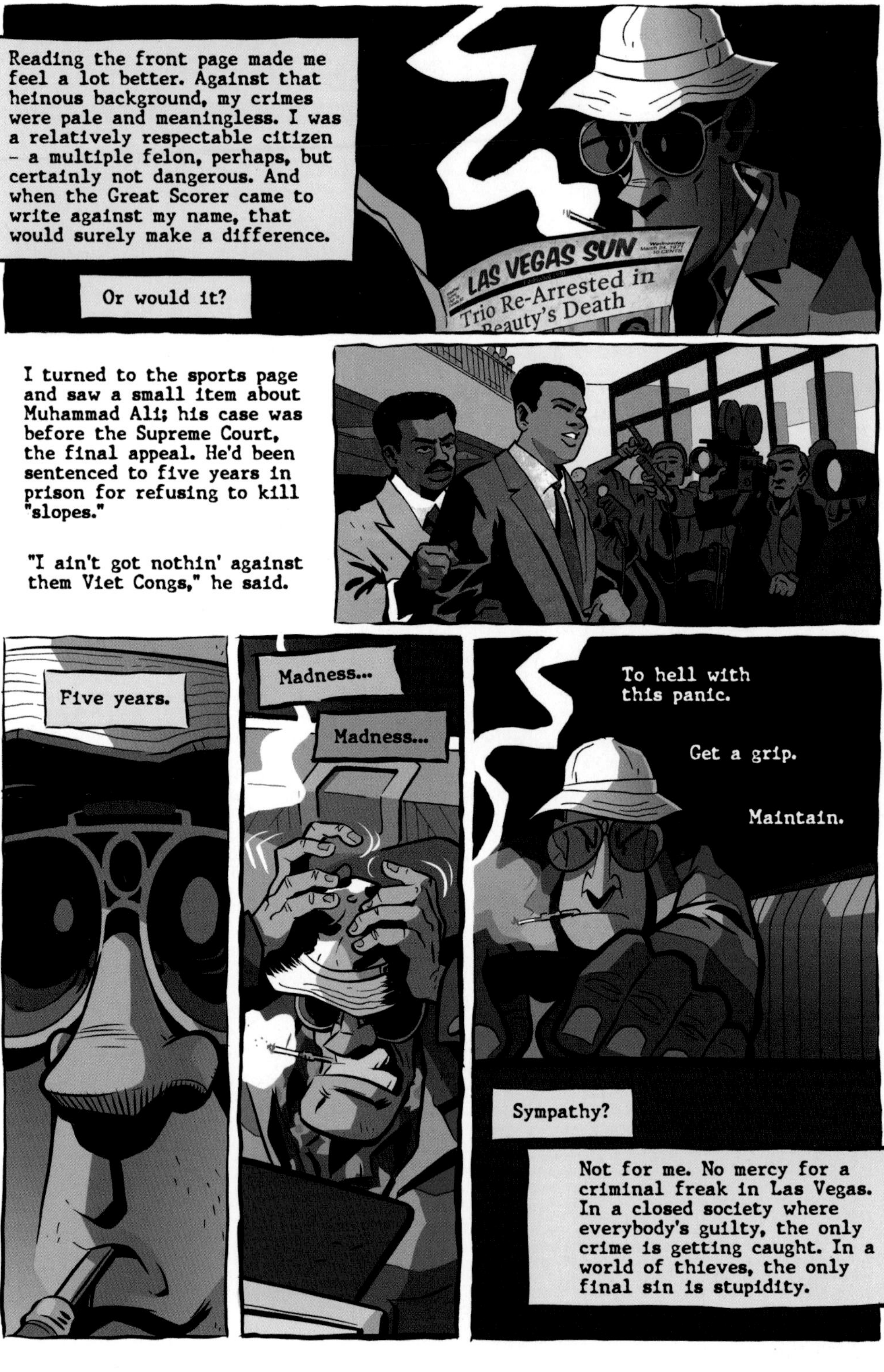
Reading the front page made me feel a lot better. Against that heinous background, my crimes were pale and meaningless. I was a relatively respectable citizen - a multiple felon, perhaps, but certainly not dangerous. And when the Great Scorer came to write against my name, that would surely make a difference.
LAS VEGAS SUN
Trio Re-Arrested in
Or would it?
I turned to the sports page and saw a small item about Muhammad Ali; his case was before the Supreme Court, the final appeal. He'd been sentenced to five years in prison for refusing to kill "slopes."
"I ain't got nothin' against them Viet Congs," he said.
Five years.
Madness...
Madness...
To hell with this panic.
Get a grip.
Maintain.
Sympathy?
Not for me. No mercy for a criminal freak in Las Vegas. In a closed society where everybody's guilty, the only crime is getting caught. In a world of thieves, the only final sin is stupidity.

10. Western Union Intervenes: A Warning from Mr. Heem... New Assignment from the Sports Desk and a Savage Invitation from the Police

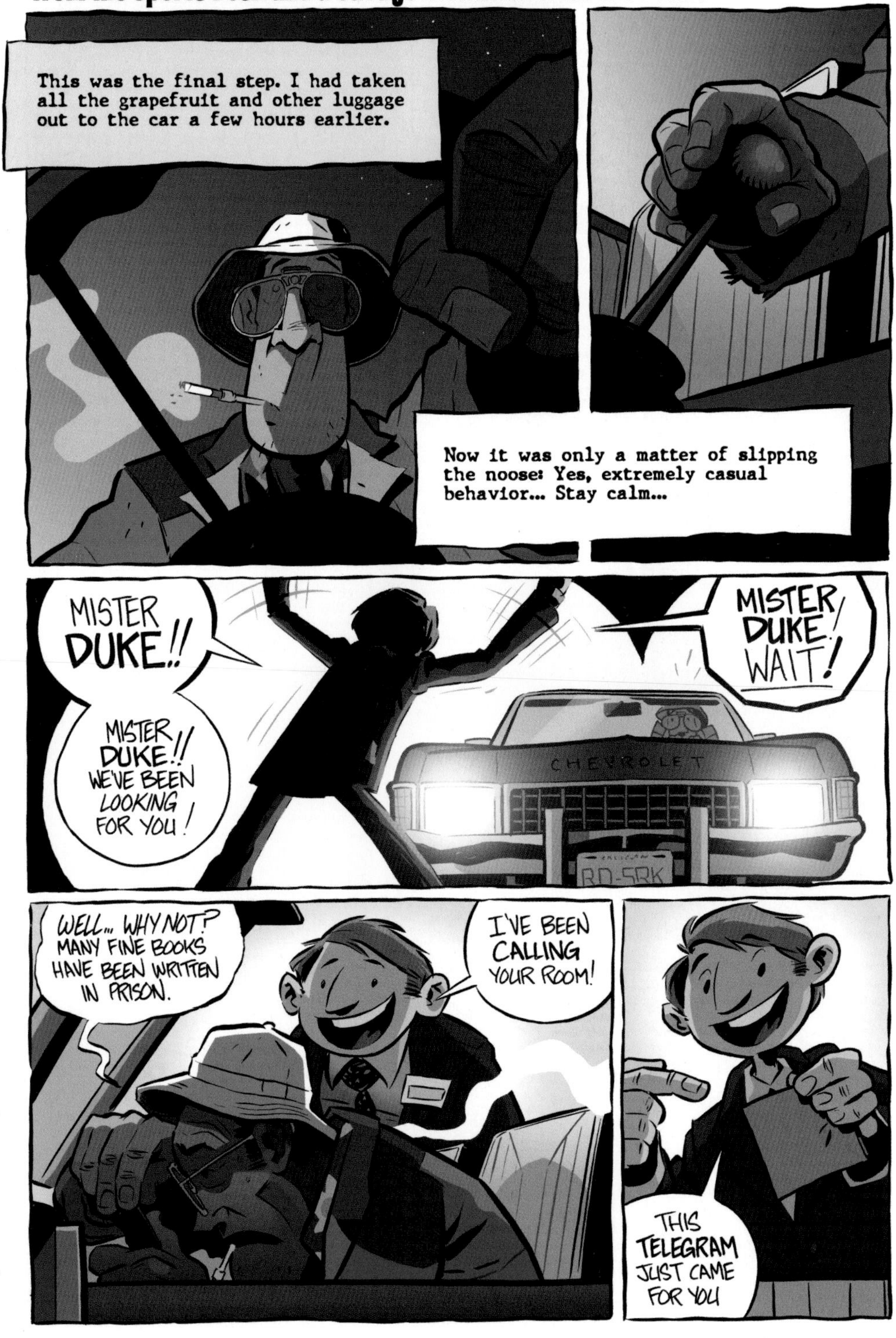
This was the final step. I had taken all the grapefruit and other luggage out to the car a few hours earlier.
Now it was only a matter of slipping the noose: Yes, extremely casual behavior... Stay calm...
MISTER DUKE!!
MISTER DUKE!! WE'VE BEEN LOOKING FOR YOU!
MISTER DUKE! WAIT!
CHEVROLET
I'VE BEEN CALLING YOUR ROOM!
WELL... WHY NOT? MANY FINE BOOKS HAVE BEEN WRITTEN IN PRISON.
THIS TELEGRAM JUST CAME FOR YOU

BUT ACTUALLY IT ISN'T FOR *YOU*. IT'S FOR SOMEBODY NAMED *THOMPSON*, BUT IT SAYS 'CARE OF *RAOUL DUKE*'. DOES THAT MAKE SENSE?

I felt dizzy. It was too much to absorb all at once. From freedom, to prison, and then back to freedom again — all in thirty seconds.

YES, IT MAKES SENSE.

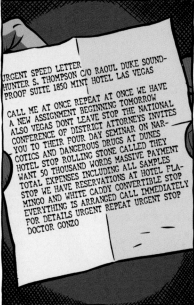

URGENT SPEED LETTER
HUNTER S. THOMPSON C/O RAOUL DUKE SOUND-
PROOF SUITE 1850 MINT HOTEL LAS VEGAS

CALL ME AT ONCE REPEAT AT ONCE WE HAVE
A NEW ASSIGNMENT BEGINNING TOMORROW
ALSO VEGAS DONT LEAVE STOP THE NATIONAL
CONFERENCE OF DISTRICT ATTORNEYS INVITES
YOU TO THEIR FOUR DAY SEMINAR ON NAR-
COTICS AND DANGEROUS DRUGS AT DUNES
HOTEL STOP ROLLING STONE CALLED THEY
WANT 50 THOUSAND WORDS MASSIVE PAYMENT
TOTAL EXPENSES INCLUDING ALL SAMPLES
STOP WE HAVE RESERVATIONS AT HOTEL FLA-
MINGO AND WHITE CADDY CONVERTIBLE STOP
EVERYTHING IS ARRANGED CALL IMMEDIATELY
FOR DETAILS URGENT REPEAT URGENT STOP
DOCTOR GONZO

HOLY SHIT!

THIS *CAN'T* BE TRUE!

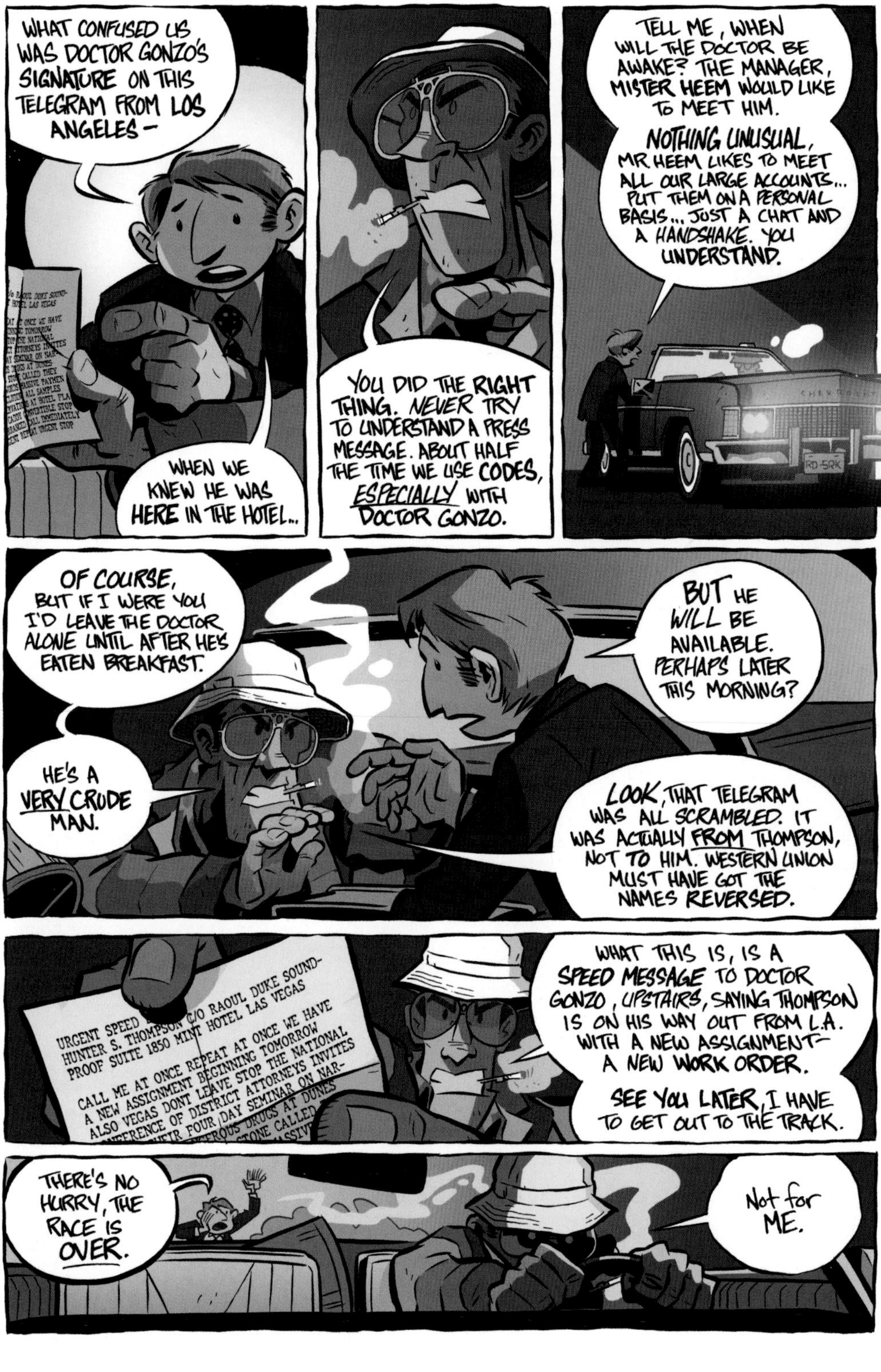
WHAT CONFUSED US WAS DOCTOR GONZO'S SIGNATURE ON THIS TELEGRAM FROM LOS ANGELES –
WHEN WE KNEW HE WAS HERE IN THE HOTEL...
YOU DID THE RIGHT THING. NEVER TRY TO UNDERSTAND A PRESS MESSAGE. ABOUT HALF THE TIME WE USE CODES, ESPECIALLY WITH DOCTOR GONZO.
TELL ME, WHEN WILL THE DOCTOR BE AWAKE? THE MANAGER, MISTER HEEM WOULD LIKE TO MEET HIM.
NOTHING UNUSUAL, MR HEEM LIKES TO MEET ALL OUR LARGE ACCOUNTS... PUT THEM ON A PERSONAL BASIS... JUST A CHAT AND A HANDSHAKE. YOU UNDERSTAND.
RD-5RK
OF COURSE, BUT IF I WERE YOU I'D LEAVE THE DOCTOR ALONE UNTIL AFTER HE'S EATEN BREAKFAST.
HE'S A VERY CRUDE MAN.
BUT HE WILL BE AVAILABLE. PERHAPS LATER THIS MORNING?
LOOK, THAT TELEGRAM WAS ALL SCRAMBLED. IT WAS ACTUALLY FROM THOMPSON, NOT TO HIM. WESTERN UNION MUST HAVE GOT THE NAMES REVERSED.
URGENT SPEED
HUNTER S. THOMPSON C/O RAOUL DUKE SOUND-
PROOF SUITE 1850 MINT HOTEL LAS VEGAS
CALL ME AT ONCE REPEAT AT ONCE WE HAVE
A NEW ASSIGNMENT BEGINNING TOMORROW
ALSO VEGAS DONT LEAVE STOP THE NATIONAL
WHAT THIS IS, IS A SPEED MESSAGE TO DOCTOR GONZO, UPSTAIRS, SAYING THOMPSON IS ON HIS WAY OUT FROM L.A. WITH A NEW ASSIGNMENT – A NEW WORK ORDER.
SEE YOU LATER, I HAVE TO GET OUT TO THE TRACK.
THERE'S NO HURRY, THE RACE IS OVER.
Not for ME.

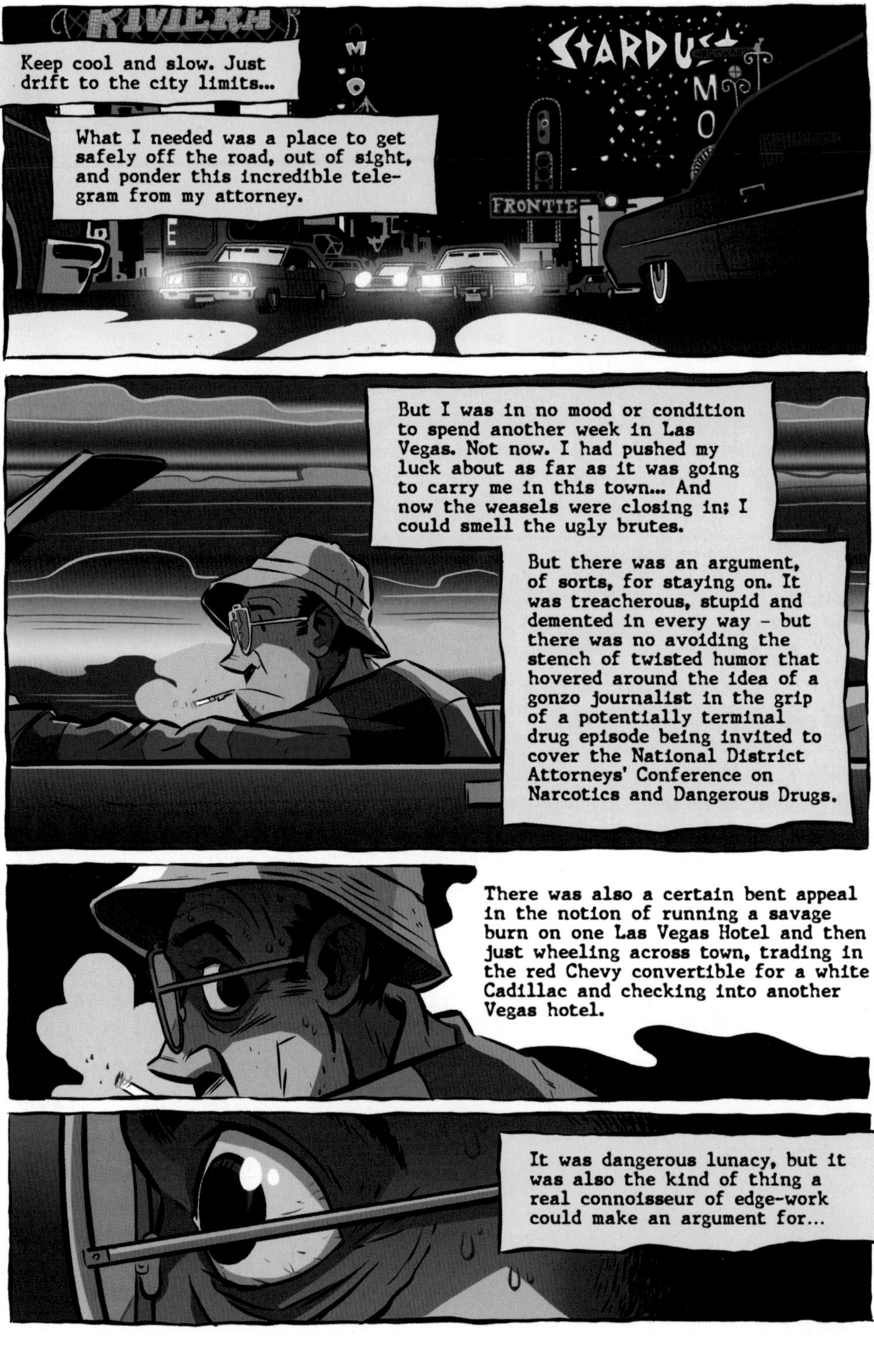
Keep cool and slow. Just drift to the city limits...
What I needed was a place to get safely off the road, out of sight, and ponder this incredible telegram from my attorney.
But I was in no mood or condition to spend another week in Las Vegas. Not now. I had pushed my luck about as far as it was going to carry me in this town... And now the weasels were closing in; I could smell the ugly brutes.
But there was an argument, of sorts, for staying on. It was treacherous, stupid and demented in every way - but there was no avoiding the stench of twisted humor that hovered around the idea of a gonzo journalist in the grip of a potentially terminal drug episode being invited to cover the National District Attorneys' Conference on Narcotics and Dangerous Drugs.
There was also a certain bent appeal in the notion of running a savage burn on one Las Vegas Hotel and then just wheeling across town, trading in the red Chevy convertible for a white Cadillac and checking into another Vegas hotel.
It was dangerous lunacy, but it was also the kind of thing a real connoisseur of edge-work could make an argument for...

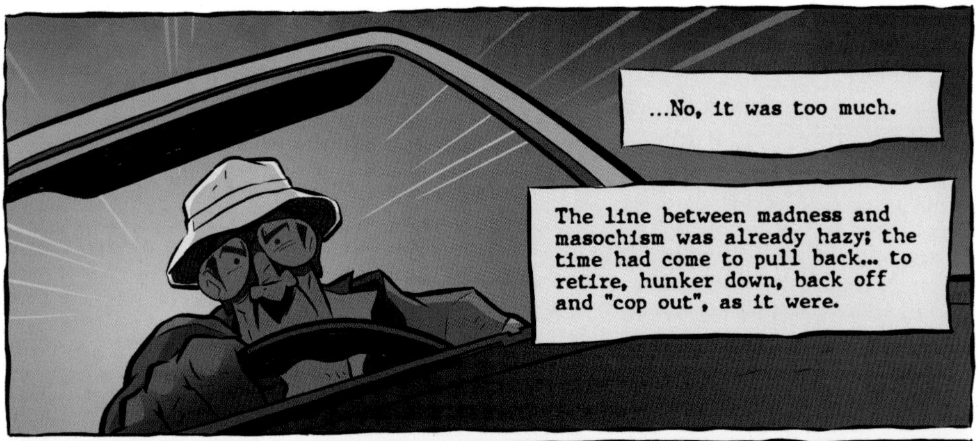
...No, it was too much.
The line between madness and masochism was already hazy; the time had come to pull back... to retire, hunker down, back off and "cop out", as it were.

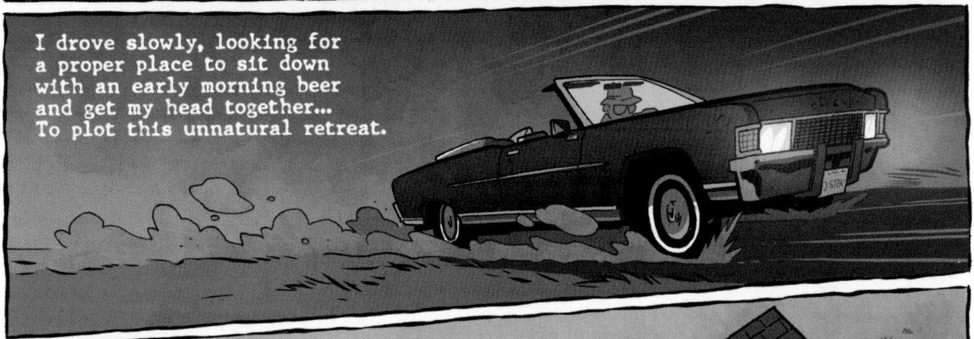
I drove slowly, looking for a proper place to sit down with an early morning beer and get my head together... To plot this unnatural retreat.

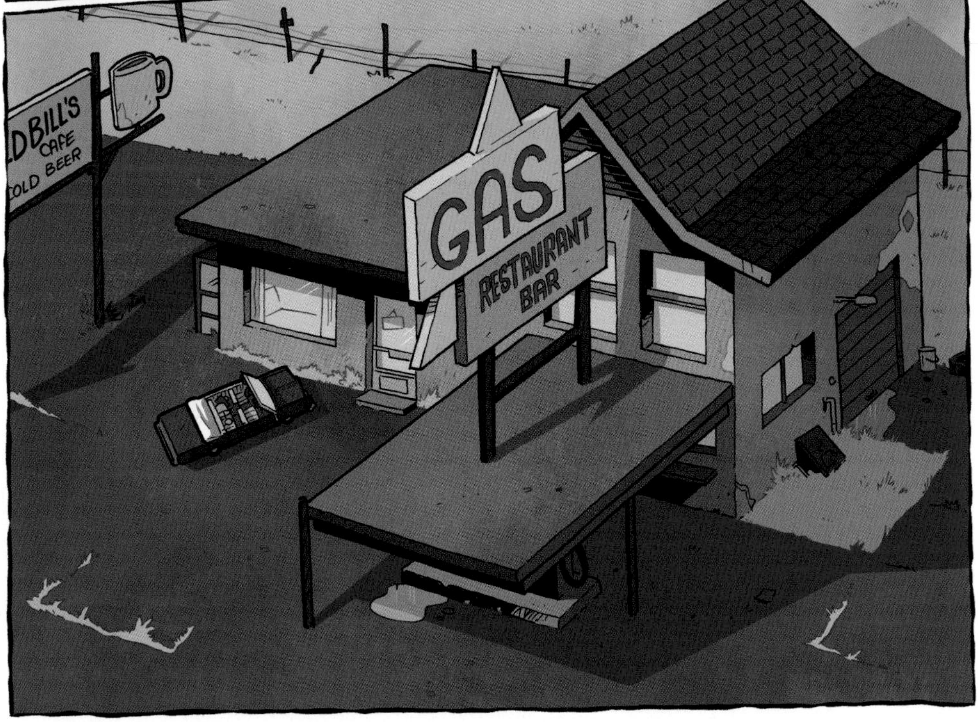
CAFE
COLD BEER
GAS
RESTAURANT
BAR

11. Aaawww, Mama, Can This Really Be the End? ... Down and Out in Vegas, with Amphetamine Psychosis Again?

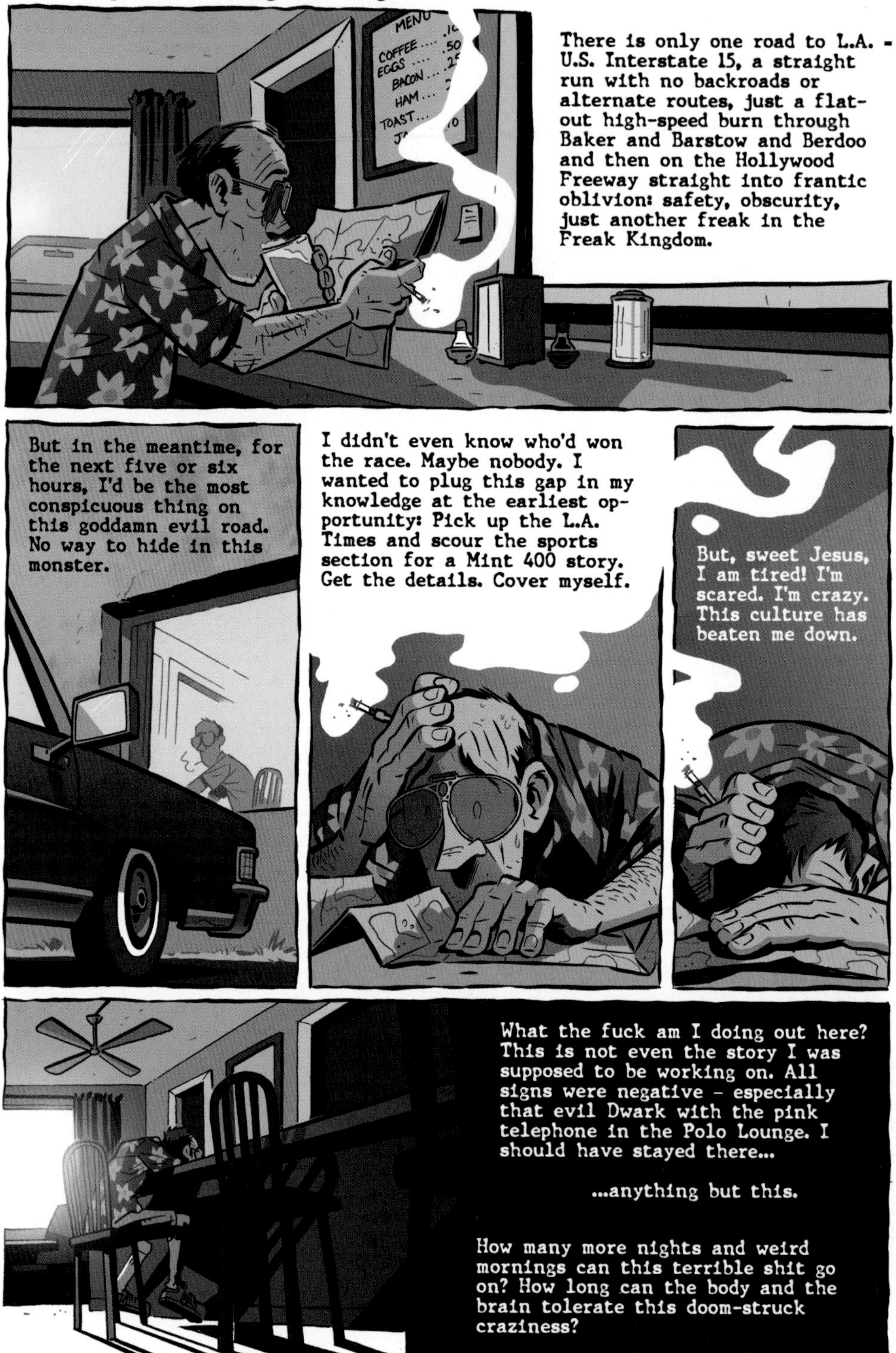
MENU
COFFEE
EGGS
BACON
HAM
TOAST
There is only one road to L.A. - U.S. Interstate 15, a straight run with no backroads or alternate routes, just a flat-out high-speed burn through Baker and Barstow and Berdoo and then on the Hollywood Freeway straight into frantic oblivion: safety, obscurity, just another freak in the Freak Kingdom.
But in the meantime, for the next five or six hours, I'd be the most conspicuous thing on this goddamn evil road. No way to hide in this monster.
I didn't even know who'd won the race. Maybe nobody. I wanted to plug this gap in my knowledge at the earliest opportunity: Pick up the L.A. Times and scour the sports section for a Mint 400 story. Get the details. Cover myself.
But, sweet Jesus, I am tired! I'm scared. I'm crazy. This culture has beaten me down.
What the fuck am I doing out here? This is not even the story I was supposed to be working on. All signs were negative - especially that evil Dwark with the pink telephone in the Polo Lounge. I should have stayed there...
...anything but this.
How many more nights and weird mornings can this terrible shit go on? How long can the body and the brain tolerate this doom-struck craziness?

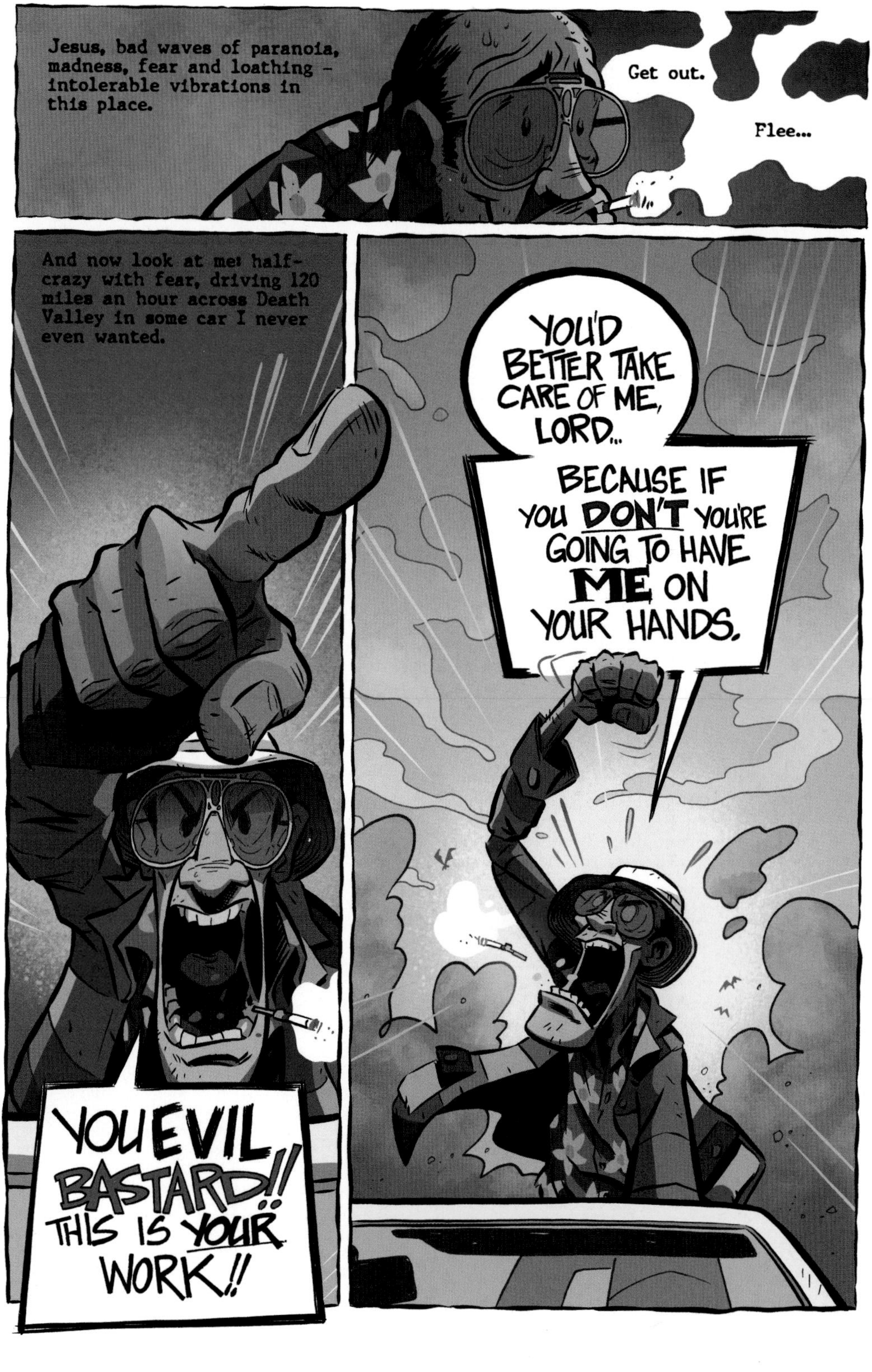
Jesus, bad waves of paranoia, madness, fear and loathing - intolerable vibrations in this place.
Get out.
Flee...
And now look at me: half-crazy with fear, driving 120 miles an hour across Death Valley in some car I never even wanted.
YOU EVIL BASTARD!! THIS IS YOUR WORK!!
YOU'D BETTER TAKE CARE OF ME, LORD...
BECAUSE IF YOU DON'T YOU'RE GOING TO HAVE ME ON YOUR HANDS.

12. Hellish Speed... Grappling with the California Highway Patrol... Mano a Mano on Highway 61

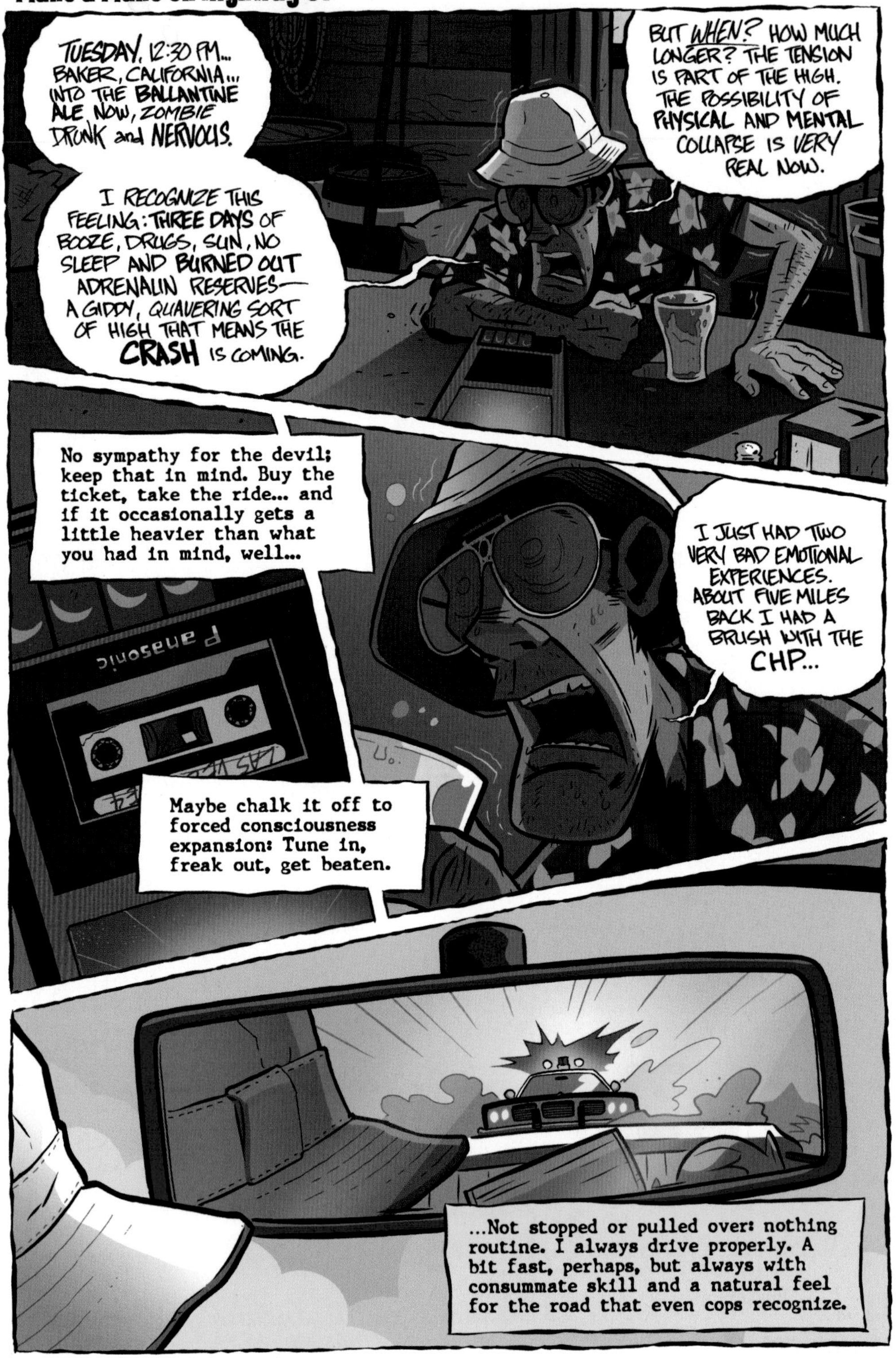

TUESDAY, 12:30 PM... BAKER, CALIFORNIA... INTO THE BALLANTINE ALE NOW, ZOMBIE DRUNK and NERVOUS.
I RECOGNIZE THIS FEELING: THREE DAYS OF BOOZE, DRUGS, SUN, NO SLEEP AND BURNED OUT ADRENALIN RESERVES— A GIDDY, QUAVERING SORT OF HIGH THAT MEANS THE CRASH IS COMING.
BUT WHEN? HOW MUCH LONGER? THE TENSION IS PART OF THE HIGH. THE POSSIBILITY OF PHYSICAL AND MENTAL COLLAPSE IS VERY REAL NOW.
No sympathy for the devil; keep that in mind. Buy the ticket, take the ride... and if it occasionally gets a little heavier than what you had in mind, well...
I JUST HAD TWO VERY BAD EMOTIONAL EXPERIENCES. ABOUT FIVE MILES BACK I HAD A BRUSH WITH THE CHP...
Maybe chalk it off to forced consciousness expansion: Tune in, freak out, get beaten.
...Not stopped or pulled over: nothing routine. I always drive properly. A bit fast, perhaps, but always with consummate skill and a natural feel for the road that even cops recognize.

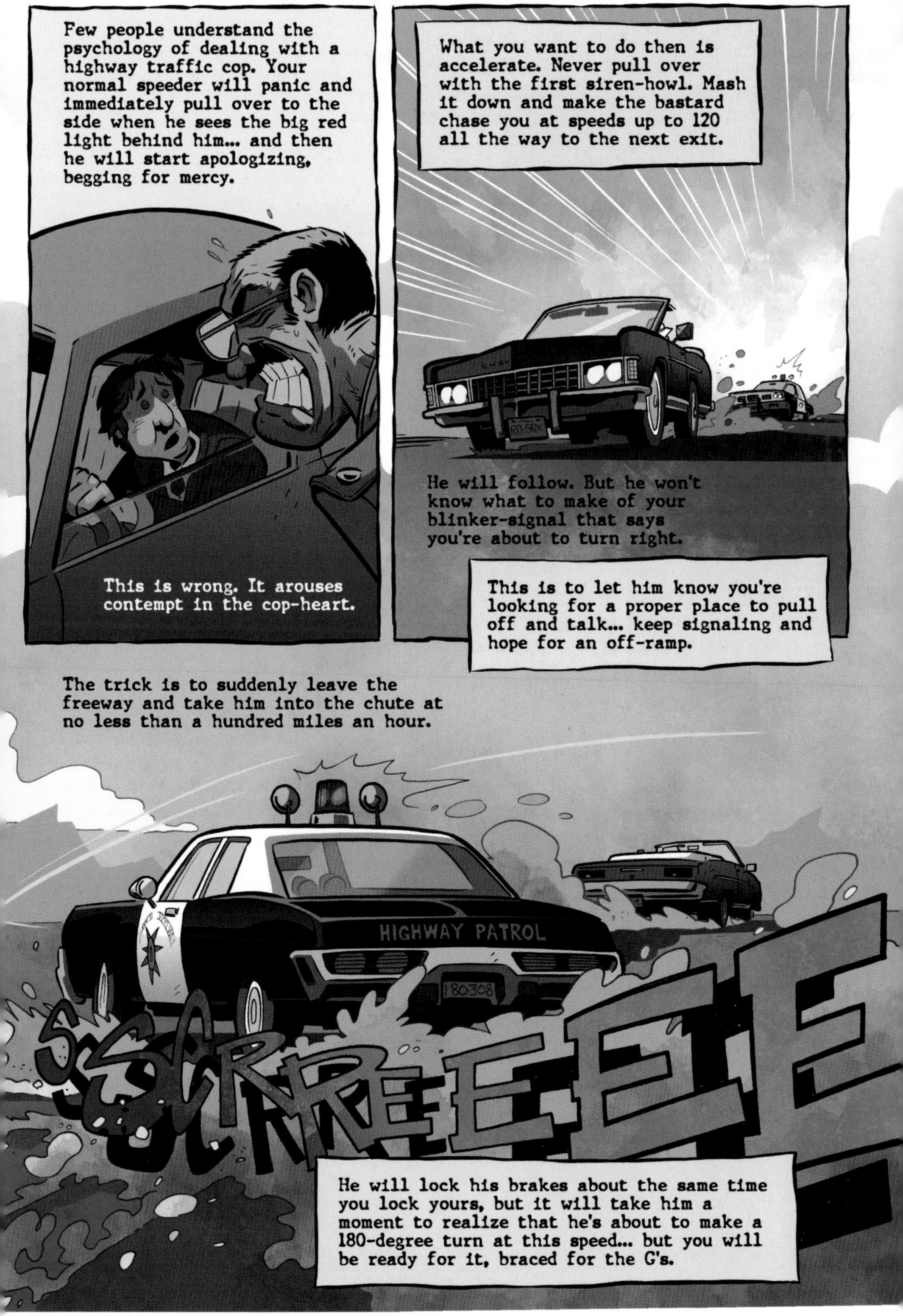
Few people understand the psychology of dealing with a highway traffic cop. Your normal speeder will panic and immediately pull over to the side when he sees the big red light behind him... and then he will start apologizing, begging for mercy.
This is wrong. It arouses contempt in the cop-heart.
What you want to do then is accelerate. Never pull over with the first siren-howl. Mash it down and make the bastard chase you at speeds up to 120 all the way to the next exit.
He will follow. But he won't know what to make of your blinker-signal that says you're about to turn right.
This is to let him know you're looking for a proper place to pull off and talk... keep signaling and hope for an off-ramp.
The trick is to suddenly leave the freeway and take him into the chute at no less than a hundred miles an hour.
HIGHWAY PATROL
180308
He will lock his brakes about the same time you lock yours, but it will take him a moment to realize that he's about to make a 180-degree turn at this speed... but you will be ready for it, braced for the G's.

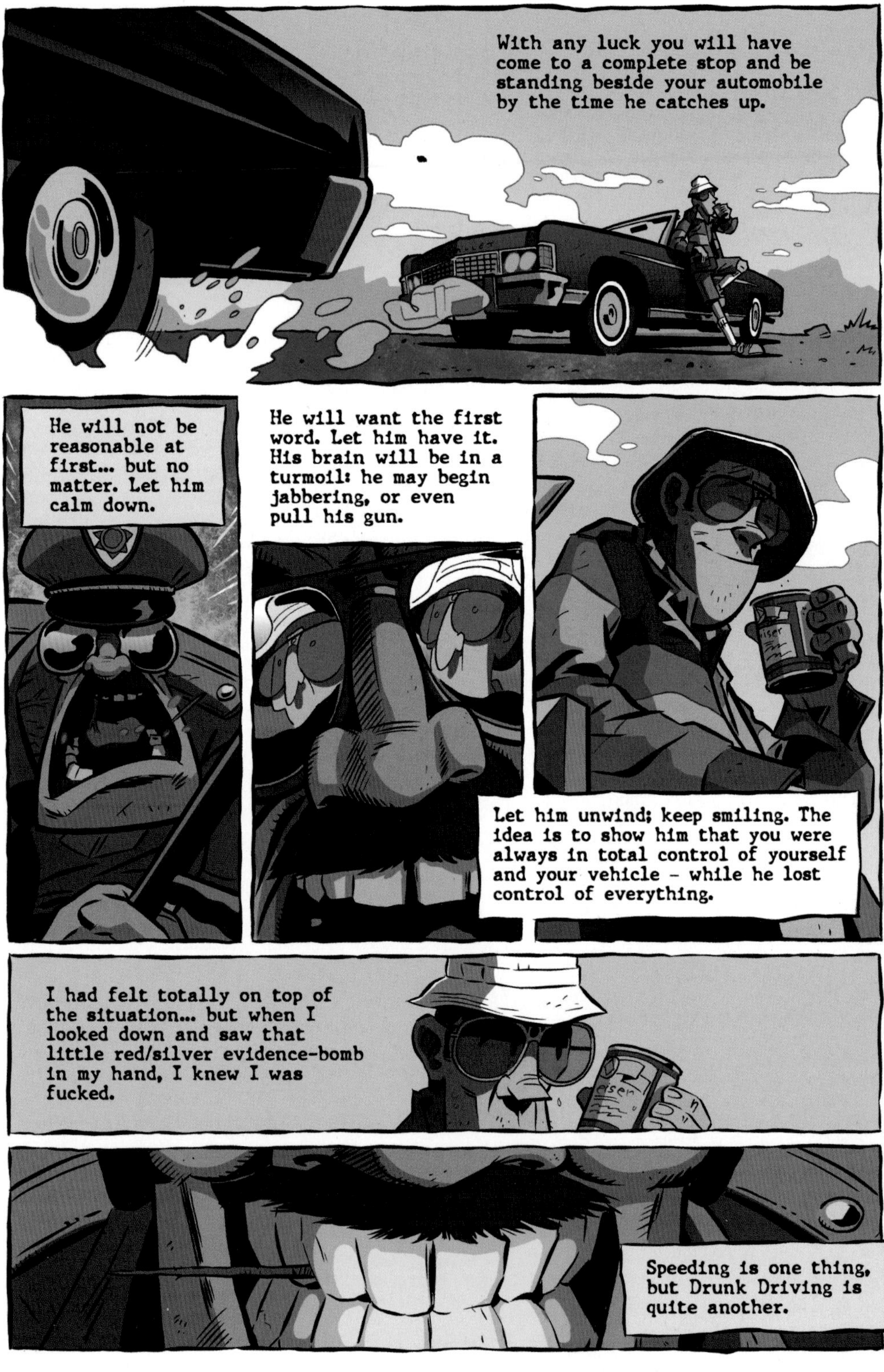
With any luck you will have come to a complete stop and be standing beside your automobile by the time he catches up.
He will not be reasonable at first... but no matter. Let him calm down.
He will want the first word. Let him have it. His brain will be in a turmoil: he may begin jabbering, or even pull his gun.
Let him unwind; keep smiling. The idea is to show him that you were always in total control of yourself and your vehicle - while he lost control of everything.
I had felt totally on top of the situation... but when I looked down and saw that little red/silver evidence-bomb in my hand, I knew I was fucked.
Speeding is one thing, but Drunk Driving is quite another.

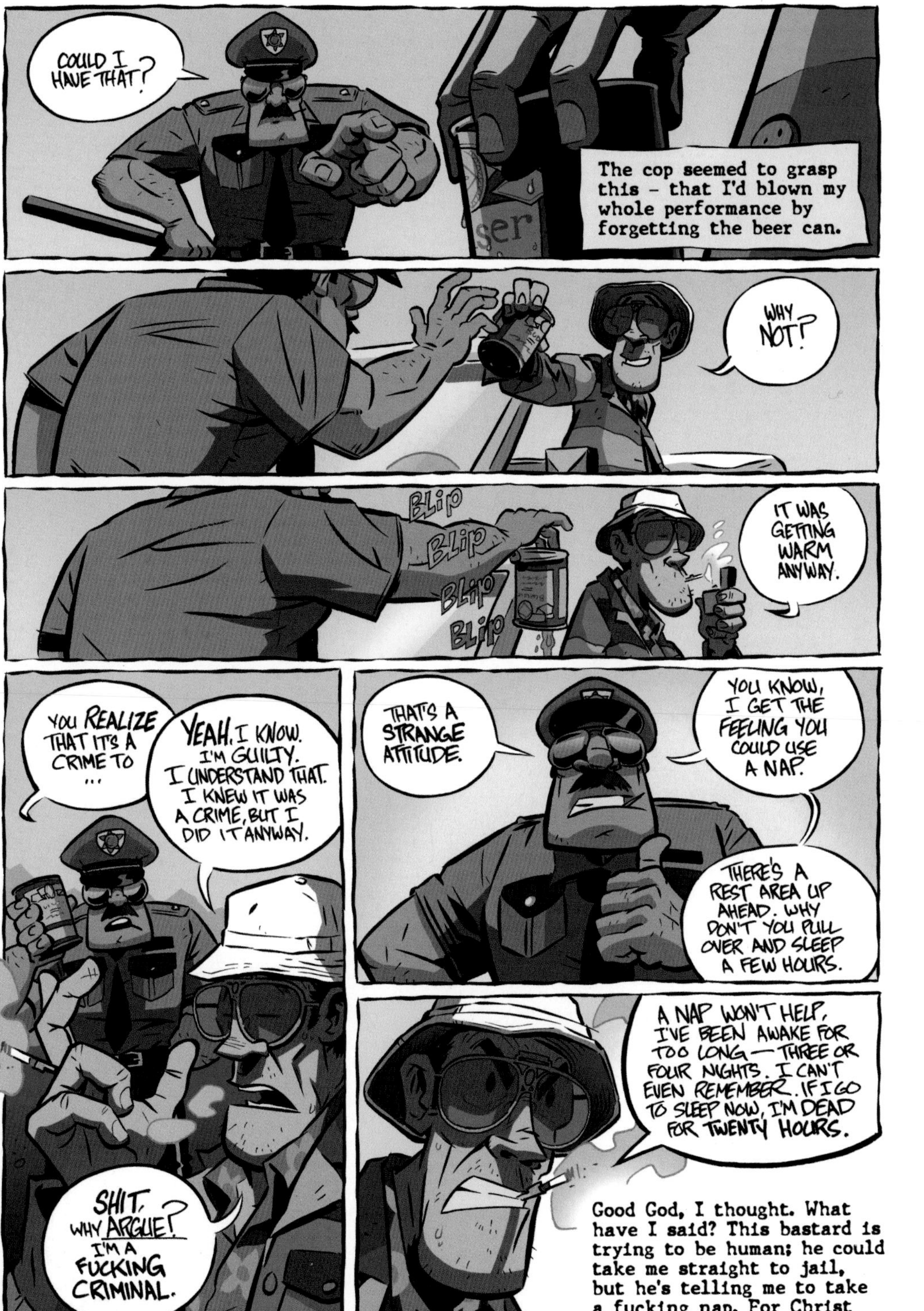
COULD I HAVE THAT?
The cop seemed to grasp this - that I'd blown my whole performance by forgetting the beer can.
ser
WHY NOT?
BLIP
BLIP
BLIP
BLIP
IT WAS GETTING WARM ANYWAY.
YOU REALIZE THAT IT'S A CRIME TO ...
YEAH, I KNOW. I'M GUILTY. I UNDERSTAND THAT. I KNEW IT WAS A CRIME, BUT I DID IT ANYWAY.
SHIT, WHY ARGUE? I'M A FUCKING CRIMINAL.
THAT'S A STRANGE ATTITUDE.
YOU KNOW, I GET THE FEELING YOU COULD USE A NAP.
THERE'S A REST AREA UP AHEAD. WHY DON'T YOU PULL OVER AND SLEEP A FEW HOURS.
A NAP WON'T HELP. I'VE BEEN AWAKE FOR TOO LONG — THREE OR FOUR NIGHTS. I CAN'T EVEN REMEMBER. IF I GO TO SLEEP NOW, I'M DEAD FOR TWENTY HOURS.
Good God, I thought. What have I said? This bastard is trying to be human; he could take me straight to jail, but he's telling me to take a fucking nap. For Christ sake, agree with him!

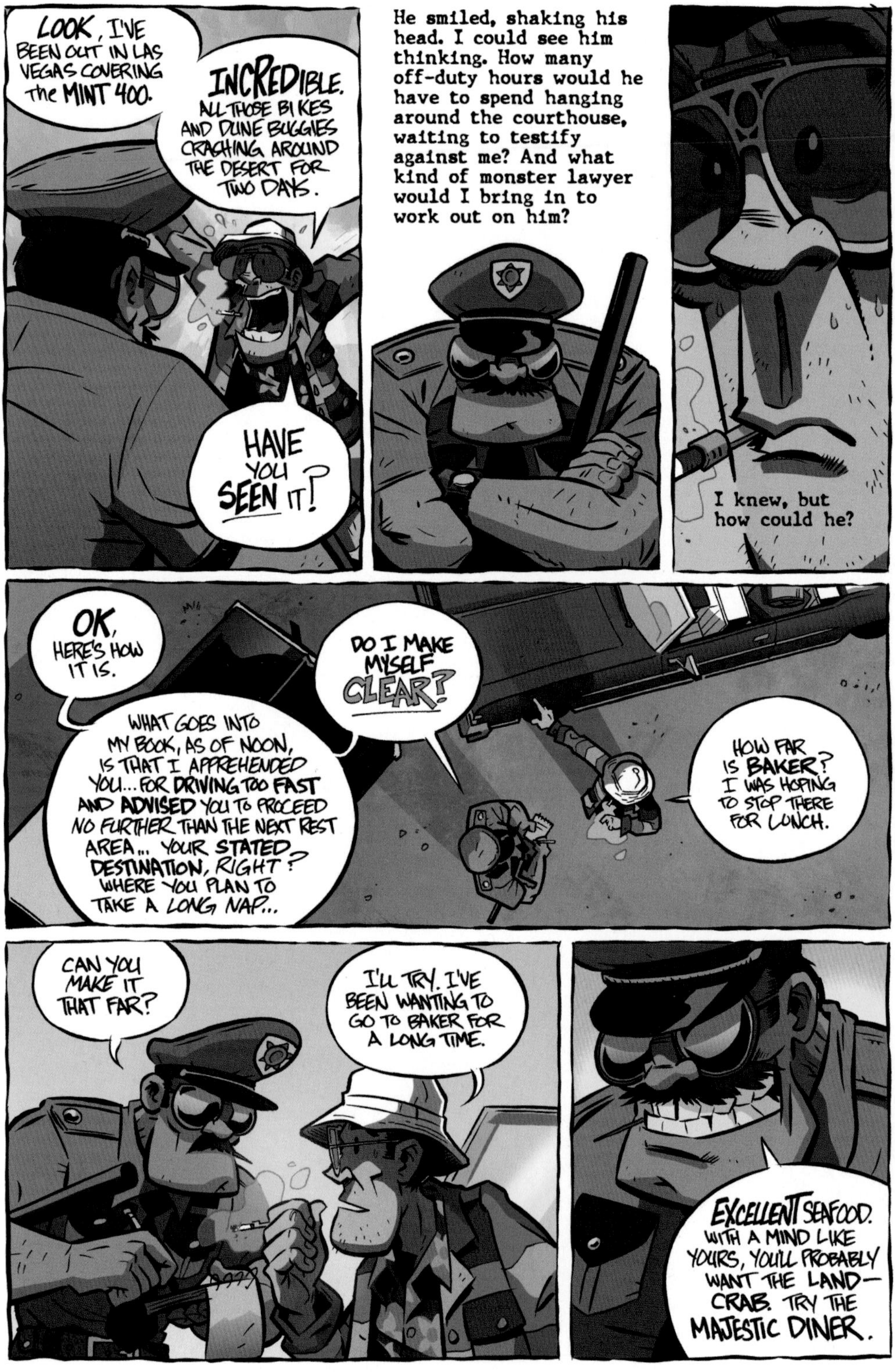
LOOK, I'VE BEEN OUT IN LAS VEGAS COVERING the MINT 400.
INCREDIBLE. ALL THOSE BIKES AND DUNE BUGGIES CRASHING AROUND THE DESERT FOR TWO DAYS.
HAVE YOU SEEN IT?
He smiled, shaking his head. I could see him thinking. How many off-duty hours would he have to spend hanging around the courthouse, waiting to testify against me? And what kind of monster lawyer would I bring in to work out on him?
I knew, but how could he?
OK, HERE'S HOW IT IS.
WHAT GOES INTO MY BOOK, AS OF NOON, IS THAT I APPREHENDED YOU... FOR DRIVING TOO FAST AND ADVISED YOU TO PROCEED NO FURTHER THAN THE NEXT REST AREA... YOUR STATED DESTINATION, RIGHT? WHERE YOU PLAN TO TAKE A LONG NAP...
DO I MAKE MYSELF CLEAR?
HOW FAR IS BAKER? I WAS HOPING TO STOP THERE FOR LUNCH.
CAN YOU MAKE IT THAT FAR?
I'LL TRY. I'VE BEEN WANTING TO GO TO BAKER FOR A LONG TIME.
EXCELLENT SEAFOOD. WITH A MIND LIKE YOURS, YOU'LL PROBABLY WANT THE LAND-CRAB. TRY THE MAJESTIC DINER.

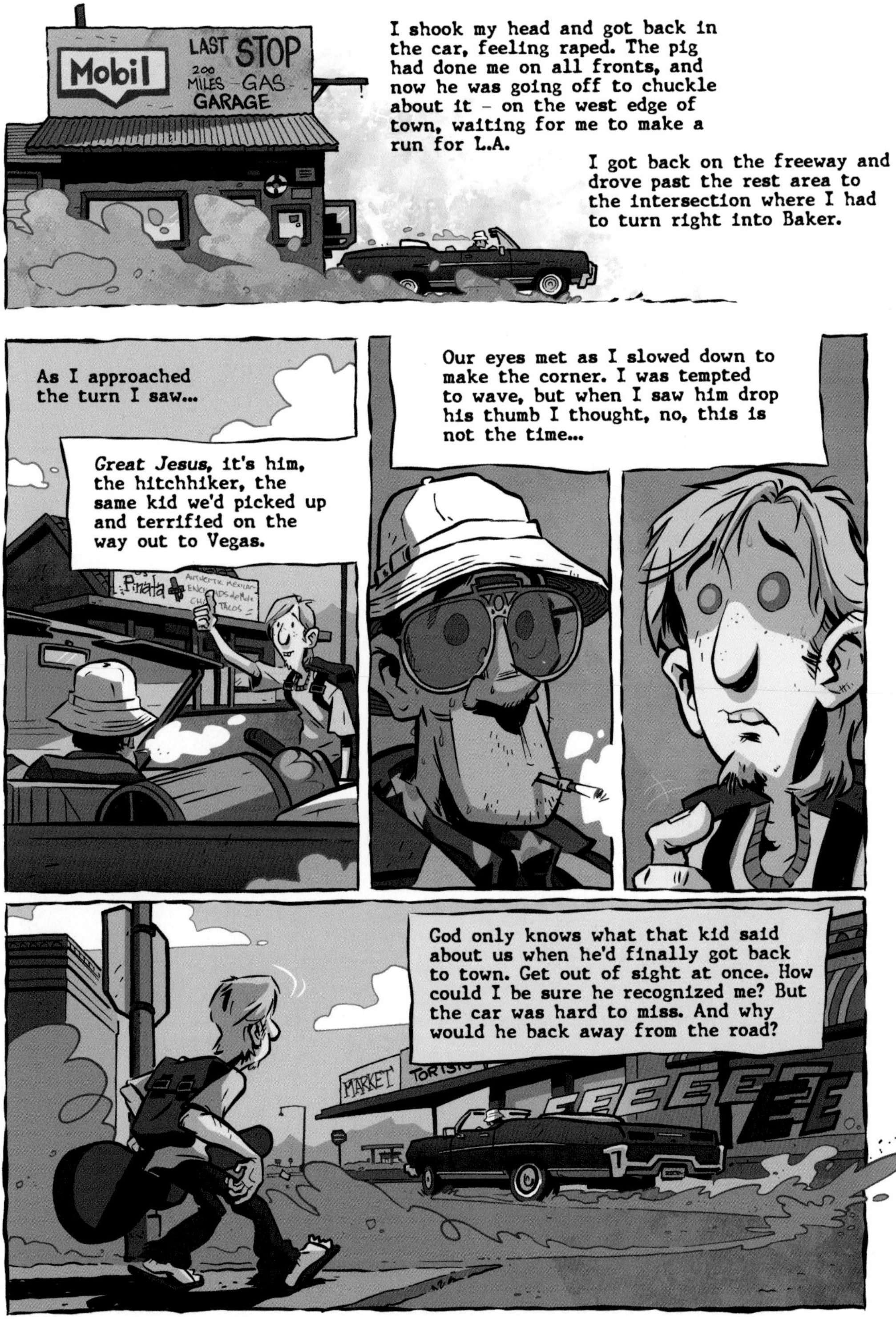
Mobil
LAST STOP
200 MILES GAS
GARAGE
I shook my head and got back in the car, feeling raped. The pig had done me on all fronts, and now he was going off to chuckle about it – on the west edge of town, waiting for me to make a run for L.A.
I got back on the freeway and drove past the rest area to the intersection where I had to turn right into Baker.
As I approached the turn I saw...
Great Jesus, it's him, the hitchhiker, the same kid we'd picked up and terrified on the way out to Vegas.
Piñata
Our eyes met as I slowed down to make the corner. I was tempted to wave, but when I saw him drop his thumb I thought, no, this is not the time...
God only knows what that kid said about us when he'd finally got back to town. Get out of sight at once. How could I be sure he recognized me? But the car was hard to miss. And why would he back away from the road?
MARKET
EEEEEEE

Suddenly I had two personal enemies in this godforsaken town. The CHP cop would bust me for sure if I tried to go on through to L.A., and this goddamn rotten kid/hitchhiker would have me hunted down like a beast if I stayed. Either way, it was horrible.

This was it: The crisis.

I found a telephone booth on the northern outskirts. I placed an emergency collect call to my attorney in Malibu.

THEY'VE **NAILED** ME! I'M TRAPPED IN SOME STINKING DESERT CROSSROADS CALLED BAKER.

YOU SOUND A LITTLE PARANOID.

I DON'T HAVE MUCH TIME. THE FUCKERS ARE CLOSING IN.

YOU BASTARD! FIRST I GOT RUN DOWN BY THE CHP, THEN THAT KID SPOTTED ME!

I NEED A LAWYER IMMEDIATELY!

YOU'RE SUPPOSED TO BE IN VEGAS. WE HAVE A SUITE AT THE FLAMINGO. I WAS JUST ABOUT TO LEAVE FOR THE AIRPORT.

YOU WORTHLESS BASTARD! I'LL CRIPPLE YOUR ASS FOR THIS! ALL THAT SHIT IN THE CAR IS YOURS! YOU UNDERSTAND THAT? WHEN I FINISH TESTIFYING OUT HERE YOU'LL BE DISBARRED!

YOU BRAINLESS SCUM-BAG! I SENT YOU A TELEGRAM! YOU'RE SUPPOSED TO BE COVERING THE NATIONAL DISTRICT ATTORNEYS' CONFERENCE!

I MADE ALL THE RESERVATIONS... RENTED A WHITE CADILLAC CONVERTIBLE... THE WHOLE THING IS ARRANGED!

WHAT THE HELL ARE YOU DOING OUT THERE IN THE MIDDLE OF THE FUCKING DESERT?

NEVER MIND. IT'S ALL A BIG JOKE. I'M ACTUALLY SITTING BESIDE THE POOL AT THE FLAMINGO. I'M TALKING FROM A PORTABLE PHONE. I HAVE TOTAL CREDIT!

CAN YOU GRASP THAT?

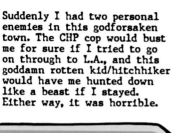

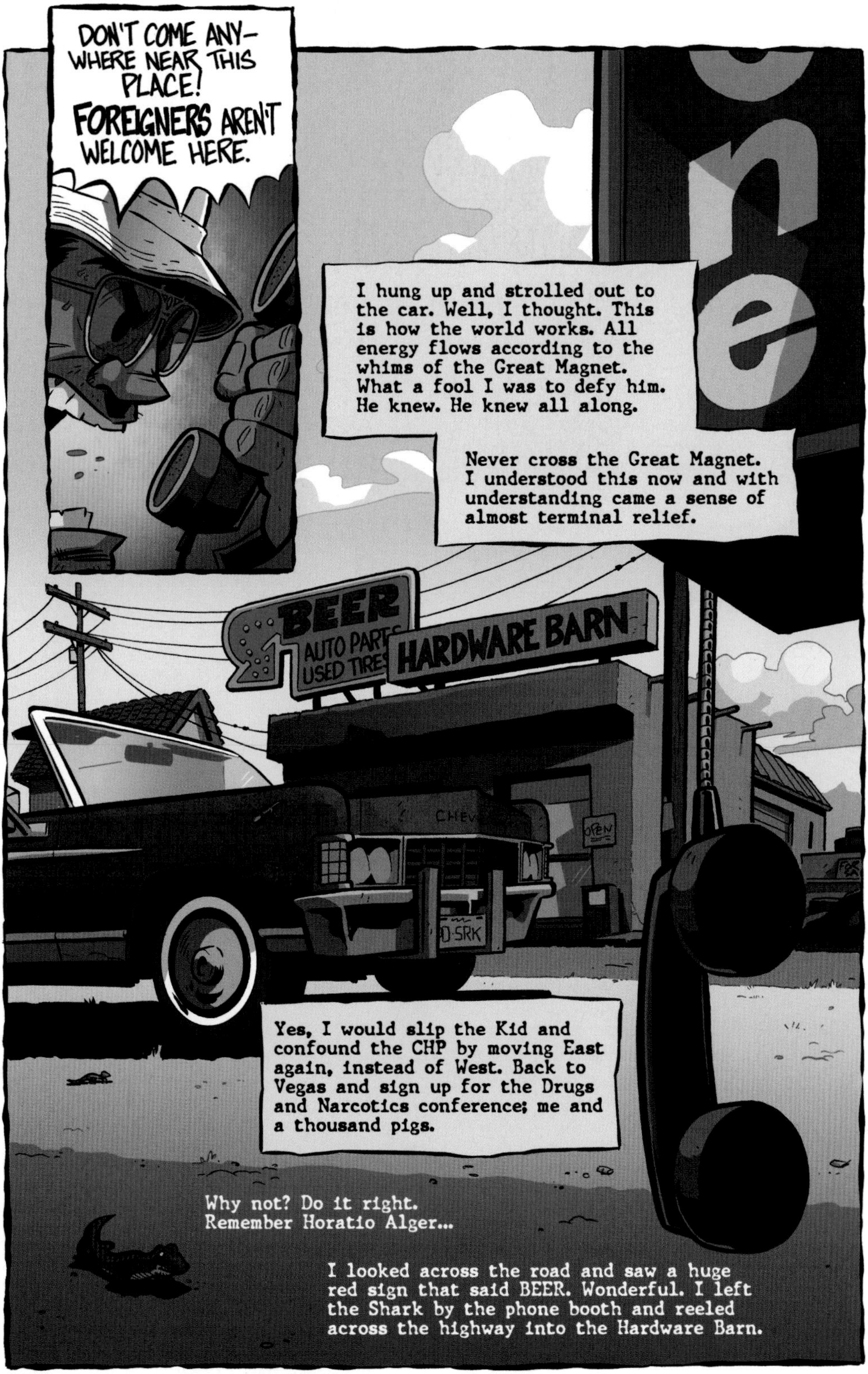
DON'T COME ANYWHERE NEAR THIS PLACE! FOREIGNERS AREN'T WELCOME HERE.
I hung up and strolled out to the car. Well, I thought. This is how the world works. All energy flows according to the whims of the Great Magnet. What a fool I was to defy him. He knew. He knew all along.
Never cross the Great Magnet. I understood this now and with understanding came a sense of almost terminal relief.
BEER
AUTO PARTS
USED TIRES
HARDWARE BARN
Yes, I would slip the Kid and confound the CHP by moving East again, instead of West. Back to Vegas and sign up for the Drugs and Narcotics conference; me and a thousand pigs.
Why not? Do it right. Remember Horatio Alger...
I looked across the road and saw a huge red sign that said BEER. Wonderful. I left the Shark by the phone booth and reeled across the highway into the Hardware Barn.

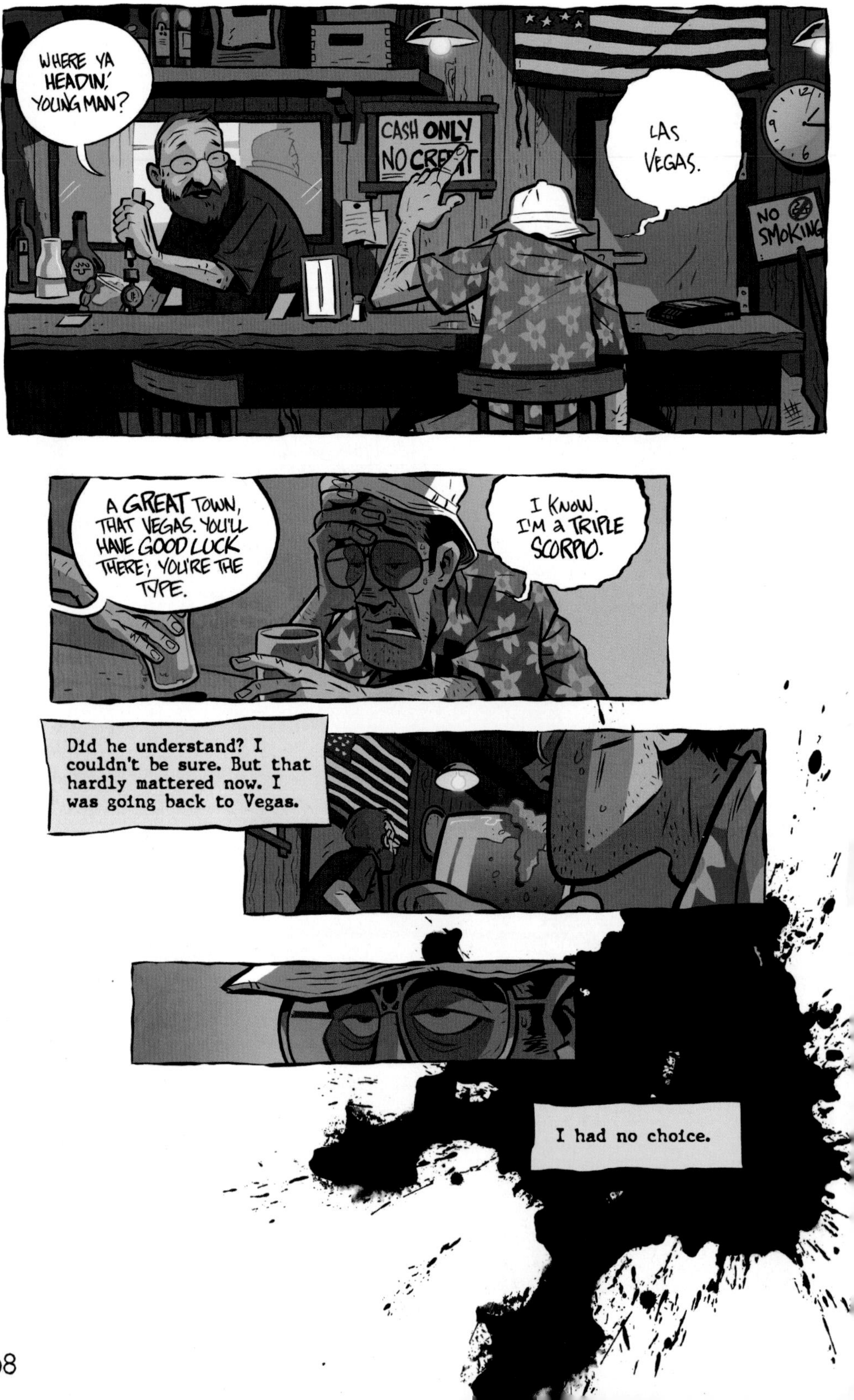
WHERE YA HEADIN', YOUNG MAN?
CASH ONLY NO CREDIT
LAS VEGAS.
NO SMOKING
A GREAT TOWN, THAT VEGAS. YOU'LL HAVE GOOD LUCK THERE; YOU'RE THE TYPE.
I KNOW. I'M a TRIPLE SCORPIO.
Did he understand? I couldn't be sure. But that hardly mattered now. I was going back to Vegas.
I had no choice.

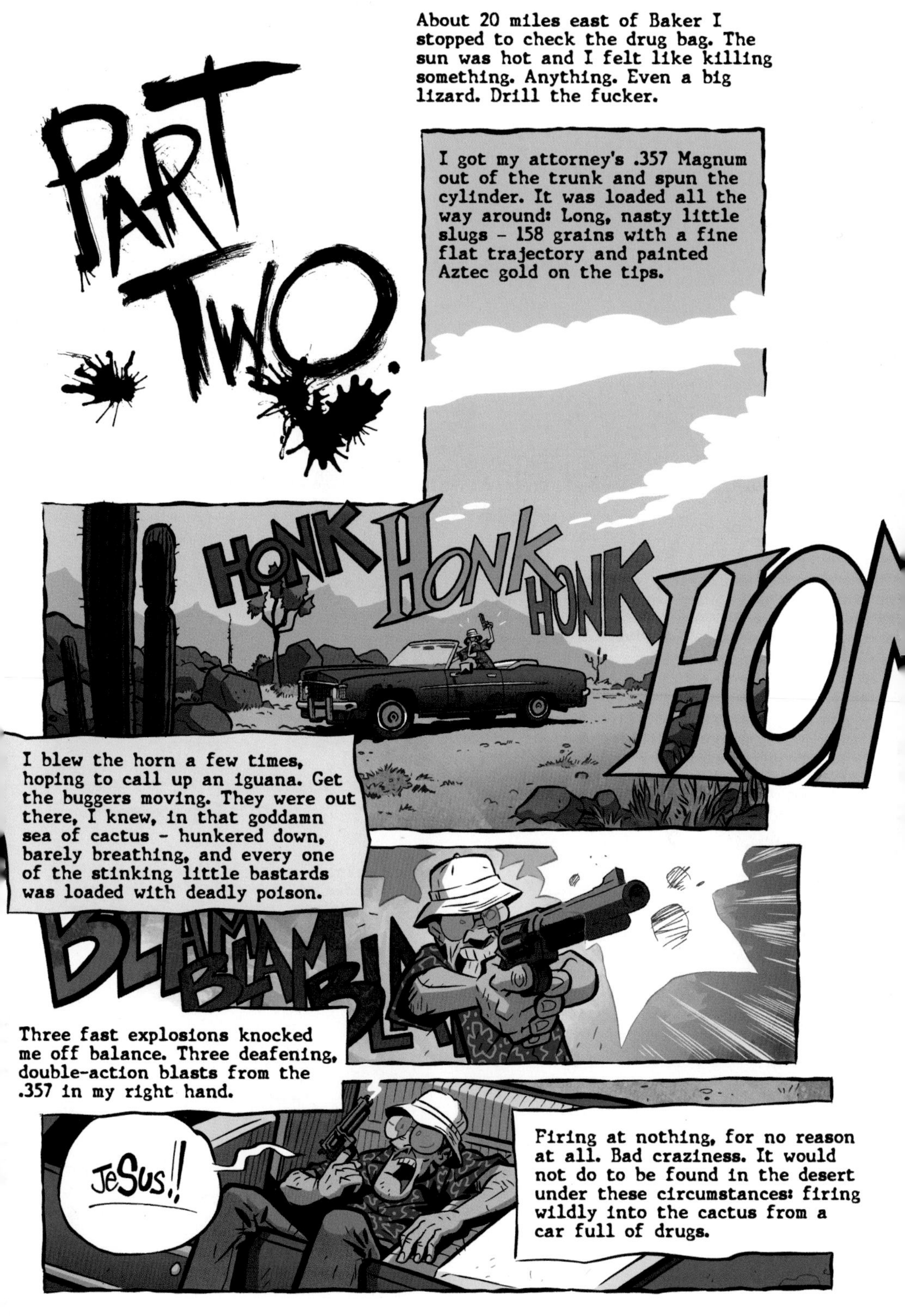
PART TWO.
About 20 miles east of Baker I stopped to check the drug bag. The sun was hot and I felt like killing something. Anything. Even a big lizard. Drill the fucker.
I got my attorney's .357 Magnum out of the trunk and spun the cylinder. It was loaded all the way around: Long, nasty little slugs - 158 grains with a fine flat trajectory and painted Aztec gold on the tips.
HONK HONK HONK
I blew the horn a few times, hoping to call up an iguana. Get the buggers moving. They were out there, I knew, in that goddamn sea of cactus - hunkered down, barely breathing, and every one of the stinking little bastards was loaded with deadly poison.
BLAM BLAM
Three fast explosions knocked me off balance. Three deafening, double-action blasts from the .357 in my right hand.
JeSus!!
Firing at nothing, for no reason at all. Bad craziness. It would not do to be found in the desert under these circumstances: firing wildly into the cactus from a car full of drugs.

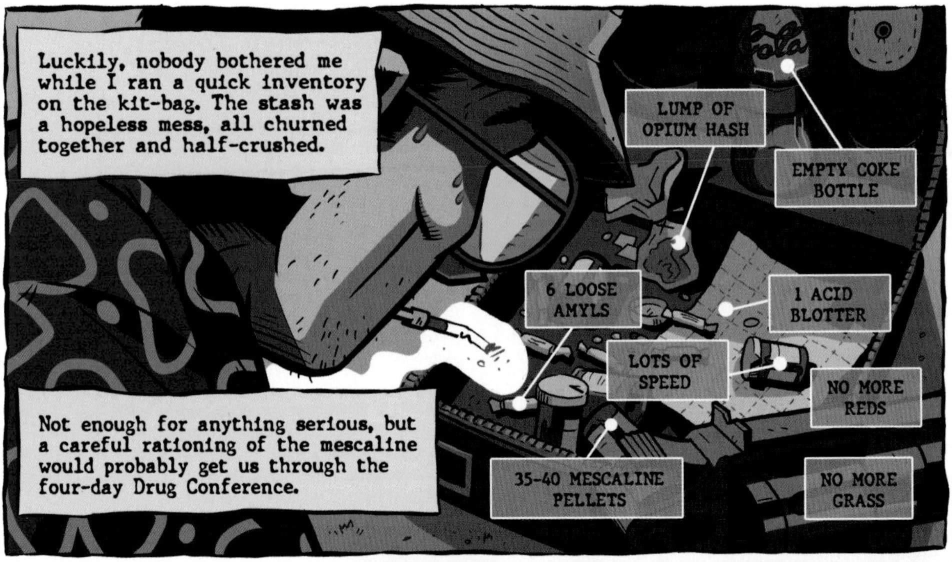
Luckily, nobody bothered me while I ran a quick inventory on the kit-bag. The stash was a hopeless mess, all churned together and half-crushed.
LUMP OF OPIUM HASH
EMPTY COKE BOTTLE
6 LOOSE AMYLS
1 ACID BLOTTER
LOTS OF SPEED
NO MORE REDS
35-40 MESCALINE PELLETS
NO MORE GRASS
Not enough for anything serious, but a careful rationing of the mescaline would probably get us through the four-day Drug Conference.

On the outskirts of Vegas I stopped at a neighborhood pharmacy and bought two quarts of Gold tequila, two fifths of Chivas Regal and a pint of ether. I was tempted to ask for some amyls but the druggist had the eyes of a mean Baptist hysteric.

I wondered what he would say if I asked him for $22 worth of Romilar and a tank of nitrous oxide. Probably he would have sold it to me. Why not? Free enterprise...

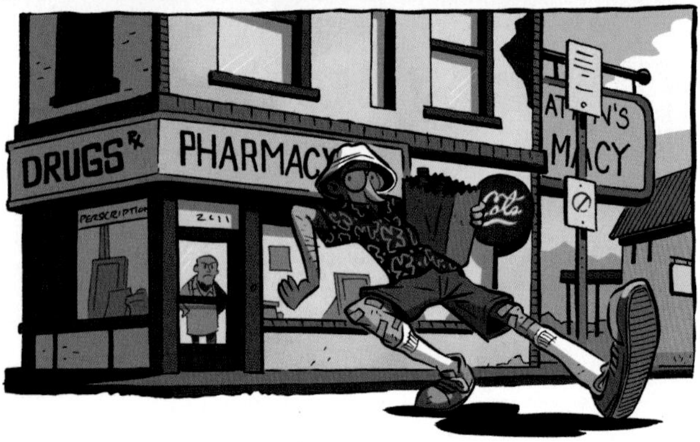
DRUGS ℞
PHARMAC

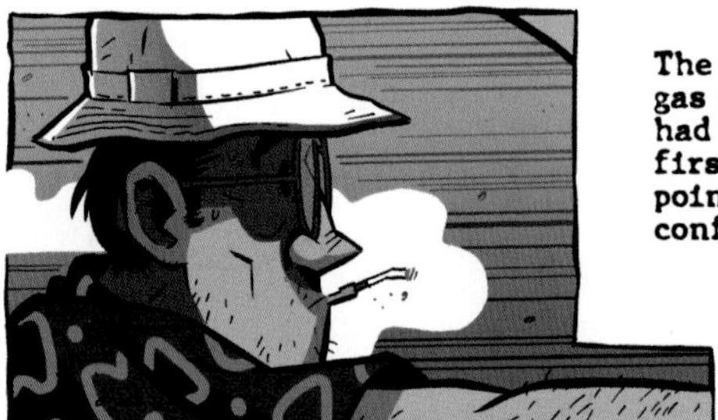

The idea of going completely crazy on laughing gas in the middle of a DAs' drug conference had a definite warped appeal. But not on the first day, I thought. Save that for later. No point getting busted and committed before the conference even starts.

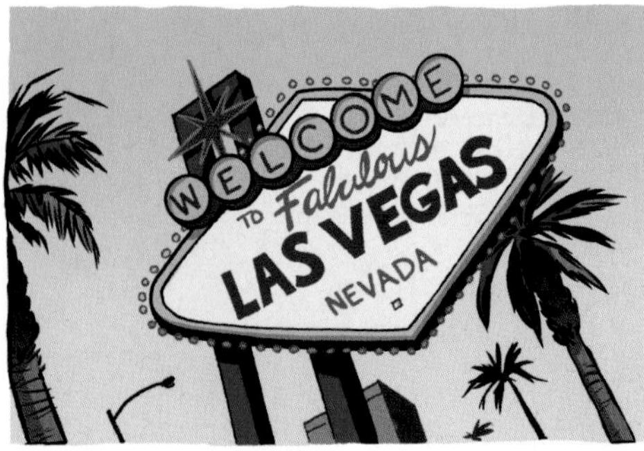
WELCOME
TO Fabulous
LAS VEGAS
NEVADA

The first order of business was to get rid of the Red Shark. It was too obvious. Too many people might recognize it, especially the Vegas police. The last place they would look for it, I felt, was in a rental-car lot at the airport. I had to go out there anyway, to meet my attorney. He would be arriving from L.A. in the late afternoon.

2. Another Day, Another Convertible... & Another Hotel Full of Cops

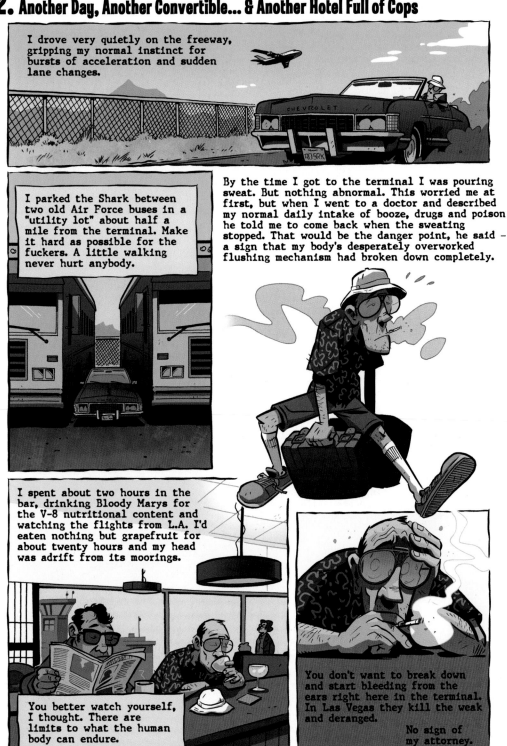

I drove very quietly on the freeway, gripping my normal instinct for bursts of acceleration and sudden lane changes.

I parked the Shark between two old Air Force buses in a "utility lot" about half a mile from the terminal. Make it hard as possible for the fuckers. A little walking never hurt anybody.

By the time I got to the terminal I was pouring sweat. But nothing abnormal. This worried me at first, but when I went to a doctor and described my normal daily intake of booze, drugs and poison he told me to come back when the sweating stopped. That would be the danger point, he said – a sign that my body's desperately overworked flushing mechanism had broken down completely.

I spent about two hours in the bar, drinking Bloody Marys for the V-8 nutritional content and watching the flights from L.A. I'd eaten nothing but grapefruit for about twenty hours and my head was adrift from its moorings.

You better watch yourself, I thought. There are limits to what the human body can endure.

You don't want to break down and start bleeding from the ears right here in the terminal. In Las Vegas they kill the weak and deranged.

No sign of my attorney.

101

Down to the VIP car-rental booth, where I traded the Red Shark in for a White Cadillac Convertible.

WHAT YOU NEED, I THINK, IS ONE OF OUR **MERCEDES 600** TOWNE-CRUISER SPECIALS, WITH AIR CONDITIONING.

DO I **LOOK** LIKE A GODDAMN **NAZI?** I'LL HAVE A NATURAL AMERICAN CAR, or NOTHING AT ALL!

They called up the white Coupe de Ville at once. Everything was automatic. I could sit in the red-leather driver's seat and make every inch of the car jump, by touching the proper buttons.

It was a wonderful machine: Ten grand worth of gimmicks and high-priced Special Effects.

The Caddy wouldn't get off the line quite as fast as the Red Shark, but once it got rolling – around eighty – it was pure smooth hell... all that elegant, upholstered weight lashing across the desert was like rolling through midnight on the old California Zephyr.

I drove straight to the hotel after renting the car. There was still no sign of my attorney, so I decided to check in on my own.

WELCOME NATIONAL DISTRICT ATTORNEYS CONFERENCE

Our room was at the Flamingo, in the nerve-center of the Strip: right across the street from Caesar's Palace and the Dunes – site of the Drug Conference.

102

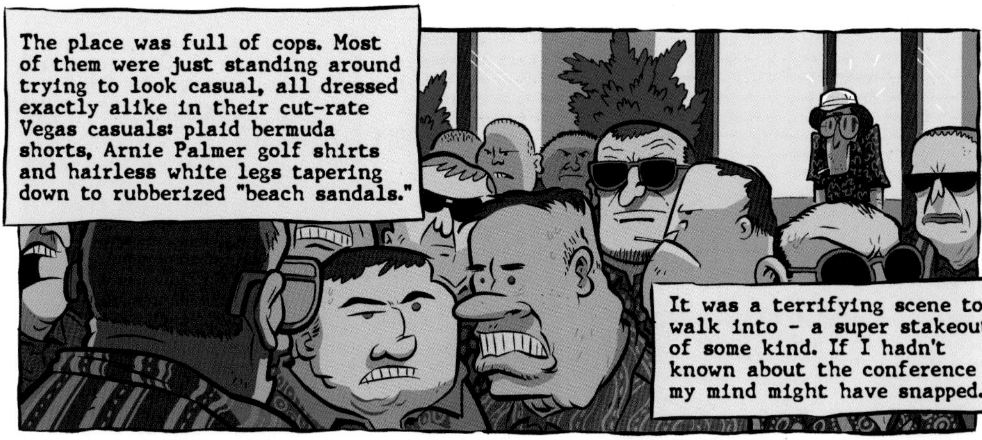
The place was full of cops. Most of them were just standing around trying to look casual, all dressed exactly alike in their cut-rate Vegas casuals: plaid bermuda shorts, Arnie Palmer golf shirts and hairless white legs tapering down to rubberized "beach sandals."
It was a terrifying scene to walk into - a super stakeout of some kind. If I hadn't known about the conference my mind might have snapped.

I waded up to the desk and got in line. The man in front of me was a Police Chief from some small town in Michigan.

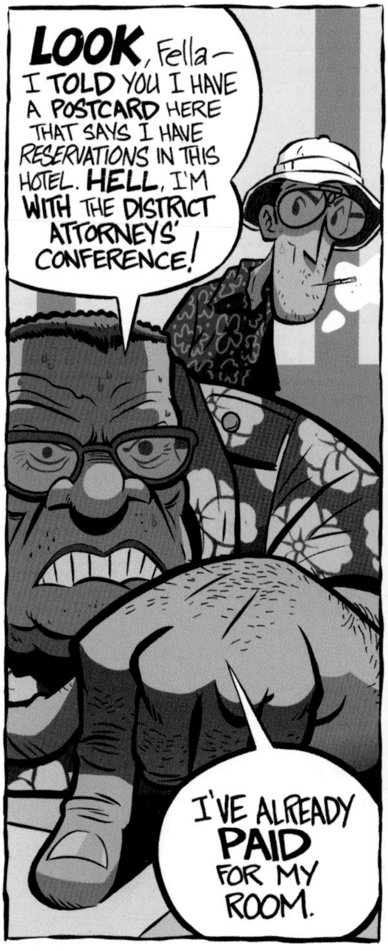
LOOK, Fella— I TOLD YOU I HAVE A POSTCARD HERE THAT SAYS I HAVE RESERVATIONS IN THIS HOTEL. HELL, I'M WITH THE DISTRICT ATTORNEYS' CONFERENCE!
I'VE ALREADY PAID FOR MY ROOM.

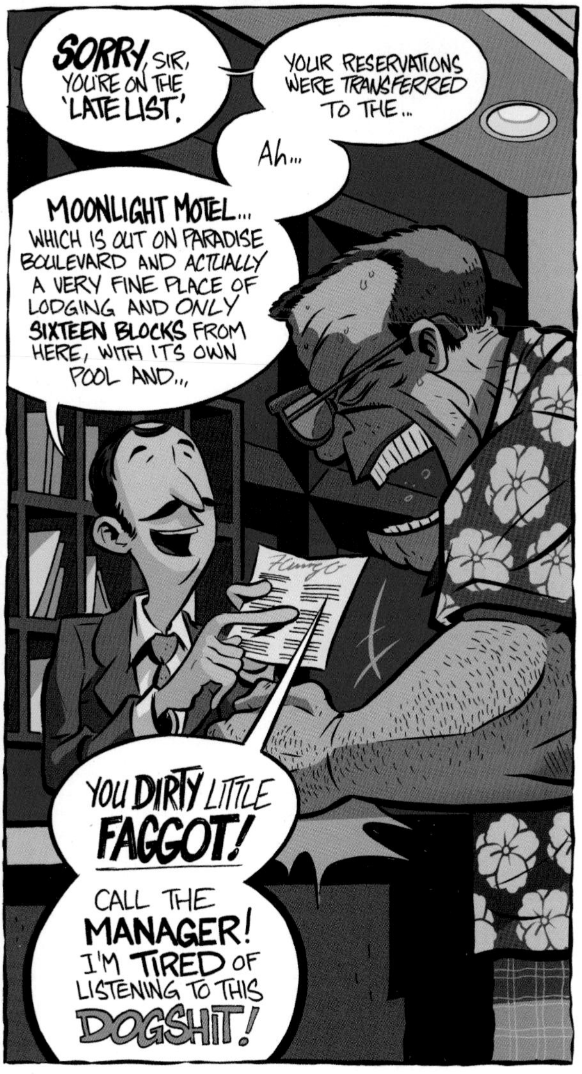
SORRY, SIR, YOU'RE ON THE 'LATE LIST.'
YOUR RESERVATIONS WERE TRANSFERRED TO THE...
Ah...
MOONLIGHT MOTEL... WHICH IS OUT ON PARADISE BOULEVARD AND ACTUALLY A VERY FINE PLACE OF LODGING AND ONLY SIXTEEN BLOCKS FROM HERE, WITH ITS OWN POOL AND...
YOU DIRTY LITTLE FAGGOT!
CALL THE MANAGER! I'M TIRED OF LISTENING TO THIS DOGSHIT!

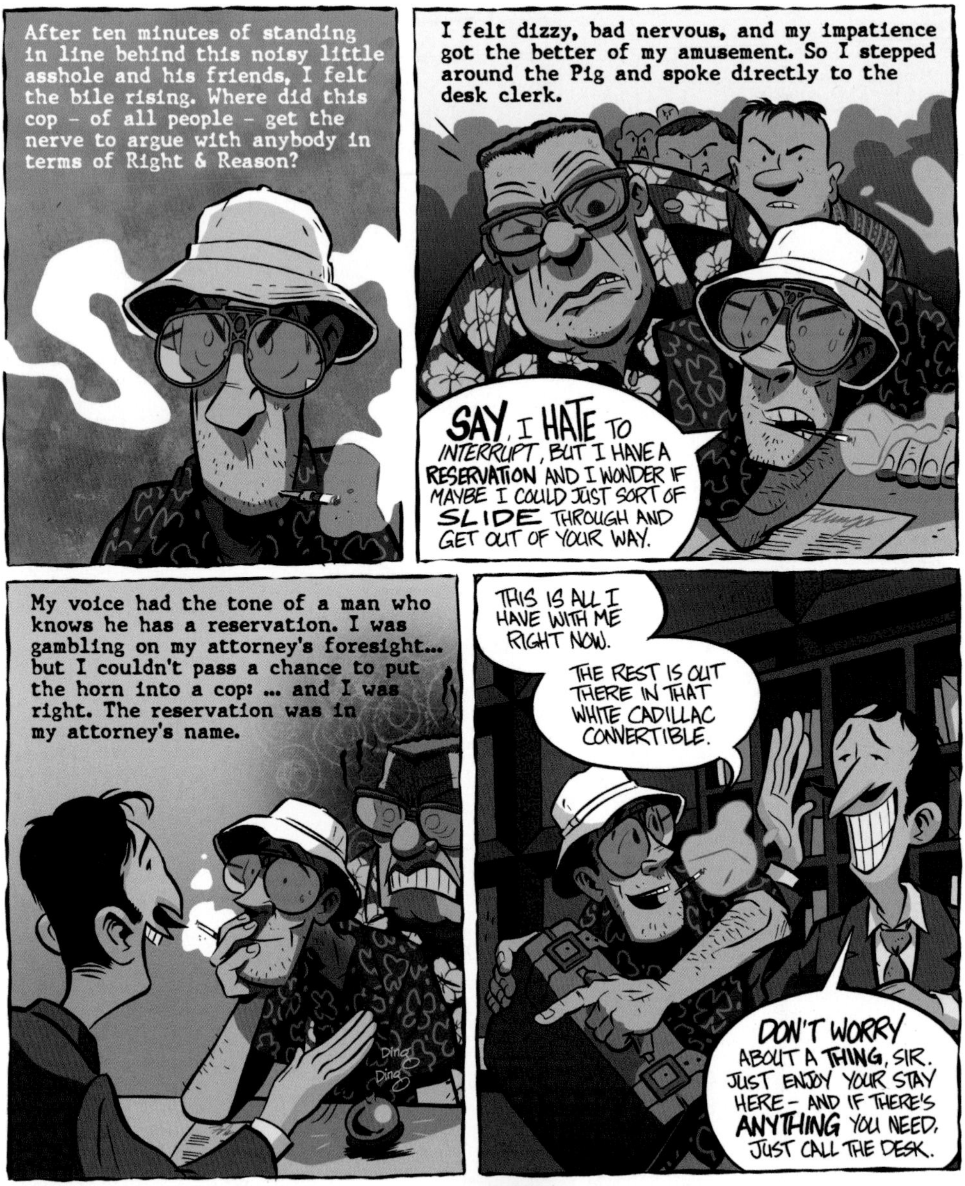
After ten minutes of standing in line behind this noisy little asshole and his friends, I felt the bile rising. Where did this cop - of all people - get the nerve to argue with anybody in terms of Right & Reason?
I felt dizzy, bad nervous, and my impatience got the better of my amusement. So I stepped around the Pig and spoke directly to the desk clerk.
SAY, I HATE TO INTERRUPT, BUT I HAVE A RESERVATION AND I WONDER IF MAYBE I COULD JUST SORT OF SLIDE THROUGH AND GET OUT OF YOUR WAY.
My voice had the tone of a man who knows he has a reservation. I was gambling on my attorney's foresight... but I couldn't pass a chance to put the horn into a cop: ... and I was right. The reservation was in my attorney's name.
Ding
Ding
THIS IS ALL I HAVE WITH ME RIGHT NOW.
THE REST IS OUT THERE IN THAT WHITE CADILLAC CONVERTIBLE.
DON'T WORRY ABOUT A THING, SIR. JUST ENJOY YOUR STAY HERE - AND IF THERE'S ANYTHING YOU NEED, JUST CALL THE DESK.

I nodded and smiled, half-watching the stunned reaction of the cop-crowd right next to me. Here they were arguing with every piece of leverage they could command, for a room they'd already paid for - and suddenly their whole act gets side-swiped by some crusty drifter who looks like something out of an upper-Michigan hobo jungle.

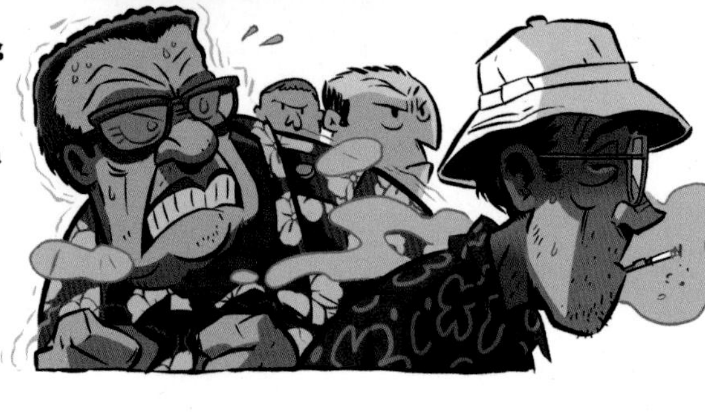

3. Savage Lucy... 'Teeth Like Baseballs, Eyes Like Jellied Fire'

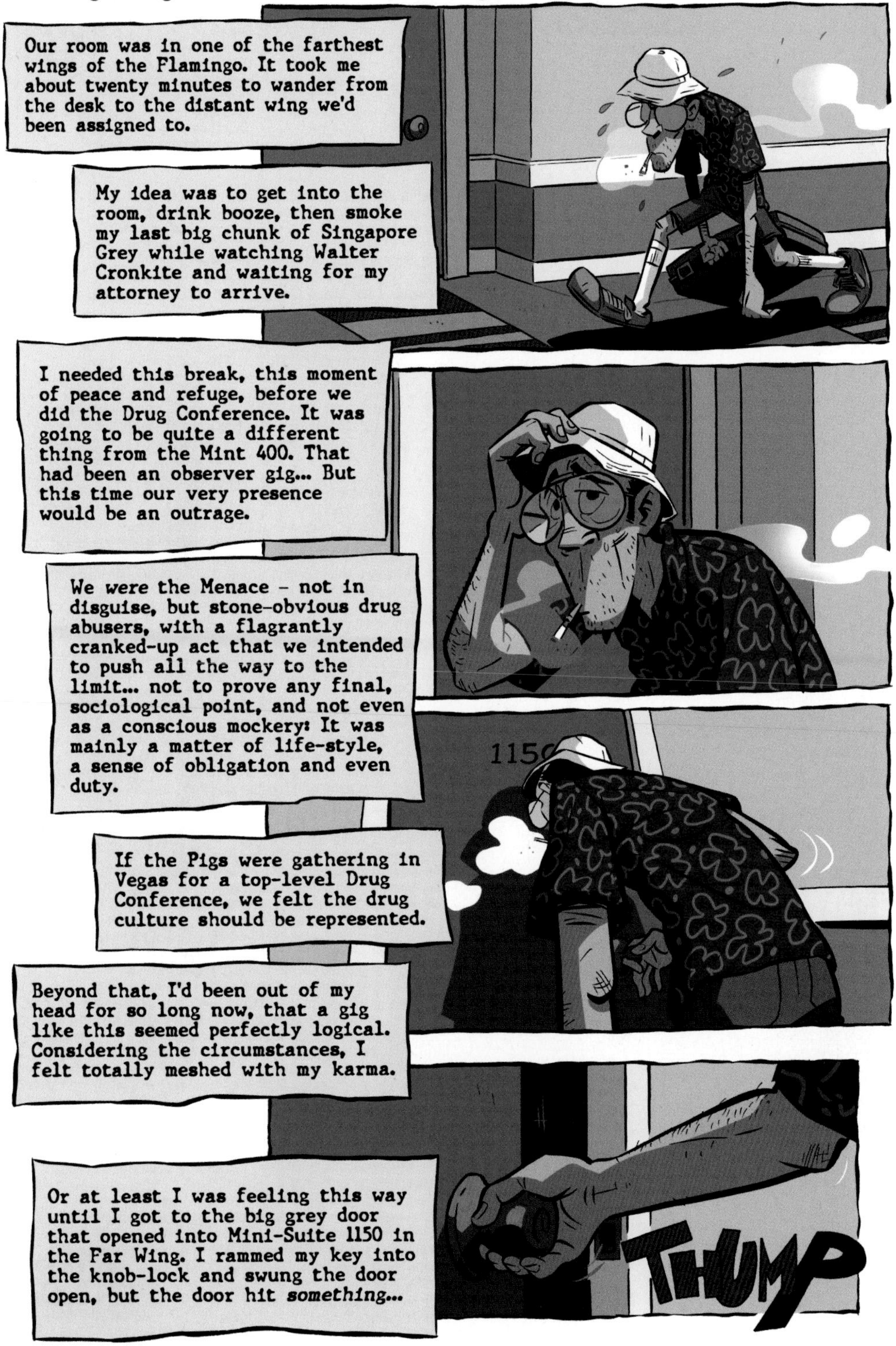

Our room was in one of the farthest wings of the Flamingo. It took me about twenty minutes to wander from the desk to the distant wing we'd been assigned to.
My idea was to get into the room, drink booze, then smoke my last big chunk of Singapore Grey while watching Walter Cronkite and waiting for my attorney to arrive.
I needed this break, this moment of peace and refuge, before we did the Drug Conference. It was going to be quite a different thing from the Mint 400. That had been an observer gig... But this time our very presence would be an outrage.
We were the Menace - not in disguise, but stone-obvious drug abusers, with a flagrantly cranked-up act that we intended to push all the way to the limit... not to prove any final, sociological point, and not even as a conscious mockery: It was mainly a matter of life-style, a sense of obligation and even duty.
If the Pigs were gathering in Vegas for a top-level Drug Conference, we felt the drug culture should be represented.
Beyond that, I'd been out of my head for so long now, that a gig like this seemed perfectly logical. Considering the circumstances, I felt totally meshed with my karma.
Or at least I was feeling this way until I got to the big grey door that opened into Mini-Suite 1150 in the Far Wing. I rammed my key into the knob-lock and swung the door open, but the door hit *something*...
THUMP

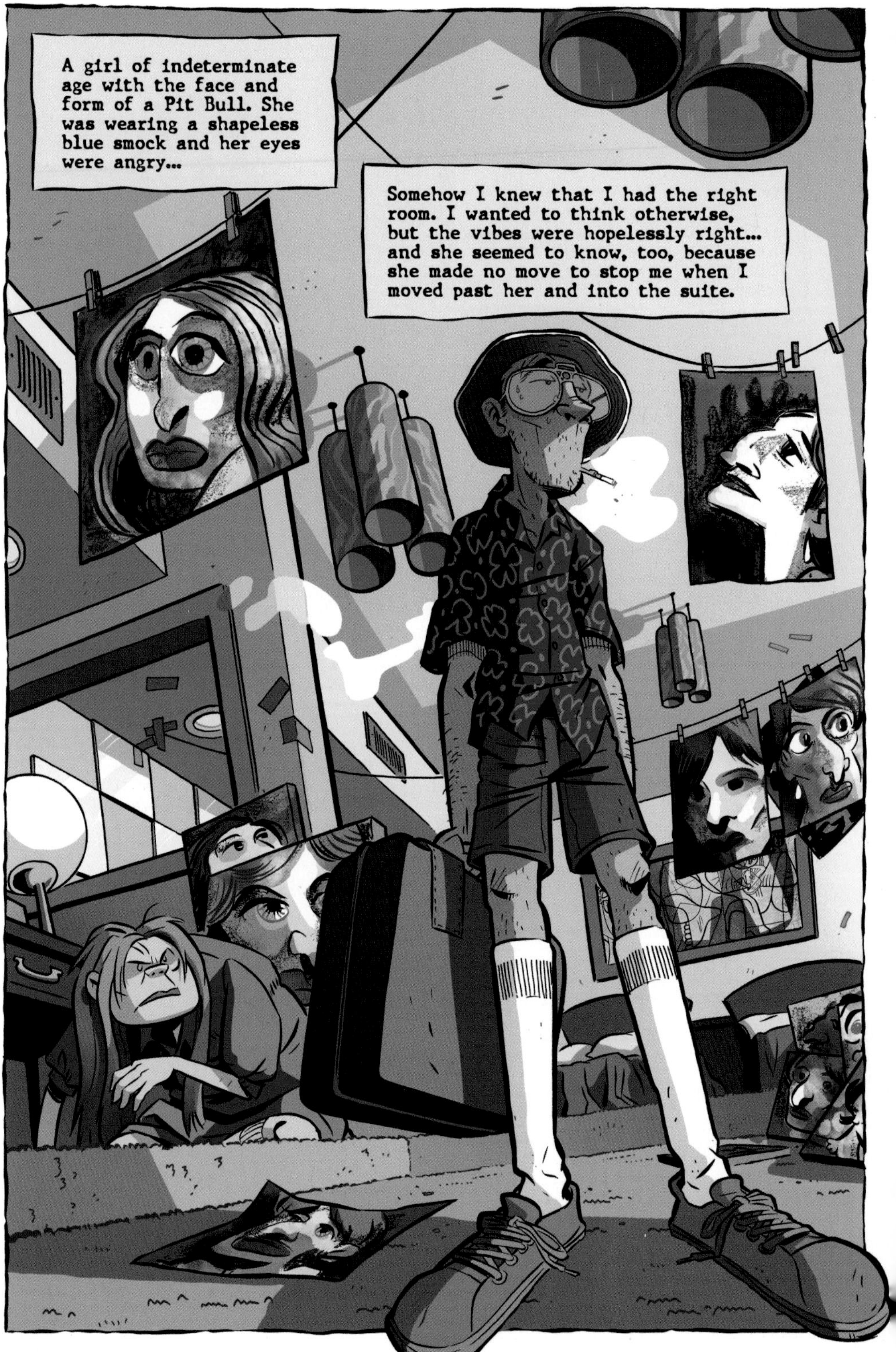
A girl of indeterminate age with the face and form of a Pit Bull. She was wearing a shapeless blue smock and her eyes were angry...
Somehow I knew that I had the right room. I wanted to think otherwise, but the vibes were hopelessly right... and she seemed to know, too, because she made no move to stop me when I moved past her and into the suite.

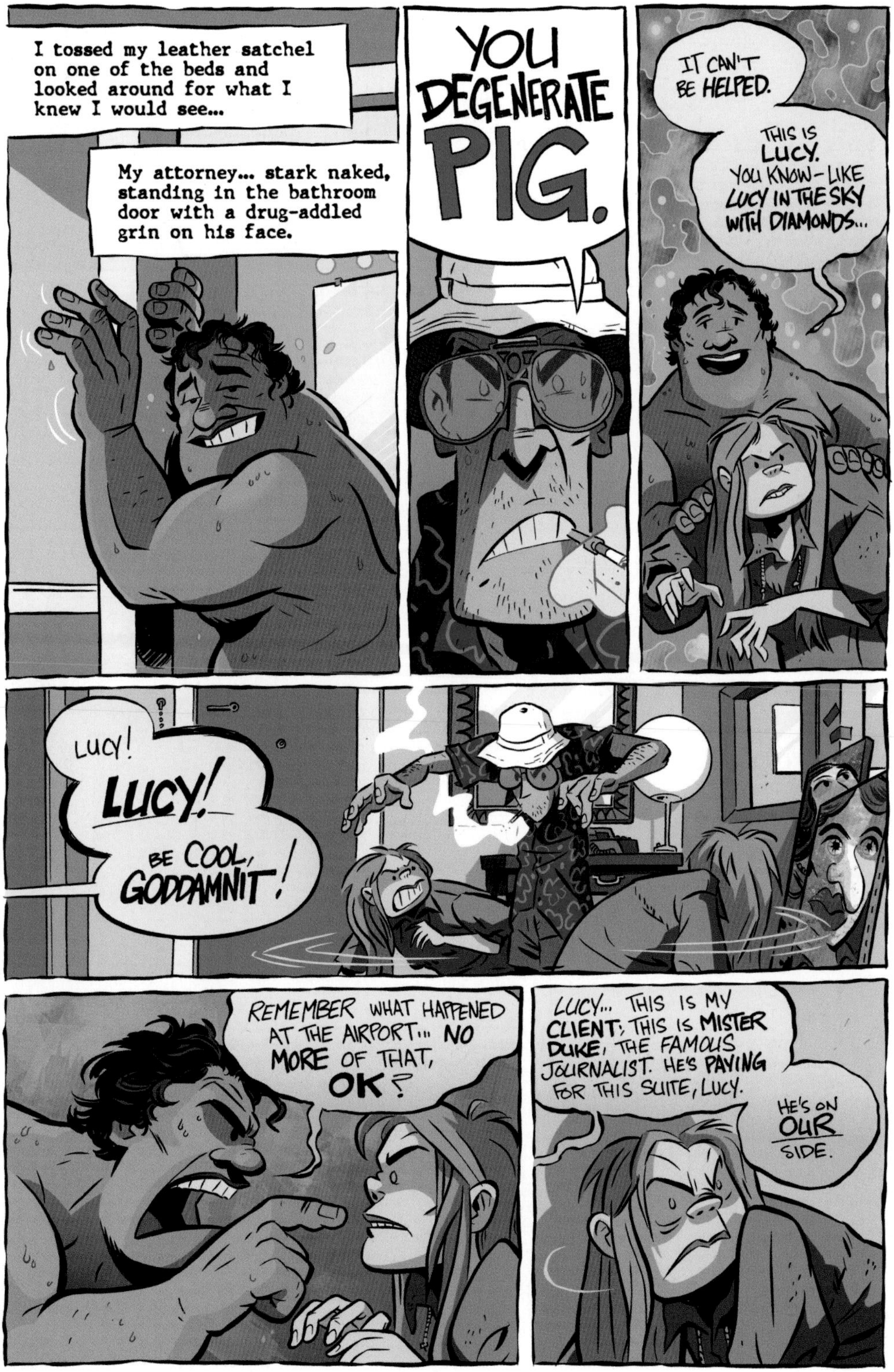
I tossed my leather satchel on one of the beds and looked around for what I knew I would see...
My attorney... stark naked, standing in the bathroom door with a drug-addled grin on his face.
YOU DEGENERATE PIG.
IT CAN'T BE HELPED.
THIS IS LUCY. YOU KNOW—LIKE LUCY IN THE SKY WITH DIAMONDS...
LUCY! LUCY!
BE COOL, GODDAMNIT!
REMEMBER WHAT HAPPENED AT THE AIRPORT... NO MORE OF THAT, OK?
LUCY... THIS IS MY CLIENT; THIS IS MISTER DUKE, THE FAMOUS JOURNALIST. HE'S PAYING FOR THIS SUITE, LUCY.
HE'S ON OUR SIDE.

I casually reached for the Mace can. I was tempted to jerk the thing out and soak her down on general principles, I desperately needed rest. The last thing I wanted was a fight to the finish with some kind of drug-crazed hormone monster. My attorney seemed to understand this; he knew why my hand was in the satchel.

NO! NOT HERE! WE'LL HAVE TO MOVE OUT!

MISTER DUKE IS MY FRIEND, HE LOVES ARTISTS. LET'S SHOW HIM YOUR PAINTINGS.

AKRR
GGRRRR
GRR

He was twisted. I could see that. And so was Lucy. Her eyes were feverish and crazy. She was staring at me like I was something that would have to be rendered helpless before life could get back to whatever she considered normal.

For the first time, I noticed that the room was full of artwork — maybe forty or fifty portraits, some in oil, some charcoal, all more or less the same size and all the same face.

It was a girl with a broad mouth, a big nose and extremely glittering eyes — a demonically sensual face; the kind of over-stated, embarrassingly dramatic renderings that you find in the bedrooms of young female art students who get hung up on horses.

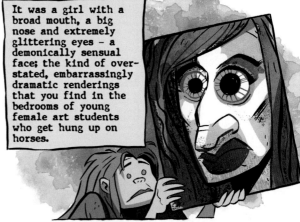

LUCY PAINTS PORTRAITS OF BARBRA STREISAND. SHE'S AN ARTIST UP IN MONTANA...

SHE CAME ALL THE WAY DOWN HERE JUST TO GIVE ALL THESE PORTRAITS TO BARBRA. WE'RE GOING OVER TO THE AMERICANA HOTEL TONIGHT, AND MEET HER BACKSTAGE.

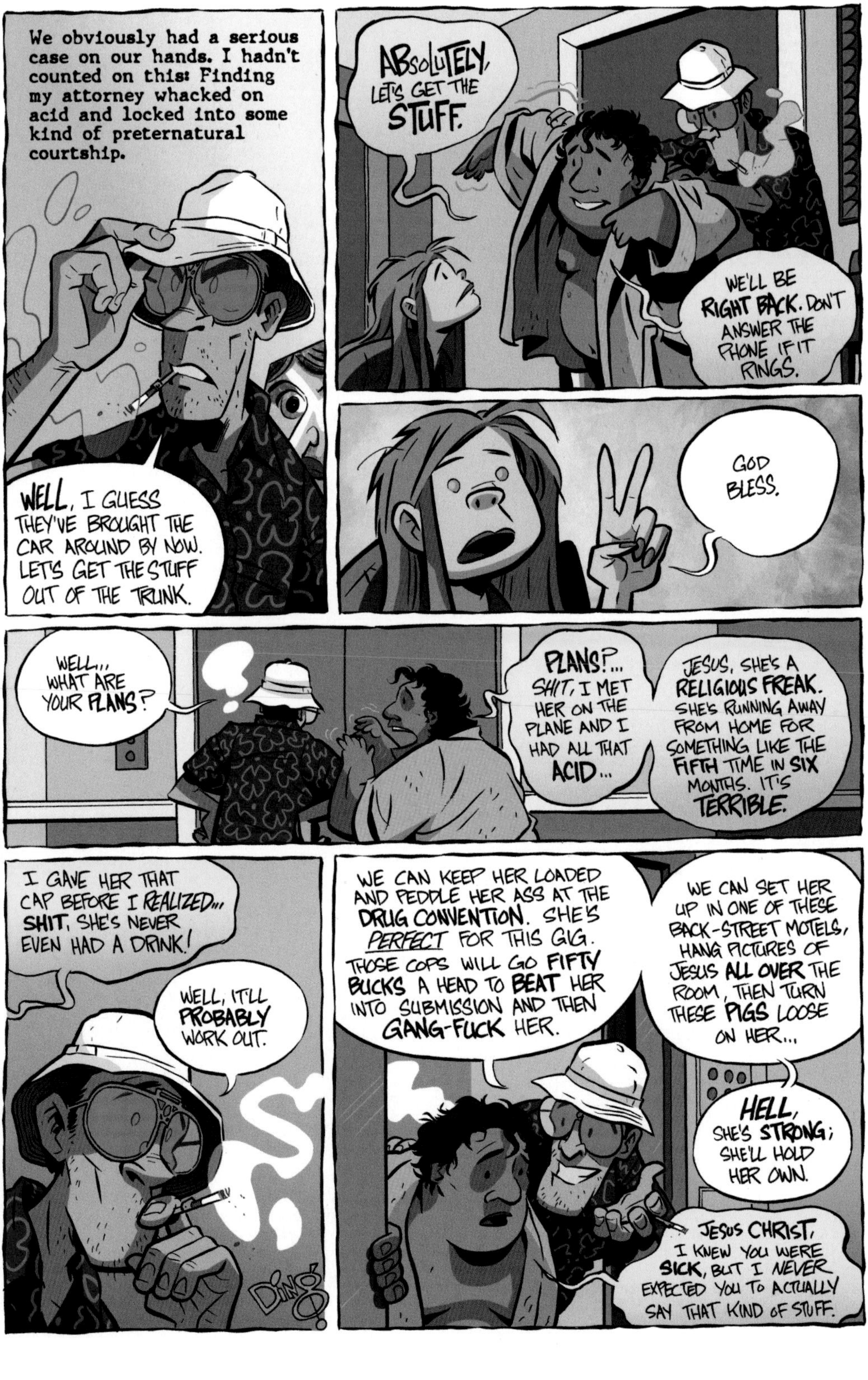
We obviously had a serious case on our hands. I hadn't counted on this: Finding my attorney whacked on acid and locked into some kind of preternatural courtship.
WELL, I GUESS THEY'VE BROUGHT THE CAR AROUND BY NOW. LET'S GET THE STUFF OUT OF THE TRUNK.
ABSOLUTELY, LET'S GET THE STUFF.
WE'LL BE RIGHT BACK. DON'T ANSWER THE PHONE IF IT RINGS.
GOD BLESS.
WELL,,, WHAT ARE YOUR PLANS?
PLANS?... SHIT, I MET HER ON THE PLANE AND I HAD ALL THAT ACID...
JESUS, SHE'S A RELIGIOUS FREAK. SHE'S RUNNING AWAY FROM HOME FOR SOMETHING LIKE THE FIFTH TIME IN SIX MONTHS. IT'S TERRIBLE.
I GAVE HER THAT CAP BEFORE I REALIZED,,, SHIT, SHE'S NEVER EVEN HAD A DRINK!
WELL, IT'LL PROBABLY WORK OUT.
WE CAN KEEP HER LOADED AND PEDDLE HER ASS AT THE DRUG CONVENTION. SHE'S PERFECT FOR THIS GIG. THOSE COPS WILL GO FIFTY BUCKS A HEAD TO BEAT HER INTO SUBMISSION AND THEN GANG-FUCK HER.
WE CAN SET HER UP IN ONE OF THESE BACK-STREET MOTELS, HANG PICTURES OF JESUS ALL OVER THE ROOM, THEN TURN THESE PIGS LOOSE ON HER...
HELL, SHE'S STRONG; SHE'LL HOLD HER OWN.
JESUS CHRIST, I KNEW YOU WERE SICK, BUT I NEVER EXPECTED YOU TO ACTUALLY SAY THAT KIND OF STUFF.

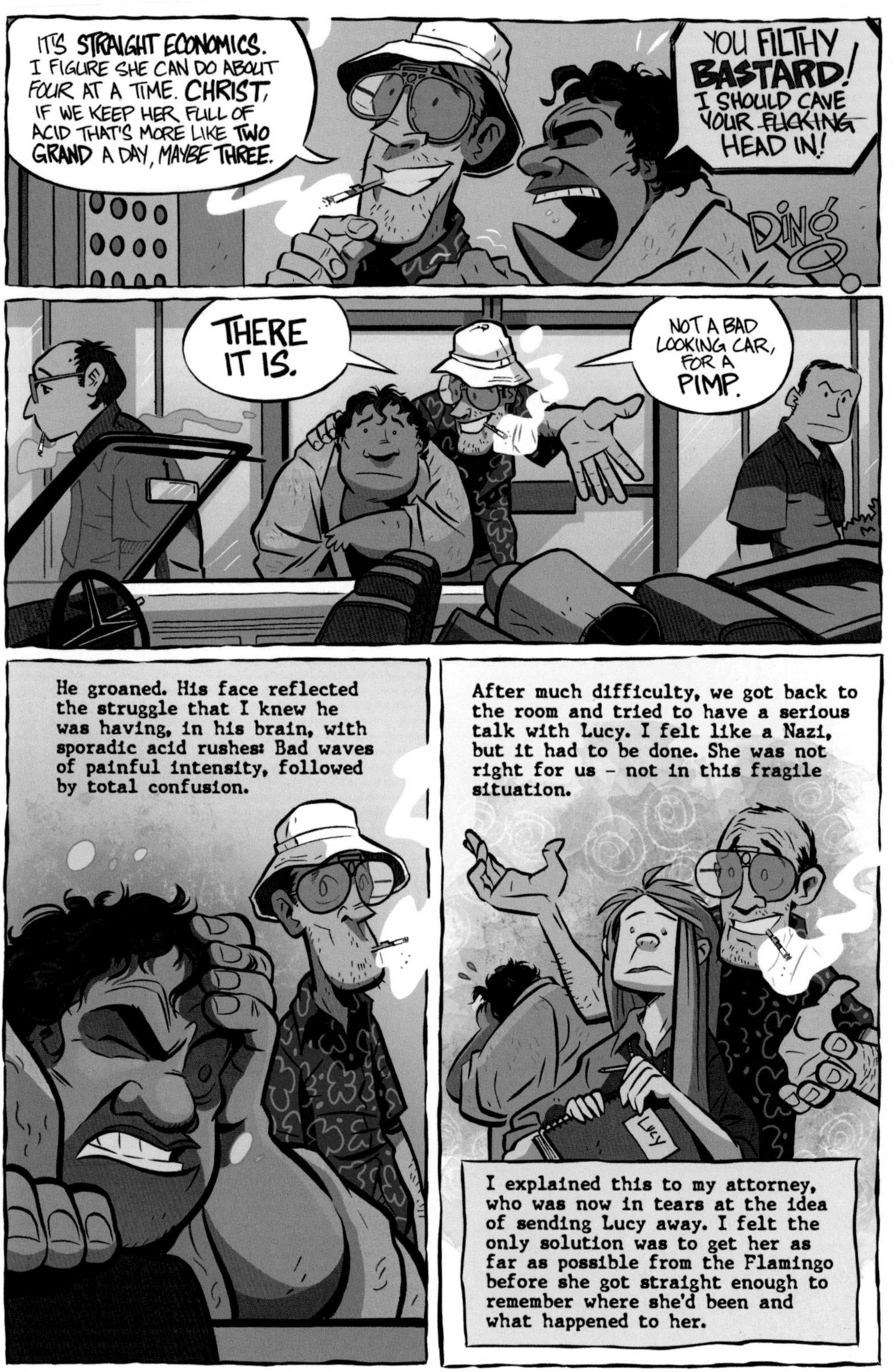
IT'S STRAIGHT ECONOMICS. I FIGURE SHE CAN DO ABOUT FOUR AT A TIME. CHRIST, IF WE KEEP HER FULL OF ACID THAT'S MORE LIKE TWO GRAND A DAY, MAYBE THREE.
YOU FILTHY BASTARD! I SHOULD CAVE YOUR FUCKING HEAD IN!
DING
THERE IT IS.
NOT A BAD LOOKING CAR, FOR A PIMP.
He groaned. His face reflected the struggle that I knew he was having, in his brain, with sporadic acid rushes: Bad waves of painful intensity, followed by total confusion.
After much difficulty, we got back to the room and tried to have a serious talk with Lucy. I felt like a Nazi, but it had to be done. She was not right for us - not in this fragile situation.
Lucy
I explained this to my attorney, who was now in tears at the idea of sending Lucy away. I felt the only solution was to get her as far as possible from the Flamingo before she got straight enough to remember where she'd been and what happened to her.

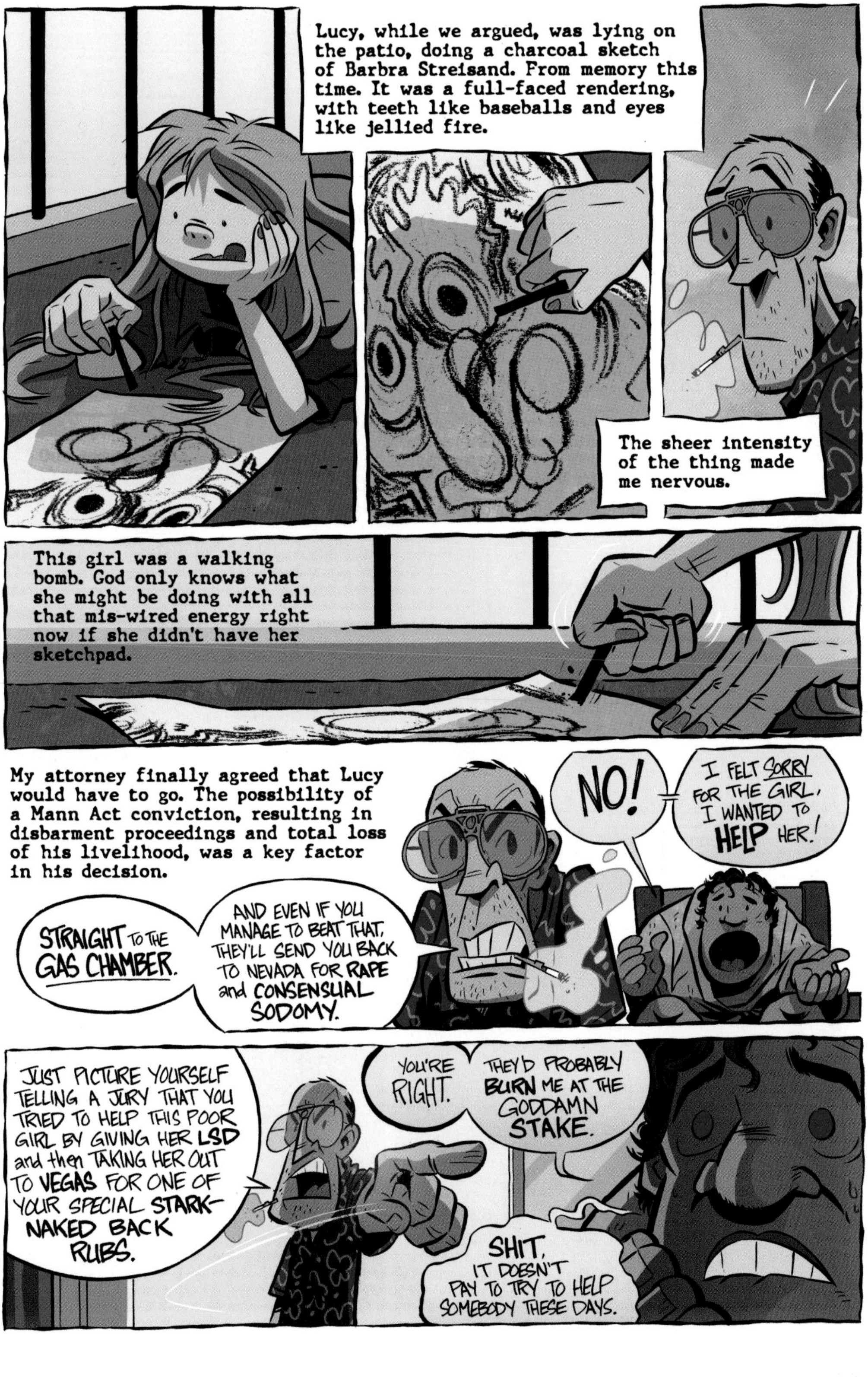
Lucy, while we argued, was lying on the patio, doing a charcoal sketch of Barbra Streisand. From memory this time. It was a full-faced rendering, with teeth like baseballs and eyes like jellied fire.
The sheer intensity of the thing made me nervous.
This girl was a walking bomb. God only knows what she might be doing with all that mis-wired energy right now if she didn't have her sketchpad.
My attorney finally agreed that Lucy would have to go. The possibility of a Mann Act conviction, resulting in disbarment proceedings and total loss of his livelihood, was a key factor in his decision.
NO!
I FELT SORRY FOR THE GIRL, I WANTED TO HELP HER!
STRAIGHT TO THE GAS CHAMBER.
AND EVEN IF YOU MANAGE TO BEAT THAT, THEY'LL SEND YOU BACK TO NEVADA FOR RAPE and CONSENSUAL SODOMY.
JUST PICTURE YOURSELF TELLING A JURY THAT YOU TRIED TO HELP THIS POOR GIRL BY GIVING HER LSD and then TAKING HER OUT TO VEGAS FOR ONE OF YOUR SPECIAL STARK-NAKED BACK RUBS.
YOU'RE RIGHT.
THEY'D PROBABLY BURN ME AT THE GODDAMN STAKE.
SHIT, IT DOESN'T PAY TO TRY TO HELP SOMEBODY THESE DAYS.

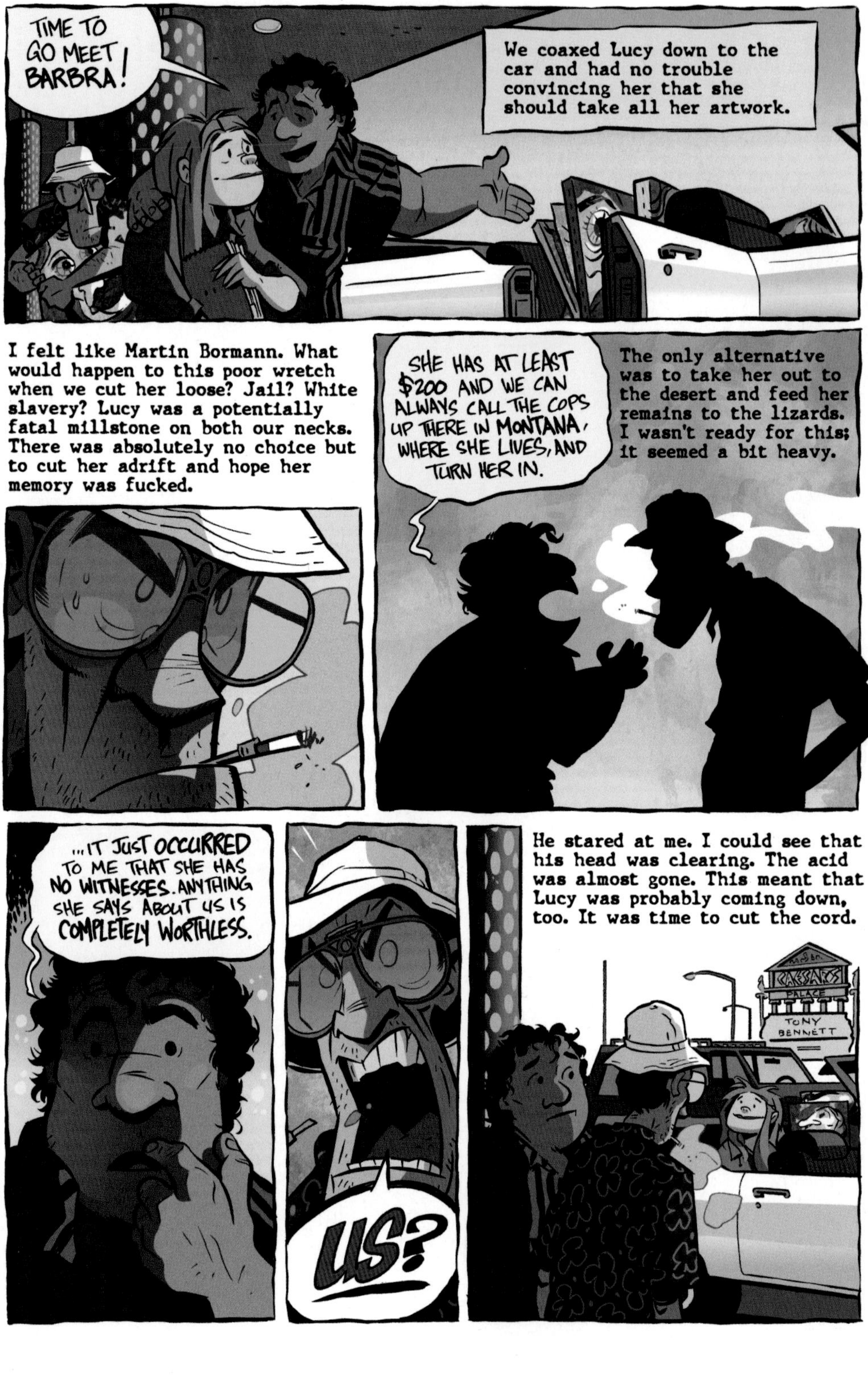
TIME TO GO MEET BARBRA!
We coaxed Lucy down to the car and had no trouble convincing her that she should take all her artwork.
I felt like Martin Bormann. What would happen to this poor wretch when we cut her loose? Jail? White slavery? Lucy was a potentially fatal millstone on both our necks. There was absolutely no choice but to cut her adrift and hope her memory was fucked.
SHE HAS AT LEAST $200 AND WE CAN ALWAYS CALL THE COPS UP THERE IN MONTANA, WHERE SHE LIVES, AND TURN HER IN.
The only alternative was to take her out to the desert and feed her remains to the lizards. I wasn't ready for this; it seemed a bit heavy.
...IT JUST OCCURRED TO ME THAT SHE HAS NO WITNESSES. ANYTHING SHE SAYS ABOUT US IS COMPLETELY WORTHLESS.
US?
He stared at me. I could see that his head was clearing. The acid was almost gone. This meant that Lucy was probably coming down, too. It was time to cut the cord.
PALACE
TONY BENNETT

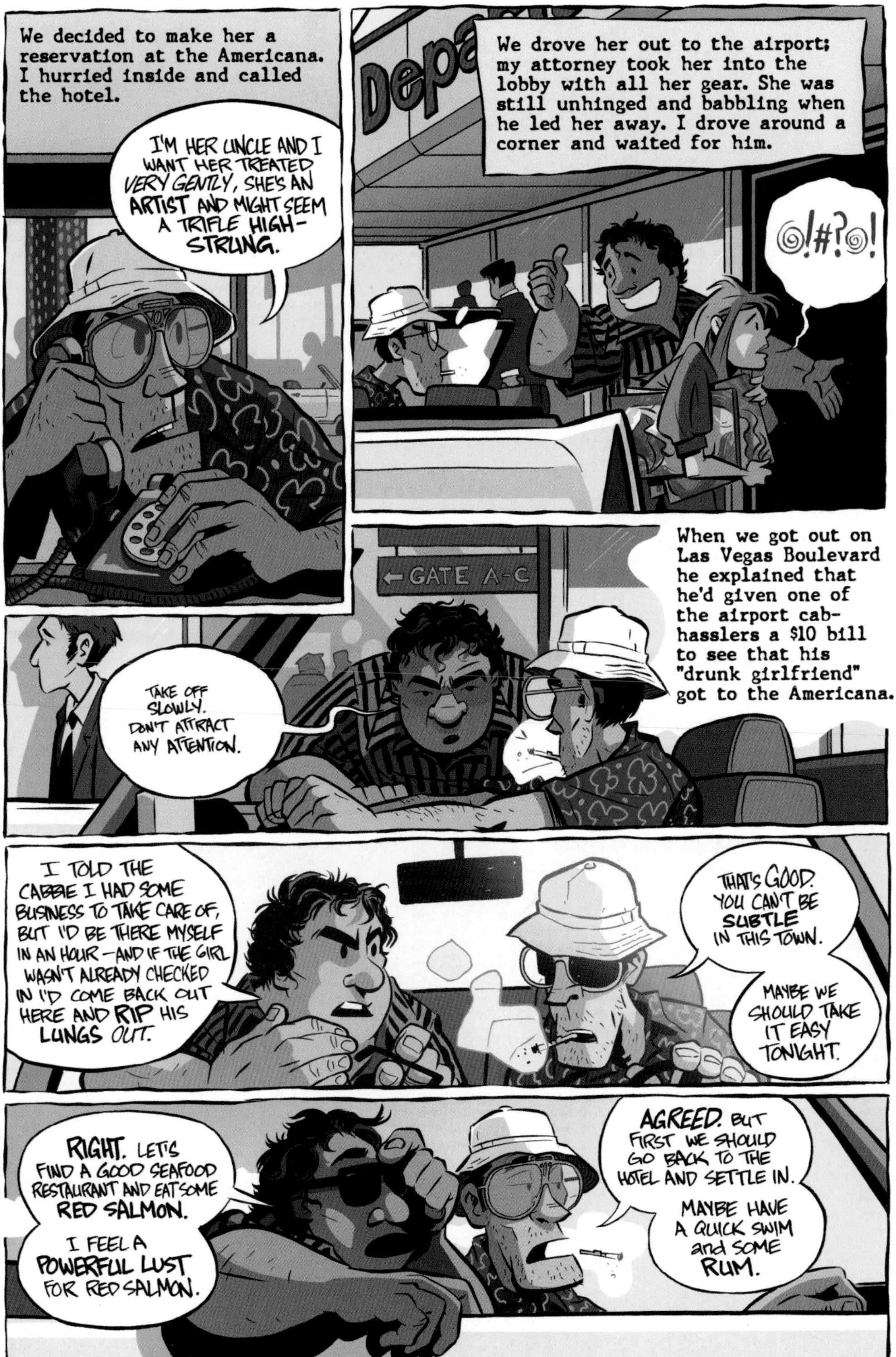

We decided to make her a reservation at the Americana. I hurried inside and called the hotel.
I'M HER UNCLE AND I WANT HER TREATED VERY GENTLY, SHE'S AN ARTIST AND MIGHT SEEM A TRIFLE HIGH-STRUNG.
Depa
We drove her out to the airport; my attorney took her into the lobby with all her gear. She was still unhinged and babbling when he led her away. I drove around a corner and waited for him.
!#?!
GATE A-C
When we got out on Las Vegas Boulevard he explained that he'd given one of the airport cab-hasslers a $10 bill to see that his "drunk girlfriend" got to the Americana.
TAKE OFF SLOWLY. DON'T ATTRACT ANY ATTENTION.
I TOLD THE CABBIE I HAD SOME BUSINESS TO TAKE CARE OF, BUT I'D BE THERE MYSELF IN AN HOUR—AND IF THE GIRL WASN'T ALREADY CHECKED IN I'D COME BACK OUT HERE AND RIP HIS LUNGS OUT.
THAT'S GOOD. YOU CAN'T BE SUBTLE IN THIS TOWN.
MAYBE WE SHOULD TAKE IT EASY TONIGHT.
RIGHT. LET'S FIND A GOOD SEAFOOD RESTAURANT AND EAT SOME RED SALMON.
I FEEL A POWERFUL LUST FOR RED SALMON.
AGREED. BUT FIRST WE SHOULD GO BACK TO THE HOTEL AND SETTLE IN.
MAYBE HAVE A QUICK SWIM and SOME RUM.

4. No Refuge for Degenerates... Reflections on a Murderous Junkie

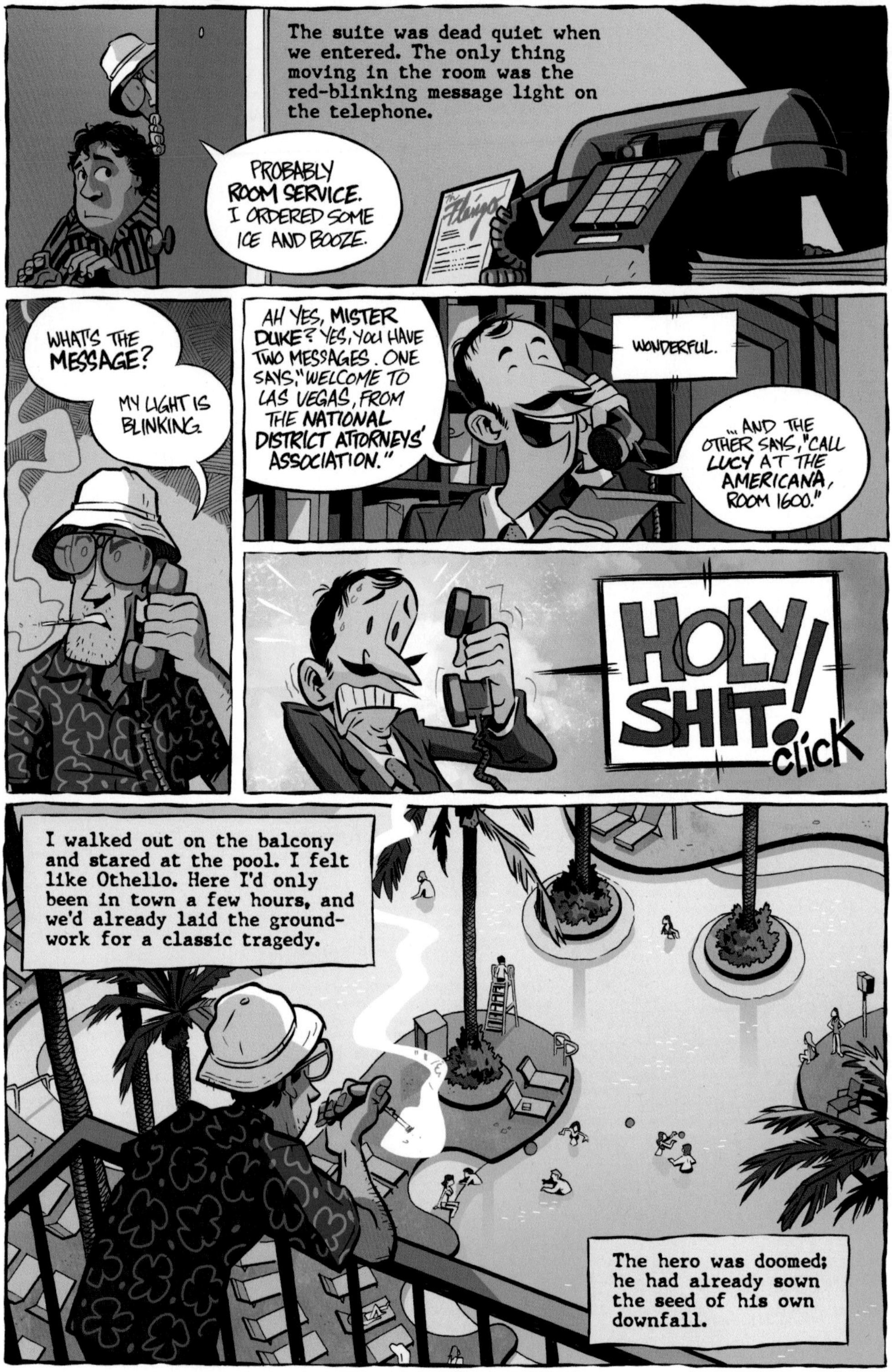

The suite was dead quiet when we entered. The only thing moving in the room was the red-blinking message light on the telephone.
PROBABLY ROOM SERVICE. I ORDERED SOME ICE AND BOOZE.
WHAT'S THE MESSAGE?
MY LIGHT IS BLINKING.
AH YES, MISTER DUKE? YES, YOU HAVE TWO MESSAGES. ONE SAYS, "WELCOME TO LAS VEGAS, FROM THE NATIONAL DISTRICT ATTORNEYS' ASSOCIATION."
WONDERFUL.
...AND THE OTHER SAYS, "CALL LUCY AT THE AMERICANA, ROOM 1600."
HOLY SHIT!
CLICK
I walked out on the balcony and stared at the pool. I felt like Othello. Here I'd only been in town a few hours, and we'd already laid the groundwork for a classic tragedy.
The hero was doomed; he had already sown the seed of his own downfall.

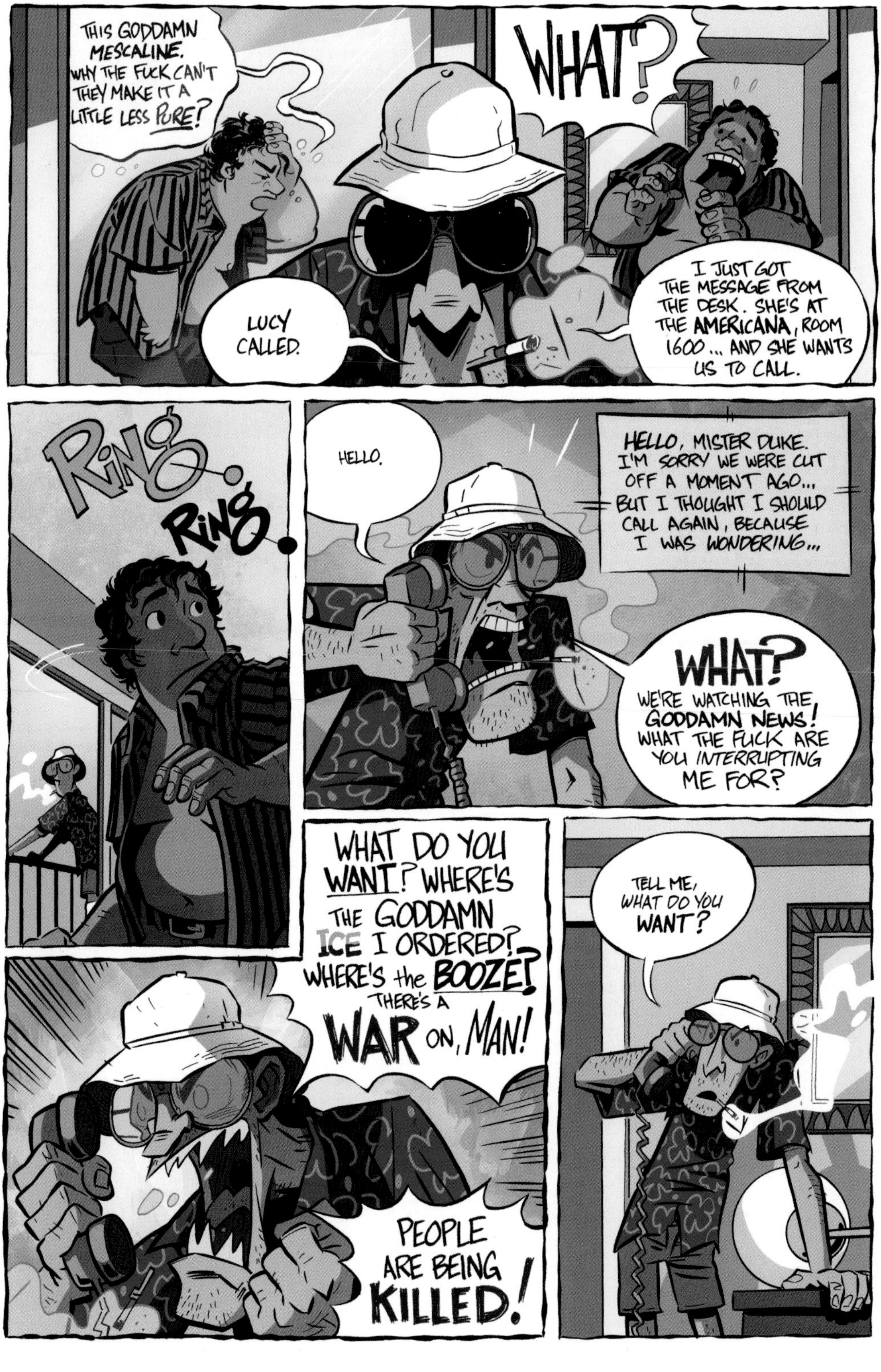
THIS GODDAMN MESCALINE. WHY THE FUCK CAN'T THEY MAKE IT A LITTLE LESS PURE?
WHAT?
LUCY CALLED.
I JUST GOT THE MESSAGE FROM THE DESK. SHE'S AT THE AMERICANA, ROOM 1600... AND SHE WANTS US TO CALL.
RING
RING
HELLO.
HELLO, MISTER DUKE. I'M SORRY WE WERE CUT OFF A MOMENT AGO... BUT I THOUGHT I SHOULD CALL AGAIN, BECAUSE I WAS WONDERING...
WHAT? WE'RE WATCHING THE GODDAMN NEWS! WHAT THE FUCK ARE YOU INTERRUPTING ME FOR?
WHAT DO YOU WANT? WHERE'S THE GODDAMN ICE I ORDERED? WHERE'S the BOOZE? THERE'S A WAR ON, MAN!
PEOPLE ARE BEING KILLED!
TELL ME, WHAT DO YOU WANT?

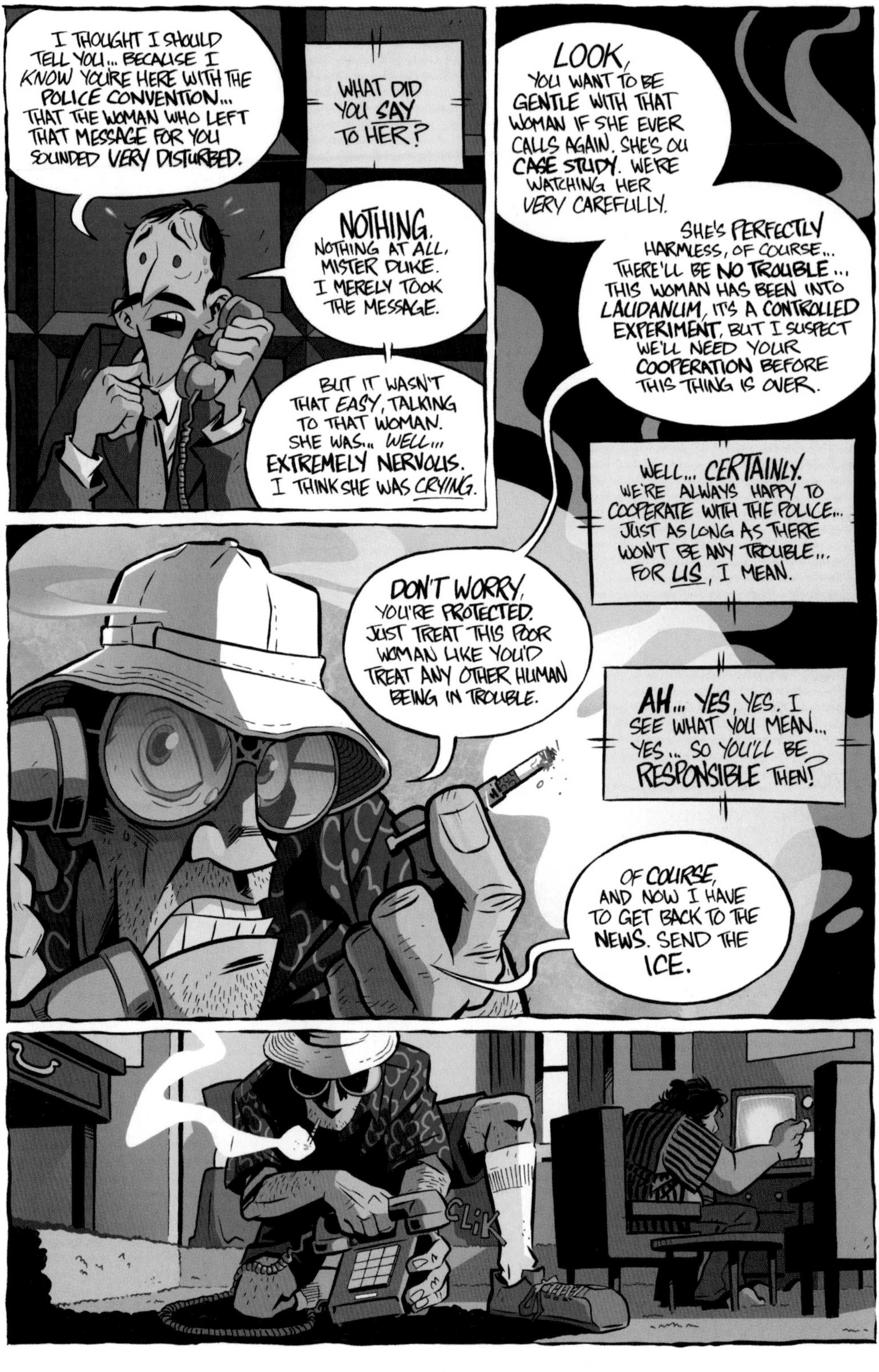
I THOUGHT I SHOULD TELL YOU... BECAUSE I KNOW YOU'RE HERE WITH THE POLICE CONVENTION... THAT THE WOMAN WHO LEFT THAT MESSAGE FOR YOU SOUNDED VERY DISTURBED.
WHAT DID YOU SAY TO HER?
NOTHING. NOTHING AT ALL, MISTER DUKE. I MERELY TOOK THE MESSAGE.
BUT IT WASN'T THAT EASY, TALKING TO THAT WOMAN. SHE WAS... WELL... EXTREMELY NERVOUS. I THINK SHE WAS CRYING.
LOOK, YOU WANT TO BE GENTLE WITH THAT WOMAN IF SHE EVER CALLS AGAIN. SHE'S OU CASE STUDY. WE'RE WATCHING HER VERY CAREFULLY.
SHE'S PERFECTLY HARMLESS, OF COURSE... THERE'LL BE NO TROUBLE... THIS WOMAN HAS BEEN INTO LAUDANUM, IT'S A CONTROLLED EXPERIMENT, BUT I SUSPECT WE'LL NEED YOUR COOPERATION BEFORE THIS THING IS OVER.
WELL... CERTAINLY. WE'RE ALWAYS HAPPY TO COOPERATE WITH THE POLICE... JUST AS LONG AS THERE WON'T BE ANY TROUBLE... FOR US, I MEAN.
DON'T WORRY, YOU'RE PROTECTED. JUST TREAT THIS POOR WOMAN LIKE YOU'D TREAT ANY OTHER HUMAN BEING IN TROUBLE.
AH... YES, YES. I SEE WHAT YOU MEAN... YES... SO YOU'LL BE RESPONSIBLE THEN?
OF COURSE, AND NOW I HAVE TO GET BACK TO THE NEWS. SEND THE ICE.
CLIK

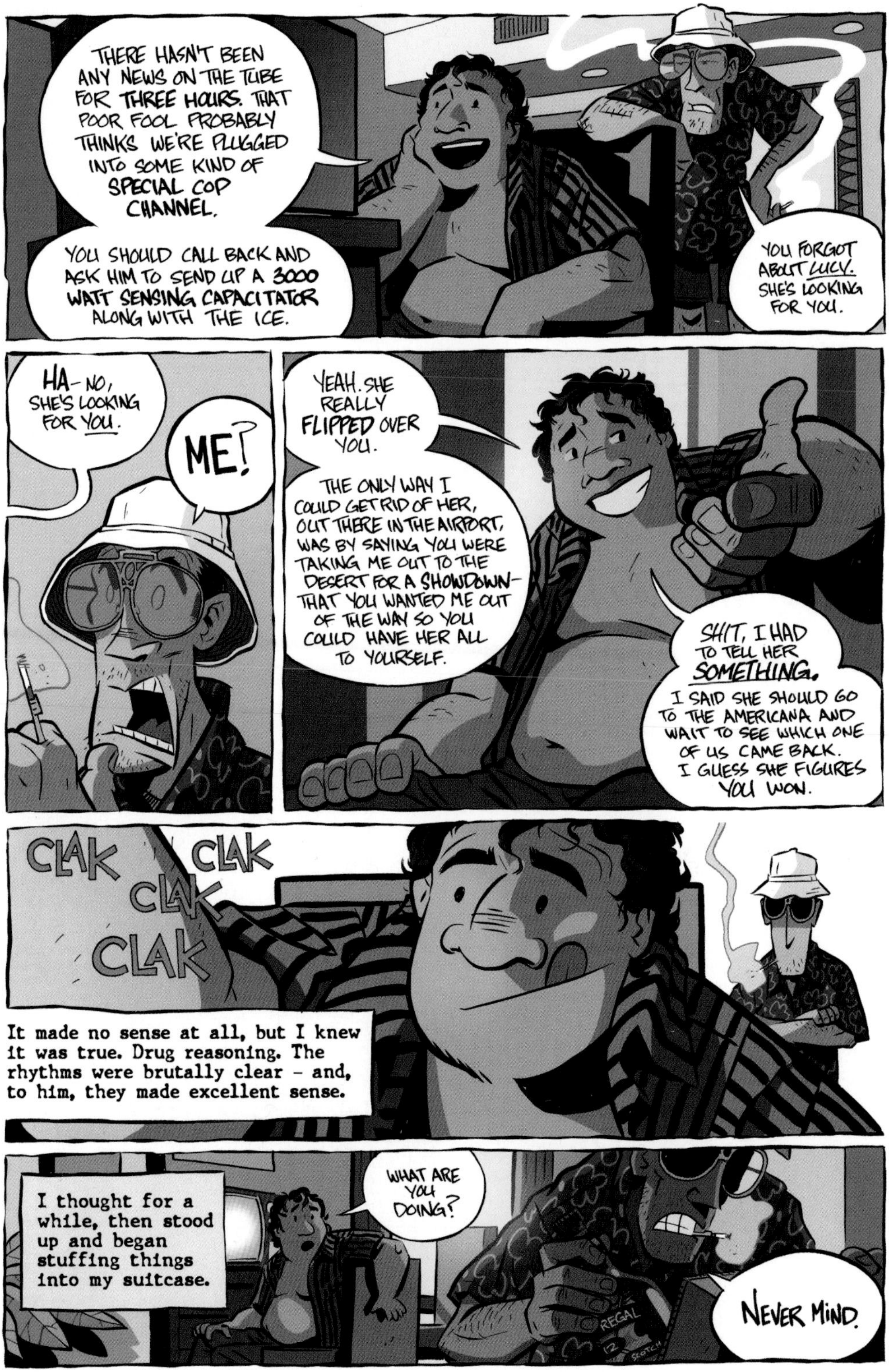
THERE HASN'T BEEN ANY NEWS ON THE TUBE FOR THREE HOURS. THAT POOR FOOL PROBABLY THINKS WE'RE PLUGGED INTO SOME KIND OF SPECIAL COP CHANNEL.
YOU SHOULD CALL BACK AND ASK HIM TO SEND UP A 3000 WATT SENSING CAPACITATOR ALONG WITH THE ICE.
YOU FORGOT ABOUT LUCY. SHE'S LOOKING FOR YOU.
HA- NO, SHE'S LOOKING FOR YOU.
ME?
YEAH. SHE REALLY FLIPPED OVER YOU.
THE ONLY WAY I COULD GET RID OF HER, OUT THERE IN THE AIRPORT, WAS BY SAYING YOU WERE TAKING ME OUT TO THE DESERT FOR A SHOWDOWN- THAT YOU WANTED ME OUT OF THE WAY SO YOU COULD HAVE HER ALL TO YOURSELF.
SHIT, I HAD TO TELL HER SOMETHING.
I SAID SHE SHOULD GO TO THE AMERICANA AND WAIT TO SEE WHICH ONE OF US CAME BACK. I GUESS SHE FIGURES YOU WON.
CLAK CLAK CLAK CLAK
It made no sense at all, but I knew it was true. Drug reasoning. The rhythms were brutally clear - and, to him, they made excellent sense.
I thought for a while, then stood up and began stuffing things into my suitcase.
WHAT ARE YOU DOING?
NEVER MIND.
REGAL
12
SCOTCH

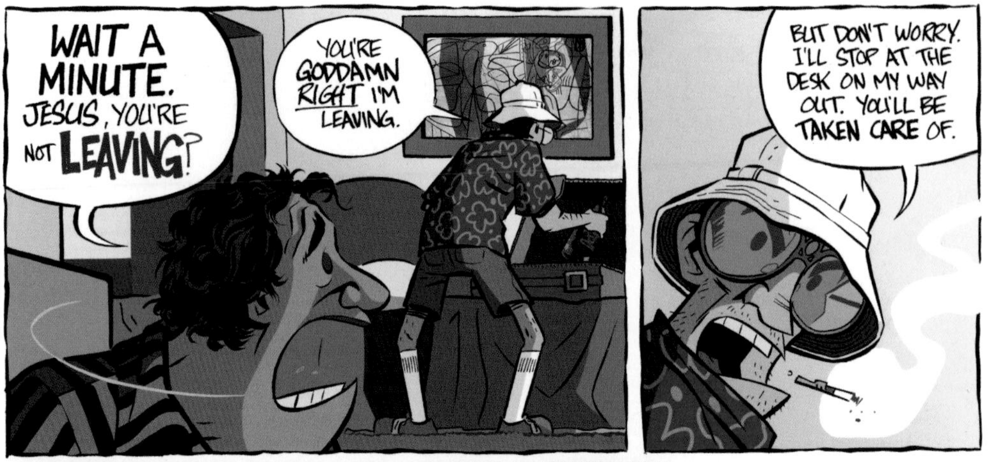
WAIT A MINUTE. JESUS, YOU'RE NOT LEAVING?
YOU'RE GODDAMN RIGHT I'M LEAVING.
BUT DON'T WORRY. I'LL STOP AT THE DESK ON MY WAY OUT. YOU'LL BE TAKEN CARE OF.

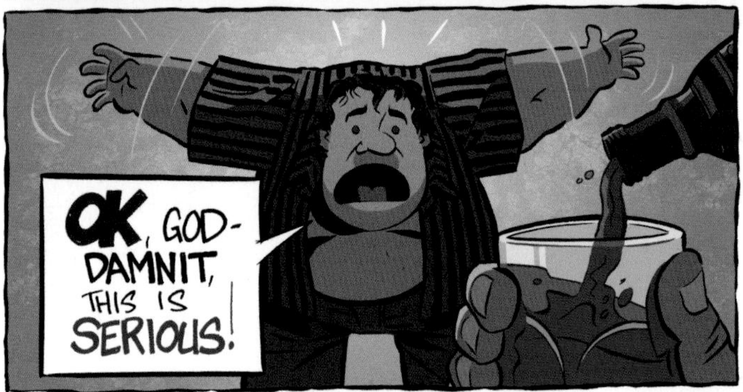
OK, GOD-DAMNIT, THIS IS SERIOUS!

I laughed, tossing my luggage together in a lump at the foot of the bed while I sat down to finish my drink. I actually intended to leave. I didn't really want to, but I figured that nothing I could possibly do with this gig was worth the risk of getting tangled up with Lucy.

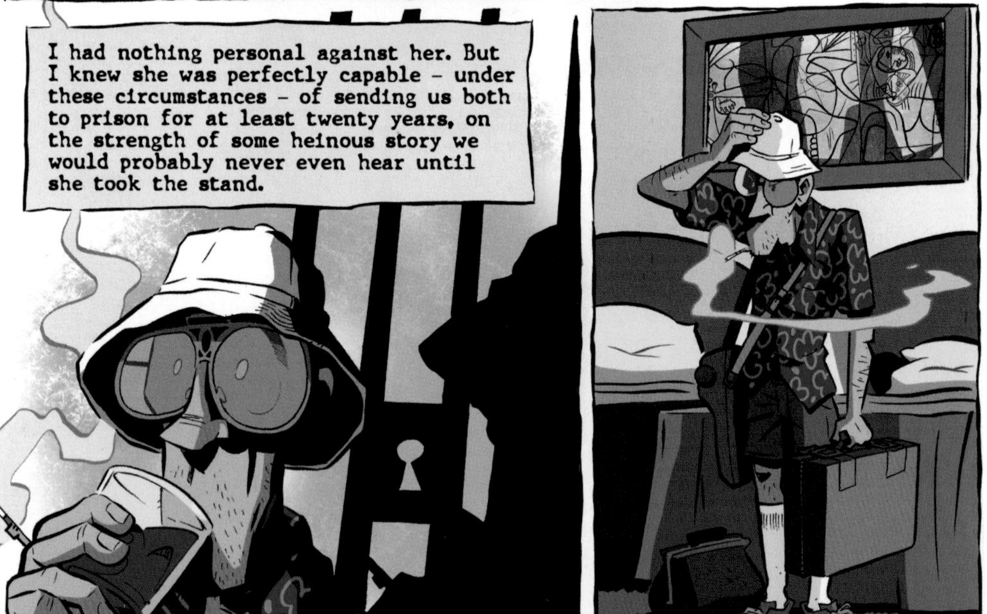
I had nothing personal against her. But I knew she was perfectly capable - under these circumstances - of sending us both to prison for at least twenty years, on the strength of some heinous story we would probably never even hear until she took the stand.

5. A Terrible Experience with Extremely Dangerous Drugs

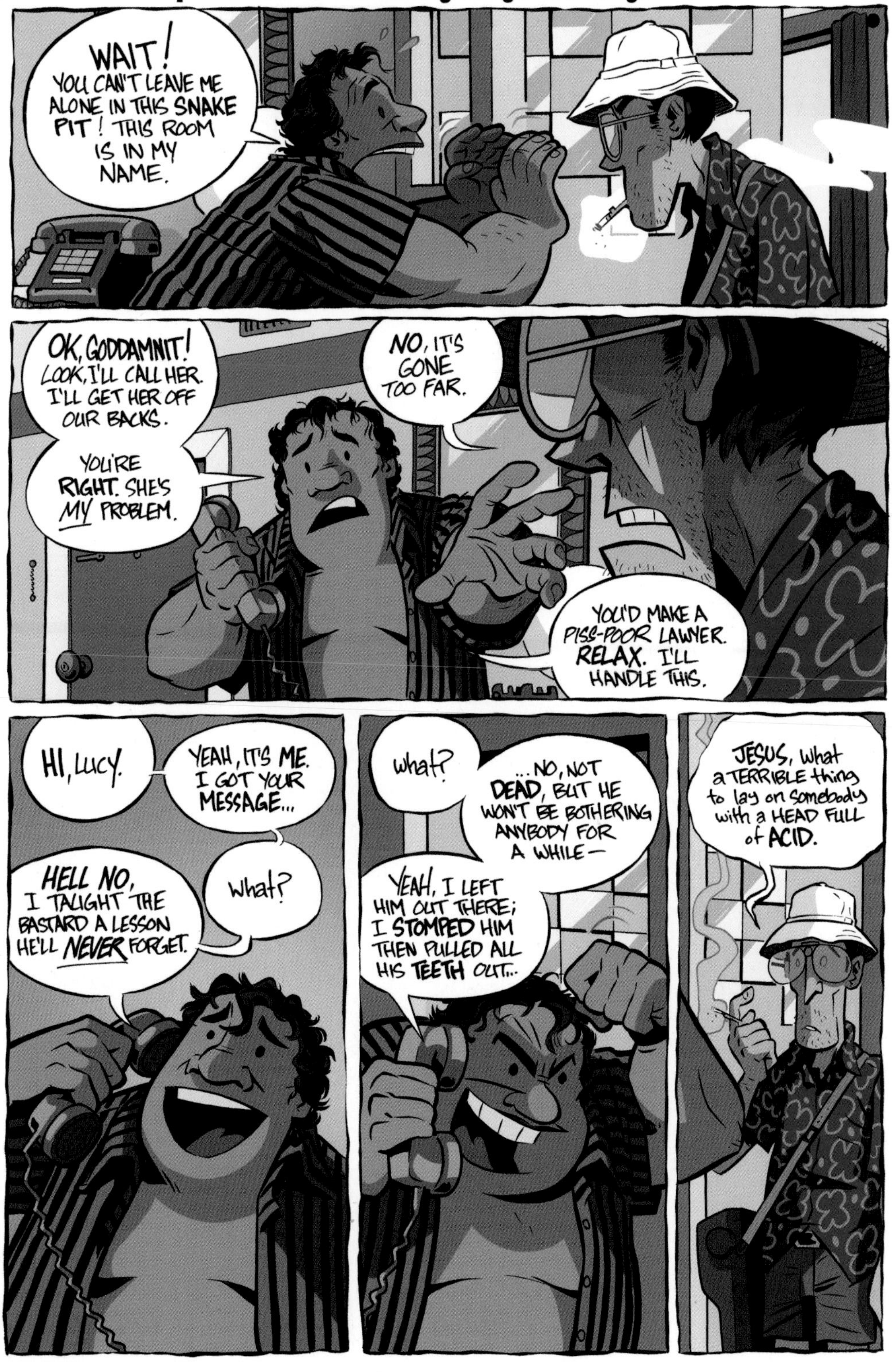
WAIT! YOU CAN'T LEAVE ME ALONE IN THIS SNAKE PIT! THIS ROOM IS IN MY NAME.
OK, GODDAMNIT! LOOK, I'LL CALL HER. I'LL GET HER OFF OUR BACKS.
NO, IT'S GONE TOO FAR.
YOU'RE RIGHT. SHE'S MY PROBLEM.
YOU'D MAKE A PISS-POOR LAWYER. RELAX. I'LL HANDLE THIS.
HI, LUCY.
YEAH, IT'S ME. I GOT YOUR MESSAGE...
HELL NO, I TAUGHT THE BASTARD A LESSON HE'LL NEVER FORGET.
what?
what?
...NO, NOT DEAD, BUT HE WON'T BE BOTHERING ANYBODY FOR A WHILE—
YEAH, I LEFT HIM OUT THERE; I STOMPED HIM THEN PULLED ALL HIS TEETH OUT...
JESUS, what a TERRIBLE thing to lay on somebody with a HEAD FULL of ACID.

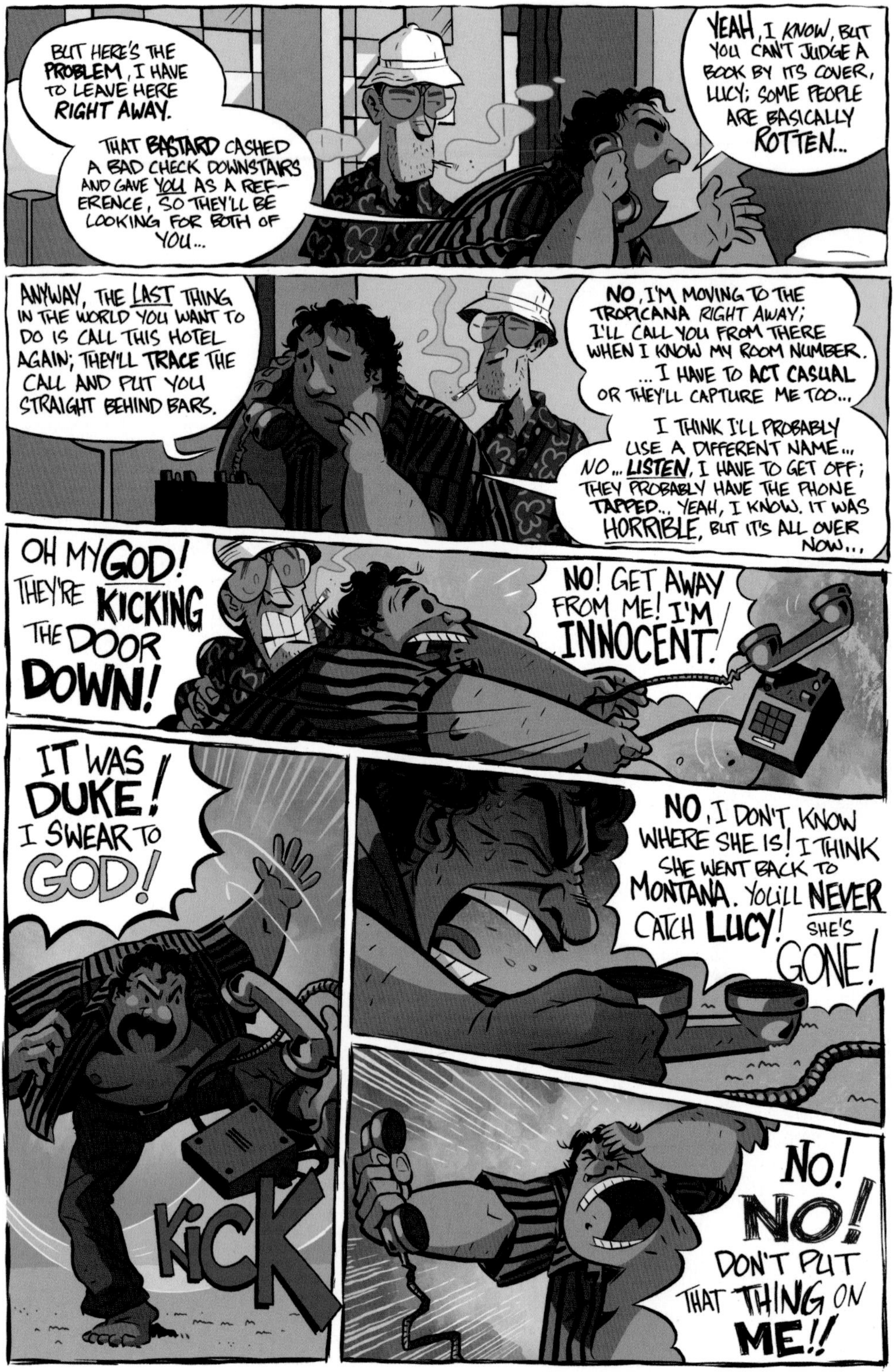
BUT HERE'S THE PROBLEM, I HAVE TO LEAVE HERE RIGHT AWAY.
THAT BASTARD CASHED A BAD CHECK DOWNSTAIRS AND GAVE YOU AS A REFERENCE, SO THEY'LL BE LOOKING FOR BOTH OF YOU...
YEAH, I KNOW, BUT YOU CAN'T JUDGE A BOOK BY ITS COVER, LUCY; SOME PEOPLE ARE BASICALLY ROTTEN...
ANYWAY, THE LAST THING IN THE WORLD YOU WANT TO DO IS CALL THIS HOTEL AGAIN; THEY'LL TRACE THE CALL AND PUT YOU STRAIGHT BEHIND BARS.
NO, I'M MOVING TO THE TROPICANA RIGHT AWAY; I'LL CALL YOU FROM THERE WHEN I KNOW MY ROOM NUMBER.
... I HAVE TO ACT CASUAL OR THEY'LL CAPTURE ME TOO...
I THINK I'LL PROBABLY USE A DIFFERENT NAME... NO... LISTEN, I HAVE TO GET OFF; THEY PROBABLY HAVE THE PHONE TAPPED... YEAH, I KNOW. IT WAS HORRIBLE, BUT IT'S ALL OVER NOW...
OH MY GOD! THEY'RE KICKING THE DOOR DOWN!
NO! GET AWAY FROM ME! I'M INNOCENT!
IT WAS DUKE! I SWEAR TO GOD!
KICK
NO, I DON'T KNOW WHERE SHE IS! I THINK SHE WENT BACK TO MONTANA. YOU'LL NEVER CATCH LUCY! SHE'S GONE!
NO! NO! DON'T PUT THAT THING ON ME!!

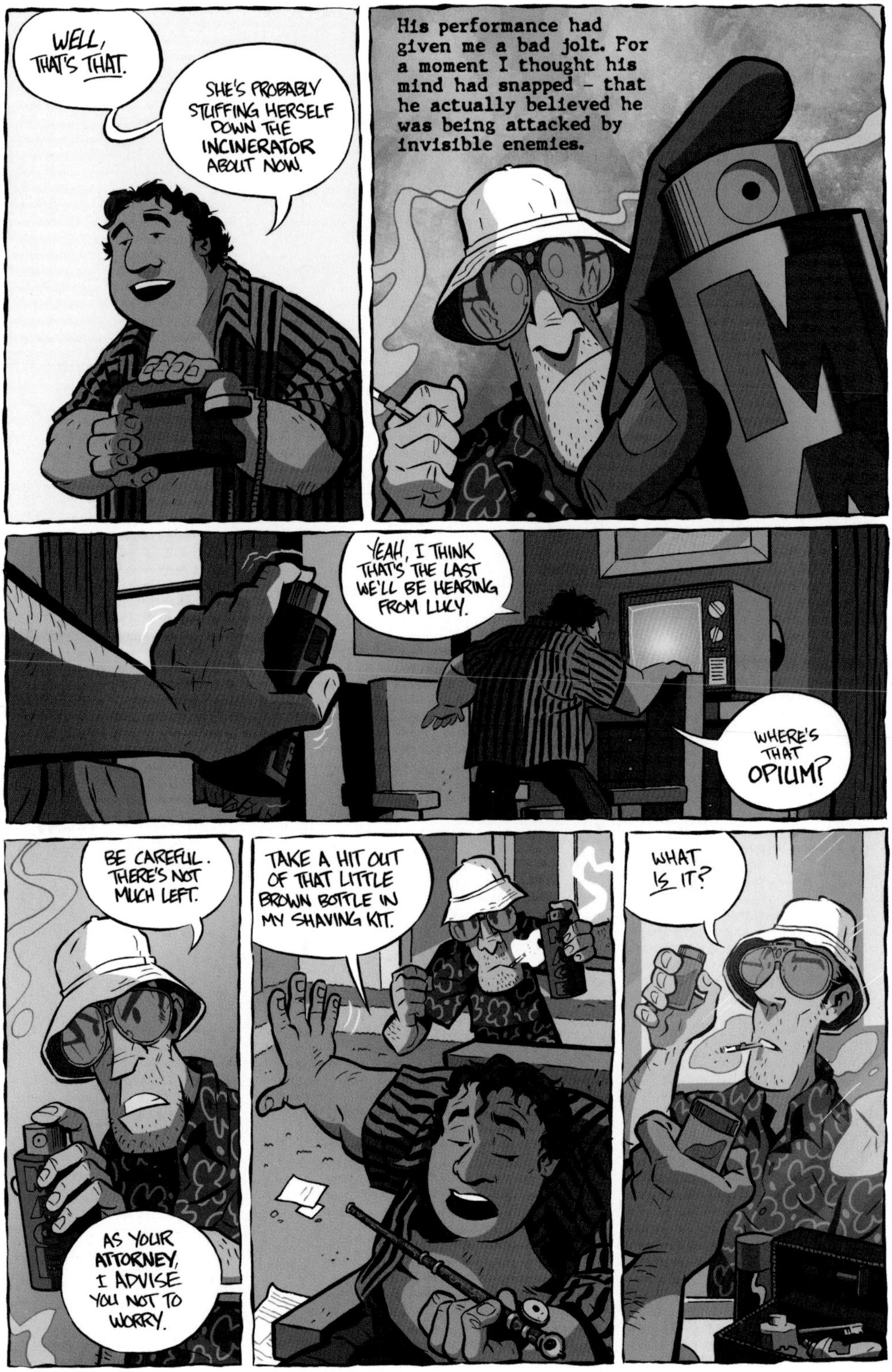
WELL, THAT'S THAT.
SHE'S PROBABLY STUFFING HERSELF DOWN THE INCINERATOR ABOUT NOW.
His performance had given me a bad jolt. For a moment I thought his mind had snapped - that he actually believed he was being attacked by invisible enemies.
YEAH, I THINK THAT'S THE LAST WE'LL BE HEARING FROM LUCY.
WHERE'S THAT OPIUM?
BE CAREFUL. THERE'S NOT MUCH LEFT.
AS YOUR ATTORNEY, I ADVISE YOU NOT TO WORRY.
TAKE A HIT OUT OF THAT LITTLE BROWN BOTTLE IN MY SHAVING KIT.
WHAT IS IT?

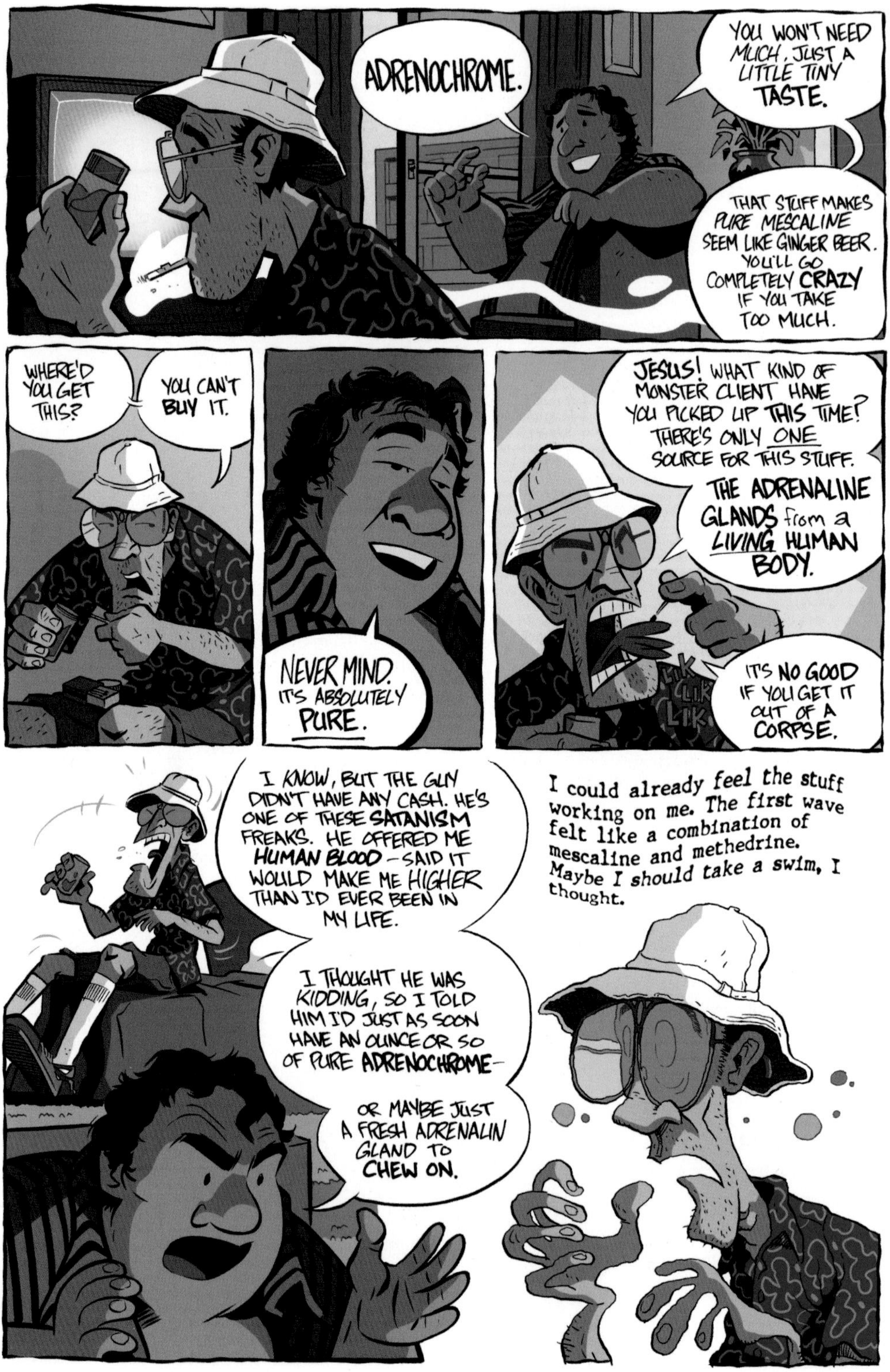
ADRENOCHROME.
YOU WON'T NEED MUCH, JUST A LITTLE TINY TASTE.
THAT STUFF MAKES PURE MESCALINE SEEM LIKE GINGER BEER. YOU'LL GO COMPLETELY CRAZY IF YOU TAKE TOO MUCH.
WHERE'D YOU GET THIS?
YOU CAN'T BUY IT.
NEVER MIND. IT'S ABSOLUTELY PURE.
JESUS! WHAT KIND OF MONSTER CLIENT HAVE YOU PICKED UP THIS TIME? THERE'S ONLY ONE SOURCE FOR THIS STUFF.
THE ADRENALINE GLANDS from a LIVING HUMAN BODY.
LIK CLIK LIK
IT'S NO GOOD IF YOU GET IT OUT OF A CORPSE.
I KNOW, BUT THE GUY DIDN'T HAVE ANY CASH. HE'S ONE OF THESE SATANISM FREAKS. HE OFFERED ME HUMAN BLOOD — SAID IT WOULD MAKE ME HIGHER THAN I'D EVER BEEN IN MY LIFE.
I THOUGHT HE WAS KIDDING, SO I TOLD HIM I'D JUST AS SOON HAVE AN OUNCE OR SO OF PURE ADRENOCHROME—
OR MAYBE JUST A FRESH ADRENALIN GLAND TO CHEW ON.
I could already feel the stuff working on me. The first wave felt like a combination of mescaline and methedrine. Maybe I should take a swim, I thought.

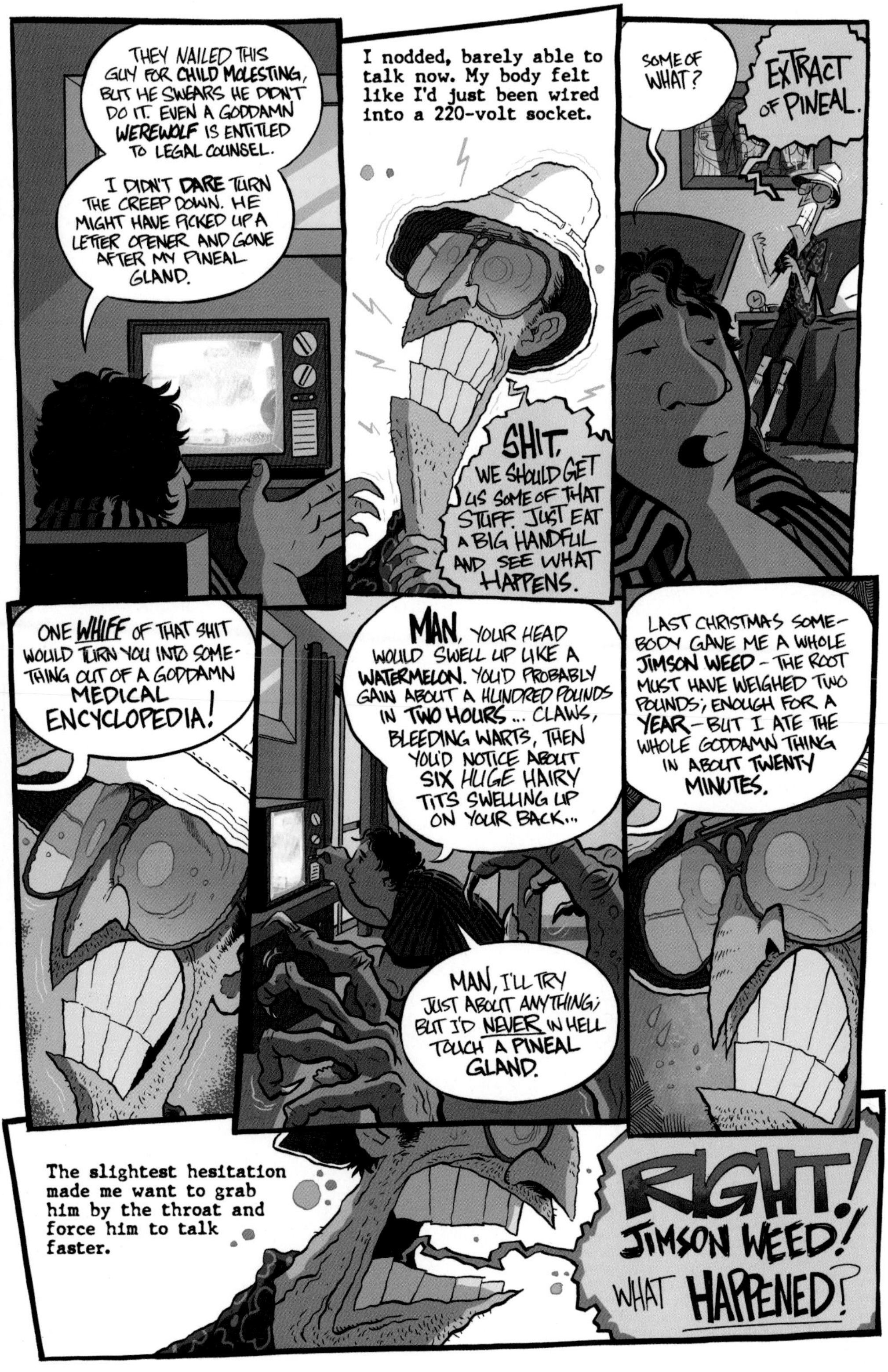
THEY NAILED THIS GUY FOR CHILD MOLESTING, BUT HE SWEARS HE DIDN'T DO IT. EVEN A GODDAMN WEREWOLF IS ENTITLED TO LEGAL COUNSEL.
I DIDN'T DARE TURN THE CREEP DOWN. HE MIGHT HAVE PICKED UP A LETTER OPENER AND GONE AFTER MY PINEAL GLAND.
I nodded, barely able to talk now. My body felt like I'd just been wired into a 220-volt socket.
SHIT, WE SHOULD GET US SOME OF THAT STUFF. JUST EAT A BIG HANDFUL AND SEE WHAT HAPPENS.
SOME OF WHAT?
EXTRACT OF PINEAL.
ONE WHIFF OF THAT SHIT WOULD TURN YOU INTO SOMETHING OUT OF A GODDAMN MEDICAL ENCYCLOPEDIA!
MAN, YOUR HEAD WOULD SWELL UP LIKE A WATERMELON. YOU'D PROBABLY GAIN ABOUT A HUNDRED POUNDS IN TWO HOURS... CLAWS, BLEEDING WARTS, THEN YOU'D NOTICE ABOUT SIX HUGE HAIRY TITS SWELLING UP ON YOUR BACK...
MAN, I'LL TRY JUST ABOUT ANYTHING; BUT I'D NEVER IN HELL TOUCH A PINEAL GLAND.
LAST CHRISTMAS SOMEBODY GAVE ME A WHOLE JIMSON WEED - THE ROOT MUST HAVE WEIGHED TWO POUNDS; ENOUGH FOR A YEAR - BUT I ATE THE WHOLE GODDAMN THING IN ABOUT TWENTY MINUTES.
The slightest hesitation made me want to grab him by the throat and force him to talk faster.
RIGHT! JIMSON WEED! WHAT HAPPENED?

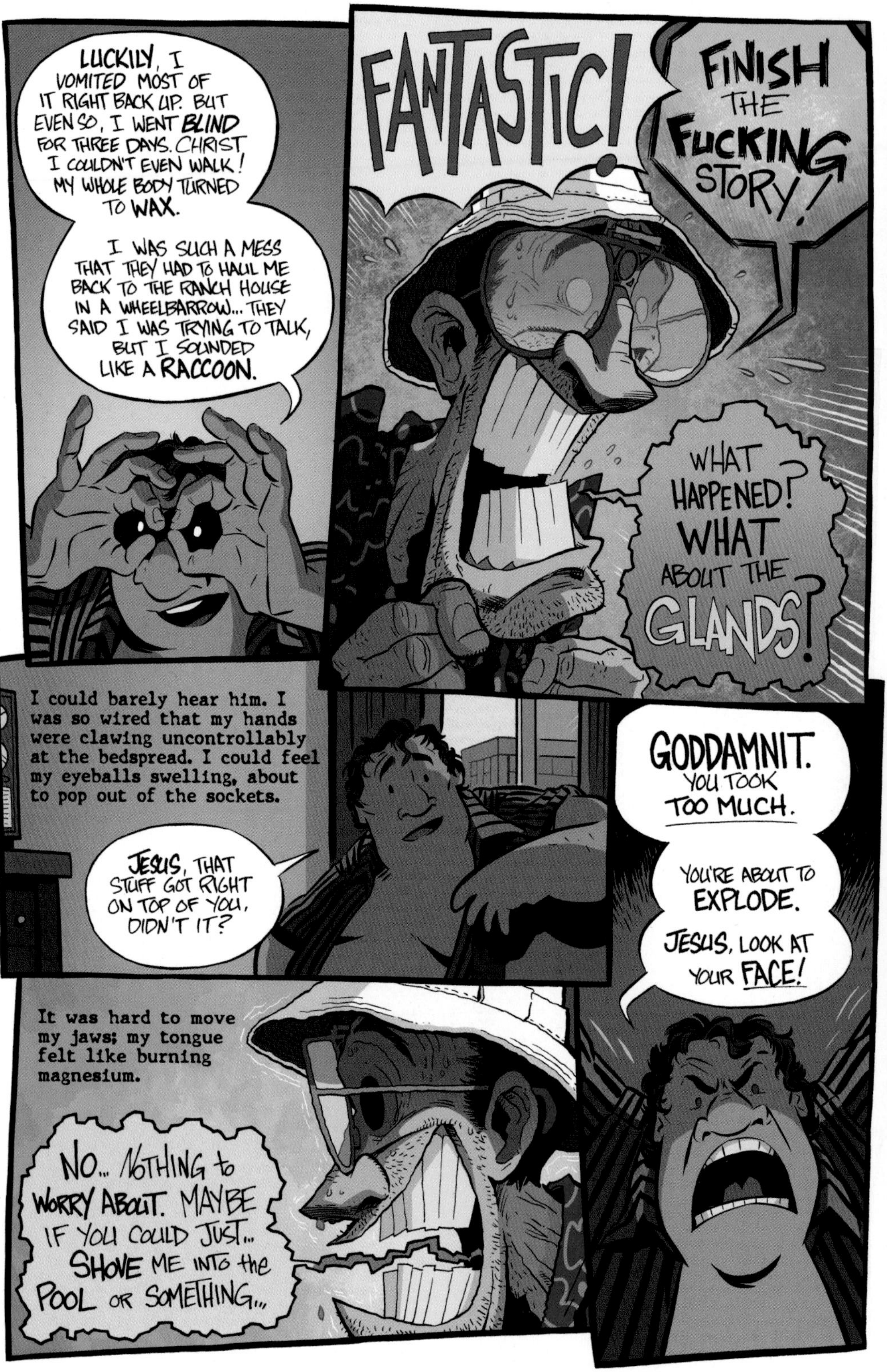
LUCKILY, I VOMITED MOST OF IT RIGHT BACK UP. BUT EVEN SO, I WENT BLIND FOR THREE DAYS. CHRIST, I COULDN'T EVEN WALK! MY WHOLE BODY TURNED TO WAX.
I WAS SUCH A MESS THAT THEY HAD TO HAUL ME BACK TO THE RANCH HOUSE IN A WHEELBARROW... THEY SAID I WAS TRYING TO TALK, BUT I SOUNDED LIKE A RACCOON.
FANTASTIC!
FINISH THE FUCKING STORY!
WHAT HAPPENED? WHAT ABOUT THE GLANDS?
I could barely hear him. I was so wired that my hands were clawing uncontrollably at the bedspread. I could feel my eyeballs swelling, about to pop out of the sockets.
JESUS, THAT STUFF GOT RIGHT ON TOP OF YOU, DIDN'T IT?
GODDAMNIT. YOU TOOK TOO MUCH.
YOU'RE ABOUT TO EXPLODE.
JESUS, LOOK AT YOUR FACE!
It was hard to move my jaws; my tongue felt like burning magnesium.
NO... NOTHING to WORRY ABOUT. MAYBE IF YOU COULD JUST... SHOVE ME INTO the POOL OR SOMETHING...

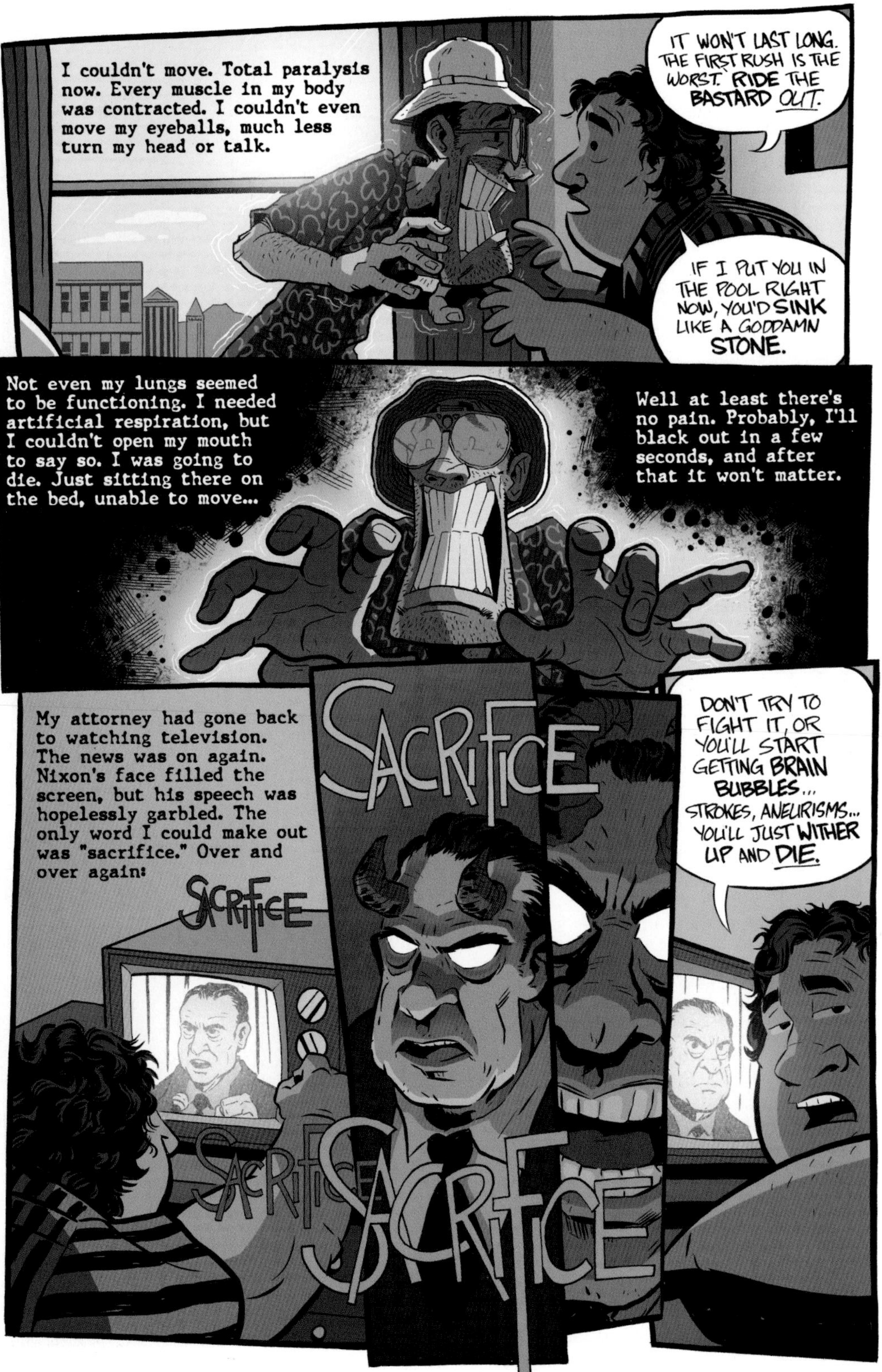
I couldn't move. Total paralysis now. Every muscle in my body was contracted. I couldn't even move my eyeballs, much less turn my head or talk.
IT WON'T LAST LONG. THE FIRST RUSH IS THE WORST. RIDE THE BASTARD OUT.
IF I PUT YOU IN THE POOL RIGHT NOW, YOU'D SINK LIKE A GODDAMN STONE.
Not even my lungs seemed to be functioning. I needed artificial respiration, but I couldn't open my mouth to say so. I was going to die. Just sitting there on the bed, unable to move...
Well at least there's no pain. Probably, I'll black out in a few seconds, and after that it won't matter.
My attorney had gone back to watching television. The news was on again. Nixon's face filled the screen, but his speech was hopelessly garbled. The only word I could make out was "sacrifice." Over and over again:
SACRIFICE
SACRIFICE
DON'T TRY TO FIGHT IT, OR YOU'LL START GETTING BRAIN BUBBLES... STROKES, ANEURISMS... YOU'LL JUST WITHER UP AND DIE.
SACRIFICE
SACRIFICE

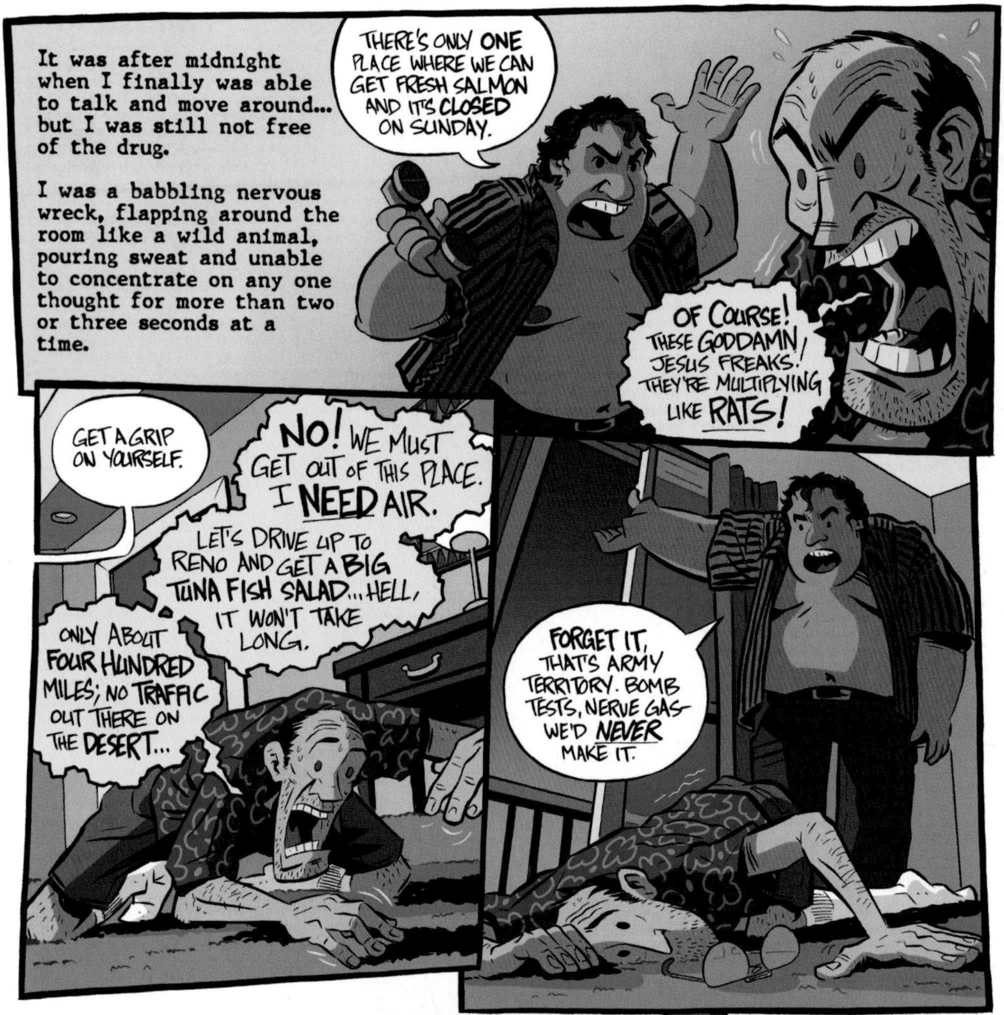
It was after midnight when I finally was able to talk and move around... but I was still not free of the drug.
I was a babbling nervous wreck, flapping around the room like a wild animal, pouring sweat and unable to concentrate on any one thought for more than two or three seconds at a time.
THERE'S ONLY ONE PLACE WHERE WE CAN GET FRESH SALMON AND IT'S CLOSED ON SUNDAY.
OF COURSE! THESE GODDAMN JESUS FREAKS! THEY'RE MULTIPLYING LIKE RATS!
GET A GRIP ON YOURSELF.
NO! WE MUST GET OUT OF THIS PLACE. I NEED AIR.
LET'S DRIVE UP TO RENO AND GET A BIG TUNA FISH SALAD... HELL, IT WON'T TAKE LONG.
ONLY ABOUT FOUR HUNDRED MILES; NO TRAFFIC OUT THERE ON THE DESERT...
FORGET IT, THAT'S ARMY TERRITORY. BOMB TESTS, NERVE GAS- WE'D NEVER MAKE IT.

We wound up at a place called The Big Flip about halfway downtown. I had a "New York steak" for $1.88. My attorney ordered the "Coyote Bush Basket" for $2.09... and after that we drank off a pot of watery coffee.

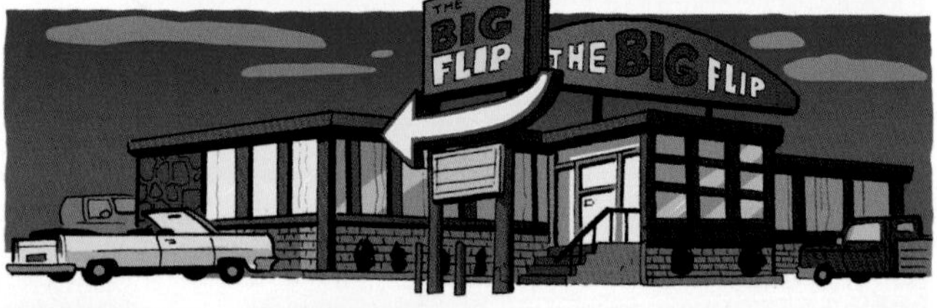
THE BIG FLIP
THE BIG FLIP

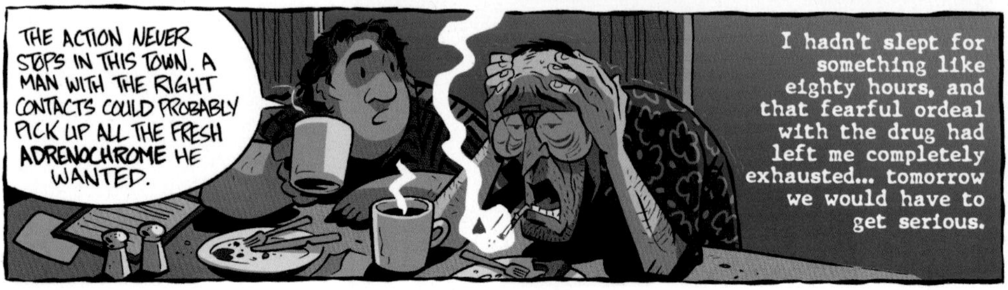
THE ACTION NEVER STOPS IN THIS TOWN. A MAN WITH THE RIGHT CONTACTS COULD PROBABLY PICK UP ALL THE FRESH ADRENOCHROME HE WANTED.
I hadn't slept for something like eighty hours, and that fearful ordeal with the drug had left me completely exhausted... tomorrow we would have to get serious.

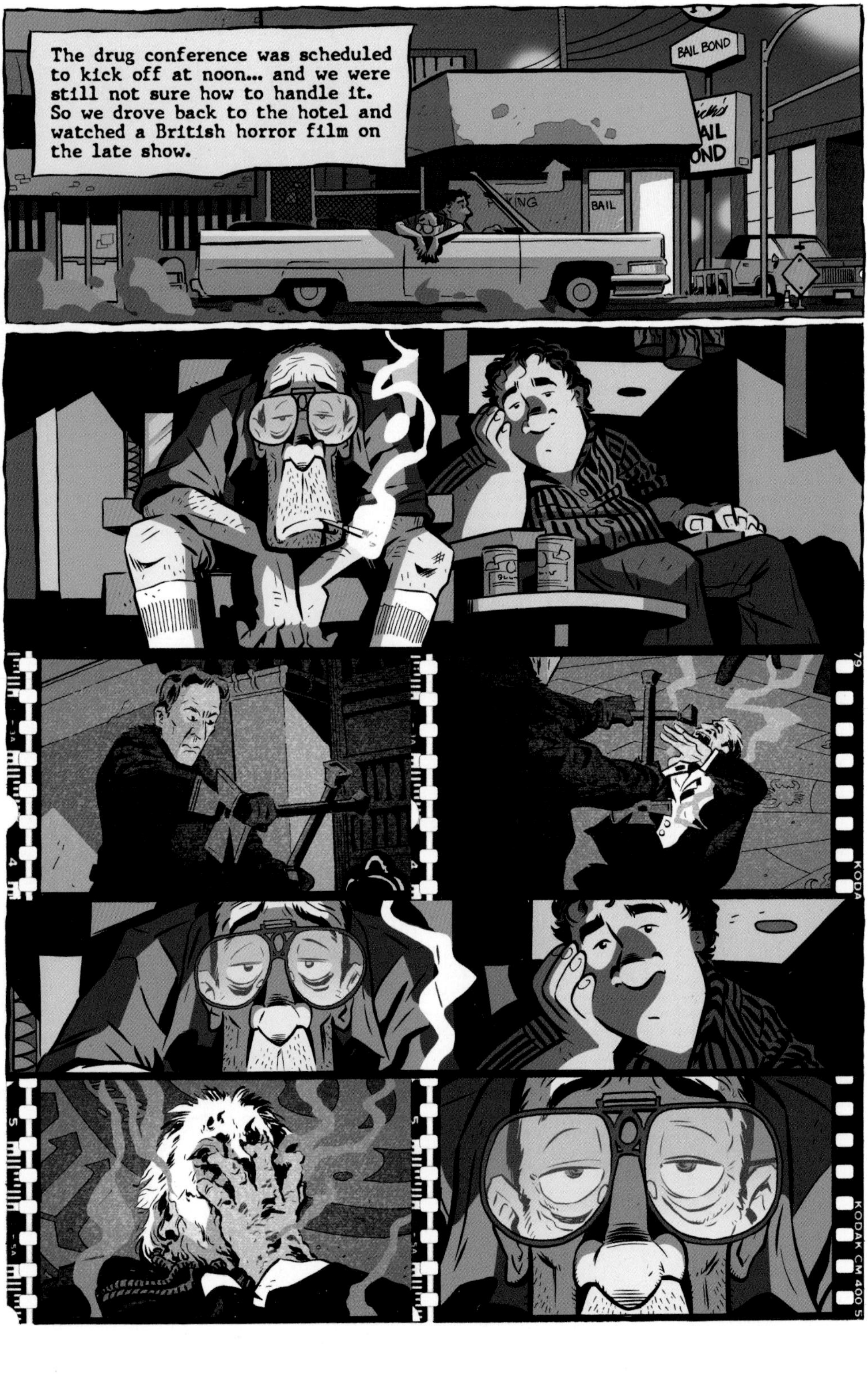
The drug conference was scheduled to kick off at noon... and we were still not sure how to handle it. So we drove back to the hotel and watched a British horror film on the late show.
BAIL BOND
BAIL

6. Getting Down to Business... Opening Day at the Drug Convention

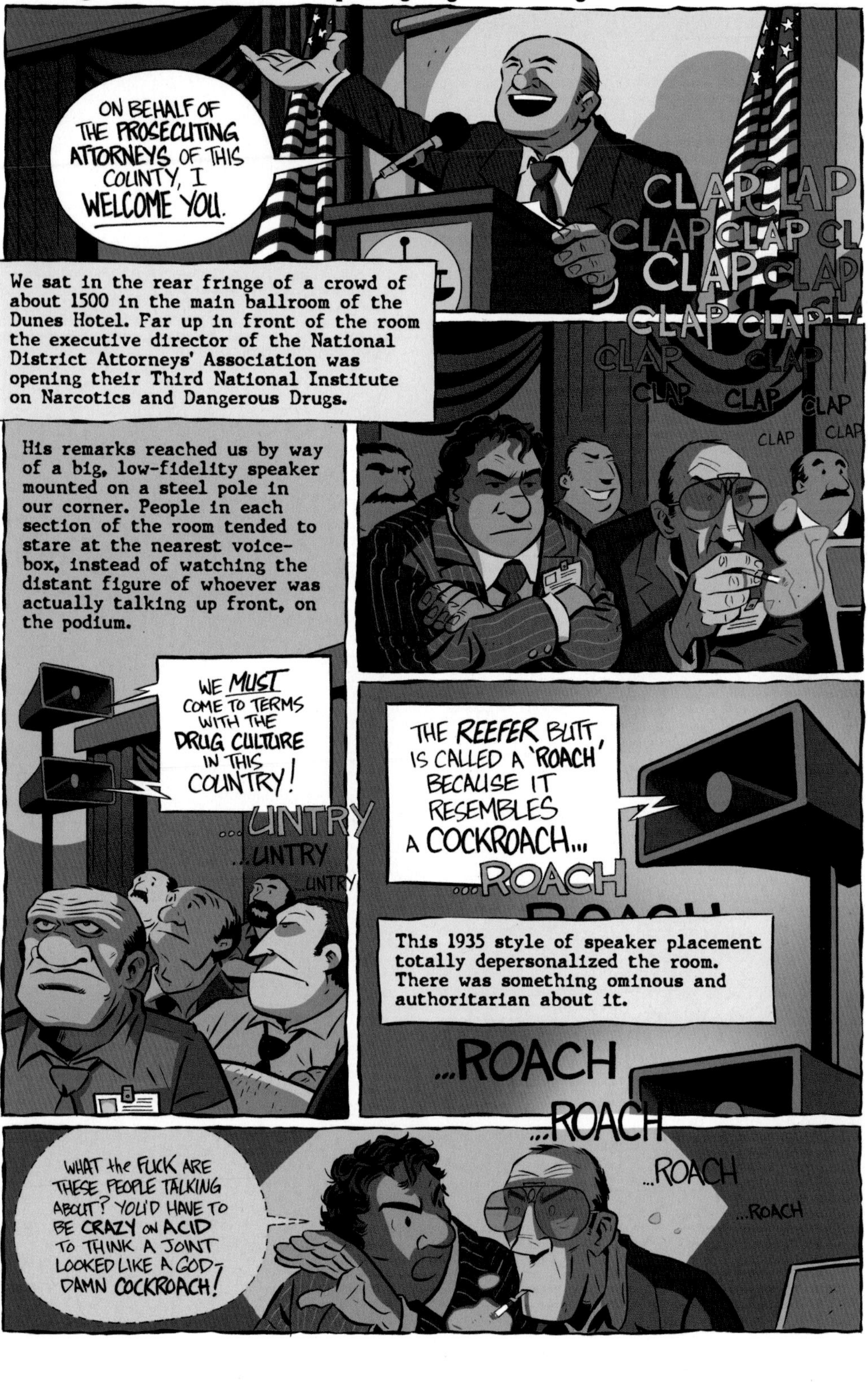

ON BEHALF OF THE PROSECUTING ATTORNEYS OF THIS COUNTY, I WELCOME YOU.
CLAP CLAP CLAP CLAP CLAP CLAP CLAP CLAP CLAP CLAP CLAP CLAP CLAP CLAP CLAP CLAP
We sat in the rear fringe of a crowd of about 1500 in the main ballroom of the Dunes Hotel. Far up in front of the room the executive director of the National District Attorneys' Association was opening their Third National Institute on Narcotics and Dangerous Drugs.
His remarks reached us by way of a big, low-fidelity speaker mounted on a steel pole in our corner. People in each section of the room tended to stare at the nearest voice-box, instead of watching the distant figure of whoever was actually talking up front, on the podium.
WE MUST COME TO TERMS WITH THE DRUG CULTURE IN THIS COUNTRY!
...UNTRY
...UNTRY
...UNTRY
THE REEFER BUTT, IS CALLED A 'ROACH' BECAUSE IT RESEMBLES A COCKROACH...
...ROACH
This 1935 style of speaker placement totally depersonalized the room. There was something ominous and authoritarian about it.
...ROACH
...ROACH
WHAT the FUCK ARE THESE PEOPLE TALKING ABOUT? YOU'D HAVE TO BE CRAZY ON ACID TO THINK A JOINT LOOKED LIKE A GOD-DAMN COCKROACH!
...ROACH
...ROACH

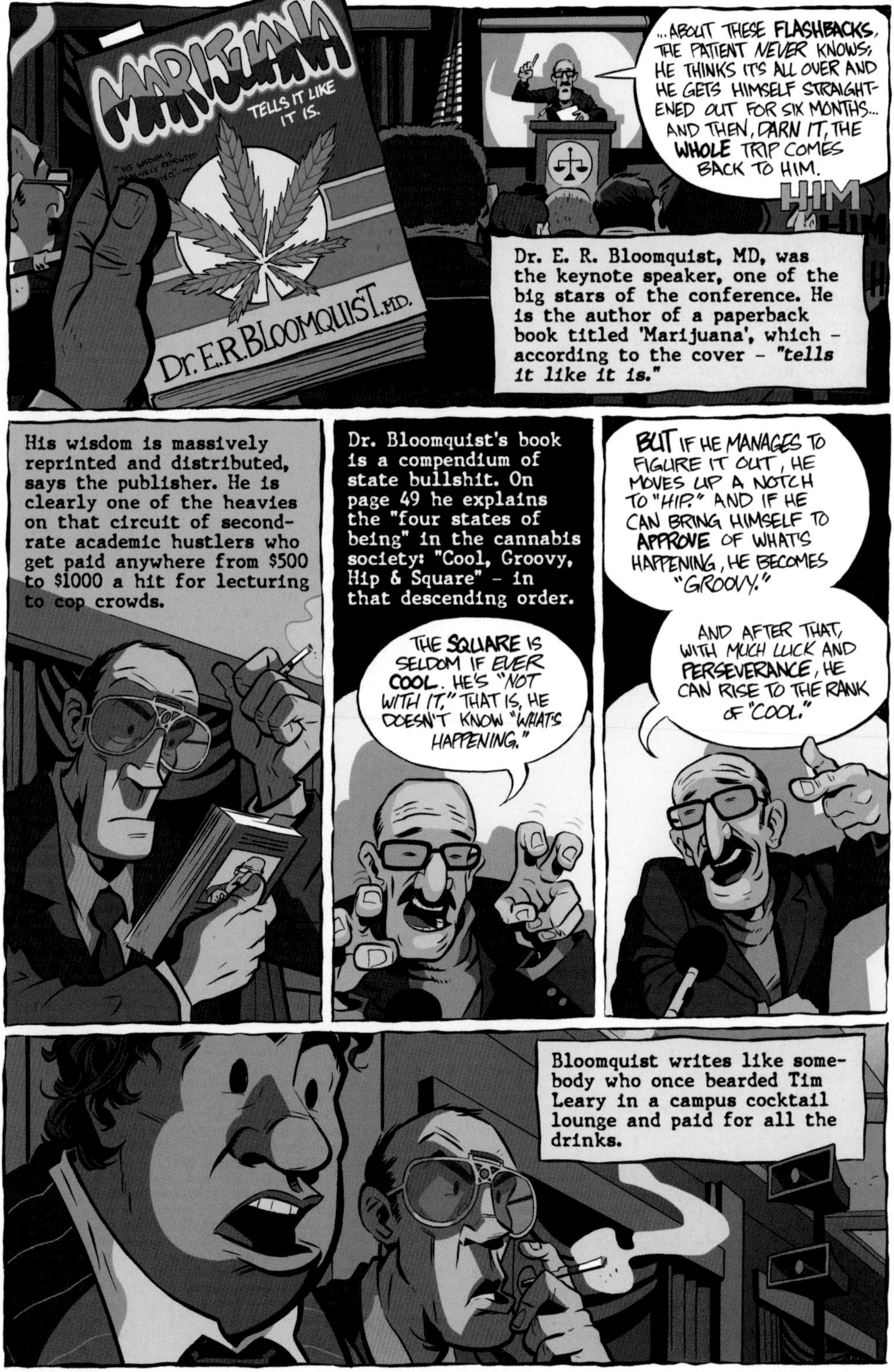
MARIJUANA
TELLS IT LIKE IT IS.
Dr. E.R. BLOOMQUIST, M.D.
...ABOUT THESE **FLASHBACKS**, THE PATIENT *NEVER* KNOWS; HE THINKS IT'S ALL OVER AND HE GETS HIMSELF STRAIGHTENED OUT FOR SIX MONTHS... AND THEN, *DARN IT*, THE **WHOLE** TRIP COMES BACK TO HIM.
HIM
Dr. E. R. Bloomquist, MD, was the keynote speaker, one of the big stars of the conference. He is the author of a paperback book titled 'Marijuana', which - according to the cover - *"tells it like it is."*
His wisdom is massively reprinted and distributed, says the publisher. He is clearly one of the heavies on that circuit of second-rate academic hustlers who get paid anywhere from $500 to $1000 a hit for lecturing to cop crowds.
Dr. Bloomquist's book is a compendium of state bullshit. On page 49 he explains the "four states of being" in the cannabis society: "Cool, Groovy, Hip & Square" - in that descending order.
THE **SQUARE** IS SELDOM IF *EVER* **COOL**. HE'S *"NOT WITH IT,"* THAT IS, HE DOESN'T KNOW *"WHAT'S HAPPENING."*
BUT IF HE **MANAGES** TO FIGURE IT OUT, HE MOVES UP A NOTCH TO "HIP." AND IF HE CAN BRING HIMSELF TO **APPROVE** OF WHAT'S HAPPENING, HE BECOMES "GROOVY."
AND AFTER THAT, WITH MUCH LUCK AND **PERSEVERANCE**, HE CAN RISE TO THE RANK OF "COOL."
Bloomquist writes like somebody who once bearded Tim Leary in a campus cocktail lounge and paid for all the drinks.

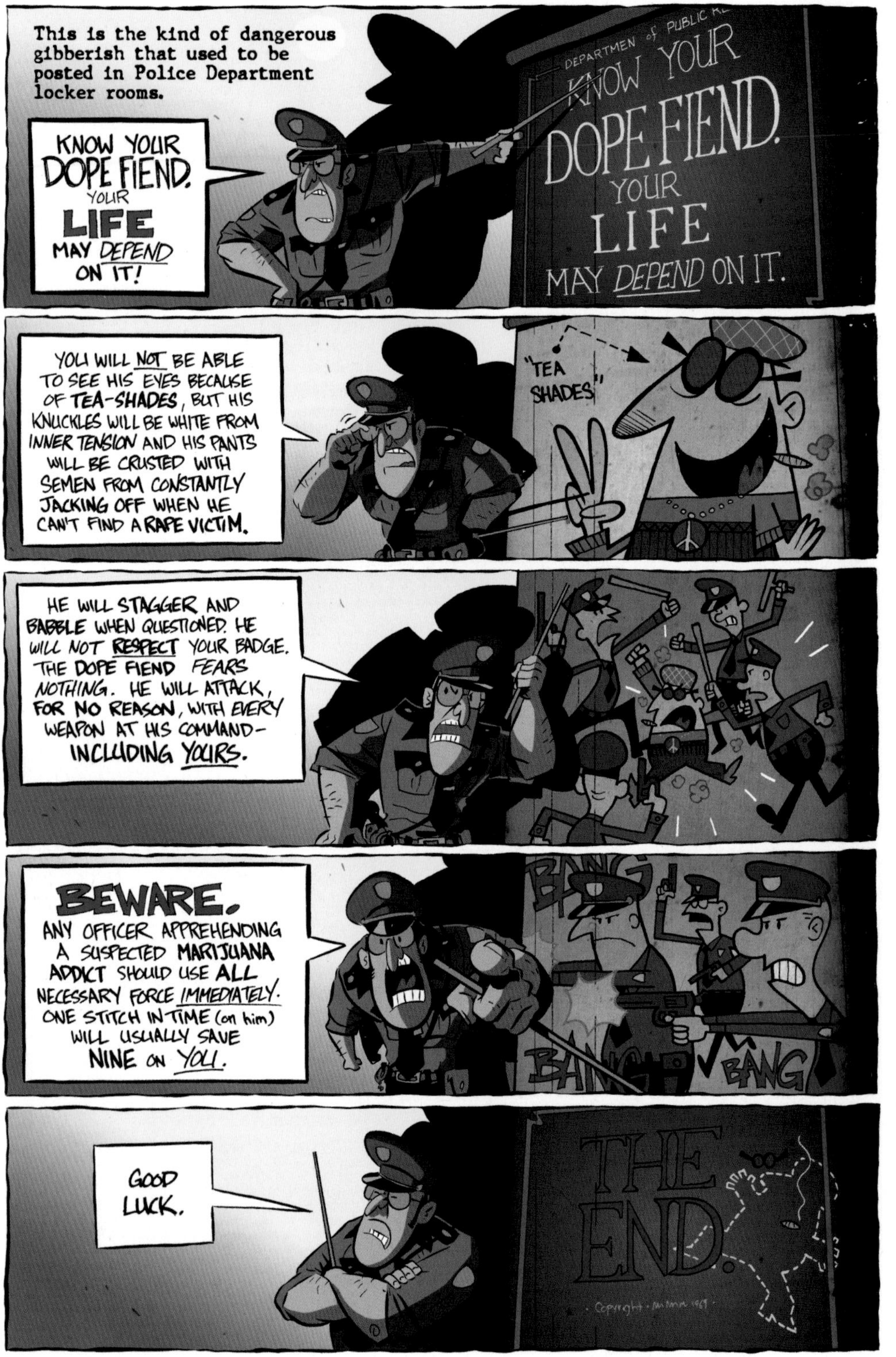
This is the kind of dangerous gibberish that used to be posted in Police Department locker rooms.
KNOW YOUR DOPE FIEND. YOUR LIFE MAY DEPEND ON IT!
KNOW YOUR DOPE FIEND. YOUR LIFE MAY DEPEND ON IT.
YOU WILL NOT BE ABLE TO SEE HIS EYES BECAUSE OF TEA-SHADES, BUT HIS KNUCKLES WILL BE WHITE FROM INNER TENSION AND HIS PANTS WILL BE CRUSTED WITH SEMEN FROM CONSTANTLY JACKING OFF WHEN HE CAN'T FIND A RAPE VICTIM.
"TEA SHADES"
HE WILL STAGGER AND BABBLE WHEN QUESTIONED. HE WILL NOT RESPECT YOUR BADGE. THE DOPE FIEND FEARS NOTHING. HE WILL ATTACK, FOR NO REASON, WITH EVERY WEAPON AT HIS COMMAND- INCLUDING YOURS.
BEWARE. ANY OFFICER APPREHENDING A SUSPECTED MARIJUANA ADDICT SHOULD USE ALL NECESSARY FORCE IMMEDIATELY. ONE STITCH IN TIME (on him) WILL USUALLY SAVE NINE ON YOU.
BANG
BANG
BANG
GOOD LUCK.
THE END.

7. If You Don't Know, Come to Learn... If You Know, Come to Teach

It was clear at a glance that this Drug Conference was not what we'd planned on. The room fairly bristled with beards, mustaches and super-Mod dress. The DAs' conference had obviously drawn a goodly contingent of undercover narcs and other twilight types.

These were the people who made my attorney nervous. Like most Californians, he was shocked to actually see these people from The Outback. Jesus, they looked and talked like a gang of drunken pig farmers!

THEY'RE ACTUALLY NICE PEOPLE ONCE YOU GET TO KNOW THEM.

KNOW THEM? ARE YOU **KIDDING!**

MAN, I KNOW THESE PEOPLE IN MY GODDAMN **BLOOD!**

DON'T MENTION THAT WORD AROUND HERE, YOU'LL GET THEM **EXCITED.**

YOU'RE RIGHT. I SAW THESE **BASTARDS** IN "EASY RIDER," BUT I DIDN'T BELIEVE THEY WERE **REAL.**

NOT LIKE **THIS.**

NOT HUNDREDS/ OF THEM!

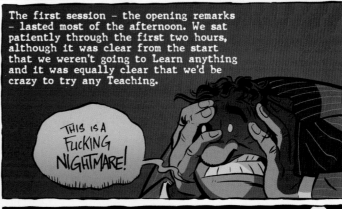

The first session – the opening remarks – lasted most of the afternoon. We sat patiently through the first two hours, although it was clear from the start that we weren't going to Learn anything and it was equally clear that we'd be crazy to try any Teaching.

THIS IS A **FUCKING NIGHTMARE!**

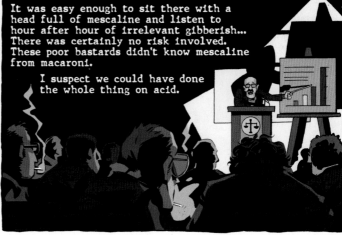

It was easy enough to sit there with a head full of mescaline and listen to hour after hour of irrelevant gibberish... There was certainly no risk involved. These poor bastards didn't know mescaline from macaroni.

I suspect we could have done the whole thing on acid.

131

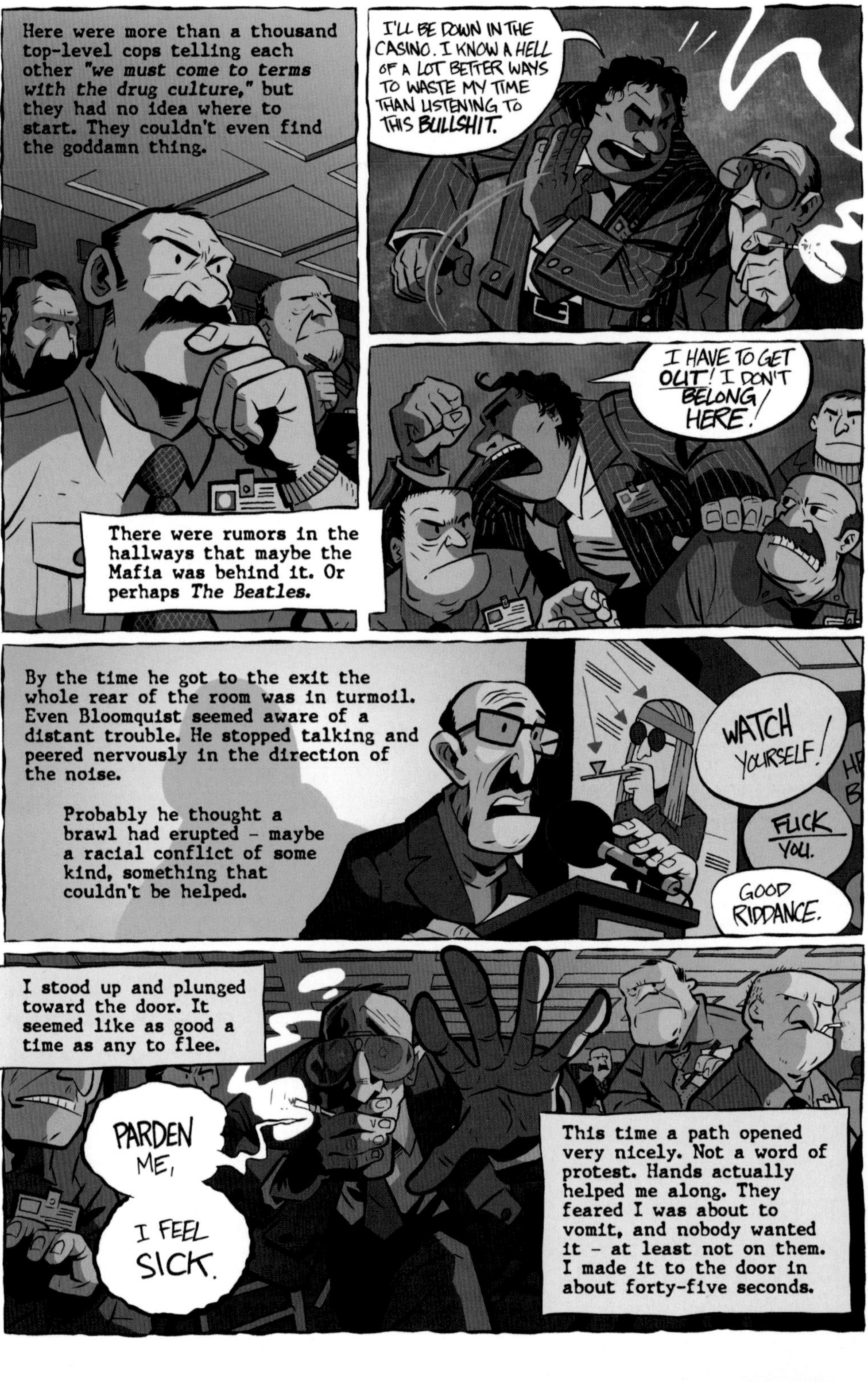
Here were more than a thousand top-level cops telling each other "we must come to terms with the drug culture," but they had no idea where to start. They couldn't even find the goddamn thing.
There were rumors in the hallways that maybe the Mafia was behind it. Or perhaps The Beatles.
I'LL BE DOWN IN THE CASINO. I KNOW A HELL OF A LOT BETTER WAYS TO WASTE MY TIME THAN LISTENING TO THIS BULLSHIT.
I HAVE TO GET OUT! I DON'T BELONG HERE!
By the time he got to the exit the whole rear of the room was in turmoil. Even Bloomquist seemed aware of a distant trouble. He stopped talking and peered nervously in the direction of the noise.
Probably he thought a brawl had erupted - maybe a racial conflict of some kind, something that couldn't be helped.
WATCH YOURSELF!
FUCK YOU.
GOOD RIDDANCE.
I stood up and plunged toward the door. It seemed like as good a time as any to flee.
PARDEN ME,
I FEEL SICK.
This time a path opened very nicely. Not a word of protest. Hands actually helped me along. They feared I was about to vomit, and nobody wanted it - at least not on them. I made it to the door in about forty-five seconds.

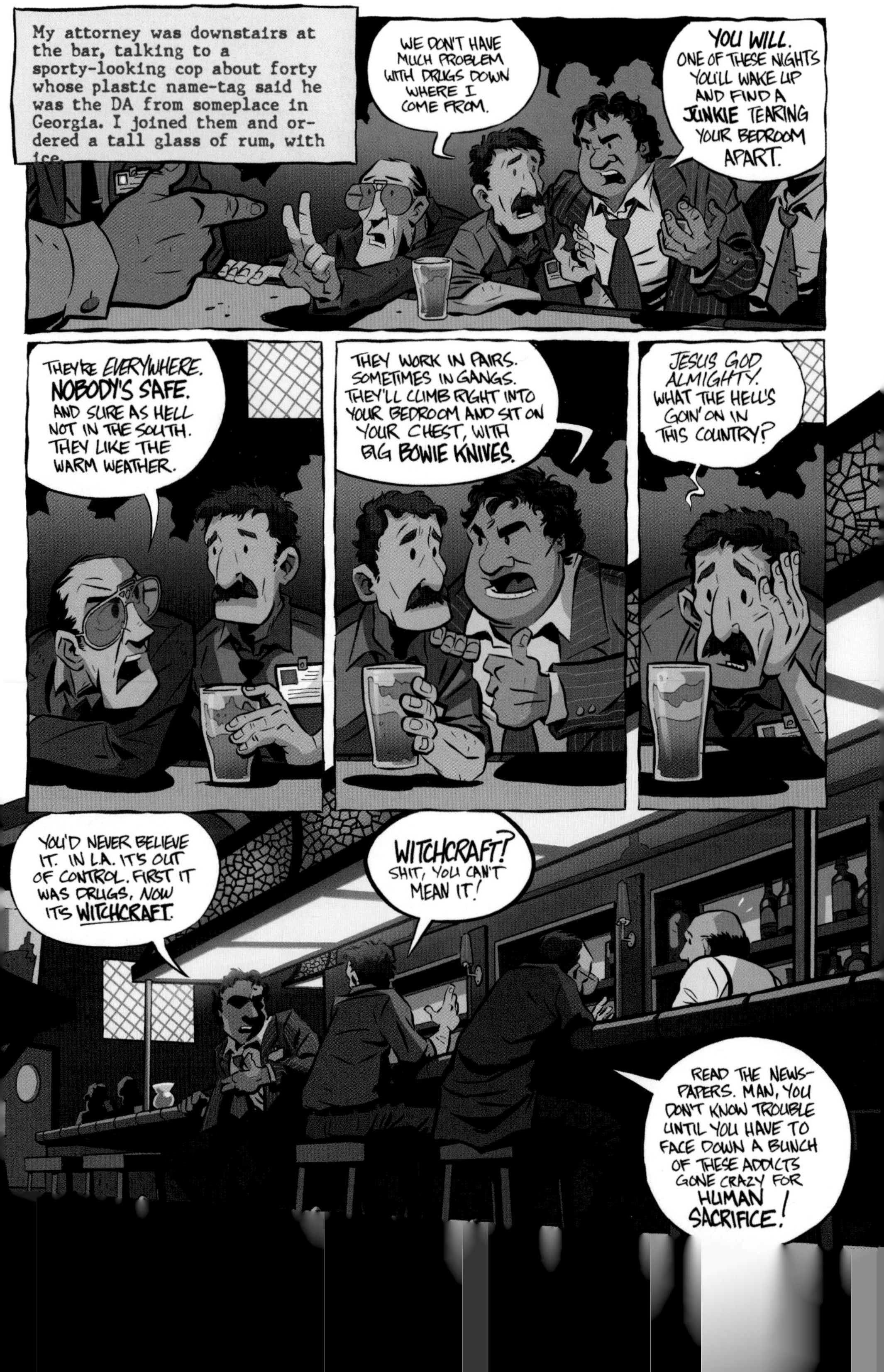
My attorney was downstairs at the bar, talking to a sporty-looking cop about forty whose plastic name-tag said he was the DA from someplace in Georgia. I joined them and ordered a tall glass of rum, with ice.
WE DON'T HAVE MUCH PROBLEM WITH DRUGS DOWN WHERE I COME FROM.
YOU WILL. ONE OF THESE NIGHTS YOU'LL WAKE UP AND FIND A JUNKIE TEARING YOUR BEDROOM APART.
THEY'RE EVERYWHERE. NOBODY'S SAFE. AND SURE AS HELL NOT IN THE SOUTH. THEY LIKE THE WARM WEATHER.
THEY WORK IN PAIRS. SOMETIMES IN GANGS. THEY'LL CLIMB RIGHT INTO YOUR BEDROOM AND SIT ON YOUR CHEST, WITH BIG BOWIE KNIVES.
JESUS GOD ALMIGHTY. WHAT THE HELL'S GOIN' ON IN THIS COUNTRY?
YOU'D NEVER BELIEVE IT. IN L.A. IT'S OUT OF CONTROL. FIRST IT WAS DRUGS, NOW IT'S WITCHCRAFT.
WITCHCRAFT? SHIT, YOU CAN'T MEAN IT!
READ THE NEWSPAPERS. MAN, YOU DON'T KNOW TROUBLE UNTIL YOU HAVE TO FACE DOWN A BUNCH OF THESE ADDICTS GONE CRAZY FOR HUMAN SACRIFICE!

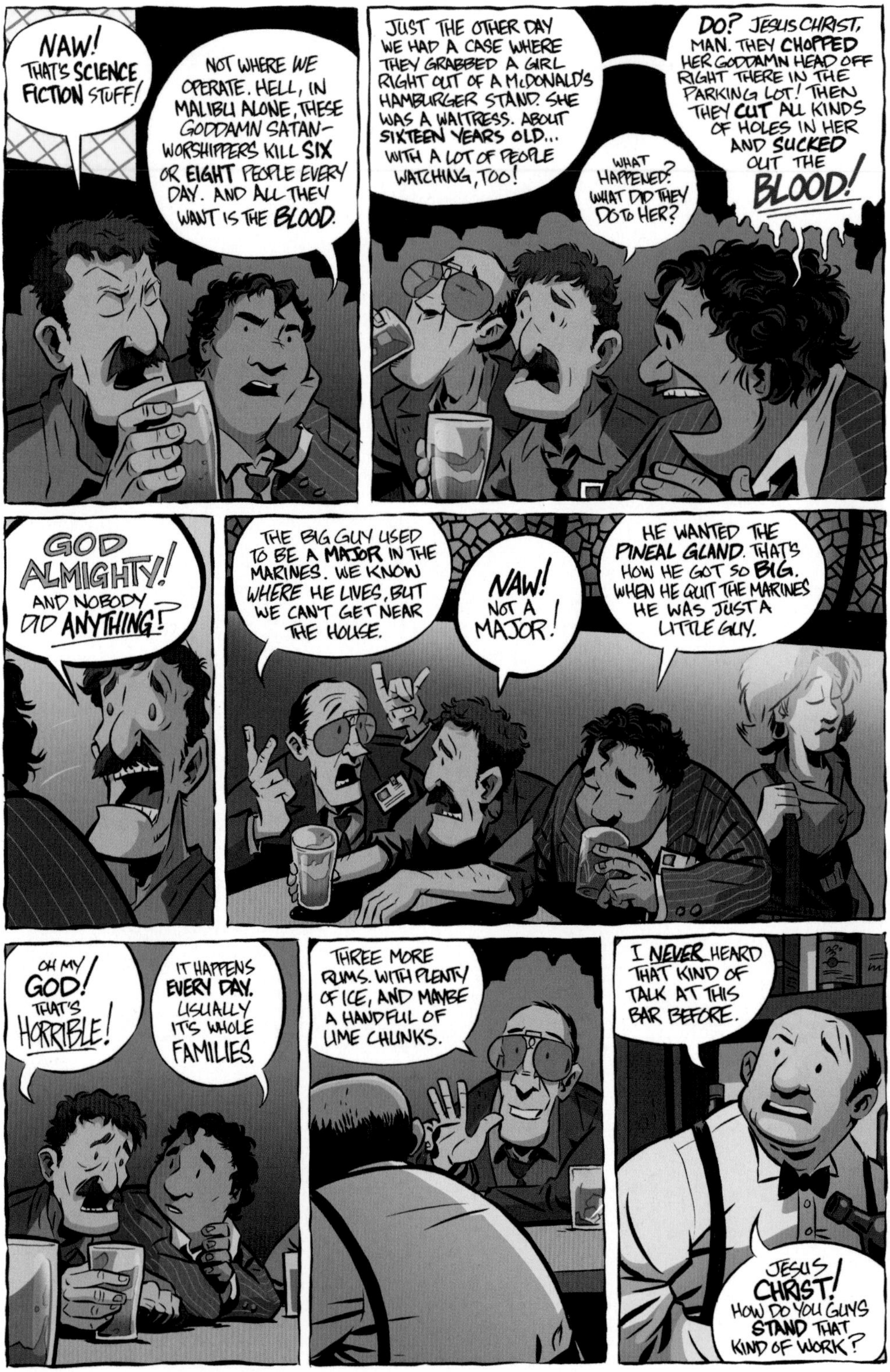

NAW! THAT'S SCIENCE FICTION STUFF!
NOT WHERE WE OPERATE. HELL, IN MALIBU ALONE, THESE GODDAMN SATAN-WORSHIPPERS KILL SIX OR EIGHT PEOPLE EVERY DAY. AND ALL THEY WANT IS THE BLOOD.
JUST THE OTHER DAY WE HAD A CASE WHERE THEY GRABBED A GIRL RIGHT OUT OF A McDONALD'S HAMBURGER STAND. SHE WAS A WAITRESS. ABOUT SIXTEEN YEARS OLD... WITH A LOT OF PEOPLE WATCHING, TOO!
WHAT HAPPENED? WHAT DID THEY DO TO HER?
DO? JESUS CHRIST, MAN. THEY CHOPPED HER GODDAMN HEAD OFF RIGHT THERE IN THE PARKING LOT! THEN THEY CUT ALL KINDS OF HOLES IN HER AND SUCKED OUT THE BLOOD!
GOD ALMIGHTY! AND NOBODY DID ANYTHING?
THE BIG GUY USED TO BE A MAJOR IN THE MARINES. WE KNOW WHERE HE LIVES, BUT WE CAN'T GET NEAR THE HOUSE.
NAW! NOT A MAJOR!
HE WANTED THE PINEAL GLAND. THAT'S HOW HE GOT SO BIG. WHEN HE QUIT THE MARINES HE WAS JUST A LITTLE GUY.
OH MY GOD! THAT'S HORRIBLE!
IT HAPPENS EVERY DAY. USUALLY IT'S WHOLE FAMILIES.
THREE MORE RUMS. WITH PLENTY OF ICE, AND MAYBE A HANDFUL OF LIME CHUNKS.
I NEVER HEARD THAT KIND OF TALK AT THIS BAR BEFORE.
JESUS CHRIST! HOW DO YOU GUYS STAND THAT KIND OF WORK?

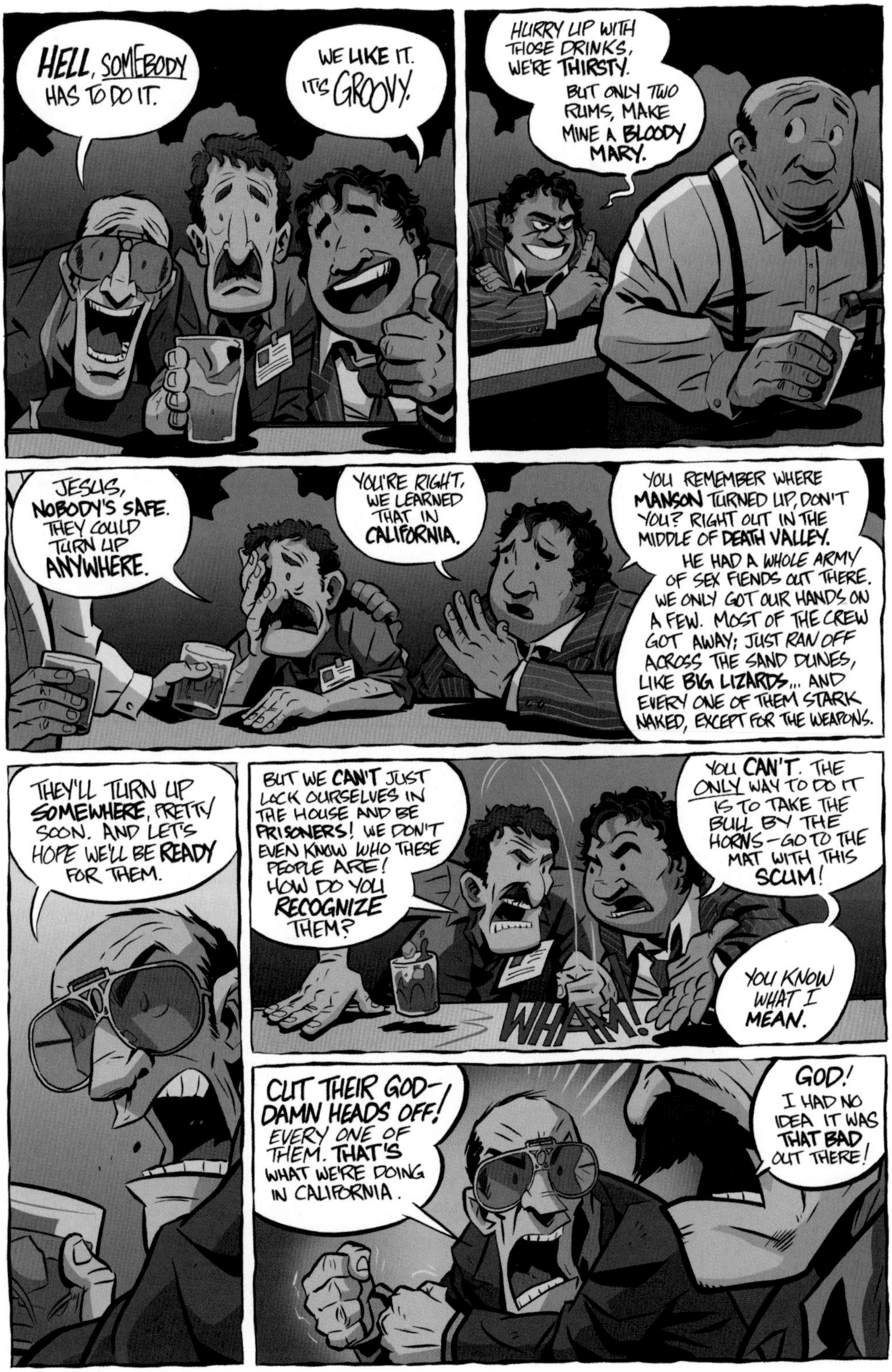
HELL, SOMEBODY HAS TO DO IT.
WE LIKE IT. IT'S GROOVY.
HURRY UP WITH THOSE DRINKS, WE'RE THIRSTY.
BUT ONLY TWO RUMS, MAKE MINE A BLOODY MARY.
JESUS, NOBODY'S SAFE. THEY COULD TURN UP ANYWHERE.
YOU'RE RIGHT, WE LEARNED THAT IN CALIFORNIA.
YOU REMEMBER WHERE MANSON TURNED UP, DON'T YOU? RIGHT OUT IN THE MIDDLE OF DEATH VALLEY.
HE HAD A WHOLE ARMY OF SEX FIENDS OUT THERE. WE ONLY GOT OUR HANDS ON A FEW. MOST OF THE CREW GOT AWAY; JUST RAN OFF ACROSS THE SAND DUNES, LIKE BIG LIZARDS... AND EVERY ONE OF THEM STARK NAKED, EXCEPT FOR THE WEAPONS.
THEY'LL TURN UP SOMEWHERE, PRETTY SOON. AND LET'S HOPE WE'LL BE READY FOR THEM.
BUT WE CAN'T JUST LOCK OURSELVES IN THE HOUSE AND BE PRISONERS! WE DON'T EVEN KNOW WHO THESE PEOPLE ARE! HOW DO YOU RECOGNIZE THEM?
YOU CAN'T. THE ONLY WAY TO DO IT IS TO TAKE THE BULL BY THE HORNS—GO TO THE MAT WITH THIS SCUM!
WHAM!
YOU KNOW WHAT I MEAN.
CUT THEIR GOD-DAMN HEADS OFF! EVERY ONE OF THEM. THAT'S WHAT WE'RE DOING IN CALIFORNIA.
GOD! I HAD NO IDEA IT WAS THAT BAD OUT THERE!

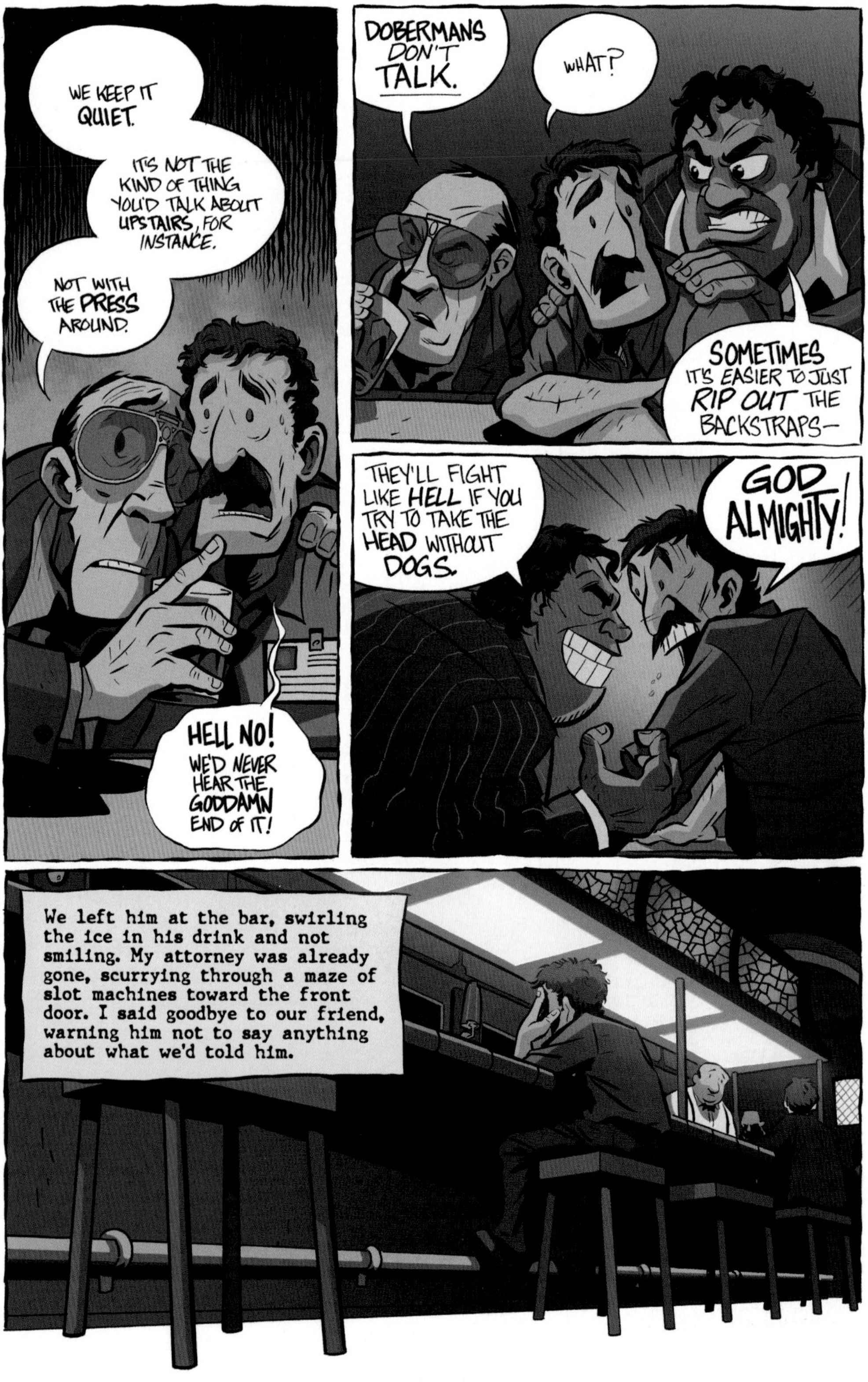
WE KEEP IT QUIET.
IT'S NOT THE KIND OF THING YOU'D TALK ABOUT UPSTAIRS, FOR INSTANCE.
NOT WITH THE PRESS AROUND.
HELL NO! WE'D NEVER HEAR THE GODDAMN END OF IT!
DOBERMANS DON'T TALK.
WHAT?
SOMETIMES IT'S EASIER TO JUST RIP OUT THE BACKSTRAPS—
THEY'LL FIGHT LIKE HELL IF YOU TRY TO TAKE THE HEAD WITHOUT DOGS.
GOD ALMIGHTY!
We left him at the bar, swirling the ice in his drink and not smiling. My attorney was already gone, scurrying through a maze of slot machines toward the front door. I said goodbye to our friend, warning him not to say anything about what we'd told him.

8. Back Door Beauty... & Finally a Bit of Serious Drag Racing on the Strip

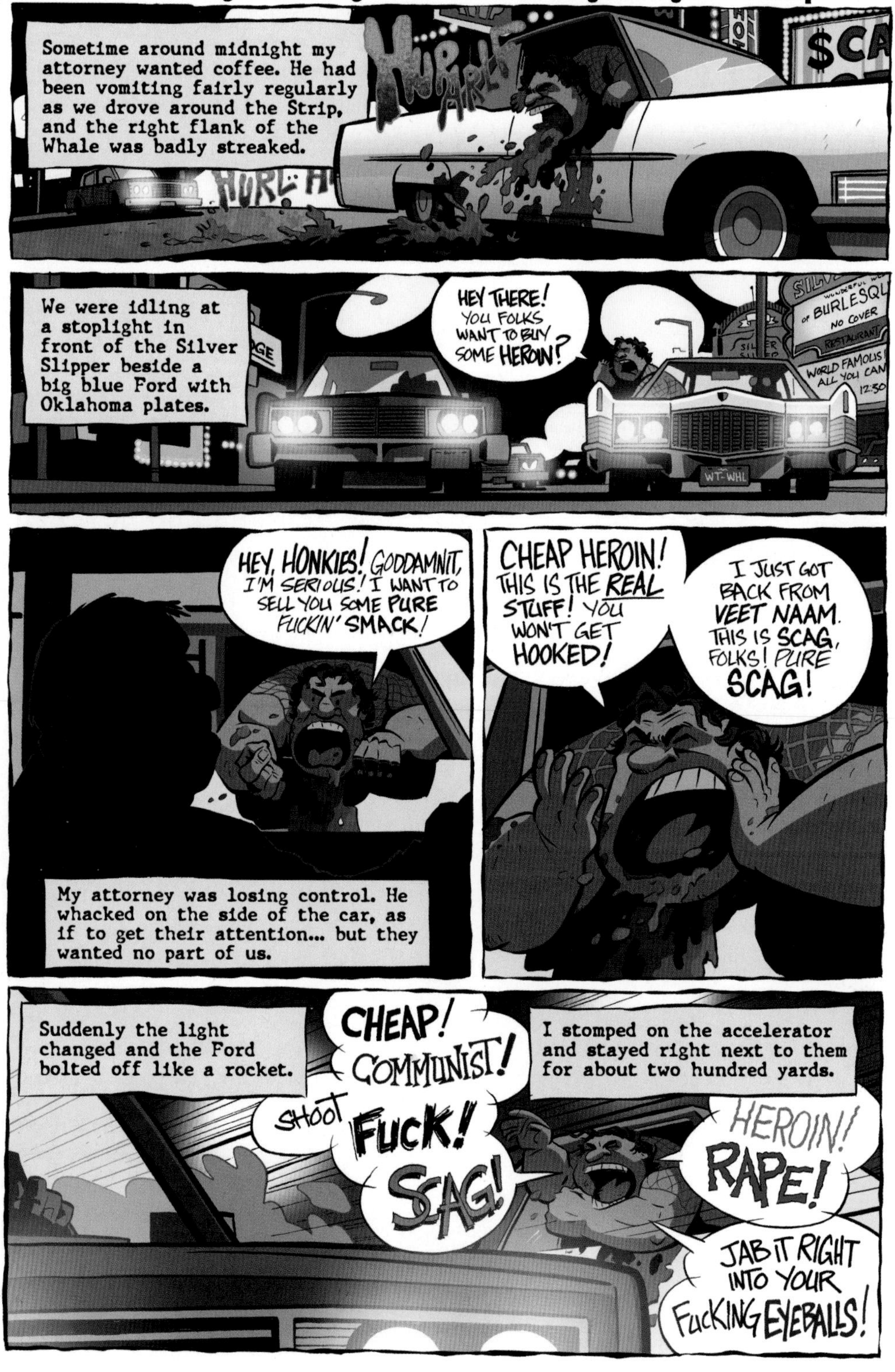
Sometime around midnight my attorney wanted coffee. He had been vomiting fairly regularly as we drove around the Strip, and the right flank of the Whale was badly streaked.
HURL
We were idling at a stoplight in front of the Silver Slipper beside a big blue Ford with Oklahoma plates.
HEY THERE! YOU FOLKS WANT TO BUY SOME HEROIN?
OF BURLESQU
NO COVER
RESTAURANT
WT-WHL
HEY, HONKIES! GODDAMNIT, I'M SERIOUS! I WANT TO SELL YOU SOME PURE FUCKIN' SMACK!
My attorney was losing control. He whacked on the side of the car, as if to get their attention... but they wanted no part of us.
CHEAP HEROIN! THIS IS THE REAL STUFF! YOU WON'T GET HOOKED!
I JUST GOT BACK FROM VEET NAAM. THIS IS SCAG, FOLKS! PURE SCAG!
Suddenly the light changed and the Ford bolted off like a rocket.
CHEAP! COMMUNIST!
SHOOT
FUCK!
SCAG!
I stomped on the accelerator and stayed right next to them for about two hundred yards.
HEROIN!
RAPE!
JAB IT RIGHT INTO YOUR FUCKING EYEBALLS!

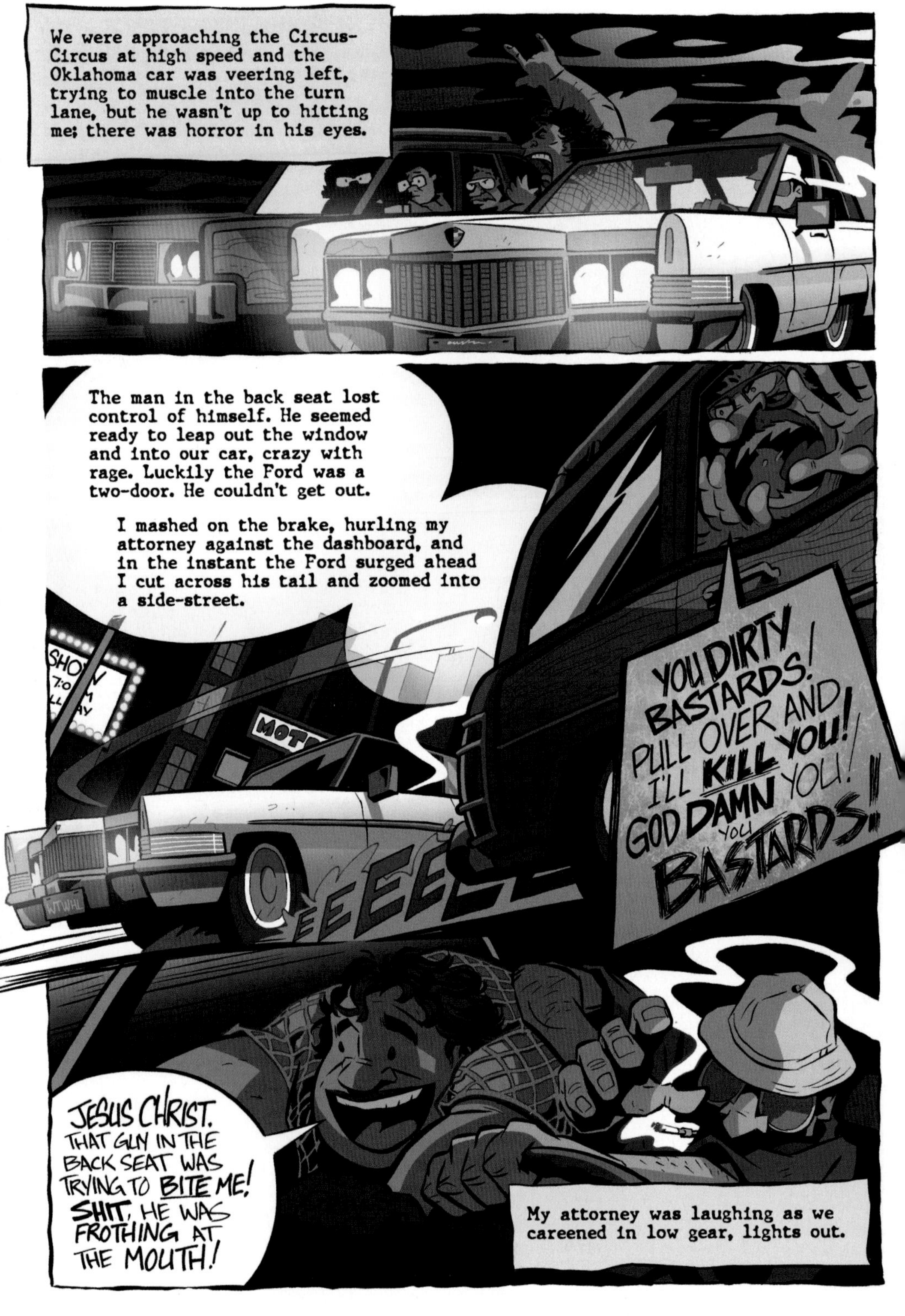

We were approaching the Circus-Circus at high speed and the Oklahoma car was veering left, trying to muscle into the turn lane, but he wasn't up to hitting me; there was horror in his eyes.
The man in the back seat lost control of himself. He seemed ready to leap out the window and into our car, crazy with rage. Luckily the Ford was a two-door. He couldn't get out.
I mashed on the brake, hurling my attorney against the dashboard, and in the instant the Ford surged ahead I cut across his tail and zoomed into a side-street.
YOU DIRTY BASTARDS! PULL OVER AND I'LL KILL YOU! GOD DAMN YOU! YOU BASTARDS!!
EEEEE
JESUS CHRIST. THAT GUY IN THE BACK SEAT WAS TRYING TO BITE ME! SHIT, HE WAS FROTHING AT THE MOUTH!
My attorney was laughing as we careened in low gear, lights out.

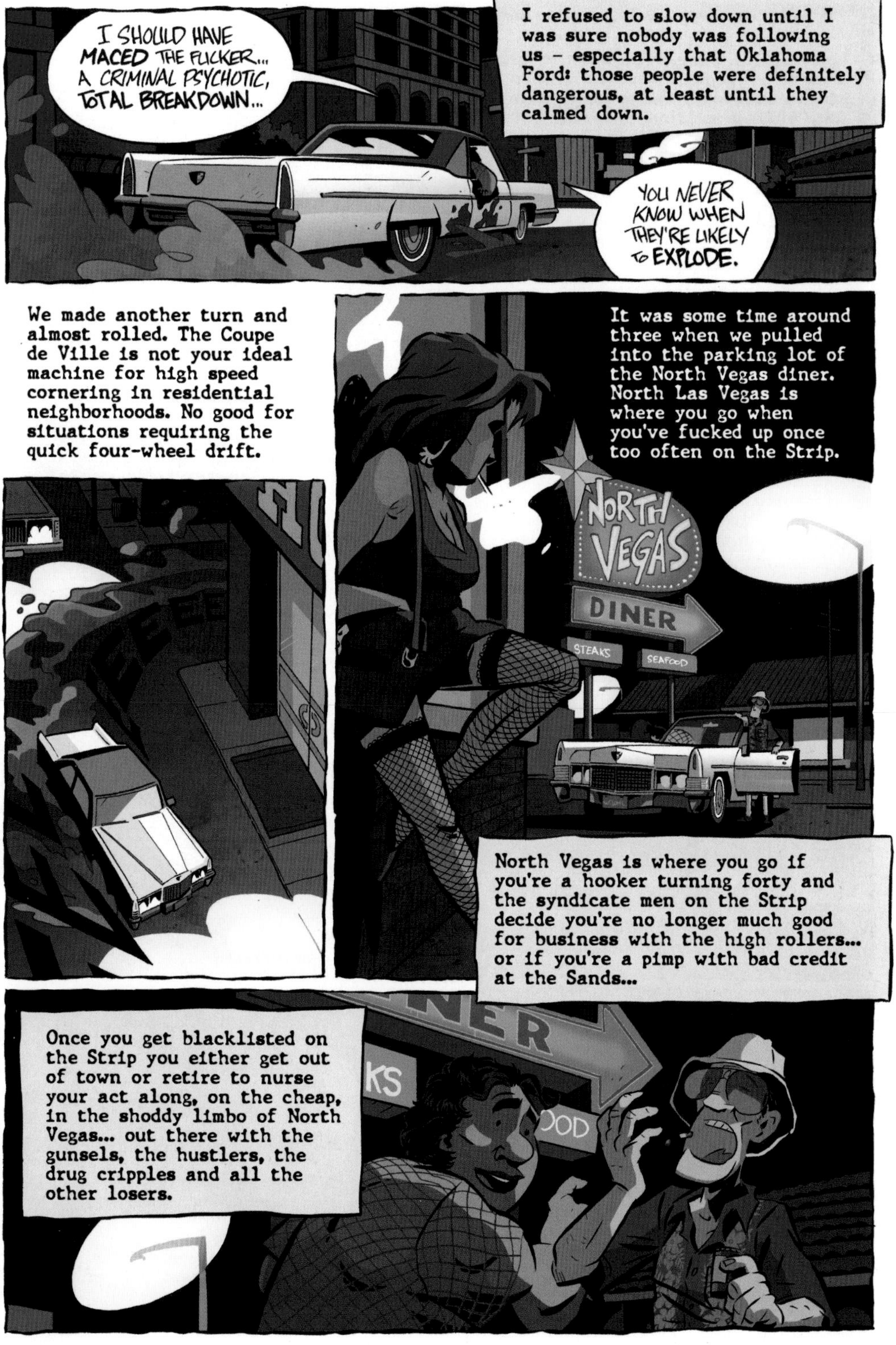
I refused to slow down until I was sure nobody was following us - especially that Oklahoma Ford: those people were definitely dangerous, at least until they calmed down.
I SHOULD HAVE MACED THE FUCKER... A CRIMINAL PSYCHOTIC, TOTAL BREAKDOWN...
YOU NEVER KNOW WHEN THEY'RE LIKELY TO EXPLODE.
We made another turn and almost rolled. The Coupe de Ville is not your ideal machine for high speed cornering in residential neighborhoods. No good for situations requiring the quick four-wheel drift.
It was some time around three when we pulled into the parking lot of the North Vegas diner. North Las Vegas is where you go when you've fucked up once too often on the Strip.
NORTH VEGAS
DINER
STEAKS
SEAFOOD
North Vegas is where you go if you're a hooker turning forty and the syndicate men on the Strip decide you're no longer much good for business with the high rollers... or if you're a pimp with bad credit at the Sands...
Once you get blacklisted on the Strip you either get out of town or retire to nurse your act along, on the cheap, in the shoddy limbo of North Vegas... out there with the gunsels, the hustlers, the drug cripples and all the other losers.

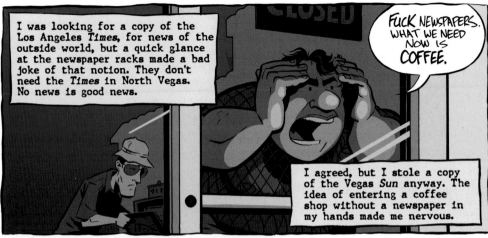

I was looking for a copy of the Los Angeles *Times*, for news of the outside world, but a quick glance at the newspaper racks made a bad joke of that notion. They don't need the *Times* in North Vegas. No news is good news.

FUCK NEWSPAPERS. WHAT WE NEED NOW IS COFFEE.

I agreed, but I stole a copy of the Vegas *Sun* anyway. The idea of entering a coffee shop without a newspaper in my hands made me nervous.

The North Star Coffee Lounge seemed like a fairly safe haven from our storms. There was nothing in the atmosphere to put me on my guard.

A CUP OF BLACK COFFEE ...

The waitress was passively hostile, but I was accustomed to that. She was a big woman. Not fat, but large in every way, long sinewy arms and a brawler's jawbone. Big head of dark hair, face slashed with lipstick and a 48 Double-E chest that was probably spec- tacular about twenty years ago.

YOU?

... AND A 29 CENT HAMBURGER WITH PICKLES AND ONION.

TWO GLASSES OF ICE WATER—

WITH ICE.

My attorney had no newspaper or anything else to compel his attention. So he focused, out of boredom, on the waitress.

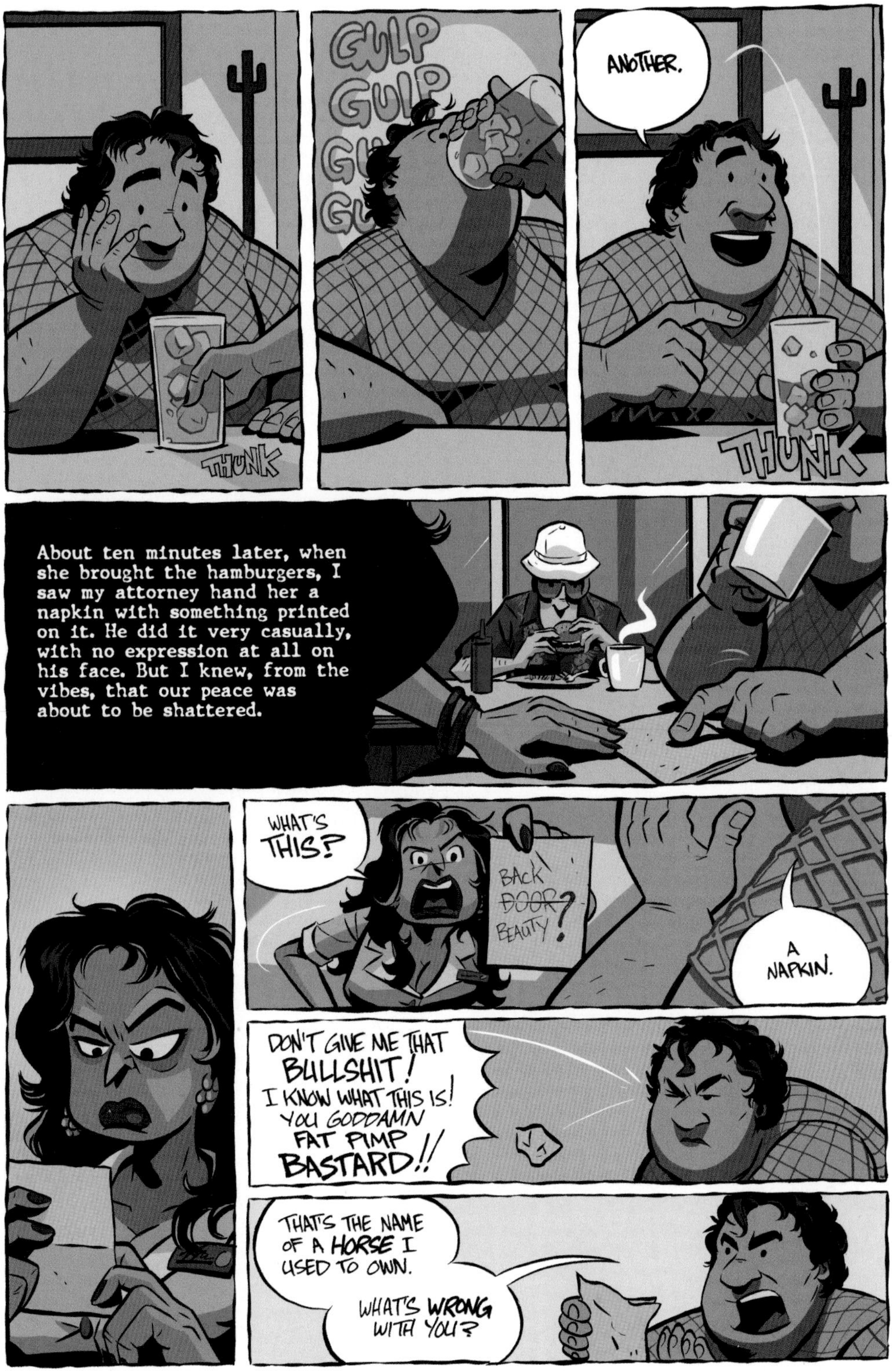

GULP
GULP
GU
GU
THUNK
ANOTHER.
THUNK
About ten minutes later, when she brought the hamburgers, I saw my attorney hand her a napkin with something printed on it. He did it very casually, with no expression at all on his face. But I knew, from the vibes, that our peace was about to be shattered.
WHAT'S THIS?
BACK DOOR? BEAUTY?
A NAPKIN.
DON'T GIVE ME THAT BULLSHIT! I KNOW WHAT THIS IS! YOU GODDAMN FAT PIMP BASTARD!!
THAT'S THE NAME OF A HORSE I USED TO OWN.
WHAT'S WRONG WITH YOU?

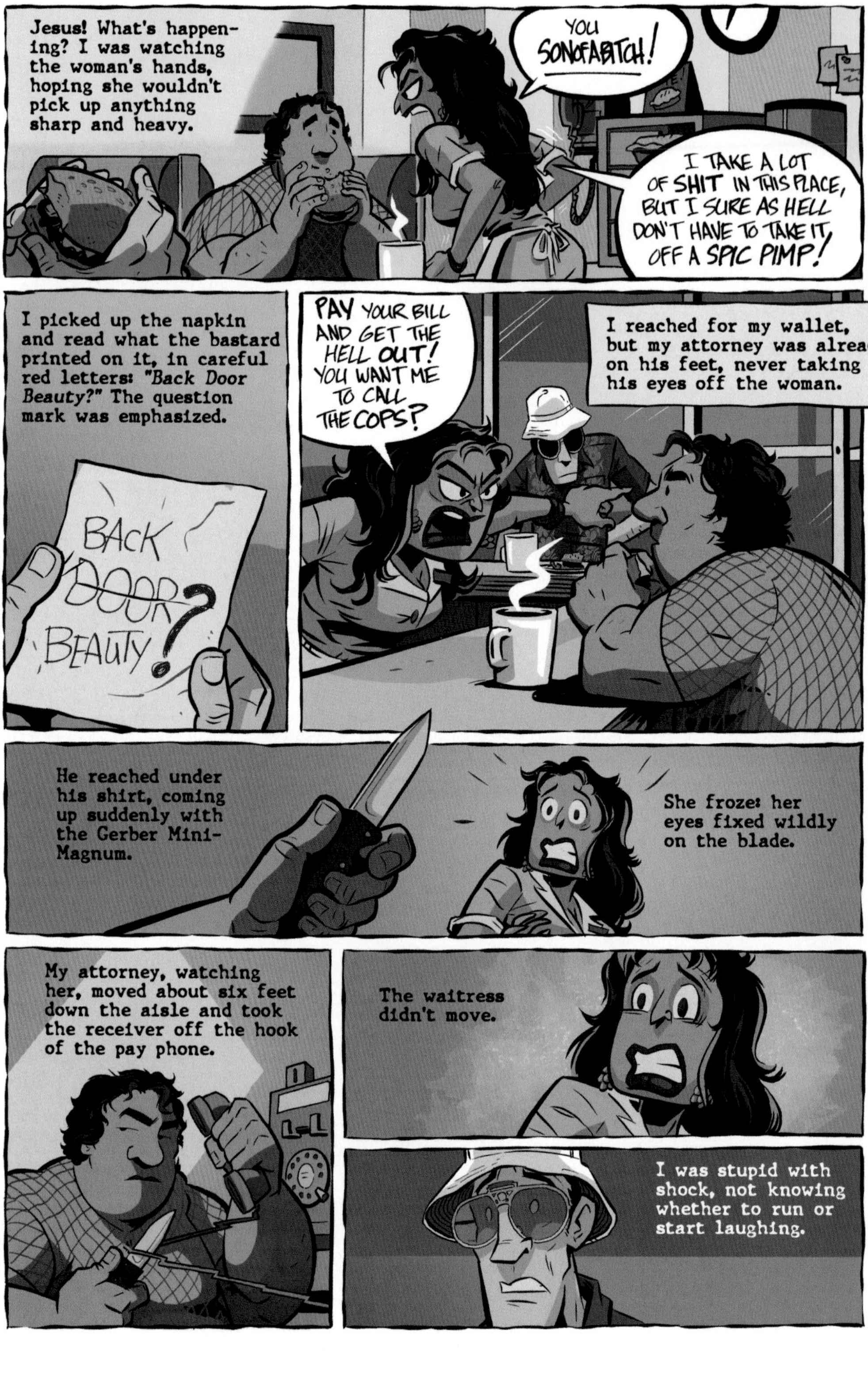
Jesus! What's happening? I was watching the woman's hands, hoping she wouldn't pick up anything sharp and heavy.
YOU SONOFABITCH!
I TAKE A LOT OF SHIT IN THIS PLACE, BUT I SURE AS HELL DON'T HAVE TO TAKE IT OFF A SPIC PIMP!
I picked up the napkin and read what the bastard printed on it, in careful red letters: "Back Door Beauty?" The question mark was emphasized.
BACK DOOR BEAUTY?
PAY YOUR BILL AND GET THE HELL OUT! YOU WANT ME TO CALL THE COPS?
I reached for my wallet, but my attorney was already on his feet, never taking his eyes off the woman.
He reached under his shirt, coming up suddenly with the Gerber Mini-Magnum.
She froze: her eyes fixed wildly on the blade.
My attorney, watching her, moved about six feet down the aisle and took the receiver off the hook of the pay phone.
The waitress didn't move.
I was stupid with shock, not knowing whether to run or start laughing.

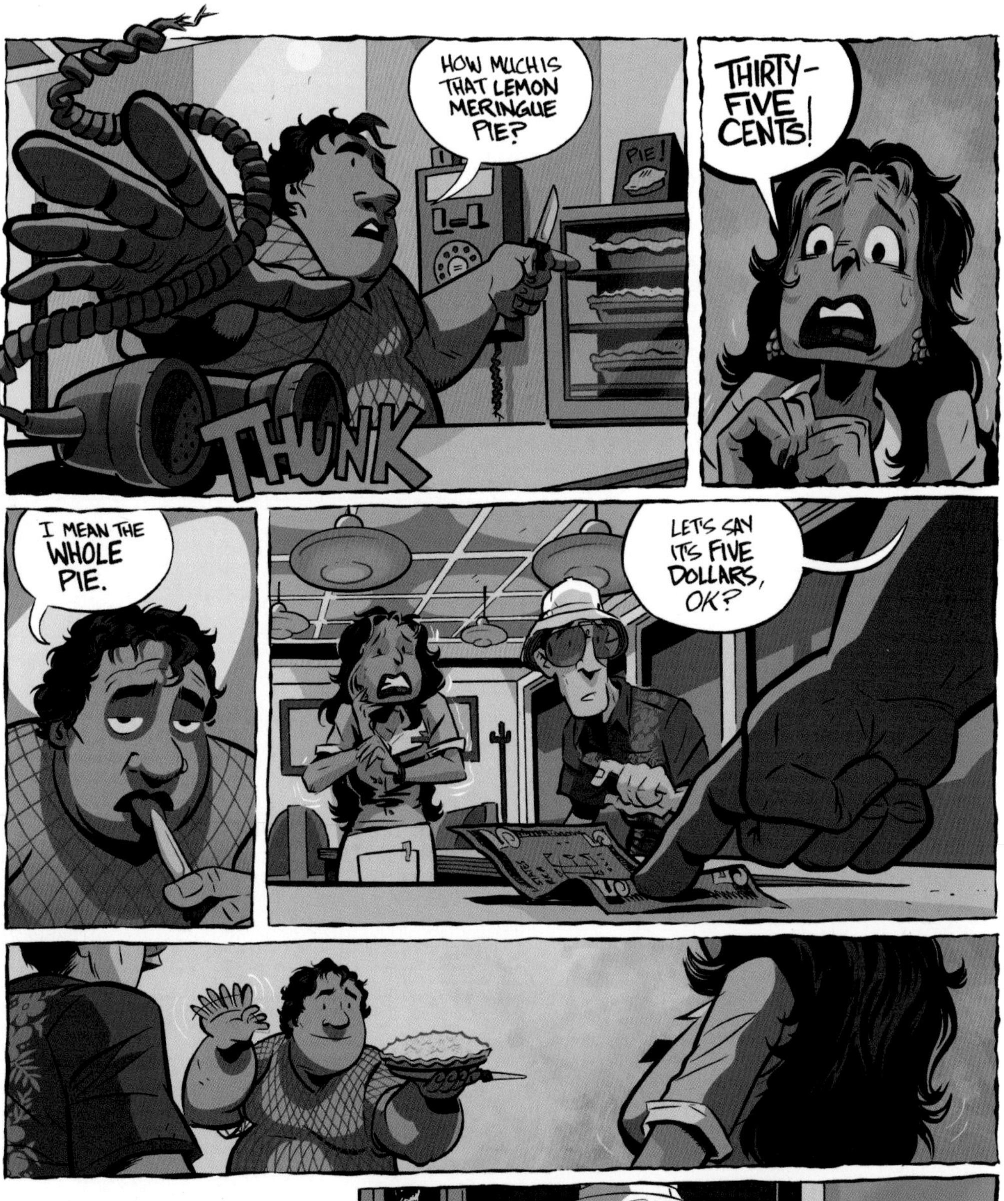
HOW MUCH IS THAT LEMON MERINGUE PIE?
PIE!
THUNK
THIRTY-FIVE CENTS!
I MEAN THE WHOLE PIE.
LET'S SAY IT'S FIVE DOLLARS, OK?

The waitress was clearly in shock. The sight of the blade, jerked out in the heat of an argument, had apparently triggered bad memories.

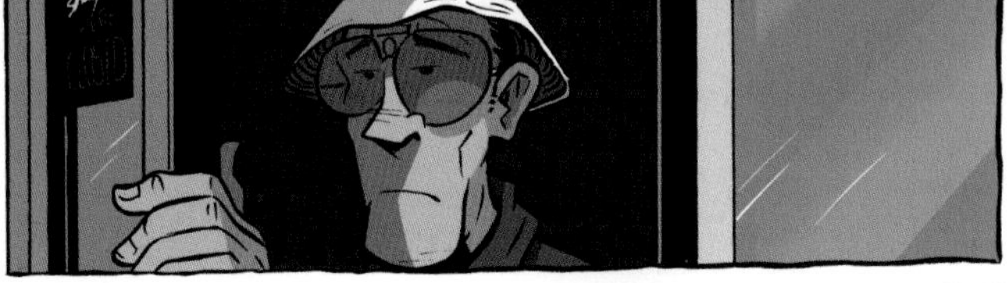

The glazed look in her eyes said her throat had been cut. She was still in the grip of paralysis when we left.

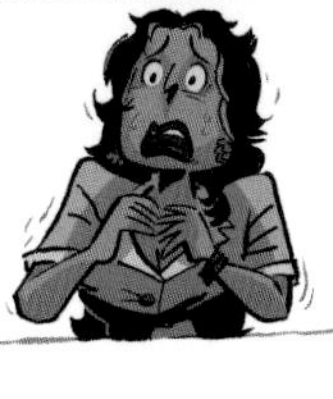

9. Breakdown on Paradise Blvd.

EDITOR'S NOTE:

At this point in the chronology, Dr. Duke appears to have broken down completely; the original manuscript is so splintered that we were forced to seek out the original tape recording and transcribe it verbatim.

According to the tape, this section follows an episode involving Duke, his attorney and a waitress at an all-night diner in North Vegas. The rationale for the following transaction appears to be based on a feeling - shared by both Duke and his attorney - that the American Dream would have to be sought out somewhere far beyond the dreary confines of the District Attorneys' Conference on Narcotics and Dangerous Drugs.

The transcription begins somewhere on the Northeast outskirts of Las Vegas - zooming along Paradise Road in the White Whale...

Att'y: Boulder City is to the right. Is that a town?

Duke: Yeah.

Att'y: Let's go to Boulder City.

Duke: All right. Let's get some coffee somewhere...

Att'y: Right up here, Terry's Taco Stand, USA. I could go for a taco. Five for a buck.

Duke: Sounds horrible. I'd rather go somewhere where's there's one for 50 cents.

Att'y: No... This might be the last chance we get for tacos.

Duke: I need some coffee.

Att'y: I want tacos...

Duke: Five for a buck, that's like... <u>five hamburgers</u> for a buck.

Att'y: Don't judge a taco by its price.

Duke: You think you might make a deal?

Att'y: I might. There's a hamburger for 29 cents. Tacos are 29 cents. It's just a cheap place, that's all.

Duke: Go bargain with them.

TERRY'S
5 TACOS
U.S.A.
TACOS FOR $1.00

[Only garbled sounds here. – Ed.]

Att'y: Hello.

Waitress: May I help you?

Att'y: Yeah, you have tacos here? Are they Mexican tacos or just regular tacos? I mean, do you have chili in them and things like that?

Waitress: We have cheese and lettuce, and we have sauce, you know, put on them.

Att'y: I mean do you guarantee that they are authentic Mexican tacos?

Waitress: ...I don't know. Hey Lou, do we have authentic Mexican tacos?

Woman's voice from kitchen: What?

Waitress: Authentic Mexican tacos.

Lou: We have tacos. I don't know how Mexican they are.

Att'y: You just started working here?

Waitress: Today.

Att'y: I thought so.

Att'y: As your attorney I advise you to get the chiliburger, a hamburger with chili on it.

Duke: That's too heavy for me.

Att'y: Then I advise you to get a taco burger, try that one.

Duke: ...the taco has meat in it. I'll try that one. And some coffee now. Right now. So I can drink it while I'm waiting.

Waitress: Aren't you from Nevada?

Att'y: No. We've never been here before. Just traveling through.

Att'y: Let me run it down just briefly if I can. We're looking for the American Dream, and we were told it was somewhere in this area... Well, we're here looking for it, 'cause they sent us out here all the way from San Francisco to look for it. That's why they gave us this white Cadillac, they figure that we could catch up with it in that...

Waitress: Hey Lou, you know where the American Dream is?

145

Att'y: We were sent out here from San Francisco to look for the American Dream, by a magazine, to cover it.

Lou: Oh, you mean a place.

Att'y: A place called the American Dream.

Lou: Is that the old Psychiatrist's Club?

Waitress: I think so.

Att'y: The old Psychiatrist's Club?

Lou: Old Psychiatrist's Club, it's on Paradise. Are you guys serious?

Att'y: All we were told was, go till you find the American Dream. Take this white Cadillac and go find the American Dream. It's somewhere in the Las Vegas area.

Lou: ...Did somebody just send you on a goose chase?

Att'y: It's sort of a wild goose chase, more or less, but personally we're dead serious.

Lou: That has to be the old Psychiatrist's Club, but the only people who hang out there is a bunch of pushers, peddlers, uppers and downers, and all that stuff.

Att'y: Maybe that's it. Is it a night-time place or is it an all day...

Lou: Oh, honey, this never stops.

Att'y: Is that what it's called, the old Psychiatrist's Club?

Lou: No, that is what it used to be, but someone bought it... it's a mental joint, where all the dopers hang out.

Att'y: A mental joint? You mean like a mental hospital?

Lou: No, honey, where all the dope peddlers and all the pushers, everybody hangs out. It's a place where all the kids are potted when they go in, and everything... but it's not called what you said, the American Dream.

Att'y: Do you have any idea more or less where it might be located?

Lou: Right off of Paradise and Eastern.

Att'y: I think this place you're talking about and the way you're describing it, I think that maybe that's it.

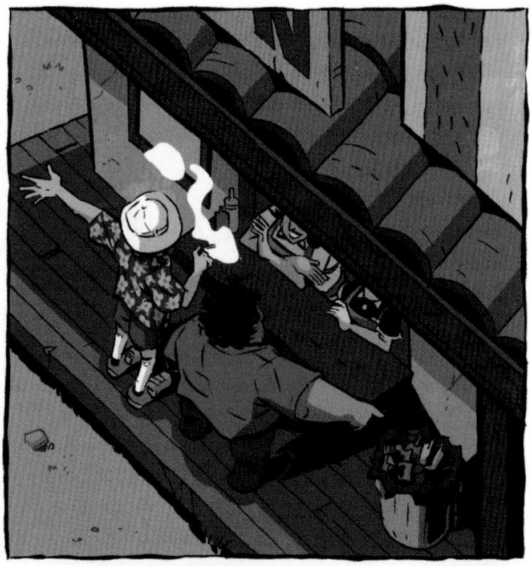

Lou: It's not a tourist joint.

Att'y: Well, that's why they sent me. He's the writer: I'm the bodyguard. 'Cause I figure it will be...

Lou: These guys are nuts... these kids are nuts.

Duke: Twenty-four-hour-a-day violence? Is that what we're saying?

Lou: Exactly. Now, right up here at the first gas station is Tropicana, take a right.

Att'y: Tropicana to the right.

Lou: Right on Tropicana, right on Paradise, you'll see a big black building, it's all painted black and real weird looking.

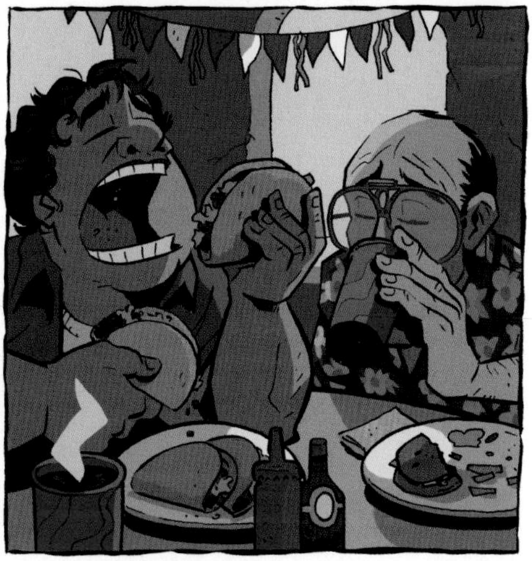

Att'y: OK. Big black building, right on Paradise: twenty-four-hour-a-day violence, drugs.

Lou: You gonna be glad you stopped here, boys.

Duke: Only if we find it.

Att'y: Only if we write the article and get it in.

Waitress: Well, why don't you come inside and sit down?

Duke: We're trying to get as much sun as we can.

Att'y: She's going to make a phone call to find out where it is.

Duke: Oh. OK, well, let's go inside.

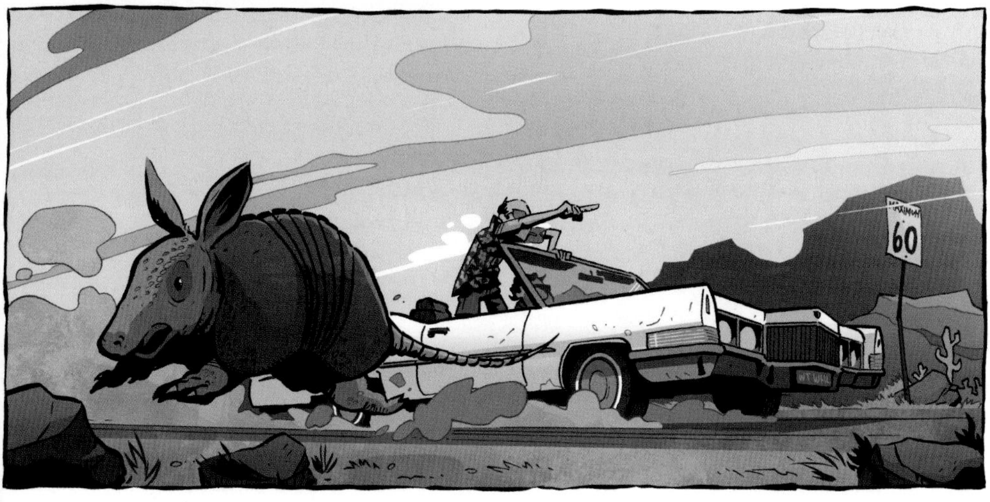
60

EDITOR'S NOTE (*cont.*):

Tape cassettes for the next sequence were impossible to transcribe due to some viscous liquid encrusted behind the heads. There is a certain consistency in the garbled sounds however, indicating that almost two hours later Dr. Duke and his attorney finally located what was left of the "Old Psychiatrist's Club" - a huge slab of cracked, scorched concrete in a vacant lot full of tall weeds. The owner of a gas station across the road said the place had "burned down about three years ago."

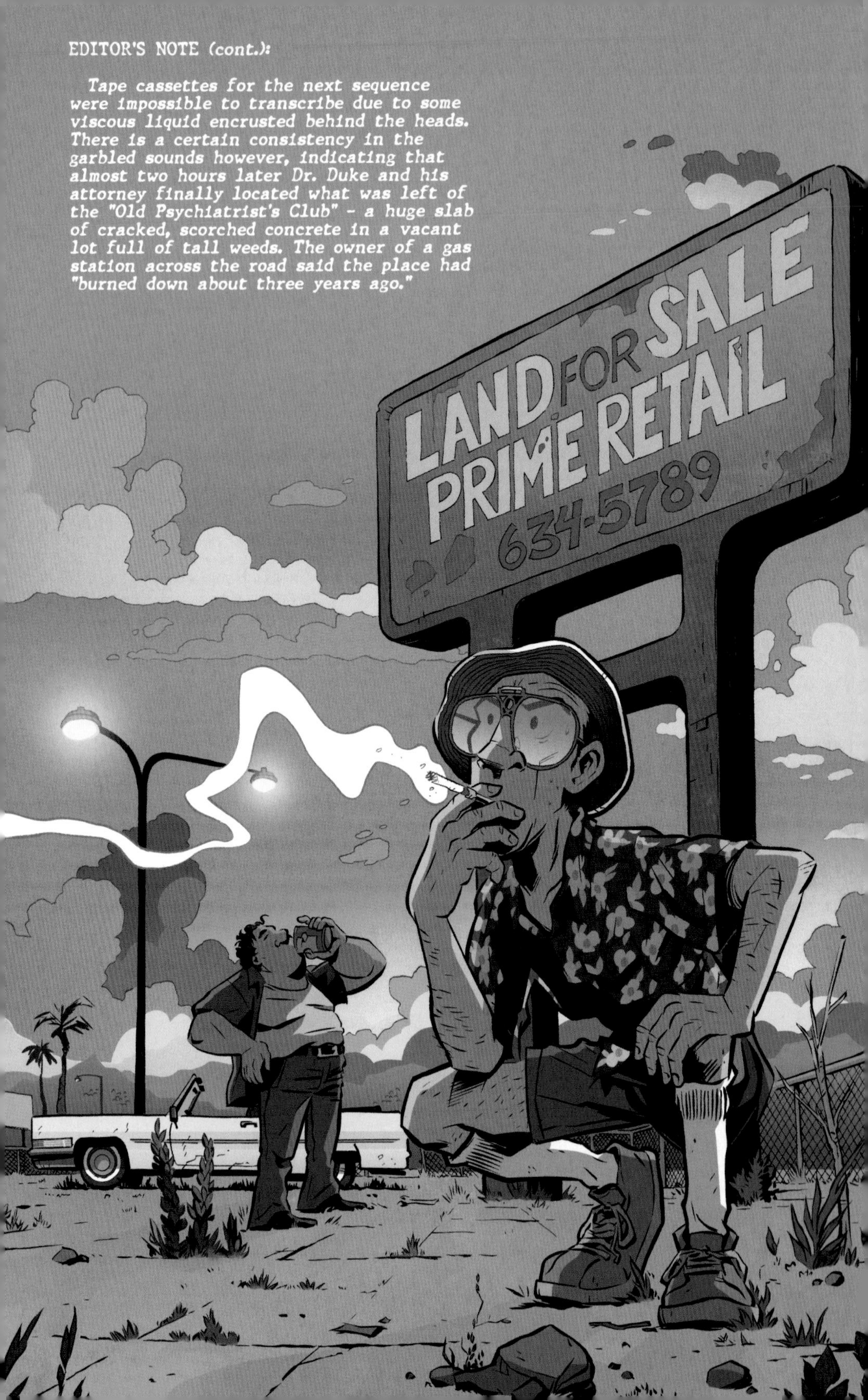
LAND FOR SALE
PRIME RETAIL
634-5789

. Heavy Duty at the Airport… Ugly Peruvian Flashback… 'No! It's Too Late! Don't Try It!'

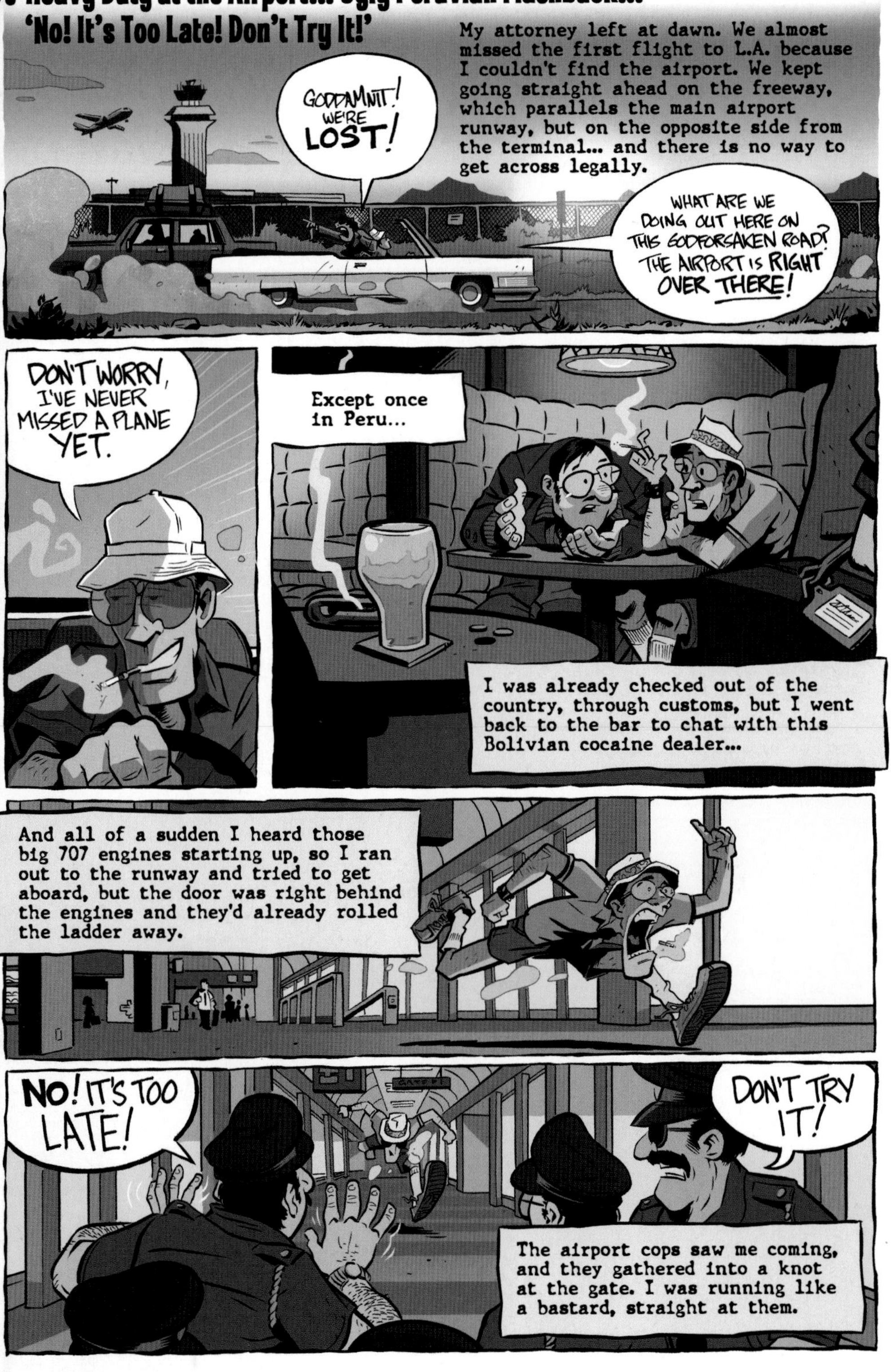

My attorney left at dawn. We almost missed the first flight to L.A. because I couldn't find the airport. We kept going straight ahead on the freeway, which parallels the main airport runway, but on the opposite side from the terminal... and there is no way to get across legally.
GODDAMNIT! WE'RE LOST!
WHAT ARE WE DOING OUT HERE ON THIS GODFORSAKEN ROAD? THE AIRPORT IS RIGHT OVER THERE!
DON'T WORRY, I'VE NEVER MISSED A PLANE YET.
Except once in Peru...
I was already checked out of the country, through customs, but I went back to the bar to chat with this Bolivian cocaine dealer...
And all of a sudden I heard those big 707 engines starting up, so I ran out to the runway and tried to get aboard, but the door was right behind the engines and they'd already rolled the ladder away.
NO! IT'S TOO LATE!
DON'T TRY IT!
The airport cops saw me coming, and they gathered into a knot at the gate. I was running like a bastard, straight at them.

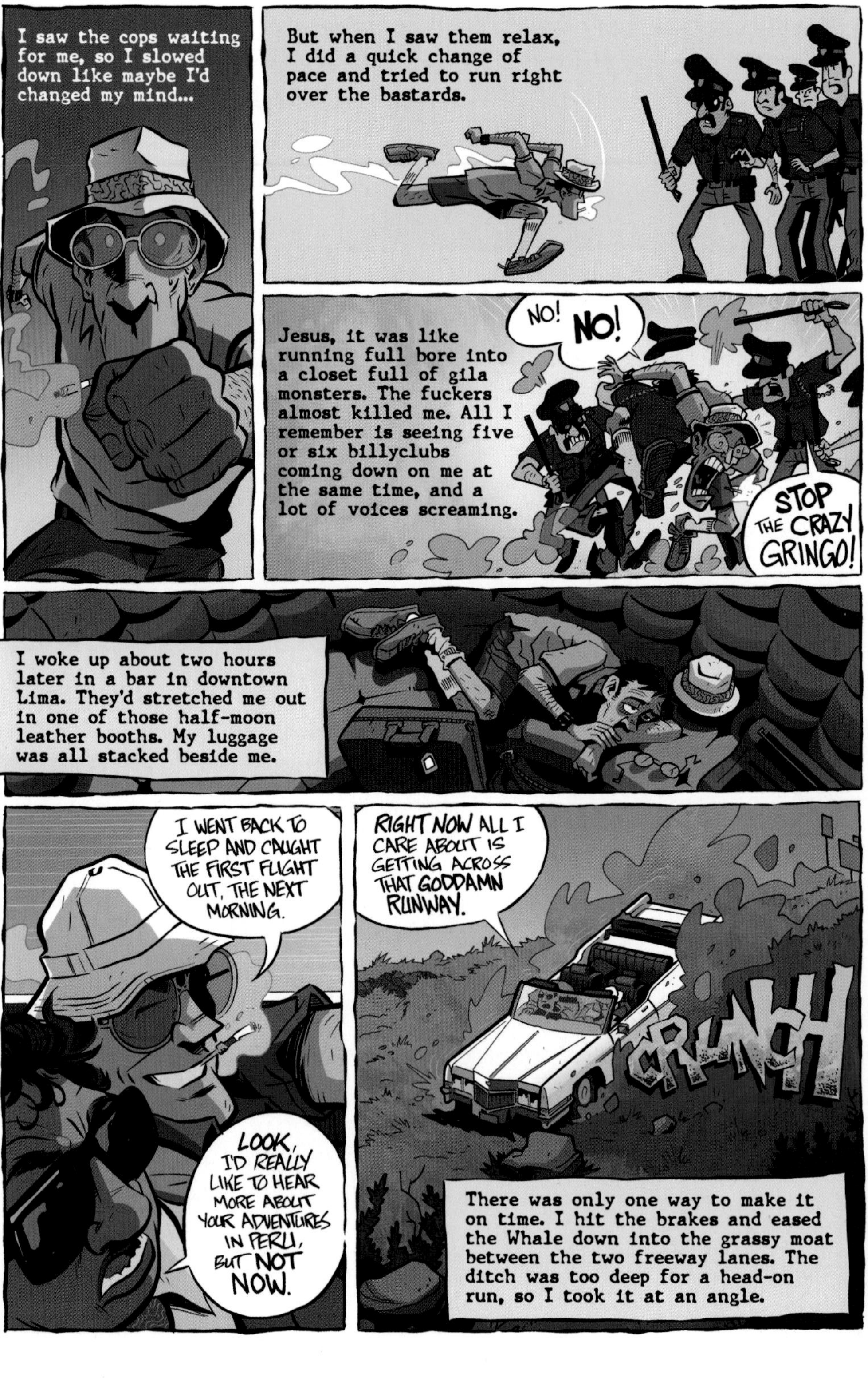

I saw the cops waiting for me, so I slowed down like maybe I'd changed my mind...
But when I saw them relax, I did a quick change of pace and tried to run right over the bastards.
Jesus, it was like running full bore into a closet full of gila monsters. The fuckers almost killed me. All I remember is seeing five or six billyclubs coming down on me at the same time, and a lot of voices screaming.
NO! NO!
STOP THE CRAZY GRINGO!
I woke up about two hours later in a bar in downtown Lima. They'd stretched me out in one of those half-moon leather booths. My luggage was all stacked beside me.
I WENT BACK TO SLEEP AND CAUGHT THE FIRST FLIGHT OUT, THE NEXT MORNING.
LOOK, I'D REALLY LIKE TO HEAR MORE ABOUT YOUR ADVENTURES IN PERU, BUT NOT NOW.
RIGHT NOW ALL I CARE ABOUT IS GETTING ACROSS THAT GODDAMN RUNWAY.
CRUNCH
There was only one way to make it on time. I hit the brakes and eased the Whale down into the grassy moat between the two freeway lanes. The ditch was too deep for a head-on run, so I took it at an angle.

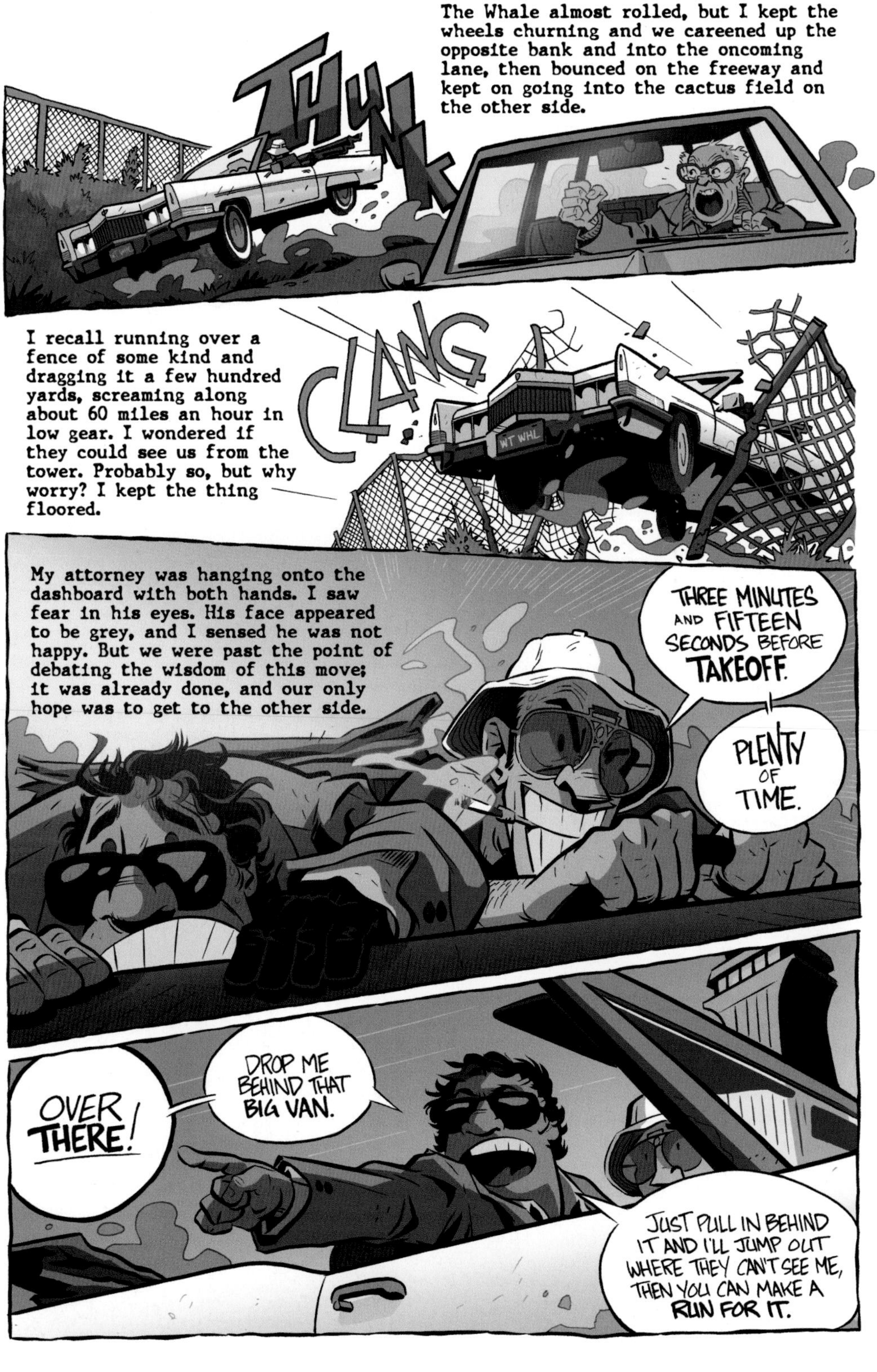
The Whale almost rolled, but I kept the wheels churning and we careened up the opposite bank and into the oncoming lane, then bounced on the freeway and kept on going into the cactus field on the other side.
THUNK
I recall running over a fence of some kind and dragging it a few hundred yards, screaming along about 60 miles an hour in low gear. I wondered if they could see us from the tower. Probably so, but why worry? I kept the thing floored.
CLANG
WT WHL
My attorney was hanging onto the dashboard with both hands. I saw fear in his eyes. His face appeared to be grey, and I sensed he was not happy. But we were past the point of debating the wisdom of this move; it was already done, and our only hope was to get to the other side.
THREE MINUTES AND FIFTEEN SECONDS BEFORE TAKEOFF.
PLENTY OF TIME.
OVER THERE!
DROP ME BEHIND THAT BIG VAN.
JUST PULL IN BEHIND IT AND I'LL JUMP OUT WHERE THEY CAN'T SEE ME, THEN YOU CAN MAKE A RUN FOR IT.

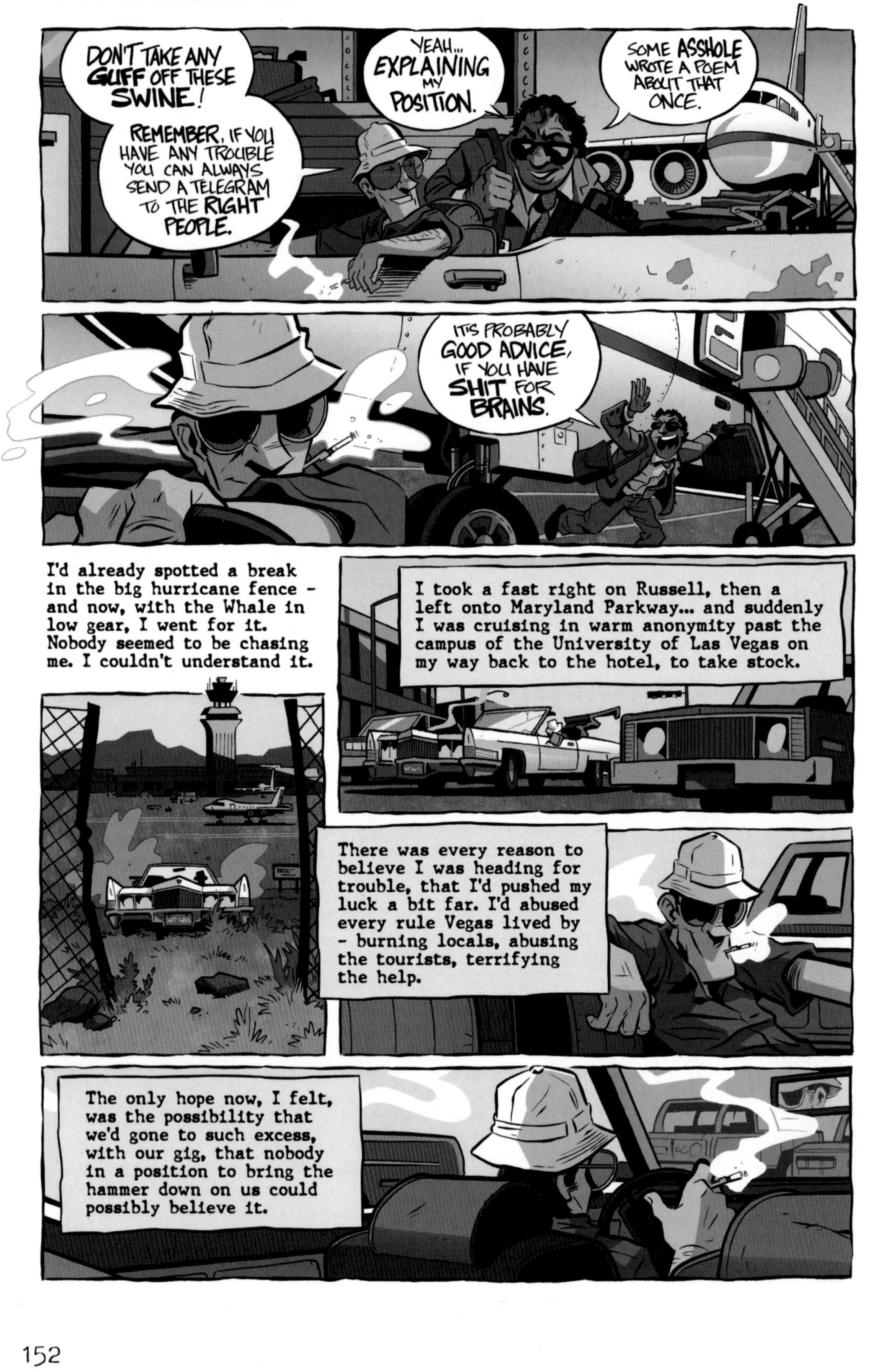
DON'T TAKE ANY GUFF OFF THESE SWINE!
REMEMBER, IF YOU HAVE ANY TROUBLE YOU CAN ALWAYS SEND A TELEGRAM TO THE RIGHT PEOPLE.
YEAH... EXPLAINING MY POSITION.
SOME ASSHOLE WROTE A POEM ABOUT THAT ONCE.
IT'S PROBABLY GOOD ADVICE, IF YOU HAVE SHIT FOR BRAINS.
I'd already spotted a break in the big hurricane fence - and now, with the Whale in low gear, I went for it. Nobody seemed to be chasing me. I couldn't understand it.
I took a fast right on Russell, then a left onto Maryland Parkway... and suddenly I was cruising in warm anonymity past the campus of the University of Las Vegas on my way back to the hotel, to take stock.
There was every reason to believe I was heading for trouble, that I'd pushed my luck a bit far. I'd abused every rule Vegas lived by - burning locals, abusing the tourists, terrifying the help.
The only hope now, I felt, was the possibility that we'd gone to such excess, with our gig, that nobody in a position to bring the hammer down on us could possibly believe it.

11. Fraud? Larceny? Rape? ... A Brutal Connection with the Alice from Linen Service

I was brooding as I eased the White Whale into the Flamingo parking lot. We are all wired into a survival trip now. No more of the speed that fueled the Sixties. Uppers are going out of style. This was the fatal flaw in Tim Leary's trip. He crashed around America selling "consciousness expansion" without ever giving a thought to the grim meat-hook realities that were lying in wait for all the people who took him too seriously.

There is not much satisfaction in knowing that he blew it very badly for himself, because he took too many others down with him. All those pathetically eager acid freaks who thought they could buy Peace and Understanding for three bucks a hit. But their failure is ours, too.

What Leary took down with him was the central illusion of a whole life-style that he helped to create... a generation of permanent cripples, failed seekers, who never understood the essential old-mystic fallacy of the Acid Culture: the desperate assumption that some-body - or at least some force - is tending that Light at the end of the tunnel.

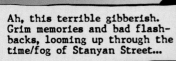

Ah, this terrible gibberish. Grim memories and bad flash-backs, looming up through the time/fog of Stanyan Street...

No solace for refugees, no point in looking back. The question, as always, is now...?

I was slumped on my bed in the Flamingo, feeling dangerously out of phase with my surroundings. Something ugly was about to happen. I was sure of it.

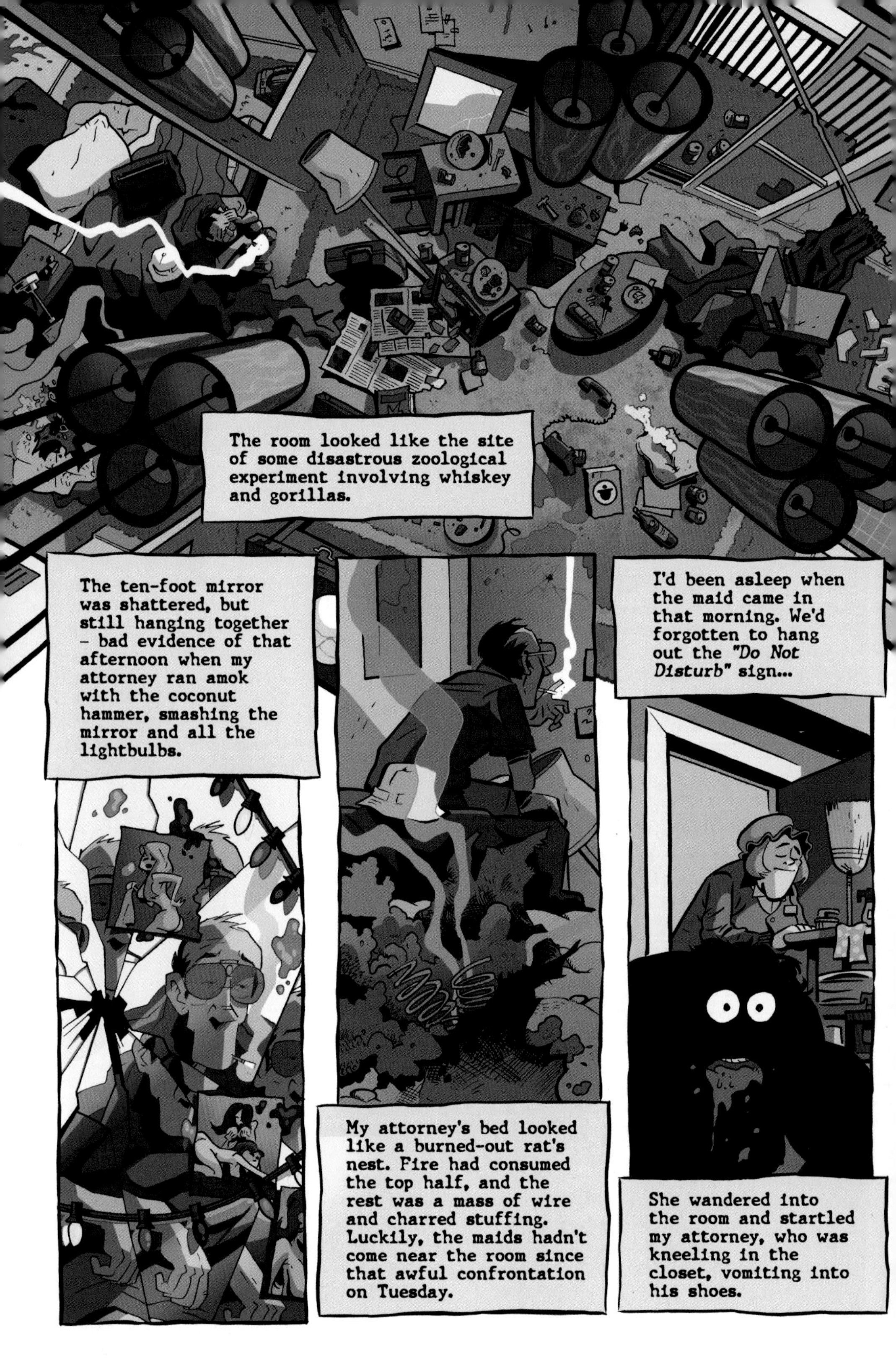
The room looked like the site of some disastrous zoological experiment involving whiskey and gorillas.
The ten-foot mirror was shattered, but still hanging together - bad evidence of that afternoon when my attorney ran amok with the coconut hammer, smashing the mirror and all the lightbulbs.
My attorney's bed looked like a burned-out rat's nest. Fire had consumed the top half, and the rest was a mass of wire and charred stuffing. Luckily, the maids hadn't come near the room since that awful confrontation on Tuesday.
I'd been asleep when the maid came in that morning. We'd forgotten to hang out the *"Do Not Disturb"* sign...
She wandered into the room and startled my attorney, who was kneeling in the closet, vomiting into his shoes.

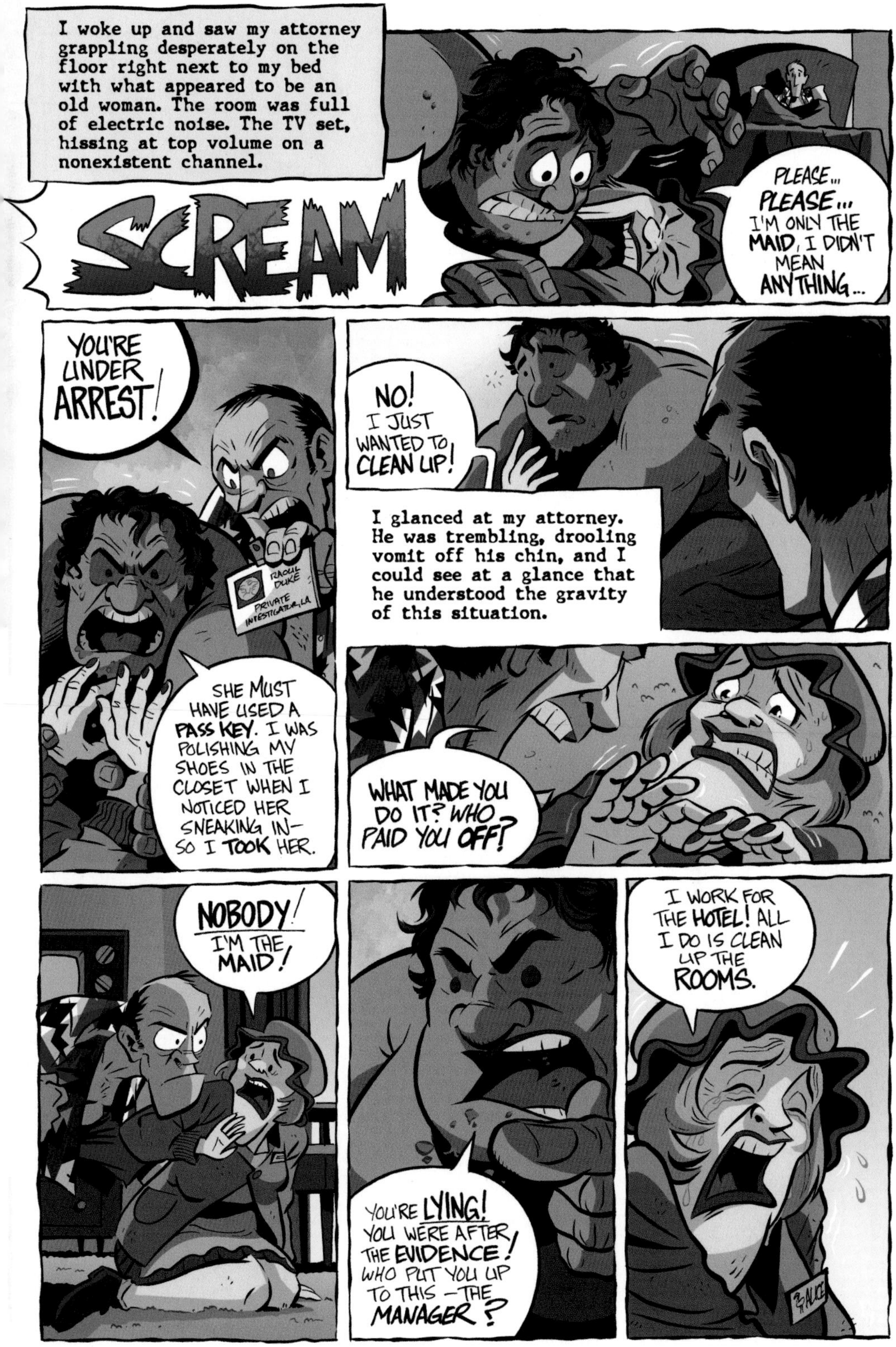
I woke up and saw my attorney grappling desperately on the floor right next to my bed with what appeared to be an old woman. The room was full of electric noise. The TV set, hissing at top volume on a nonexistent channel.
SCREAM
PLEASE... PLEASE... I'M ONLY THE MAID, I DIDN'T MEAN ANYTHING...
YOU'RE UNDER ARREST!
RAOUL DUKE PRIVATE INVESTIGATOR, LA
SHE MUST HAVE USED A PASS KEY. I WAS POLISHING MY SHOES IN THE CLOSET WHEN I NOTICED HER SNEAKING IN– SO I TOOK HER.
NO! I JUST WANTED TO CLEAN UP!
I glanced at my attorney. He was trembling, drooling vomit off his chin, and I could see at a glance that he understood the gravity of this situation.
WHAT MADE YOU DO IT? WHO PAID YOU OFF?
NOBODY! I'M THE MAID!
YOU'RE LYING! YOU WERE AFTER THE EVIDENCE! WHO PUT YOU UP TO THIS —THE MANAGER?
I WORK FOR THE HOTEL! ALL I DO IS CLEAN UP THE ROOMS.

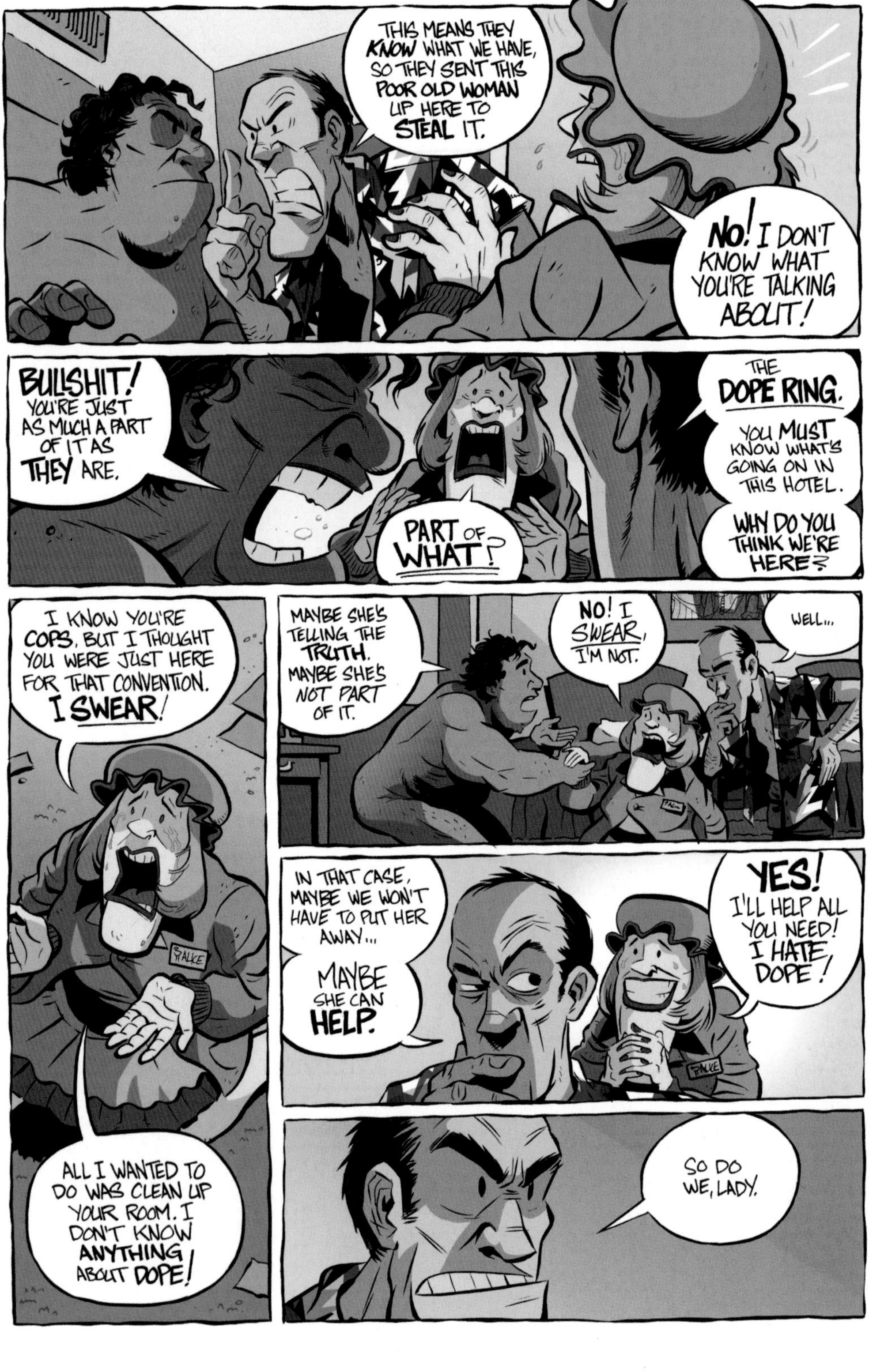

THIS MEANS THEY KNOW WHAT WE HAVE, SO THEY SENT THIS POOR OLD WOMAN UP HERE TO STEAL IT.
NO! I DON'T KNOW WHAT YOU'RE TALKING ABOUT!
BULLSHIT! YOU'RE JUST AS MUCH A PART OF IT AS THEY ARE.
PART OF WHAT?
THE DOPE RING.
YOU MUST KNOW WHAT'S GOING ON IN THIS HOTEL.
WHY DO YOU THINK WE'RE HERE?
I KNOW YOU'RE COPS, BUT I THOUGHT YOU WERE JUST HERE FOR THAT CONVENTION. I SWEAR!
ALL I WANTED TO DO WAS CLEAN UP YOUR ROOM. I DON'T KNOW ANYTHING ABOUT DOPE!
MAYBE SHE'S TELLING THE TRUTH. MAYBE SHE'S NOT PART OF IT.
NO! I SWEAR, I'M NOT.
WELL...
IN THAT CASE, MAYBE WE WON'T HAVE TO PUT HER AWAY...
MAYBE SHE CAN HELP.
YES! I'LL HELP ALL YOU NEED! I HATE DOPE!
SO DO WE, LADY.

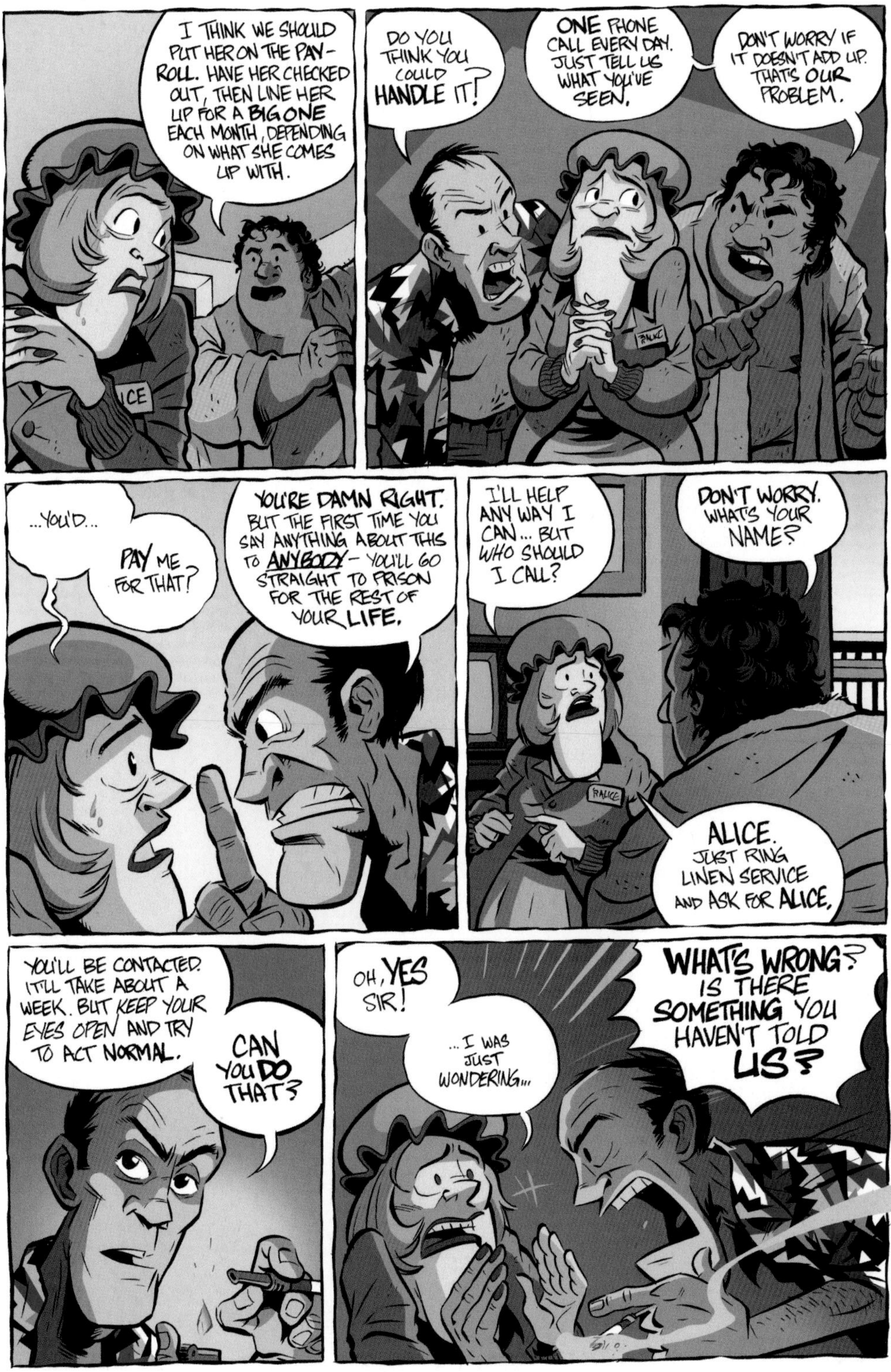
I THINK WE SHOULD PUT HER ON THE PAY-ROLL. HAVE HER CHECKED OUT, THEN LINE HER UP FOR A BIG ONE EACH MONTH, DEPENDING ON WHAT SHE COMES UP WITH.
ICE
DO YOU THINK YOU COULD HANDLE IT?
ONE PHONE CALL EVERY DAY. JUST TELL US WHAT YOU'VE SEEN.
DON'T WORRY IF IT DOESN'T ADD UP. THAT'S OUR PROBLEM.
...YOU'D...
PAY ME FOR THAT?
YOU'RE DAMN RIGHT. BUT THE FIRST TIME YOU SAY ANYTHING ABOUT THIS TO ANYBODY - YOU'LL GO STRAIGHT TO PRISON FOR THE REST OF YOUR LIFE.
I'LL HELP ANY WAY I CAN... BUT WHO SHOULD I CALL?
DON'T WORRY. WHAT'S YOUR NAME?
ALICE. JUST RING LINEN SERVICE AND ASK FOR ALICE.
YOU'LL BE CONTACTED. IT'LL TAKE ABOUT A WEEK. BUT KEEP YOUR EYES OPEN AND TRY TO ACT NORMAL.
CAN YOU DO THAT?
OH, YES SIR!
...I WAS JUST WONDERING...
WHAT'S WRONG? IS THERE SOMETHING YOU HAVEN'T TOLD US?

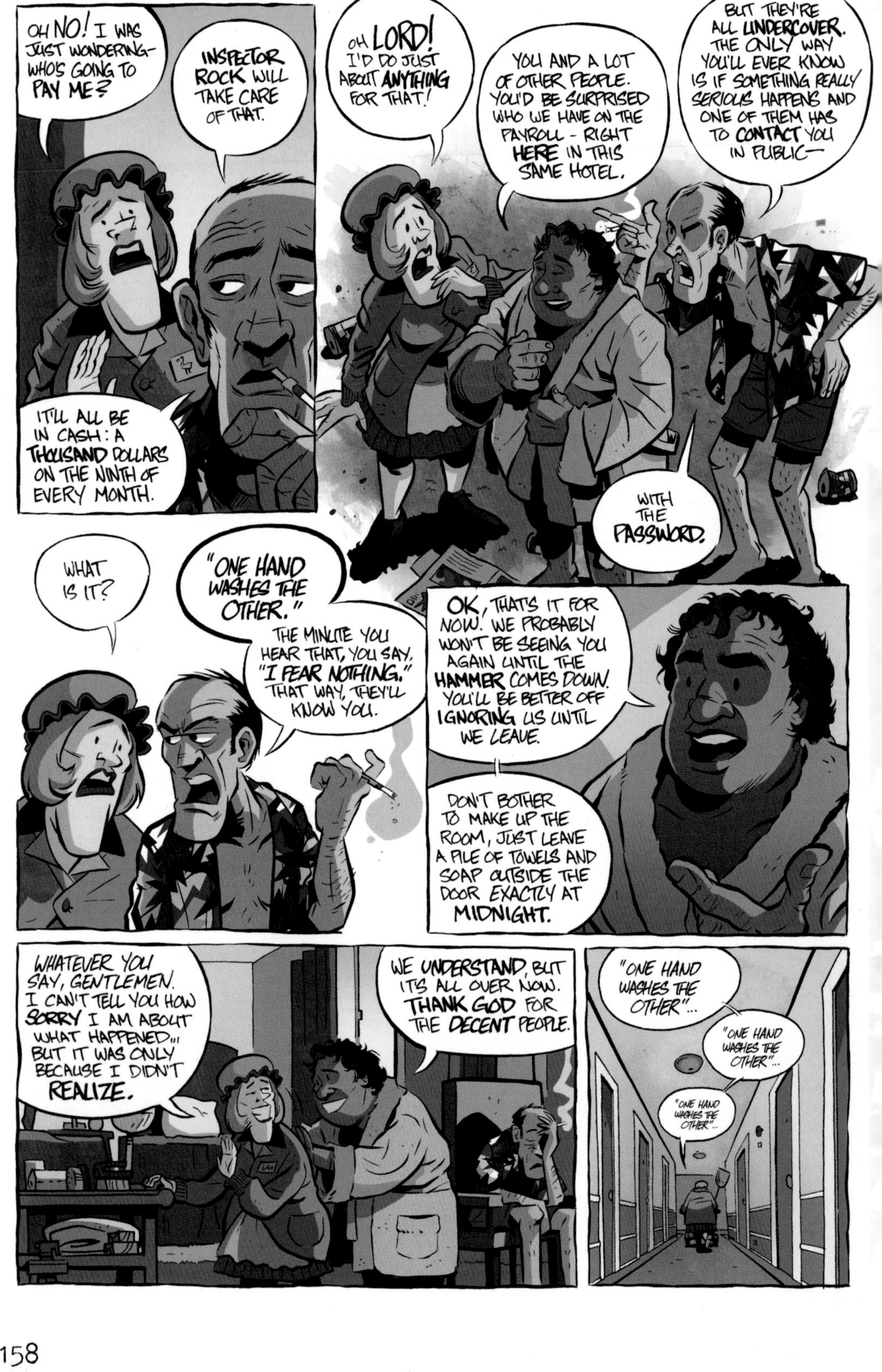
OH NO! I WAS JUST WONDERING- WHO'S GOING TO PAY ME?
INSPECTOR ROCK WILL TAKE CARE OF THAT.
IT'LL ALL BE IN CASH: A THOUSAND DOLLARS ON THE NINTH OF EVERY MONTH.
OH LORD! I'D DO JUST ABOUT ANYTHING FOR THAT!
YOU AND A LOT OF OTHER PEOPLE. YOU'D BE SURPRISED WHO WE HAVE ON THE PAYROLL - RIGHT HERE IN THIS SAME HOTEL.
BUT THEY'RE ALL UNDERCOVER. THE ONLY WAY YOU'LL EVER KNOW IS IF SOMETHING REALLY SERIOUS HAPPENS AND ONE OF THEM HAS TO CONTACT YOU IN PUBLIC—
WITH THE PASSWORD.
WHAT IS IT?
"ONE HAND WASHES THE OTHER."
THE MINUTE YOU HEAR THAT, YOU SAY, "I FEAR NOTHING." THAT WAY, THEY'LL KNOW YOU.
OK, THAT'S IT FOR NOW. WE PROBABLY WON'T BE SEEING YOU AGAIN UNTIL THE HAMMER COMES DOWN. YOU'LL BE BETTER OFF IGNORING US UNTIL WE LEAVE.
DON'T BOTHER TO MAKE UP THE ROOM, JUST LEAVE A PILE OF TOWELS AND SOAP OUTSIDE THE DOOR EXACTLY AT MIDNIGHT.
WHATEVER YOU SAY, GENTLEMEN. I CAN'T TELL YOU HOW SORRY I AM ABOUT WHAT HAPPENED... BUT IT WAS ONLY BECAUSE I DIDN'T REALIZE.
WE UNDERSTAND, BUT IT'S ALL OVER NOW. THANK GOD FOR THE DECENT PEOPLE.
"ONE HAND WASHES THE OTHER"...
"ONE HAND WASHES THE OTHER"...
"ONE HAND WASHES THE OTHER"...

2. Return to the Circus-Circus... Looking for the Ape... to Hell with the American Dream

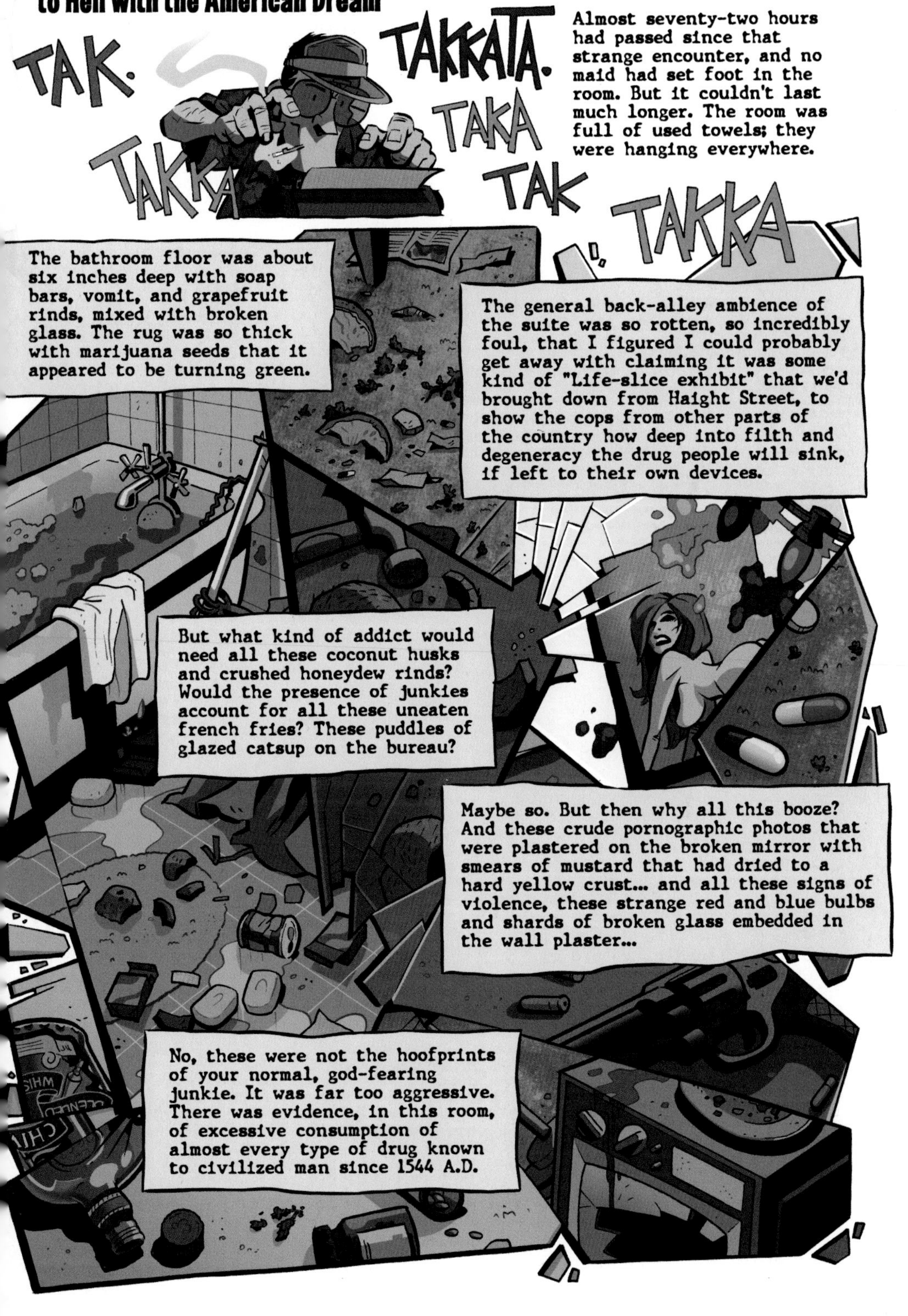
TAK. TAKKATA. TAKKA TAKA TAK TAKKA
Almost seventy-two hours had passed since that strange encounter, and no maid had set foot in the room. But it couldn't last much longer. The room was full of used towels; they were hanging everywhere.
The bathroom floor was about six inches deep with soap bars, vomit, and grapefruit rinds, mixed with broken glass. The rug was so thick with marijuana seeds that it appeared to be turning green.
The general back-alley ambience of the suite was so rotten, so incredibly foul, that I figured I could probably get away with claiming it was some kind of "Life-slice exhibit" that we'd brought down from Haight Street, to show the cops from other parts of the country how deep into filth and degeneracy the drug people will sink, if left to their own devices.
But what kind of addict would need all these coconut husks and crushed honeydew rinds? Would the presence of junkies account for all these uneaten french fries? These puddles of glazed catsup on the bureau?
Maybe so. But then why all this booze? And these crude pornographic photos that were plastered on the broken mirror with smears of mustard that had dried to a hard yellow crust... and all these signs of violence, these strange red and blue bulbs and shards of broken glass embedded in the wall plaster...
No, these were not the hoofprints of your normal, god-fearing junkie. It was far too aggressive. There was evidence, in this room, of excessive consumption of almost every type of drug known to civilized man since 1544 A.D.

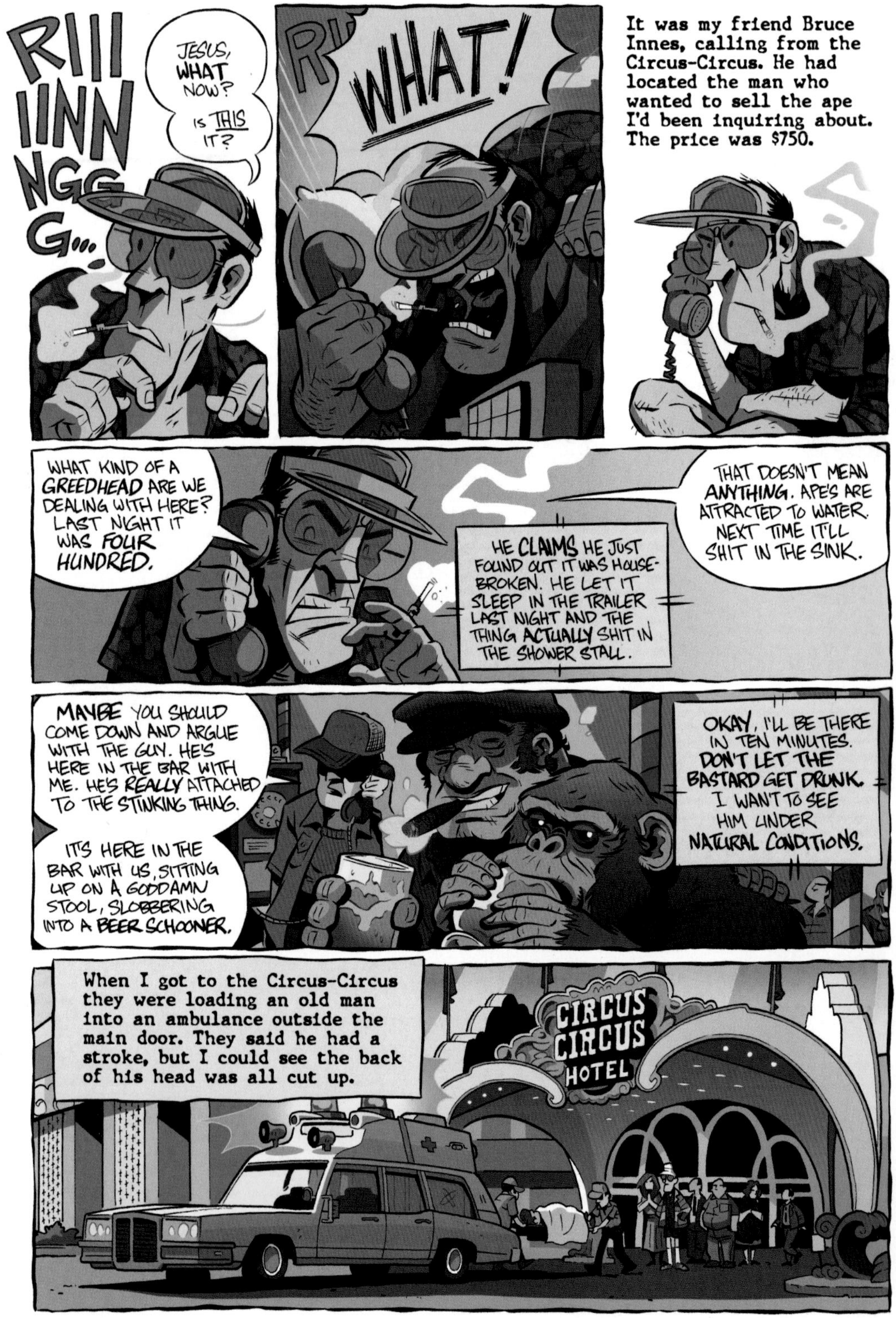
RIII IINN NGG G...
JESUS, WHAT NOW? IS THIS IT?
WHAT!
It was my friend Bruce Innes, calling from the Circus-Circus. He had located the man who wanted to sell the ape I'd been inquiring about. The price was $750.
WHAT KIND OF A GREEDHEAD ARE WE DEALING WITH HERE? LAST NIGHT IT WAS FOUR HUNDRED.
HE CLAIMS HE JUST FOUND OUT IT WAS HOUSE-BROKEN. HE LET IT SLEEP IN THE TRAILER LAST NIGHT AND THE THING ACTUALLY SHIT IN THE SHOWER STALL.
THAT DOESN'T MEAN ANYTHING. APE'S ARE ATTRACTED TO WATER. NEXT TIME IT'LL SHIT IN THE SINK.
MAYBE YOU SHOULD COME DOWN AND ARGUE WITH THE GUY. HE'S HERE IN THE BAR WITH ME. HE'S REALLY ATTACHED TO THE STINKING THING.
IT'S HERE IN THE BAR WITH US, SITTING UP ON A GODDAMN STOOL, SLOBBERING INTO A BEER SCHOONER.
OKAY, I'LL BE THERE IN TEN MINUTES. DON'T LET THE BASTARD GET DRUNK. I WANT TO SEE HIM UNDER NATURAL CONDITIONS.
When I got to the Circus-Circus they were loading an old man into an ambulance outside the main door. They said he had a stroke, but I could see the back of his head was all cut up.
CIRCUS CIRCUS HOTEL

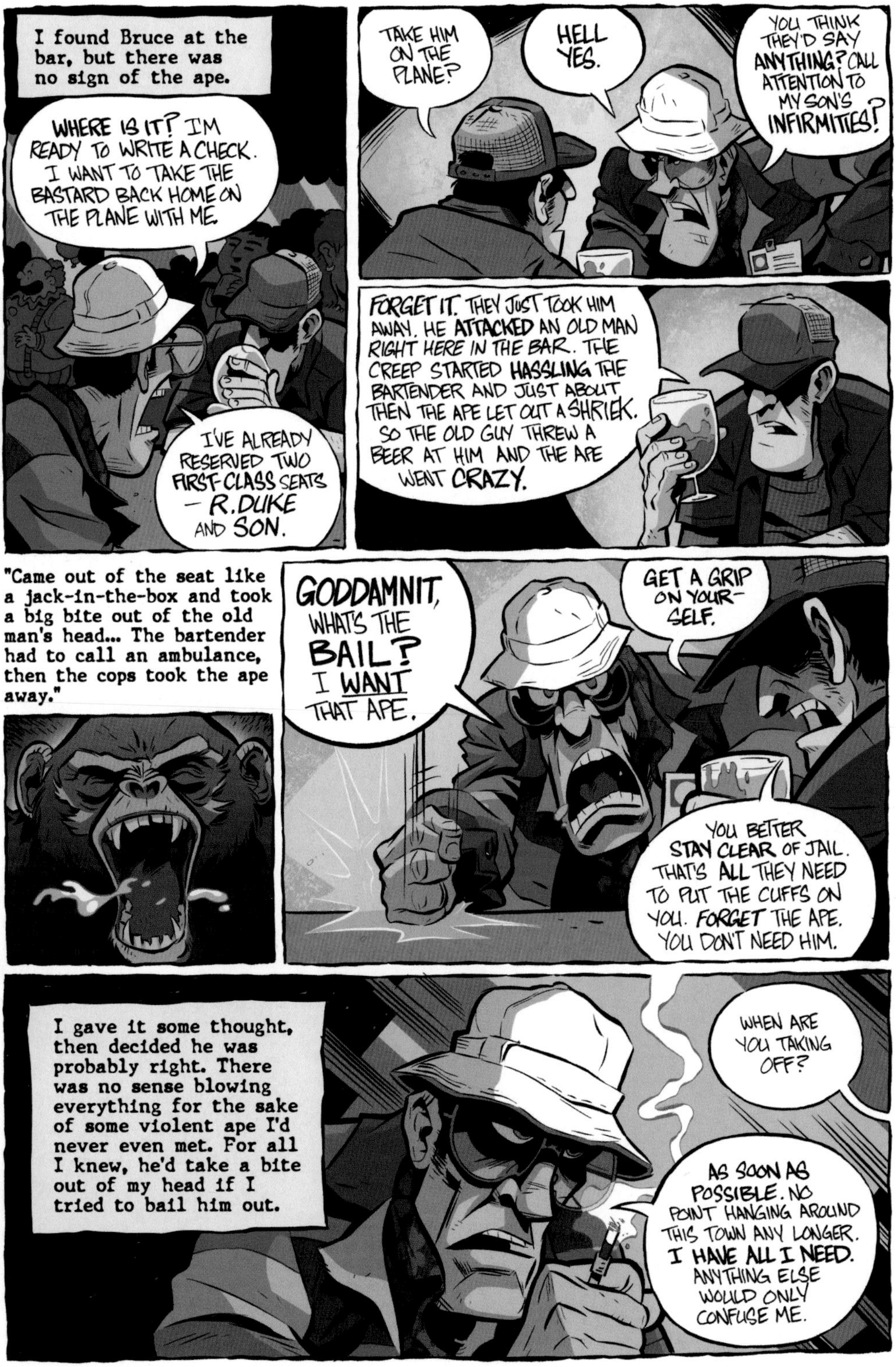
I found Bruce at the bar, but there was no sign of the ape.
WHERE IS IT? I'M READY TO WRITE A CHECK. I WANT TO TAKE THE BASTARD BACK HOME ON THE PLANE WITH ME.
I'VE ALREADY RESERVED TWO FIRST-CLASS SEATS — R. DUKE AND SON.
TAKE HIM ON THE PLANE?
HELL YES.
YOU THINK THEY'D SAY ANYTHING? CALL ATTENTION TO MY SON'S INFIRMITIES?
FORGET IT. THEY JUST TOOK HIM AWAY. HE ATTACKED AN OLD MAN RIGHT HERE IN THE BAR. THE CREEP STARTED HASSLING THE BARTENDER AND JUST ABOUT THEN THE APE LET OUT A SHRIEK. SO THE OLD GUY THREW A BEER AT HIM AND THE APE WENT CRAZY.
"Came out of the seat like a jack-in-the-box and took a big bite out of the old man's head... The bartender had to call an ambulance, then the cops took the ape away."
GODDAMNIT, WHAT'S THE BAIL? I WANT THAT APE.
GET A GRIP ON YOURSELF.
YOU BETTER STAY CLEAR OF JAIL. THAT'S ALL THEY NEED TO PUT THE CUFFS ON YOU. FORGET THE APE. YOU DON'T NEED HIM.
I gave it some thought, then decided he was probably right. There was no sense blowing everything for the sake of some violent ape I'd never even met. For all I knew, he'd take a bite out of my head if I tried to bail him out.
WHEN ARE YOU TAKING OFF?
AS SOON AS POSSIBLE. NO POINT HANGING AROUND THIS TOWN ANY LONGER. I HAVE ALL I NEED. ANYTHING ELSE WOULD ONLY CONFUSE ME.

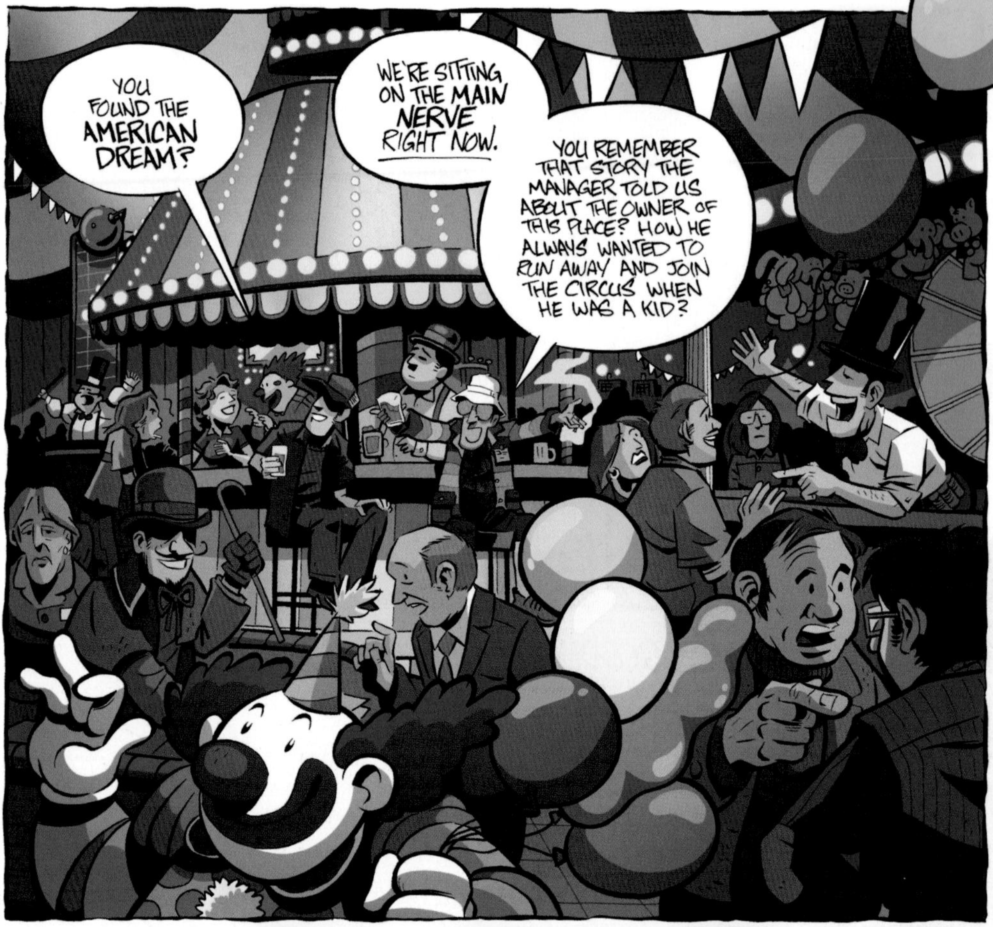
YOU FOUND THE AMERICAN DREAM?
WE'RE SITTING ON THE MAIN NERVE RIGHT NOW.
YOU REMEMBER THAT STORY THE MANAGER TOLD US ABOUT THE OWNER OF THIS PLACE? HOW HE ALWAYS WANTED TO RUN AWAY AND JOIN THE CIRCUS WHEN HE WAS A KID?

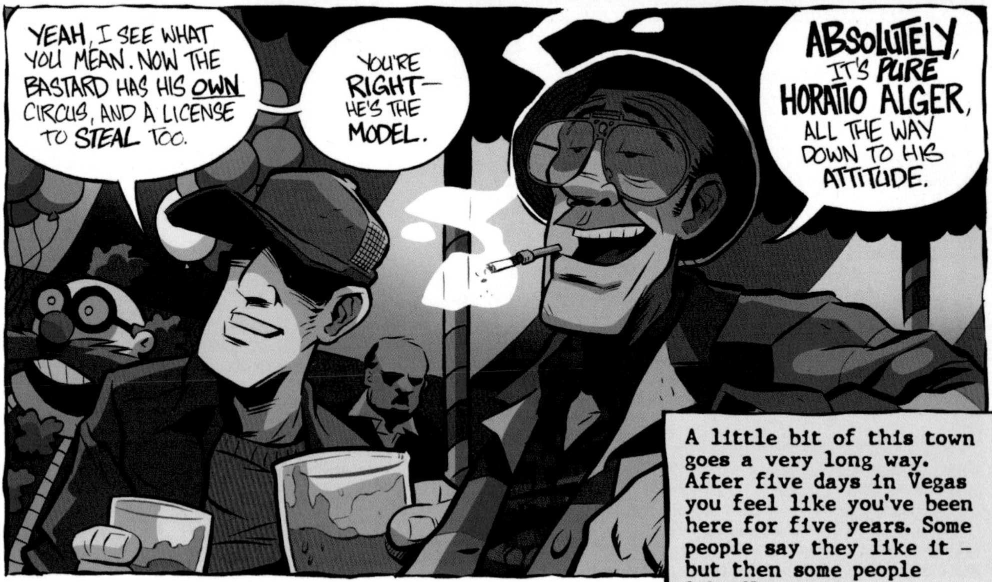
YEAH, I SEE WHAT YOU MEAN. NOW THE BASTARD HAS HIS OWN CIRCUS, AND A LICENSE TO STEAL TOO.
YOU'RE RIGHT— HE'S THE MODEL.
ABSOLUTELY, IT'S PURE HORATIO ALGER, ALL THE WAY DOWN TO HIS ATTITUDE.
A little bit of this town goes a very long way. After five days in Vegas you feel like you've been here for five years. Some people say they like it - but then some people like Nixon, too.

3. End of the Road... Death of the Whale... Soaking Sweats in the Airport

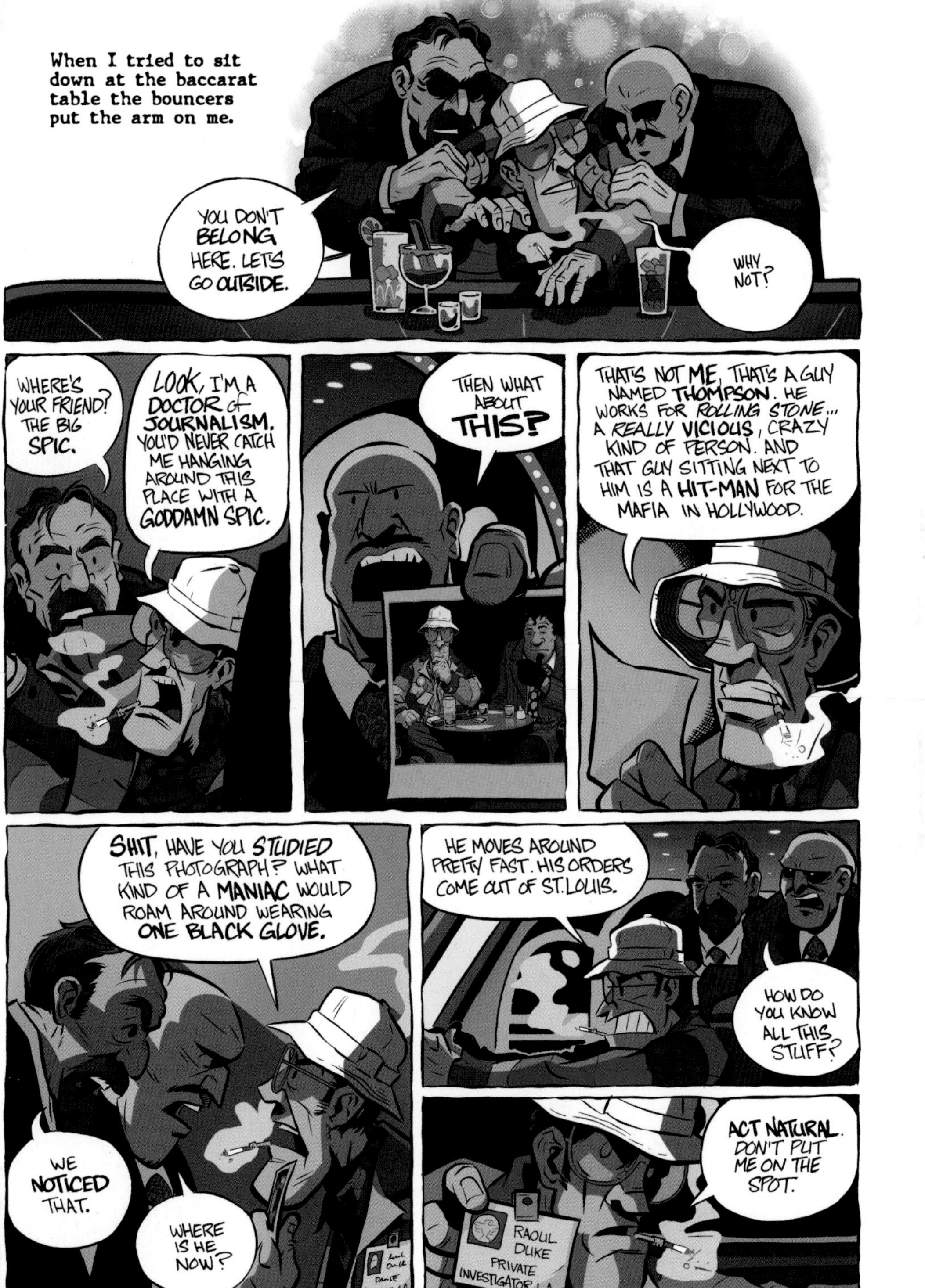

When I tried to sit down at the baccarat table the bouncers put the arm on me.
YOU DON'T BELONG HERE. LET'S GO OUTSIDE.
WHY NOT?
WHERE'S YOUR FRIEND? THE BIG SPIC.
LOOK, I'M A DOCTOR of JOURNALISM. YOU'D NEVER CATCH ME HANGING AROUND THIS PLACE WITH A GODDAMN SPIC.
THEN WHAT ABOUT THIS?
THAT'S NOT ME, THAT'S A GUY NAMED THOMPSON. HE WORKS FOR ROLLING STONE... A REALLY VICIOUS, CRAZY KIND OF PERSON. AND THAT GUY SITTING NEXT TO HIM IS A HIT-MAN FOR THE MAFIA IN HOLLYWOOD.
SHIT, HAVE YOU STUDIED THIS PHOTOGRAPH? WHAT KIND OF A MANIAC WOULD ROAM AROUND WEARING ONE BLACK GLOVE.
WE NOTICED THAT.
WHERE IS HE NOW?
HE MOVES AROUND PRETTY FAST. HIS ORDERS COME OUT OF ST. LOUIS.
HOW DO YOU KNOW ALL THIS STUFF?
ACT NATURAL. DON'T PUT ME ON THE SPOT.
RAOUL DUKE
PRIVATE INVESTIGATOR, L.A.

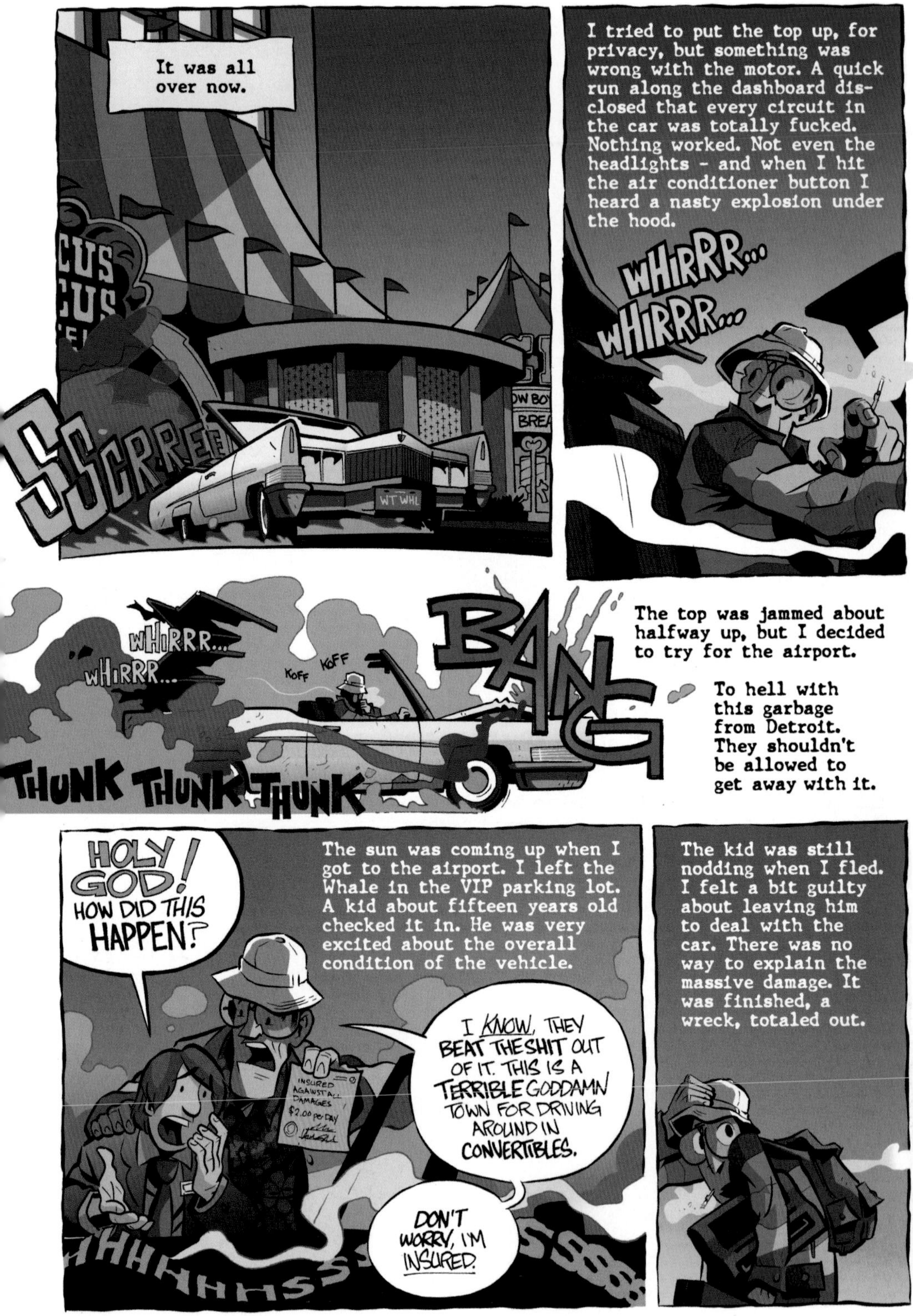
It was all over now.
SSCRREE
WT WHL
I tried to put the top up, for privacy, but something was wrong with the motor. A quick run along the dashboard disclosed that every circuit in the car was totally fucked. Nothing worked. Not even the headlights - and when I hit the air conditioner button I heard a nasty explosion under the hood.
WHIRRR...
WHIRRR...
WHIRRR...
WHIRRR...
KOFF KOFF
BANG
THUNK THUNK THUNK
The top was jammed about halfway up, but I decided to try for the airport.
To hell with this garbage from Detroit. They shouldn't be allowed to get away with it.
The sun was coming up when I got to the airport. I left the Whale in the VIP parking lot. A kid about fifteen years old checked it in. He was very excited about the overall condition of the vehicle.
HOLY GOD! HOW DID THIS HAPPEN?
I KNOW, THEY BEAT THE SHIT OUT OF IT. THIS IS A TERRIBLE GODDAMN TOWN FOR DRIVING AROUND IN CONVERTIBLES.
INSURED AGAINST ALL DAMAGES $2.00 per DAY
DON'T WORRY, I'M INSURED.
HHHHHHSSSSSSSS
The kid was still nodding when I fled. I felt a bit guilty about leaving him to deal with the car. There was no way to explain the massive damage. It was finished, a wreck, totaled out.

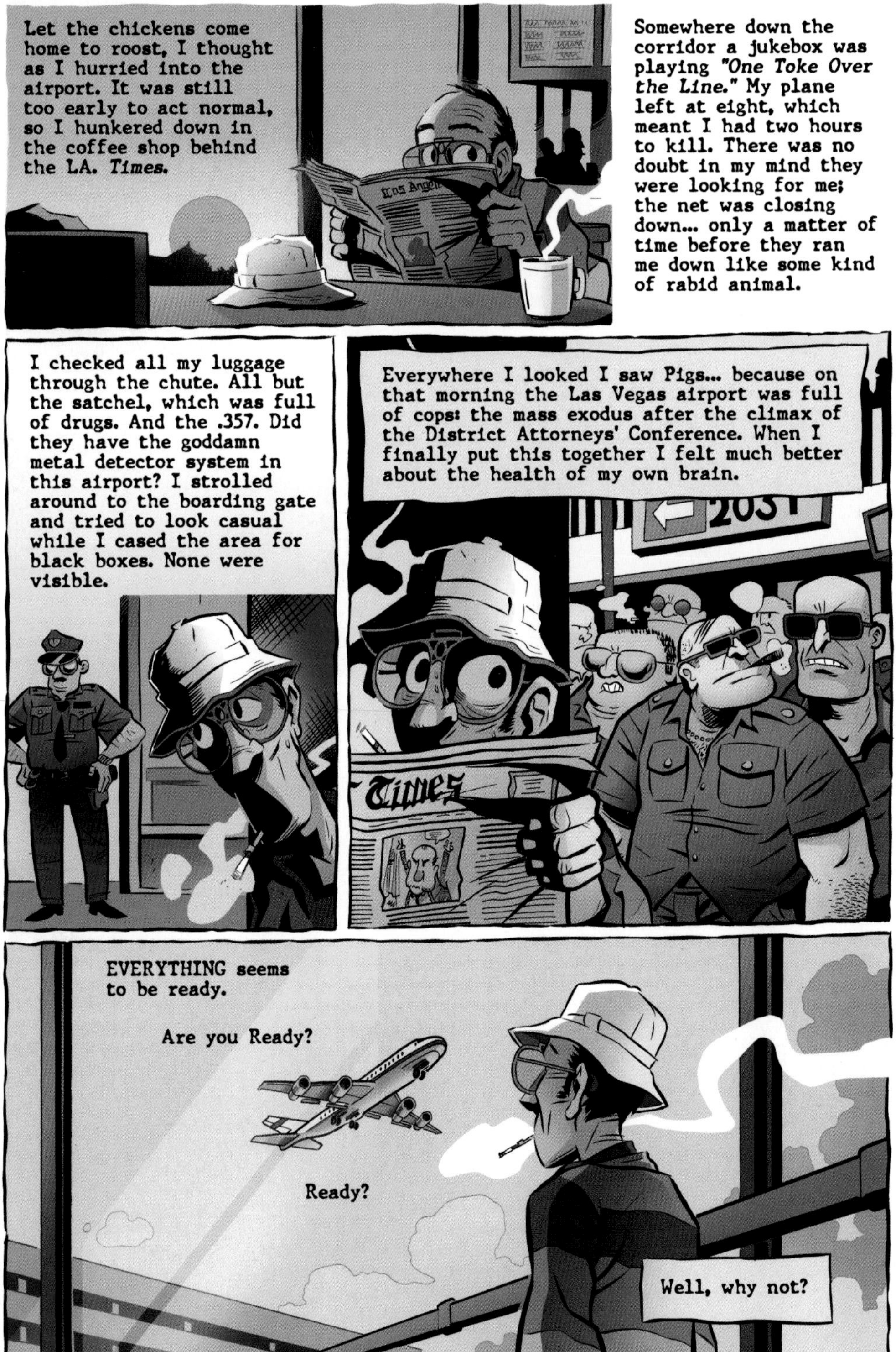
Let the chickens come home to roost, I thought as I hurried into the airport. It was still too early to act normal, so I hunkered down in the coffee shop behind the LA. *Times.*
Somewhere down the corridor a jukebox was playing *"One Toke Over the Line."* My plane left at eight, which meant I had two hours to kill. There was no doubt in my mind they were looking for me; the net was closing down... only a matter of time before they ran me down like some kind of rabid animal.
I checked all my luggage through the chute. All but the satchel, which was full of drugs. And the .357. Did they have the goddamn metal detector system in this airport? I strolled around to the boarding gate and tried to look casual while I cased the area for black boxes. None were visible.
Everywhere I looked I saw Pigs... because on that morning the Las Vegas airport was full of cops: the mass exodus after the climax of the District Attorneys' Conference. When I finally put this together I felt much better about the health of my own brain.
EVERYTHING seems to be ready.
Are you Ready?
Ready?
Well, why not?

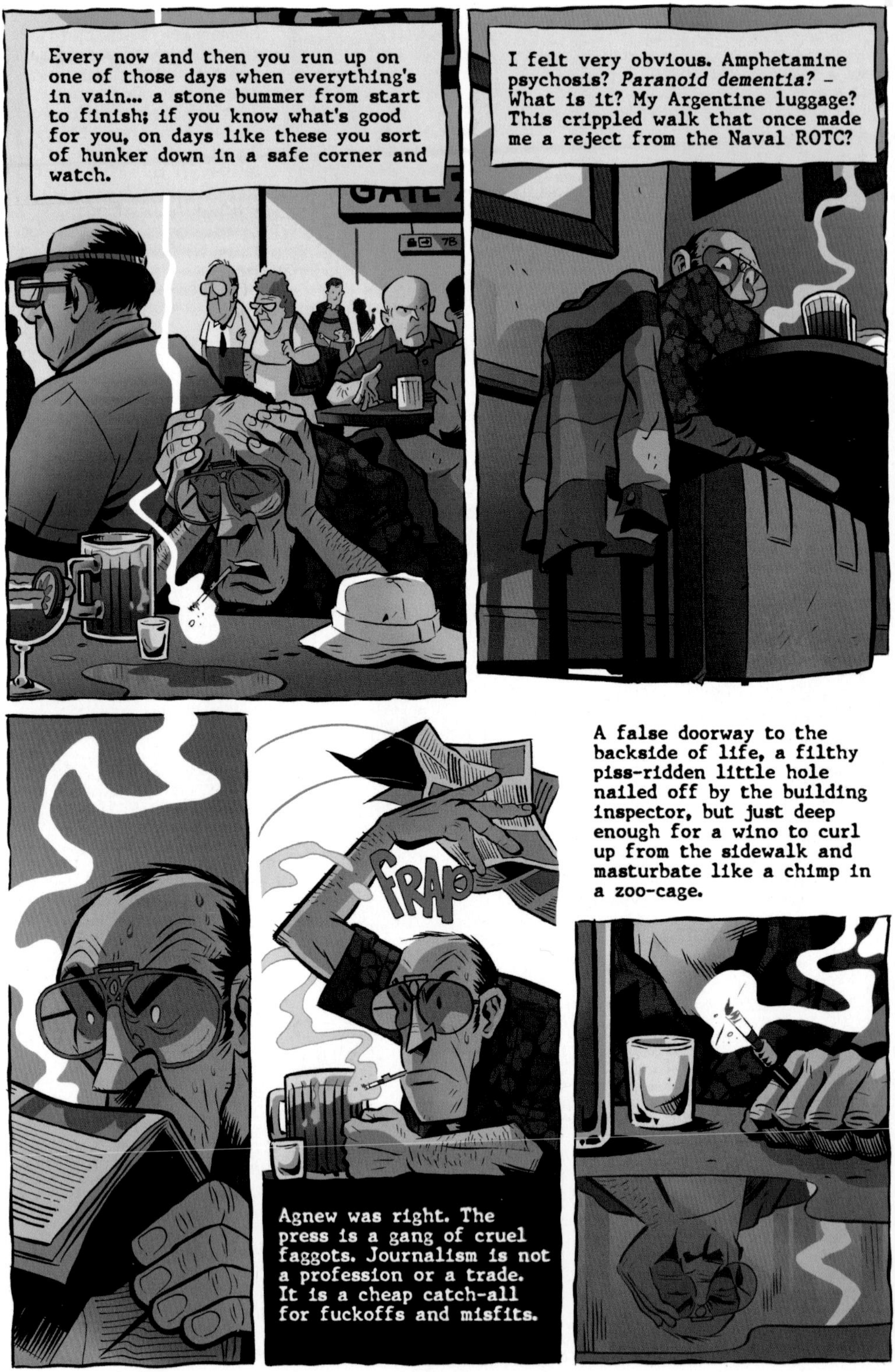
Every now and then you run up on one of those days when everything's in vain... a stone bummer from start to finish; if you know what's good for you, on days like these you sort of hunker down in a safe corner and watch.
I felt very obvious. Amphetamine psychosis? *Paranoid dementia?* - What is it? My Argentine luggage? This crippled walk that once made me a reject from the Naval ROTC?
FRAP
Agnew was right. The press is a gang of cruel faggots. Journalism is not a profession or a trade. It is a cheap catch-all for fuckoffs and misfits.
A false doorway to the backside of life, a filthy piss-ridden little hole nailed off by the building inspector, but just deep enough for a wino to curl up from the sidewalk and masturbate like a chimp in a zoo-cage.

14. Farewell to Vegas... 'God's Mercy on You Swine!'

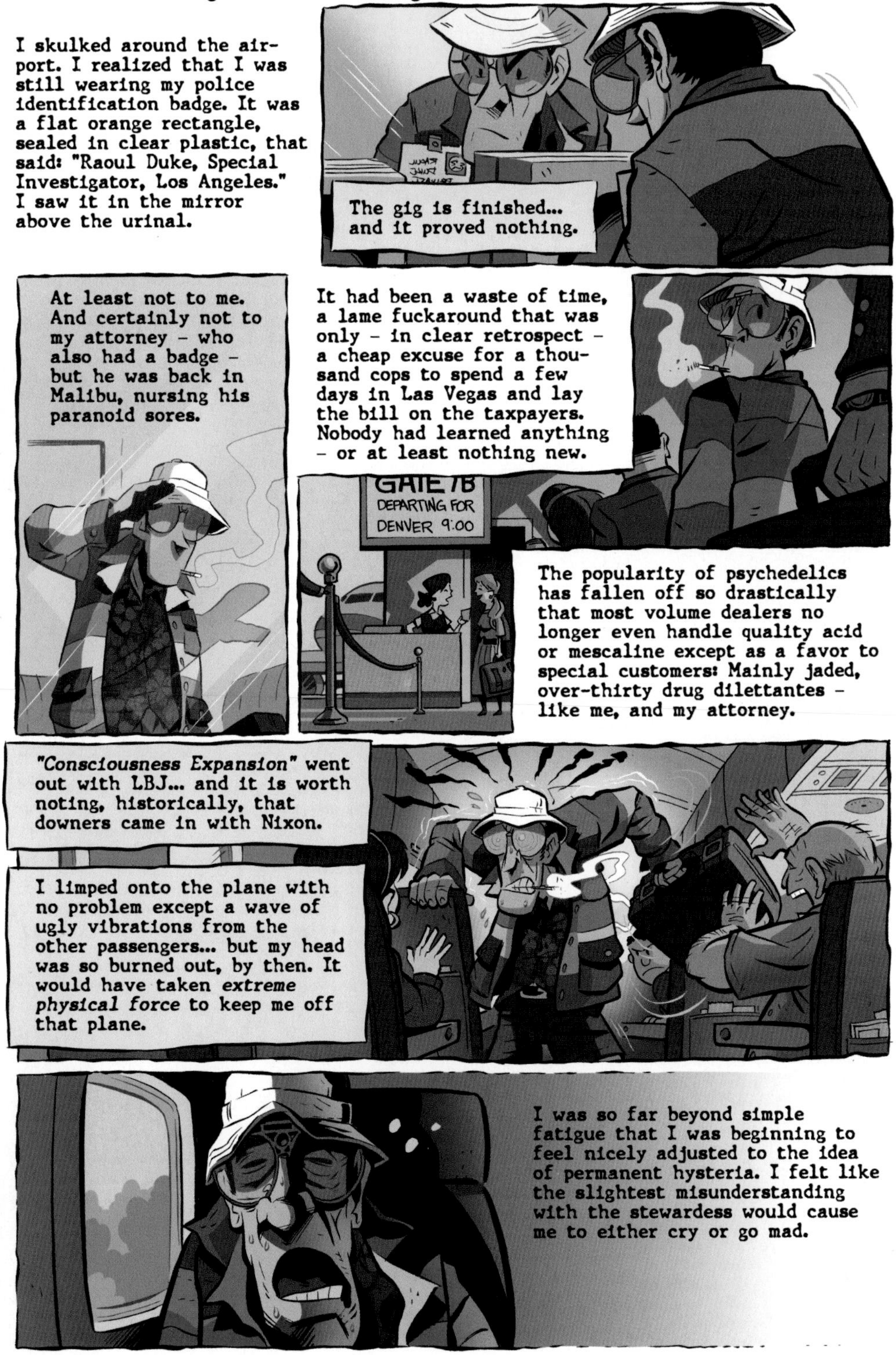
I skulked around the airport. I realized that I was still wearing my police identification badge. It was a flat orange rectangle, sealed in clear plastic, that said: "Raoul Duke, Special Investigator, Los Angeles." I saw it in the mirror above the urinal.
The gig is finished... and it proved nothing.
At least not to me. And certainly not to my attorney - who also had a badge - but he was back in Malibu, nursing his paranoid sores.
It had been a waste of time, a lame fuckaround that was only - in clear retrospect - a cheap excuse for a thousand cops to spend a few days in Las Vegas and lay the bill on the taxpayers. Nobody had learned anything - or at least nothing new.
GATE 7B
DEPARTING FOR
DENVER 9:00
The popularity of psychedelics has fallen off so drastically that most volume dealers no longer even handle quality acid or mescaline except as a favor to special customers: Mainly jaded, over-thirty drug dilettantes - like me, and my attorney.
"Consciousness Expansion" went out with LBJ... and it is worth noting, historically, that downers came in with Nixon.
I limped onto the plane with no problem except a wave of ugly vibrations from the other passengers... but my head was so burned out, by then. It would have taken *extreme physical force* to keep me off that plane.
I was so far beyond simple fatigue that I was beginning to feel nicely adjusted to the idea of permanent hysteria. I felt like the slightest misunderstanding with the stewardess would cause me to either cry or go mad.

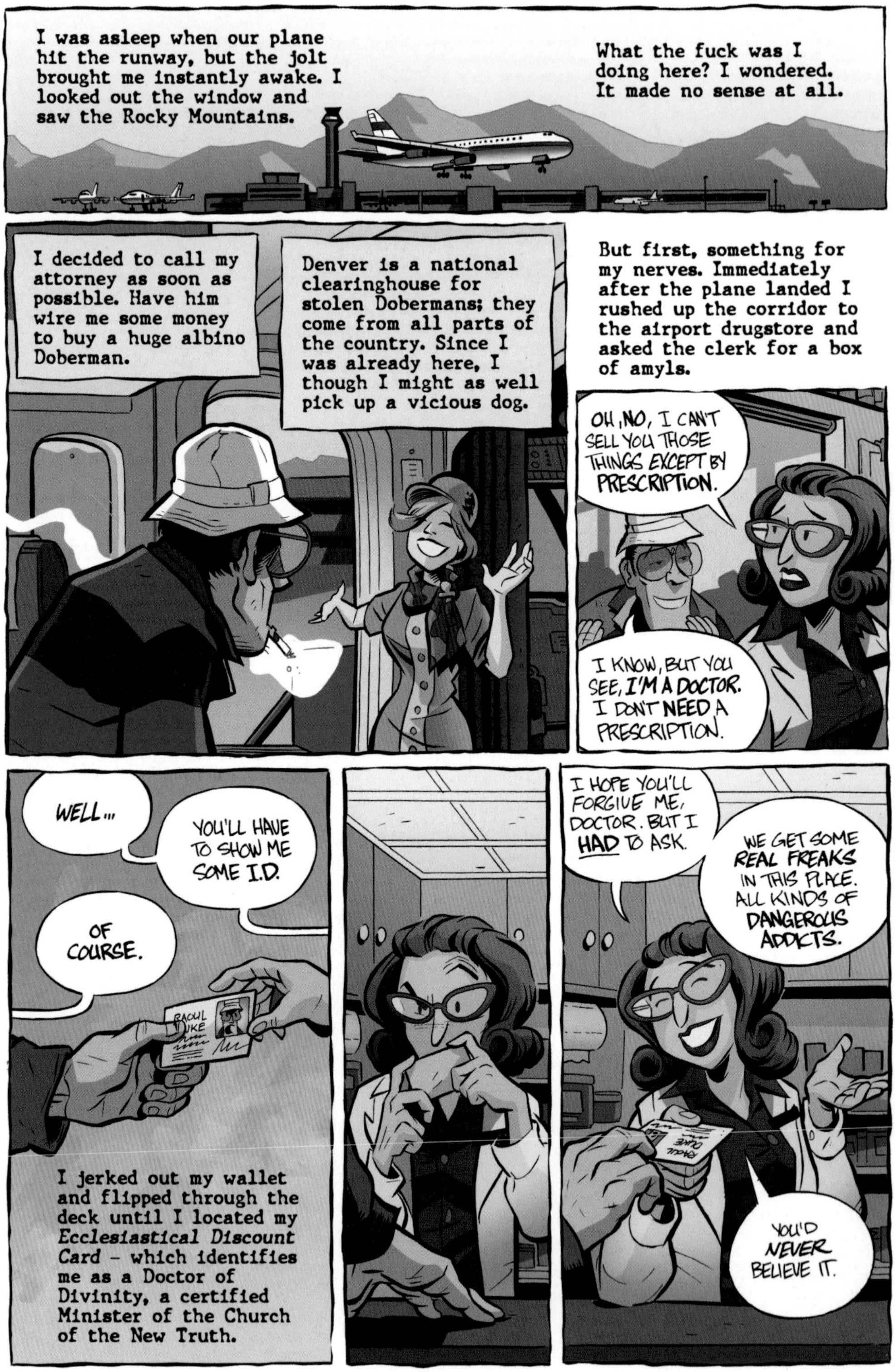
I was asleep when our plane hit the runway, but the jolt brought me instantly awake. I looked out the window and saw the Rocky Mountains.
What the fuck was I doing here? I wondered. It made no sense at all.
I decided to call my attorney as soon as possible. Have him wire me some money to buy a huge albino Doberman.
Denver is a national clearinghouse for stolen Dobermans; they come from all parts of the country. Since I was already here, I though I might as well pick up a vicious dog.
But first, something for my nerves. Immediately after the plane landed I rushed up the corridor to the airport drugstore and asked the clerk for a box of amyls.
OH, NO, I CAN'T SELL YOU THOSE THINGS EXCEPT BY PRESCRIPTION.
I KNOW, BUT YOU SEE, I'M A DOCTOR. I DON'T NEED A PRESCRIPTION.
WELL...
YOU'LL HAVE TO SHOW ME SOME I.D.
OF COURSE.
I jerked out my wallet and flipped through the deck until I located my *Ecclesiastical Discount Card* - which identifies me as a Doctor of Divinity, a certified Minister of the Church of the New Truth.
I HOPE YOU'LL FORGIVE ME, DOCTOR. BUT I HAD TO ASK.
WE GET SOME REAL FREAKS IN THIS PLACE. ALL KINDS OF DANGEROUS ADDICTS.
YOU'D NEVER BELIEVE IT.

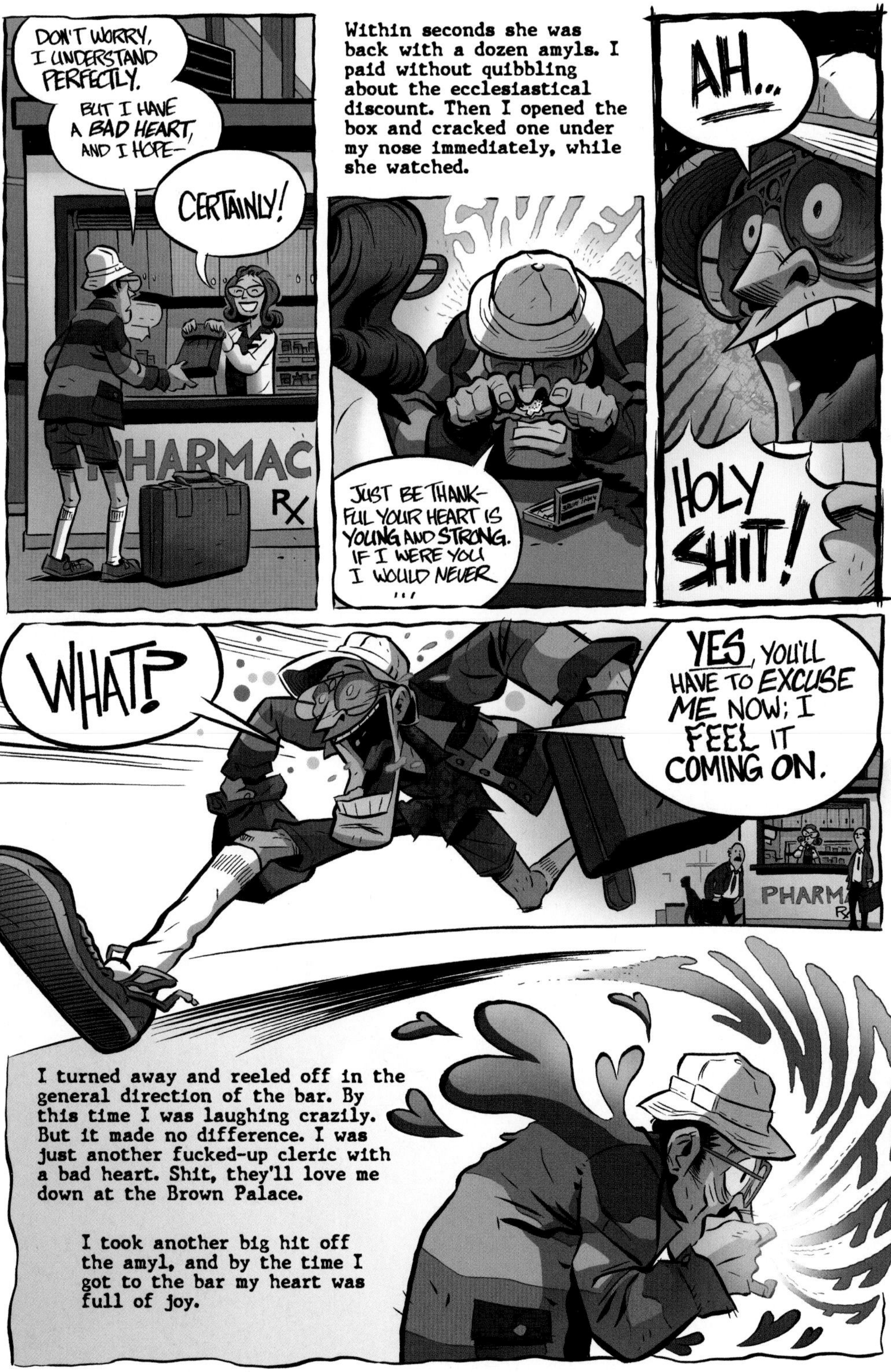
DON'T WORRY, I UNDERSTAND PERFECTLY.
BUT I HAVE A BAD HEART, AND I HOPE–
CERTAINLY!
PHARMAC
RX
Within seconds she was back with a dozen amyls. I paid without quibbling about the ecclesiastical discount. Then I opened the box and cracked one under my nose immediately, while she watched.
JUST BE THANKFUL YOUR HEART IS YOUNG AND STRONG. IF I WERE YOU I WOULD NEVER ...
AH...
HOLY SHIT!
WHAT!?
YES, YOU'LL HAVE TO EXCUSE ME NOW; I FEEL IT COMING ON.
PHARM
RX
I turned away and reeled off in the general direction of the bar. By this time I was laughing crazily. But it made no difference. I was just another fucked-up cleric with a bad heart. Shit, they'll love me down at the Brown Palace.
I took another big hit off the amyl, and by the time I got to the bar my heart was full of joy.

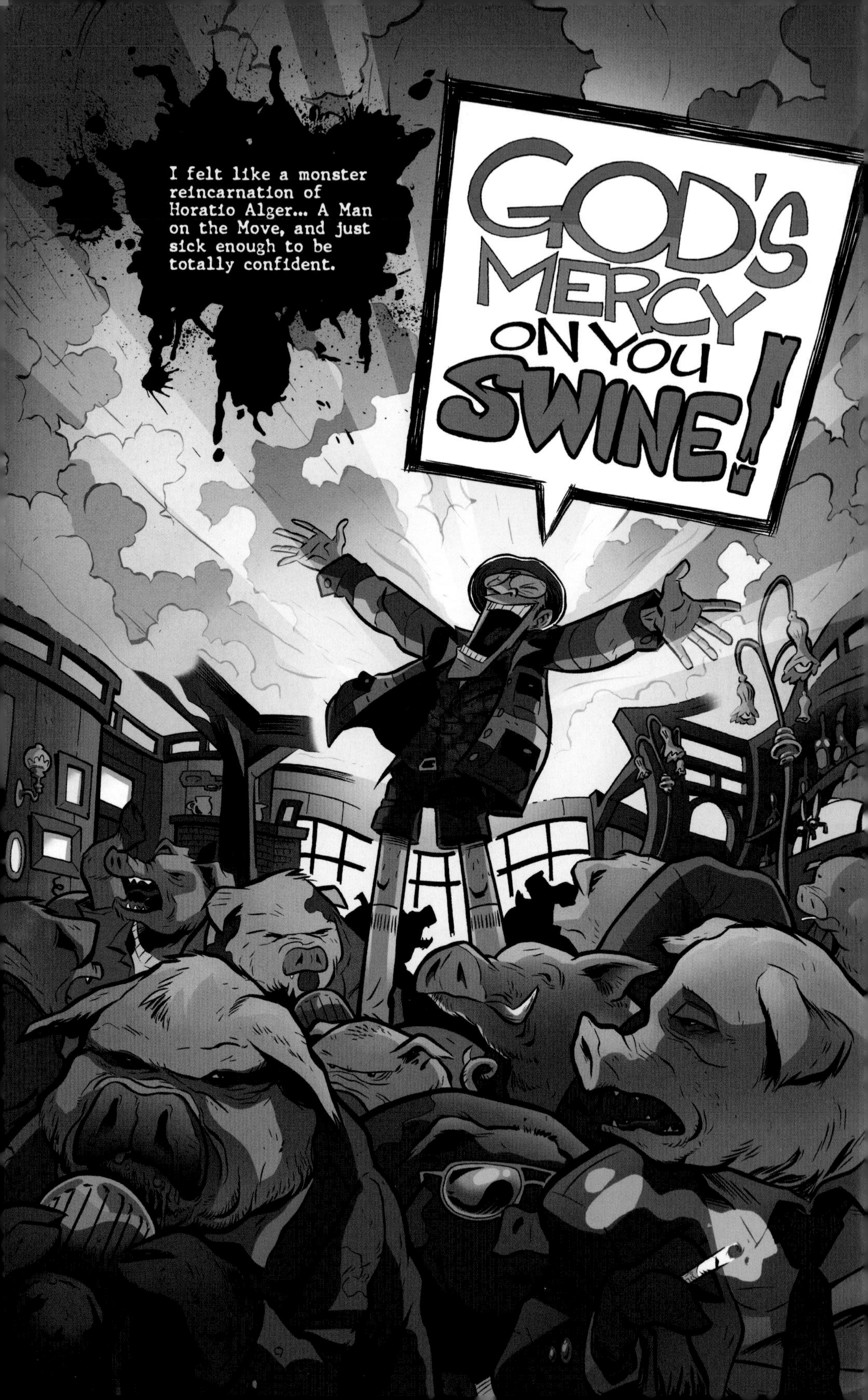
I felt like a monster reincarnation of Horatio Alger... A Man on the Move, and just sick enough to be totally confident.
GOD'S MERCY ON YOU SWINE!

Hunter S. Thompson is the author of *Hell's Angels, Fear and Loathing: On the Campaign Trail '72, The Great Shark Hunt, The Curse of Lono, Generation of Swine,* and other major statements of our time. He died in 2005.

Troy Little is the Eisner Award-nominated writer and artist of *Angora Napkin*. His other works include *Chiaroscuro: Patchwork Book 1* and other lesser statements of our time. Find his work at www.meanwhilestudios.com.

Hunter S. Thompson's Fear and Loathing in Las Vegas. Based on the work *Fear and Loathing in Las Vegas*. Copyright © 1971 by Hunter S. Thompson. All Rights Reserved. © 2015 Idea and Design Works, LLC.

Published by
Top Shelf Productions
PO Box 1282
Marietta, GA 30061-1282, USA.

Editor-in-Chief: Chris Staros.

Top Shelf Productions is an imprint of IDW Publishing, a division of Idea and Design Works, LLC. Offices: 2765 Truxtun Road, San Diego, CA 92106. Top Shelf Productions®, the Top Shelf logo, Idea and Design Works®, and the IDW logo are registered trademarks of Idea and Design Works, LLC. All Rights Reserved. This is a work of fiction. Any similarities to persons living or dead are purely coincidental. With the exception of small excerpts of artwork used for review purposes, none of the contents of this publication may be reprinted without the permission of IDW Publishing. IDW Publishing does not read or accept unsolicited submissions of ideas, stories, or artwork.

Adapted by Troy Little.
Design by Troy Little and Chris Ross.
Proofreading by Zac Boone.
Publicity and Marketing by Leigh Walton (leigh@topshelfcomix.com).
Edited by Ted Adams and Denton J. Tipton.

"Fear and Loathing in Las Vegas" by 'Raoul Duke' originally appeared in *Rolling Stone* magazine, Issue 95, November 11th, 1971, and Issue 96, November 25th 1971.

ISBN 978-1-60309-375-0

Printed in Korea.

18   17   16   15   5   4   3   2   1

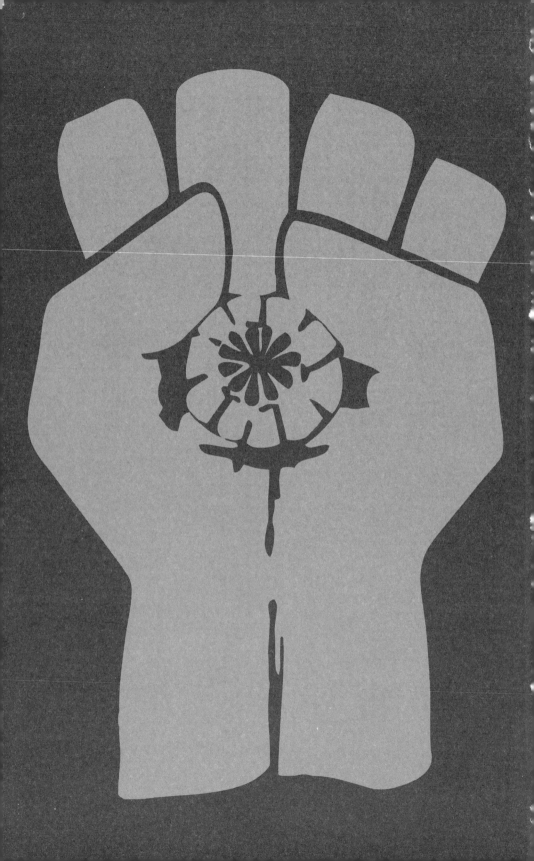